THE IBM 5100 PORTABLE COMPUTER

A Comprehensive Guide For Users and Programmers

COMPUTER SCIENCE SERIES

THE IBM 5100 PORTABLE COMPUTER
A Comprehensive Guide For Users and Programmers

HARRY KATZAN, JR.

Computer Consultant
Chairman, Computer Science Department
Pratt Institute

COMPUTER SCIENCE SERIES

VAN NOSTRAND REINHOLD COMPANY
NEW YORK   CINCINNATI   ATLANTA   DALLAS   SAN FRANCISCO
LONDON   TORONTO   MELBOURNE

Van Nostrand Reinhold Company Regional Offices:
New York   Cincinnati   Atlanta   Dallas   San Francisco

Van Nostrand Reinhold Company International Offices:
London   Toronto   Melbourne

Library of Congress Catalog Card Number: 77-2168
ISBN: 0-442-24270-0

Manufactured in the United States of America

Published by Van Nostrand Reinhold Company
450 West 33rd Street, New York. N.Y. 10001

Published simultaneously in Canada by Van Nostrand Reinhold Ltd.

15 14 13 12 11 10 9 8 7 6 5 4 3 2 1

Library of Congress Cataloging in Publication Data

Katzan, Harry.
    The IBM 5100 portable computer.

    (Computer science series)
    Includes bibliographical references and index.
    1. IBM 5100 (Computer)   2. APL (Computer
program language)   3. BASIC (Computer program
language)   I. Title.
QA76.8.I19K37   001.6′4   77-2168
ISBN 0-442-24270-0

PREFACE

The world of computers and data processing is such that new product announcements by the principle manufacturers often, directly or indirectly, affect a significant segment of the business. When a revolutionary concept is introduced, the impact is even greater.

This is the case with the IBM 5100 Portable Computer that incorporates the functions of a full-scale computer with the size of an office typewriter. The computer system allows APL and BASIC language capability and contains facilities for a display screen, magnetic tape unit, line printer, and telecommunications equipment.

This book has three main objectives: (1) to present an introduction to programming and using the IBM 5100 computer; (2) to present an introduction to the APL and BASIC languages; and (3) to present the systems concepts necessary for effectively utilizing the computer. The book is organized toward this end and the material is covered in 4 major sections, including 15 chapters, and 6 appendices. Part I, entitled *Fundamentals*, is intended to provide the reader with background material on computers and programming, and covers basic computer concepts, the foundations of programming, and the structure of the 5100 Portable Computer System. Readers with a good computer background can skip chapters 1 and 2 and go directly to chapter 3 for an overview of the 5100 system. Part II, entitled *The BASIC Language*, gives a complete description of the BASIC language, together with programming techniques and sample programs. This part also covers operational procedures and system commands relevant to the BASIC mode of operation. Part III, entitled *The APL Language*, gives a complete description of the APL language, together with programming techniques and sample applications. This part also covers operational procedures and system commands relevant to the APL mode of operation. Part IV, entitled *Systems Concepts*, covers data communications and an overview of the system development life cycle. There are six appendices. Appendix A gives sample BASIC and APL programs for amortization and payroll calculations. The programs are included to supply the reader with a realistic idea of the nature of typical 5100 Portable Computer applications and serve to supplement the systems concepts introduced in Part IV. Appendices B through F supply reference material for effectively using the 5100 system.

The book is designed to be self contained and can be used as an introduction to the 5100 Portable Computer, as an introduction to programming, as an introduction to the APL and BASIC languages, and as a 5100 reference manual. In the latter case, the book is complete with operational procedures and the syntactical forms and semantical interpretations of statements, functions, and system commands.

It is a pleasure to acknowledge the cooperation of the IBM Corporation for supplying photographs and granting permission to reproduce the reference material in appendices B through F, the assistance of the persons listed on the acknowledgment section, and most importantly, my wife Margaret for typing the manuscript and for supporting the development effort in numerous other ways.

HARRY KATZAN, JR.

ACKNOWLEDGMENT

Several persons provided valuable assistance in a variety of ways during the development of the manuscript. Accordingly, it is a pleasure to mention the following: Walt Barker, Philip Cheng, Al Dellorusso, Lee Epstein, Al Franco, Roy Larsen, Margy McCluskey, Ken Murray, Bob Pfleger, Hal Robins, Pris Teleky, Jim Yahara, and Cy Young.

CONTENTS

PART I:
Fundamentals

1 | BASIC COMPUTER CONCEPTS

The IBM 5100 is designed to be an easy-to-use portable computer that can be used by persons with varying levels of computer knowledge. For most applications, the computer can be programmed so that very little technical knowledge is required to actually operate the computer and apply it to a given problem. Operational knowledge is all that is required for this type of activity. Many persons, however, will want to program the computer themselves, because it is relatively easy to do, and because the design of the computer facilitates the programming process. Knowledge of programming methods and languages is needed for this type of activity. Lastly, the computer must be used in a productive manner in order to justify the financial investment in it. The recognition and specification of viable uses of the computer is known as systems design, for which a basic knowledge of computer applications is needed. The book covers the three types of knowledge needed to successfully use the IBM 5100 portable computer. The only prerequisite is an understanding of basic computer concepts, which are covered in this chapter.

1.1 INTRODUCTION TO COMPUTING

One of the key factors in understanding computers is the possession of a conceptual knowledge of the types of applications for which computers are used. Once the applications are recognized, then the structure of the computer and the methods for programming and using it can be presented in a straightforward manner.

Major Computer Applications

The major applications of computers tend to parallel those for which human activity is inappropriate, inconvenient, or costly. Typical examples are extensive mathematical calculations, clerical operations, and the retrieval of information. In many applications, a computer is required because the typical person cannot respond quickly enough or be sufficiently accurate to satisfy operational constraints. In the following paragraphs, several general classes of computer applications are given. The classifications are more conceptual than actual, and a given computer application could possibly be placed in more than one class—depending upon whether the computer is used for scientific, business, or administrative purposes.

Descriptive Computing. This type of computing (or if you will, problem solving) provides the user with more information on a subject, such as the design parameters of a bridge or road, the trajectory of a space vehicle, or the root of an equation. The subject under consideration is usually defined mathematically and the formulae are used in the calculations.

Data Analysis. This type of computing is used to draw conclusions and make predictions from actual or experimental data. The associated techniques normally employ statistics and mathematics but frequently involve simple comparison and logical operations for checking tolerance conditions and determining combinations of events, respectively.

Data Processing. This class of computer applications involves the storage, processing, and reporting of information. Although data processing is commonly associated with the accounting and record keeping functions of an organization, it is not generally restricted to business activity and may encompass a variety of clerical tasks, such as printing address labels, generating shipping orders, and scheduling work activities. The processing of survey and census data might also be placed in this category, as could be the computer preparation of an index for a book.

Modeling and Simulation. A *model* is an abstraction of a real-life situation from which we can draw conclusions or make predictions about the future; a *simulation* is the use of models to attain the essence of a system without having to physically develop and test it. Through the use of computers, a realistic model of a system, such as the traffic-flow in a city or the checkout procedure in a supermarket, can be developed and simulated to permit decision makers to evaluate alternatives in a reasonable time frame.

Optimization. This class of computer application uses mathematical models to obtain the best solution to a given type of problem, for which a prototype solution has been developed. Typical applications are the calculation of the exact ingredients of sausage, the optimum assignment of personnel, and the most profitable allocation of capital investments.

Process Control. This application uses a computer in conjunction with a physical process or laboratory experiment to collect data or provide real-time control of the process. Through the use of sensory or control devices, the computer can communicate with a noncomputer device that is external to the computer system. The computer is programmed to sample the input signals on a periodic basis and compare the corresponding values against prescribed limits or store them for further study. When necessary, the computer can generate output signals to control a physical system, such as a temperature control system in a chemical plant. A common example of process control is the patient monitoring system in a hospital.

On-Line and Real-Time Systems. In an on-line or real-time system, the computer is connected via telecommunications facilities to a console device or to another computer system. Typical examples are the airline reservation system in most airports, savings bank systems used for checking balances and verifying credit, and the message switching systems used in the military. *On-line* means that communication is made directly with the computer, and *real-time* means that the computer is programmed to respond within a pre-scribed time period to satisfy the user's needs.

Information Systems. An information system is a collection of computer facilities, programs, and informational resources that permit the accumulation, classification, storage, and retrieval of large amounts of information. In some cases, an information system is designed and implemented as an on-line real-time system, and in other cases, it is not. Most information systems are designed to assign meaning to data—hence the name information—in addition to storing data. Typical examples are inventory control systems, library information systems, insurance policy maintenance systems, and medical and legal information systems.

Education. One of the most rewarding applications of computers is in education where the computer is used for administration, instruction, and problem-solving. The administrative use of computers normally involves data processing and information systems and is used for record-keeping, class scheduling, and curriculum planning. In instruction, the familiar technique of computer assisted instruction (CAI) is used to enhance programmed learning. In problem-solving, descriptive computing, data analysis, and optimization, methods are used to provide the student with problem-solving and analysis experience and to extend the range of problems that can be solved.

In general, any well-defined computational or retrieval procedure that can be "broken down" into a series of successive steps can be programmed for com-puter solution. However, computers cannot do everything. Computers have well-defined characteristics that make them useful for some applications and not for others. A computer can perform arithmetic and logical operations very quickly and with great accuracy and reliability. The computer can also be used to store larger amounts of information and can be programmed to make that information available at a moment's notice. Applications that require this type of service are generally enhanced through the use of the computer. On the other hand, applications that require inductive, intuitive, or adaptive behavior are not as well defined at this stage of modern technology and normally exist as research projects or laboratory experiments.

Overview of Information Processing

Similar to the manner in which humans must be taught to perform a task, the computer must also be taught to perform a computational procedure. The process of teaching the computer is known as programming. Because computers are machines, however, they possess no innate intelligence or free will and must be guided at each stage of a computation. The directions that are given to the computer are supplied by human beings. It necessarily follows that a person could perform the same calculations if enough time were available and the person were inclined to do them. In general, the basic functions performed during information processing are independent of whether they are executed by a computer or performed by a person. These functions are summarized in succeeding paragraphs.

Recording of Information. Information, or data in the language of the computer, can originate in several ways, such as the reading of a dial, the recording of an event in symbolic form, the extraction of a value from a table, or as the result of a previous computation. The information can be recorded on paper in the form of prose, numerical data, or in graphical form, or it can be recorded on a computer-oriented medium such as punched cards or tape by a human operator. Information can also be recorded automatically on an electromechanical device, such as magnetic tape, which is a part of the experimental apparatus. When information is recorded in a form that cannot be read directly by a person, then a hard copy such as a typewritten or handwritten sheet or a computer printout is also produced for human use.

Transmittal of Information. Information is normally processed in a different location from which it is recorded. One of the advantages of the IBM 5100 Portable Computer is that information can be processed where it is recorded, thereby extending the range and convenience of computer processing. Traditionally, however, manual methods were used for transporting documents and records. Modern telecommunications facilities have reduced the need for manual methods and have provided the user with direct access to the information processing facility.

Information Storage. The storage of information is necessary before processing, during processing, and after processing. The form in which information is stored is to some extent dependent upon the processing involved but is also related to the processing device. For computer processing, information may be stored on the original recording medium, or it may pass through several stages of processing and eventually reside on a high-speed device suited to a particular application. For example, input data may be typed in at a remote console, stored in the computer during processing, and then be saved permanently on a disk storage volume. The results of the processing may be presented to the user in the form of a printed report.

Information Processing. The specific characteristics of information processing depend upon the application. For science-based computations, a small amount of input data is followed by a relatively large number of mathematical calculations, which are followed by a small amount of computed results. For data processing computations, such as payroll or accounting, there is a large amount of input and output but a relatively small number of calculations. Most computer applications fall somewhere between the two extremes. In information retrieval, for example, very little processing is performed, and the primary function is to store and retrieve large amounts of information.

Information Reporting. Information resulting from the processing must ultimately be made available to the user in the form of a printed report, an updated file, the control of a physical process, a set of plotted points, or a microfilm slide.

In later sections, it will become evident that a computer is organized to perform the same functions, i.e., input, processing, and output, along with a variety of supporting facilities for data storage and transmission.

1.2 DEVELOPMENT OF A COMPUTER APPLICATION

The popular conception of a computer is that it is an extremely complex, almost unknowable device that can solve any problem put to it—something like the Oracle at Delphi. Moreover, anyone who works with computers must certainly be a genius or, at least, close to one. Obviously, computer people do not mind the halo, even though it isn't true. The first assertion is partially true; computers *are* complex machines. However, using advanced technology, computer scientists have reduced the complexity normally associated with computation through the invention of programming languages and the use of miniaturized circuitry. As far as the Oracle-at-Delphi syndrome is concerned, the computer simply is not all knowing, and as we know from the preceding section, it must be programmed at each stage of a computation. This section goes into more detail on the development of a computer application.

Major Phases of Application Development

The development of a computer application typically involves several people and a variety of different activities. The concept does not preclude a one-person operation but does recognize the fact that more than one person are usually involved. The steps in application development include the following types of activity and normally take place in the order given:

1. Problem definition
2. Systems analysis
3. Algorithm development
4. Programming
5. Debugging and testing
6. Documentation
7. Systems implementation

Each type of activity is discussed briefly.

Problem Definition. A potential problem requiring a computer solution manifests itself through a need of some kind. For example, a scientist may need to summarize his experimental data within a given time period or to a special degree of accuracy, or a businessman may need to resolve a paperwork problem that continually increases in scope and magnitude. A bowling alley proprietor may wish to streamline his bowling league operations, thereby attracting more leagues. A direct-mail firm may wish to computerize its mailing labels, replacing inefficient and outdated methods. The problem definition phase is characterized by the fact that the person recognizing the need is often limited in one or more of several ways:

1. He does not have the resources to solve the problem and must sell the new concept to higher management or administration.
2. He recognizes the need but is not sure of the best solution.
3. He is not sure that his needs can be satisfied with a computer.
4. He is not certain of how a computer solution to his problem would fit into the total organization.
5. He is not confident of the validity of his need, is not sure that he can justify the solution, and prefers an outside opinion.

The best course of action to take in this case is to state the need precisely or formulate the problem exactly, as the originator sees it, and then call in a systems analyst from within the organization or an outside consultant to gather and analyze the facts relevant to the proposed application.

Systems Analysis. The process of analyzing a proposed computer application is performed by a person experienced in computer technology, applications, and organizational issues. More specifically, the systems analyst or consultant performs the following functions:

1. Determines whether the proposed application can be done.
2. Develops the general methodology to be employed.
3. Determines how the proposed computer application can be effectively integrated into the operational structure of the organization.

If, during the process of performing the above functions, it is determined that the proposed project is a viable one, then the systems analysis phase also includes a detailed flow analysis of the system or program and a specification of the inputs required and the outputs produced.

Algorithm Development. Algorithm development is the precise specification of the steps that comprise a computer program. In a data analysis application, for example, algorithm development would involve determining the statistical techniques and mathematical equations to be employed and the manner in which they would be used. In an inventory control application, algorithm development would involve the specification of methods for computing inventory levels, reorder points, and backorder requests. In a payroll application, algorithm development would be the identification of taxes and other deductions and the precise specification of the methods for computing gross and net pay. Algorithm development is not restricted to mathematical calculations and also includes techniques for storing and retrieving data and for editing and generating reports.

Programming. Programming is the process of writing down the steps that comprise a computer program. If detailed program specifications were generated from the systems analysis and algorithm development phases, then computer programming involves the straightforward coding of the program in a suitable programming language. If general specifications were produced during the systems analysis and algorithm development phases, then the programming phase would also involve the writing of detailed procedures in addition to coding. Computer programming is a detailed process that can easily result in a program that contains inadvertent errors. In fact, most programs contain errors that must be detected and removed.

Debugging and Testing. The process of running a program to determine if it contains errors is known as testing or program checkout, and the task of removing errors is known as debugging. Testing and debugging is achieved through the use of test cases that determine if the program operates correctly for each possible type of computation for which it was designed. Errors can occur in a variety of ways, including the following: incorrectly written program, faulty algorithm, poor systems analysis, and incorrect specification of applicable data values.

Documentation. The documentation phase includes the development of procedures for using the system or program and preparation of reports describing the procedures and internal structure of the program. Effective documentation is necessary when a person other than the original programmer is required to make changes to it.

Systems Implementation. Systems implementation is the process of putting the system or program into production. Some student, engineering, and scientific programs are developed, debugged, and computed results are obtained.

Then the program is discarded. These are referred to as "one shot" jobs. For these programs, documentation and implementation procedures are minimal. Other programs, such as those associated with information systems, data processing, and other applications, may be used for years, going through change cycles to satisfy current needs. In the latter case, the effectiveness of a program should be monitored to insure that the changing needs of the organization are satisfied.

Computational Procedures

The steps that comprise a computational procedure must be delineated before the procedure can be programmed for the computer. The notion of writing down the steps that constitute a process of some kind is not unique to the computer field. Two familiar examples from everyday life are found in a cookbook and a mechanics repair manual. As an example of a recipe, consider the following procedure for preparing fried chicken:*

Williamfburg Fried Chicken

Joint the Chickens neatly, wafh and drain. Soak in cold Milk for half an Hour. Dredge them well with Flour to which Salt and Pepper have been added. Fry in an iron Skillet in boiling Fat almoft deep enough to cover the Pieces of Chicken. Turn each Piece at leaft three Times. Fry to a nice brown, drain on brown Paper and ferve with Gravy fent up in a feparate Boat.

As an example of a repair procedure, consider the following procedure for car storage preparation:**

Car Storage Preparation—30 Days or Less

1. Wash car and inflate tires to 40 pounds pressure.
2. Provide proper cooling system protection.
3. Run engine until completely warmed up; then drain and refill with fresh oil which, according to the label on the can is intended for service "SE."
4. Run engine again with fresh oil until completely warmed up; drive car to place of storage and park. Do not restart again until end of storage period.
5. Be sure parking brake is in released position and car is on level surface.
6. If car is to be stored in a hot area, the fuel tank, lines, pump, filter, and carburetor should be drained.
7. Disconnect battery and prevent battery from discharging or freezing by keeping it fully charged.

*Bullock, Helen, Mrs., *The Williamsburg Art of Cookery*, *Colonial Williamsburg Inc.*, 1958, p. 46.
**1973 *Cadillac Shop Manual*, General Motors Corporation, Detroit, Michigan, 1972.

The procedures have two common characteristics:

1. They are each written to perform one particular task; and
2. They are each fairly general in nature, requiring a certain amount of expertise by the person involved.

These are two major areas in which a computer procedure differs from procedures found in everyday life.

Because a computer is a detailed and precise machine, the steps that comprise a computer procedure must be sufficiently detailed at each stage of a computation to permit the required calculations to be performed. Also computer procedures do not solve one problem; they are designed to solve a whole class of similar problems. The procedure for adding two signed numbers a and b serves as an example:

1. If a and b have the same sign, go to step 5. (If a and b have different signs, continue with step 2.)
2. Subtract the smaller magnitude from the larger magnitude. (Continue with step 3.)
3. Give the result the sign of the number with the larger magnitude. (Continue with step 4.)
4. Stop.
5. Add the magnitudes of the numbers a and b. (Continue with step 6.)
6. Give the result the sign of number a. (Continue with step 7.)
7. Stop.

The procedure, in this case, is fairly detailed and would work for any two numbers a and b. For example, $(-5)+(-4)=-9$, $16+(-11)=5$, $10+20=30$, and so forth. A specific procedure of this type which exists as a finite list of instructions specifying a sequence of operations that gives the answer to any problem of a given type is called an *algorithm*. Computer programs are based on the concept of an algorithm.

Another familiar algorithm is used to generate a sequence of numbers known as Fibonacci numbers, which have amazing applications in the physical world. For example, Fibonacci numbers can be used to describe the arrangement of stems on a branch and the growth in the rabbit population. The Fibonacci sequence is depicted as follows:

$$1 \ 1 \ 2 \ 3 \ 5 \ 8 \ 13 \ 21 \ 34 \ \ldots$$

The pattern can be developed by inspection. After the first two numbers, each succeeding number is the sum of the previous two numbers. An algorithm for computing Fibonacci numbers that are less than 100 is given as follows:

1. Set N1 to 0. (This is not a Fibonacci number, and it is used only to start the process.)

2. Set N2 to 1. (This is the first Fibonacci number.)
3. Write down N2.
4. Set N3 equal to N1+N2.
5. If N3 is greater than 100, then stop the calculations.
6. Write down N3.
7. Replace N1 by N2.
8. Replace N2 by N3.
9. Continue the calculations with step 4.

Clearly, an algorithm exists for each computational problem that has a general solution. The solution may exist as a set of mathematical equations that must be evaluated or as a set of procedural steps that satisfy a preestablished procedure—such as the well-known procedure for calculating income tax liability.

Descriptive Methods

For many applications, a simple list of the steps that comprise an algorithm is sufficient for stating that algorithm in a clear and unambiguous manner. However, when the procedure is complex and different options exist, then a list of instructions is hard to follow. A typical example is a list of directions for locating a particular place in an unfamiliar city. When the directions are complex, a road map is usually preferred.

A flow diagram is used in the computer field for describing a complex process. A flow diagram—usually called a *flow chart*—may be comprised of symbols that represent the following functions:

Flow direction. The flow of control is represented by an arrow. The arrow-head denotes the symbol to which control is passed.

Process. The rectangular process symbol denotes a computational operation.

Input/output. An input or output operation is denoted by a parrallelogram with slanted edges. Making information available for processing, i.e., read in, is an input function. The recording or display, i.e., read out, is an output function.

Decision. The diamond shaped decision symbol is used to denote a change in direction of flow on a conditional basis.

Start-Stop. The terminal symbol denotes the beginning or end of a computational process.

Connection. The small circle serves as a connector between different points in a flow chart.

The flow charting symbols are shown graphically in Figure 1.1.

A flow chart of the algorithm for generating Fibonacci numbers is given in

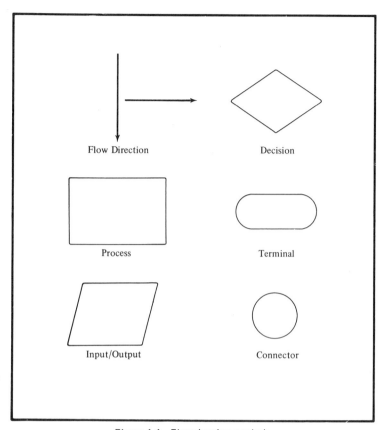

Figure 1.1 Flowcharting symbols.

Figure 1.2. One of the greatest benefits of the use of flow charts is that the existence of repetitive operations can be detected at a glance. Figure 1.3 depicts another repetitive algorithm that computes the largest factor of an integer N. As in the previous examples, the flow chart gives a visual description of a procedure, and the type of operation performed at each stage of the computation is clearly evident by the flow charting symbol used.

A computational procedure can also be described by the computer program used to perform the calculations. While a computer program has the same general characteristics as a list of instructions, the fact that meaningful statements that are computationally oriented can be used tends to reduce the complexity of this type of description. Using a program as a descriptive technique has the obvious advantage that if the program is correct, then the description of the algorithm is accurate.

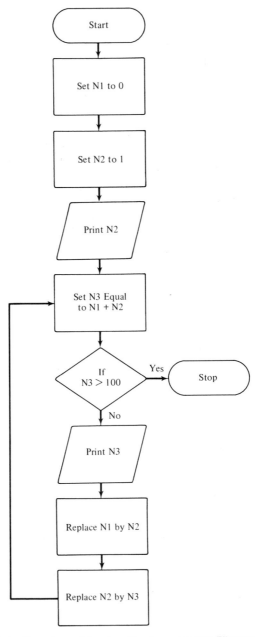

Figure 1.2   Flow chart of the algorithm for generating Fibonacci numbers.

Computer Programs

A computer representation of an algorithmic process is a *computer program*. More specifically, a program is a meaningful sequence of statements in a special language designed for programming. Internal to the computer, a program is executed by a set of specific computer-oriented instructions that effectively controls the operation of the computer.

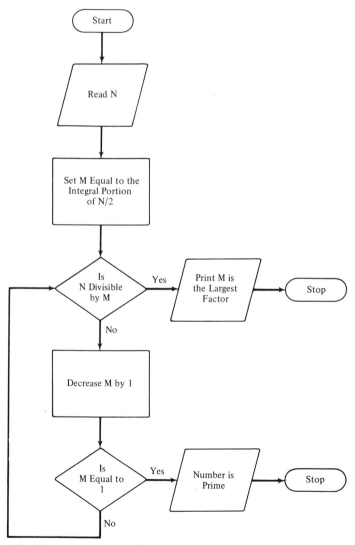

Figure 1.3 Flow chart of an algorithm for computing the largest factor of an integer N.

The statements in a program parallel the steps in an algorithmic process. Consider the problem of computing the largest factor of an integer N, given in Figure 1.3. The algorithm and the program in the BASIC language are listed as follows:

Algorithm	BASIC Program
1. Write down the number N.	10 READ N
2. Set M equal to the integer portion of N/2.	20 LET M=INT(N/2)
3. If N is divisible by M, go to step 8.	30 IF N/M=INT(N/M) GOTO 80
4. Decrease M by 1.	40 LET M=M−1
5. If M is greater than 1, go to step 3.	50 IF M>1 GOTO 30
6. Print number is prime.	60 PRINT N; 'IS PRIME'
7. Stop.	70 STOP
8. Print "largest factor is" M.	80 PRINT 'LARGEST FACTOR OF'; N; 'IS'; M
9. Stop.	90 STOP
	100 END

A computer listing and execution of the program is given in Figure 1.4, and, except for the DATA statement that supplies a data value for the program, it is identical to the program given above.

A second example of a computer program is given in Figure 1.5. It represents a simple payroll program written in the BASIC language that computes net pay as gross pay minus taxes and deductions. The program reads in the employee's name, hours, rate, tax percentage, and deductions and also pays time and one-

```
0010 READ N
0020 LET M=INT(N/2)
0030 IF N/M=INT(N/M) GOTO 0080
0040 LET M=M−1
0050 IF M>1 GOTO 0030
0060 PRINT N;'IS PRIME'
0070 STOP
0080 PRINT 'LARGEST FACTOR OF';N;'IS';M
0090 STOP
0100 DATA 477
0110 END
RUN
LARGEST FACTOR OF 477   IS 159
```

Figure 1.4 Computer listing and execution of the largest factor program.

```
0010 PRINT USING FLP,0190
0020 PRINT FLP,
0030 READ N$,H,R,P,D
0040 IF N$=' ' GOTO 0130
0050 IF H≤40 GOTO 0080
0060 LET P1=40*R+(H-40)*R*1.5
0070 GOTO 0090
0080 LET P1=H*R
0090 LET T=P1*P/100
0100 LET P2=P1-T-D
0110 PRINT USING FLP,0200,N$,H,R,T,D,P1,P2
0120 GOTO 0030
0130 STOP
0140 DATA 'A. ABLE',40,3.75,20,17
0150 DATA 'B. BAKER',35,2.5,10,17
0160 DATA 'C. CHARLY',50,6,30,25
0170 DATA 'D. DAWG',80,1,5,0
0180 DATA ' ',0,0,0,0
0190 :      NAME        HRS     RATE    TAXES   DEDUCT    GROSS     NET
0200 :###########      ###     ##.##   ###.##   ###.##   ###.##   ###.##
0210 END
```

NAME	HRS	RATE	TAXES	DEDUCT	GROSS	NET
A. ABLE	40	3.75	30.00	17.00	150.00	103.00
B. BAKER	35	2.50	8.75	17.00	87.50	61.75
C. CHARLY	50	6.00	99.00	25.00	330.00	206.00
D. DAWG	80	1.00	5.00	0.00	100.00	95.00

Figure 1.5 Computer listing and execution of a payroll program.

half for all hours over 40. At this stage, full comprehension of the program should not be expected; however, a fairly good idea of how the program works can be obtained by reading through the statements.

The structure of a program can be ascertained from the examples. The program exists as a series of statements that perform three basic functions:

1. Input,
2. Processing, and
3. Output.

In the examples, the READ statement performs the input function, the PRINT statement performs the output function, and the LET, IF, GOTO, and STOP statements perform the processing function. As mentioned previously, the DATA statement provides data on which the programs can operate. Lastly, the END statement denotes the end of the program.

Note on Programming Languages

The BASIC programming language, used in previous examples, was designed as an easy-to-use language for problem solving in an academic, business, or scientific environment. There are several other widely used programming languages that are designed for particular classes of computer applications. Some of the better known programming languages are:

FORTRAN–a mathematically oriented language designed for scientific and engineering applications.

COBOL–a common business-oriented language for data processing.

APL–a powerful mathematically oriented language for scientific and business applications.

PL/I–a multipurpose programming language for programs that span the traditional boundaries between applications.

One of the primary advantages of modern computer technology is that a user can, in most cases, select an appropriate language for a particular type of computer application.

This book covers two widely used programming languages that are available on the 5100 Portable Computer: APL and BASIC. APL, which is an acronym for *A Programming Language*, was designed by K. E. Iverson at Harvard University and implemented in collaboration with A. D. Falkoff at the IBM Corporation. The APL language is based on mathematical notation and achieves its greatest power from the fact that computer operations are defined on vectors, matrices, and arrays of higher dimension. BASIC, which is an acronym for *Beginners All Symbolic Instruction Code*, was developed at Dartmouth College under the direction of J. G. Kemeny. It was designed as an easy-to-learn language for the academic environment but has achieved great popularity as a professional programming language for business and scientific analysis.

1.3 COMPUTER SYSTEMS

The structure of a computer system parallels the three basic functions performed by a computer program: input, processing, and output. A set of hardware devices corresponds to each function, and this is the means by which the respective function is performed.

System Overview

An overview diagram of a computer system is given in Figure 1.6. The major devices are:

1. The main storage unit
2. The processing unit
3. Mass storage devices
4. Input devices
5. Output devices
6. A keyboard/display unit

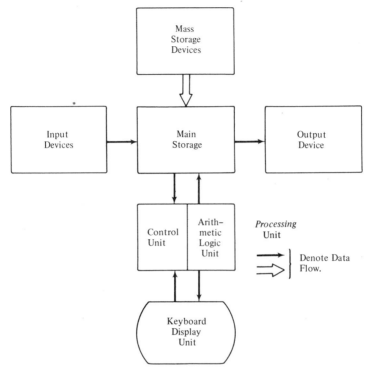

Figure 1.6   Overview of a computer system.

The heart of a computer system is the processing unit and the main storage unit that effectively control the operation of the entire system and permit the system to operate automatically without human intervention.   However, without the supporting devices in the system, the processing unit and the main storage unit would be relatively ineffective.

The devices are presented in a general fashion, even though this book describes a specific computer system.   This method of presentation will aid the reader in placing the concepts in proper perspective.

Main Storage Unit

The main storage unit is used to hold a program and its data during execution. The unit is synthesized from relatively expensive electronic components and is normally limited in size.   Therefore, the main storage unit is not used for the long-term storage of programs or data.

Before a program can be executed, it must be loaded into the main storage unit.   If the program resides on a mass storage device, then it can be loaded with a keyboard command or with a statement from an executing program.

A program may also be loaded into the main storage unit from the keyboard on a statement-by-statement basis. Normally, when a program is entered into the computer for the first time, it is entered from the keyboard. It can then be saved on a mass storage device, so that it need not be entered again manually. When the mass storage device employs a removable storage medium such as the magnetic tape cartridge on the 5100 Portable Computer, then programs and data can be stored in a secure location for safekeeping and be transferred from one computer to another.

Data is handled in a manner similar to programs. Initially, data is entered from the keyboard. If small amounts of data are involved, then they are held in the main storage unit during program execution and written to the mass storage device for long-term storage. If large amounts of data are used, then they are entered from the keyboard and written directly to the mass storage device because insufficient space would be available in the main storage unit to hold all of the data. Subsequently, when an item of data is needed during the execution of a program, it can be read from the mass storage device.

It is wise to recognize that a complete program must be in main storage in order for it to be executed. However, only the data necessary to sustain the execution of a given statement must be in main storage. Statements are available for transferring data between the main storage unit and the mass storage device, so that careful program planning can extend the range of programs that can be executed.

With nonportable computer systems, programs can also be entered from a card reader—if a program has been punched on cards, from a remote terminal device—if telecommunications facilities are used, and from a wide variety of lesser used input devices. In either case, however, the effective use of the main storage unit is dependent upon careful program planning.

The main storage unit is volatile, which means that programs and data held there are lost when electrical power to the computer is turned off. Information to be saved must be placed on a mass storage device prior to termination of a computer session.

Processing Unit

The processing unit controls the operation of the entire computer system by fetching statements from the main storage unit, interpreting them, and then executing the operations specified in the statements. The processing unit is comprised of two components: a control unit and an arithmetic-logic unit. The control unit permits the computer to operate automatically, by going from one statement to the next without human intervention. (This is in contrast to the hand or desk calculator which requires human interaction for each operation that is executed.) The control unit always keeps track of the location of the next statement in the main storage unit. When the execution of the current statement has been completed by the arithmetic-logic unit, the control unit fetches the next instruction, interprets it, and passes control signals to the arithmetic-logic unit to have the required operations executed. The arithmetic-logic unit reads the needed data from the main storage unit, performs the specified operations, and returns the computed result to the main storage unit. When a nonarithmetic statement is to be executed, the operations are performed by either the control unit or the arithmetic-logic unit, depending upon the specific function required.

Processing units differ between computer systems. Some computers require that a program be translated to primitive instructions, such as ADD, SUBTRACT, SHIFT, and STORE, and the processing unit then operates only on primitive instructions. Other computers, such as the 5100 Portable Computer, permit a program to be executed without going through the translation process. In the latter case, the processing unit checks each statement for errors and converts it into a recognizable format. The statement is then executed directly without any intervening steps.

Mass Storage Devices

Mass storage devices are used to hold programs and data for long periods of time. Two main types of mass storage devices are in widespread use: sequential devices and direct-access devices. Sequential devices employ a serial medium such as magnetic tape. With a sequential device, the computer must pass over the $(i-1)$st data element before the ith data element can be read. Direct-access devices use a rotating medium such as magnetic disk or magnetic drum. Through the use of access arms, a data element can be located directly on a direct-access medium. Before a data item on a mass storage device can be used by the process unit, it must first be read into the main storage unit. After being read into the main storage unit, the original copy of the data item on the mass storage medium remains intact. The process of placing a data item on a mass storage device is known as writing. In general, reading from a mass storage device is regarded as an input function, and writing to a mass storage device is an output function. Mass storage devices are nonvolatile, which means that information stored on them is not lost when electrical power to the device is turned off.

The 5100 Portable Computer utilizes a magnetic tape unit with a removable tape cartridge for the mass storage of programs and data. The fact that the tape cartridge can be removed means that the amount of mass storage space is potentially unlimited.

Input and Output Devices

In general, input and output devices include the following classes of equipment:

Card readers and punches
Paper tape readers and punches
Line printers

Telecommunication terminals and consoles

Special recognition equipment, such as badge readers, microfilm reader/writers, check readers, and graph plotters.

Each type of device has a specific kind of recording medium and is used for a particular application. Most computers are designed to handle a wide variety of input and output devices. Collectively, input, output, and mass storage devices are known as *peripheral devices* because they are regarded as serving in a peripheral role to the processing and main storage units.

Other than the keyboard/display unit covered in the next section, the 5100 Portable Computer permits the use of the following input and output devices: a line printer and the use of telecommunications facilities. The line printer permits printed output to be generated, and the telecommunications feature allows the 5100 Portable Computer to communicate with other computer systems under program control.

Keyboard/Display Unit

Input, output, and mass storage devices allow information to be transferred between an external device and the main storage unit. The keyboard/display unit, which consists of a keyboard unit and a display screen, allows an operator to communicate directly with the processing unit and thereby control its operation.

On large-scale computers, the keyboard/display unit is used solely to monitor computer operations. Programs and data are entered via an input device, such as the card reader, and output is received through an output device, such as the line printer.

On the 5100 Portable Computer, the keyboard/display unit can be used for four purposes:

1. As an operator console,
2. As an input device for entering data,
3. As an output device for receiving output, and
4. As an interactive device for entering, executing, and checking programs.

For many applications, all that is needed is the keyboard for input, the display screen for output, and the tape unit for storage. When printed reports are required, then the line printer can be used to obtain printed output.

Note on the 5100 Portable Computer

The preceding discussion of computer systems is not intended to be a presentation of the 5100 Portable Computer, which is covered in detail in subsequent chapters. The objective was solely to place the various concepts in perspective. Additional information on computer systems and programming can be obtained from the selected readings, which follow.

SELECTED READINGS

Crowley, T. H., *Understanding Computers*, McGraw-Hill Book Company, New York, 1967.

Feldzamen, A. N., *The Intelligent Man's Easy Guide to Computers*, David McKay Inc., New York, 1971.

Kemeny, J. G., *Man and the Computer*, Charles Scribner's Sons, New York, 1972.

Squire, E., *The Computer: An Everyday Machine*, Addison-Wesley Publishing Company, Reading, Mass., 1972.

2 | FOUNDATIONS OF PROGRAMMING AND SYSTEMS DESIGN

It is customary in professional books about computers to introduce basic concepts as they are needed. With regard to programming and programming languages, however, the full 5100 Portable Computer accepts programs written in two programming languages: APL and BASIC. Although the languages differ in scope and complexity, similar concepts apply to both languages, and to avoid duplication, the subject matter, collectively known as "foundations of programming and systems design," has been summarized in this chapter. The subject matter can be skipped by persons already familiar with the concepts. Persons who would like a brief review can read the chapter now or read it later on an "as needed" basis—depending upon whether they like their medicine in small or large doses.

2.1 NAMES

A name is used to identify an entity without having to give its attributes;* it is properly known in computing as an *identifier*. Identifiers are commonly used in the following ways:

1. To name an item of data.
2. To name a type of statement.

---

*For example, it has been said but never verified that in one German speaking country, a magnetic disk unit is called, "das recording thing das goes round and round."

3. To name a separating word in a program statement.
4. To denote a mathematical function or a computer operation.
5. To refer to a specific type of action performed by the computer system, i.e., a command.
6. To name a file of data on a mass storage device.
7. To name a program or work area.

The use of meaningful names facilitates the communication process between persons and between a person and the computer. Some names are fixed for a given computer. For example, the REWIND command instructs the computer system to rewind the tape cartridge. Other names, such as the name of an item of data, can be assigned by the user. In general, however, an identifier can be used in two well-defined instances:

1. In a statement of a program; or
2. As a command to the computer.

The two ways of using identifiers, in fact, effectively summarizes the ways a user can interact with the computer. The only other case in which a user would have to enter information is in response to an input request originating from an executable statement in a computer program.

Variables

The term *variable*, in contrast to the term constant, refers to a construct that can assume any member of a set of values. The value of a variable either varies during the course of being used, or the specific value is not significant in the validity of the assertion in which it is employed. In modern discourse, variables are also used to refer to a hypothetical or unknown concept. For example, we frequently hear declarations, such as "Let X be the . . . ."

In computing, a variable refers to a location in the main storage unit that can hold an element of data. The following statements:

In BASIC	In APL
LET A=2	$A \leftarrow 2$
LET B=3	$B \leftarrow 3$

are used to assign a value of 2 to the variable A and a value of 3 to the variable B; that is, after the statements are executed, the location identified by A contains a value of 2, and the location identified by B contains a value of 3. When a variable is used in a mathematical expression, such as A+B, the computer takes the contents of the locations specified by the respective variables, so that the expression is equivalent to 2+3. It is cumbersome to state, "the contents of the location specified by A," so that the phrases "the contents of A" and "the value of A" are commonly used substitutes in computer jargon.

Statements

In most programming languages, statements that perform specific computer functions are identified by a unique name. In the following BASIC statement, for example,

LET A=2

the key word LET is used to identify the assignment statement.* (In this case, the statement means, "assign the value 2 to the variable A.") Another example is,

GOTO 150

which means, "transfer program control to statement number 150." This is the GOTO statement in the BASIC language, and the key word GOTO is the name of the statement. The IF statement in the BASIC language uses a name that serves as a separating word, i.e., the name GOTO in the statement:

IF A>B GOTO 1630

which means, "transfer program control to statement number 1630 if the value of A is greater than the value of B; otherwise, continue with the next sequential statement."

Statement names and separating words are not used in the APL language, which is based on standard mathematical notation. However, several system variables, such as □WA that gives the remaining space in the work area, and system functions, such as □EX that excises an object from the active work area, are used to extend the range of computer facilities available to the user.

Programs

The area of main storage that can be used for loading a program and data is known as a work area or alternatively, as a workspace. In the 5100 Portable Computer, work areas and workspaces can be named so that programs and data (in the BASIC language) and functions and data (in the APL language) can be saved on a mass storage device. In the BASIC language, for example, the following system command:

SAVE 2, 'MYPROG'

saves the contents of the current work area as file numbered 2 on a tape cartridge and assigns the name MYPROG to the file. It can be subsequently loaded with a command of the form:

LOAD 2

*In modern implementations of the BASIC languages, the key word LET can be elided.

The name MYPROG is used for identification. In the APL language, the following system command:

$$)SAVE\ 2\ MYPROG$$

saves the contents of the current workspace as file numbered 2 on a tape cartridge and assigns the name MYPROG to the file. It can be subsequently loaded with a command of the form:

$$)LOAD\ 2\ MYPROG$$

In this case, the name MYPROG is used for identification and for security.

With the 5100 Portable Computer, a program is not assigned a name, per se. In the BASIC language, a program is given the name of the work area that is saved on a mass storage device. In the APL language, the user is permitted to define a function that corresponds to a program in both scope and complexity.

Functions

The term *function* has a well-defined meaning in mathematics. It is a mapping between two sets, depicted in Figure 2.1, and is expressed symbolically in a variety of ways, such as:

$$A \xrightarrow{f} B$$

$$f: A \rightarrow B$$

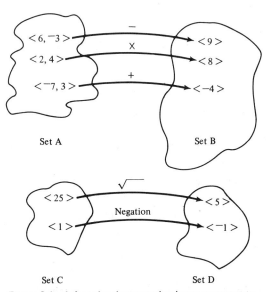

Figure 2.1   A function is a mapping between two sets.

An important characteristic of a function is the number of input values needed (known as *arguments*). For example, in the mapping:

$$<2,4>\overset{\times}{\to}<8>$$

two arguments are required, whereas in the mapping:

$$<25>\overset{\sqrt{\ }}{\to}<5>$$

one argument is required. In the BASIC and APL languages, functions are represented in the following ways:

	BASIC	APL
One argument x	f(x)	fx
Two arguments x and y	f(x,y)	x f y

where f is the name of the function.

Functions are another type of entity that must be named in computer programming languages. The BASIC language contains built-in functions, such as the square root and the absolute value, and also allows the user to define functions. The following BASIC statements demonstrate the use of the square root function, which is given the name SQR:

LET X=25
LET R=SQR (X)

The APL language contains a multiplicity of built-in functions and also allows the user to define functions. Built-in functions in APL use special symbols and user-defined functions are given names, as in the following example which performs a function named ACK on variables M and N and assigns the result to variable R:

R←M ACK N

More information on functions is given in the presentation of the BASIC and APL languages.

Commands

A command is a function performed by the computer system. Each command is assigned a meaningful name so that it can easily be remembered by a user of the 5100 Portable Computer. Typical commands are:

BASIC	APL	Function Performed
SAVE 2, 'MYPROG'	)SAVE 2 MYPROG	Saves work area (space) on tape.
LOAD 2, 'MYPROG'	)LOAD 2 MYPROG	Loads work area (space) from tape.

MARK 16,1,7	)MARK 16 1 7	Initializes tape file 7 to hold 16 thousand character positions.

Commands represent functions that normally are not needed during the execution of a computer program, so that corresponding BASIC and APL statements do not exist.

Files

When a program or a collection of data is placed on a mass storage device, it is called a *file*. Files are identified by their sequence on tape, such as the second file or the fifth file. A file can also be assigned a meaningful name, as covered above, and this name can supplement but not replace the file sequence number. Data can be placed on a tape file through the use of commands or written to a tape file from a BASIC or APL program.

2.2 DATA

The information upon which computer operations are performed is referred to as *data*. More specifically, the computer is like the human brain in the sense that it is a symbol processor. When, for example, we record an event in our brain, we actually record a symbolic image of that event. Later, only the symbolic image is required for us to think about that event. A computer operates in somewhat the same fashion by processing a symbolic representation of information known as data. The relationship of information, data, and computers is shown conceptually in Figure 2.2.

Overview

Most instances of computer data can be placed in three classes: numeric data, logical data, and descriptive data. Numeric data are normally associated with mathematical calculations and are commonly known as numbers. Logical data are used to record truth values and are commonly associated with logical oper-

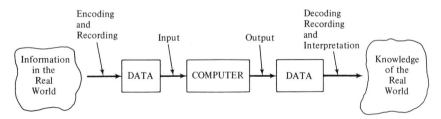

Figure 2.2 *Conceptual* view of the relationship of information, data, and computers in the real world.

ations.   Descriptive data, also known as *character data*, are used to name or identify objects and normally exist as strings of characters.

Data can be organized as single data items, such as a person's age, known as *scalars*, or they can be structured into collections of data items of the same type, but not necessarily of the same value, known as *arrays*. Examples of arrays are the ordinary vectors and matrices found in elementary mathematics.

Numeric Data

When using 5100 Portable Computer, all numeric data can be regarded as being stored in a decimal form. Internal to the computer, however, numeric data are stored in the binary number system, and computations are performed with binary values. This section is concerned with how numeric data are entered into the computer in decimal form and how they are displayed and recorded— again in decimal form. Three methods of representation are given: fixed-point form, integer form, and floating-point (or scalar) form. In general, the user of the 5100 Portable Computer has no control over how numeric data are stored internally and need not be concerned with it. External representation is the key emphasis here.

Fixed-Point Data.   In everyday calculations and in schoolbook arithmetic, calculations are performed on numbers represented in a positional* number system as a sequence of decimal digits, with possibly an algebraic sign or a decimal point. A number represented in this fashion is a *fixed-point number*, that takes the general form:

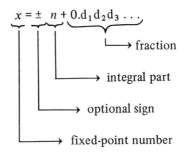

$$x = \pm\ n + 0.d_1 d_2 d_3 \ldots,$$

fraction

integral part

optional sign

fixed-point number

Clearly, the sign is optional, and the integral part, or the fractional part, or both must be present. The following are examples of fixed-point numbers:

$$
\begin{array}{cccc}
63 & 138.431 & .0000001 & 0 \\
-37 & -1.60001 & -64976200 & -.00123
\end{array}
$$

*In a positional number system (or Arabic system), the position of a digit determines its value, e.g., 44 is equal to $4 \times 10 + 4 \times 1$.

When fixed-point values are used in arithmetic calculations, the computer keeps track of the decimal point automatically, so that, for example, 1.321+63.24 is equal to 64.561 and 2.1X15 is equal to 31.5.

Unneeded constituents of a fixed-point number need not be written. In a number without a decimal point, an implied decimal point is assumed to be to the right of the rightmost digit. If, for example, it is necessary to enter a value of five, the user may simply enter 5 and need not enter +5, 5., or even 5.0— although 5.,+5, 5.1, and 5.0 are exactly equivalent values to the computer.

Fixed-point numbers are also called *decimal numbers*.

Integer Data. A fixed-point number without a fraction is an integer. An integer value participates in an arithmetic operation in precisely the same manner as a fixed-point value and may be entered into the computer in either form, as demonstrated in the preceding section. Integer values become significant in three cases.

1. When it becomes necessary to display the integral part of a fixed-point value;
2. When it is desired to index into an array (covered later in this chapter); and
3. When considering the amount of storage occupied by a program and data.

Integer values are also referred to as *whole numbers*.

Floating-Point Data. With very small and very large numbers, it is cumbersome to keep track of the decimal point, and the number of characters needed to represent the number may be large, as in the following examples:

$$.0000000012$$
$$3000000000000$$

Scientists and engineers frequently encounter values of this type and use scientific notation to represent them. Scientific notation uses a fraction and a base-10 exponential multiplier of the form:

$$x.xxxx \times 10^{y}$$

where the x's represent the fraction and the y represents an exponent. In scientific notation, .0000000012 would be expressed as $.12 \times 10^{-8}$, and 3000000000000 would be expressed as $.3 \times 10^{13}$. The objective of scientific notation is only to maintain the significant digits in a number plus a one- or two-digit exponent.

The computer equivalent of scientific notation is known as floating-point data. As with fixed-point and integer data, the computer automatically takes care of the internal representation of floating-point data, and the main concern here is over how floating-point data are entered and displayed.

Computer input and output facilities permit only a linear sequence of characters so that an alternate means of recording the exponent of a floating-point number is required. A commonly used convention is to use the letter E to denote a power of 10, demonstrated as follows:

Scientific Notation	Floating-Point Form
$.12 \times 10^{-8}$	.12E-8
$.3 \times 10^{13}$	.3E13
$-.9432 \times 10^{3}$	-.9432E3
$-.6 \times 10^{-2}$	-.6E-2

A user may enter data into the computer in the most convenient form, choosing from the fixed-point, integer, and floating-point options. When the computer is requested to display a numeric value, it selects from one of the three forms, depending upon the magnitude of the internally stored value. For display, the user may optionally program the computer to select a particular form of representation.

Floating-point form is also referred to as *scaled representation*.

Logical Data

A logical data item is used to represent a truth value that can be true or false. A value of one is used to denote the "true" case, and a value of zero is used to denote the "false" case. Because the range of logical data is small, existing only as two distinct values, it can be stored more efficiently than other types of data. The capability of using logical data is not available in all programming languages. When it is available, however, logical data can normally be entered by the user or originate through a comparison or logical operation.

Character Data

Character data serves descriptive purposes by permitting strings of characters to be entered, stored, and displayed. Character data are normally entered in quote marks and displayed without quote marks. A statement for assigning the string 'BICENTENNIAL 76' to variable T is given in BASIC and APL as:

BASIC   *APL*
LET T$ = 'BICENTENNIAL 76'   T←'BICENTENNIAL 76'

Character strings are stored differently in the various programming languages. In BASIC, for example, an entire character string is regarded as a single data item. In APL, on the other hand, each character is regarded as a single data item, and a string of characters is stored as an array. Arrays are covered in the next section.

2.3 DATA ORGANIZATION

In general, things in the real world are organized to make them easier to comprehend, describe, and use.

Constant vs. Value

An item of data that does not and cannot vary during the execution of a computer program is a *constant*. In the following examples,

$$BASIC \qquad APL$$
$$\text{LET R=Q+6} \qquad \text{R←Q+6}$$

the value 6 is a numeric constant, whereas the value of the variable Q is not regarded as a constant because it can vary during the execution of the program. Similarly, the statements given in the previous section in the BASIC and APL languages to assign the character string 'BICENTENNIAL 76' to variables T$ and T, respectively, represent the use of a character string constant, which exists as a character string enclosed in quote marks. The term *constant* is usually taken to refer to a numeric constant, and a character string constant is called a *literal*.

The terms *constant* and *literal* are used to identify data items as they exist in a computer program. When an item of data is entered by a user in response to an input request or when it participates in an input or output operation, involving the tape unit, line printer, or display, then that item of data is called a *value*. A value can be obtained in the following ways:

1. It can be read from an input unit and be assigned to a variable or an array (covered later);
2. It can be developed during the course of computation and be assigned to a variable or an array;
3. It can be written to an output unit as the value of a variable, an expression, or an element of an array.

To sum up, a constant stands for itself and does not vary during the course of computation; a value also does not vary during the course of computation) but achieves an identity through one of the methods given directly above.

Scalar Data

An ordinary item of data, expressed as a constant or value is known as a *scalar*. Common examples of scalars are the price of a computer, the age of a book, the name of a commodity, and the logical result of a comparison operation. A scalar consists of a single constant or value and an identifier that names a scalar is a scalar variable.

Array Data

When a few scalar values are involved in a computational process, it is customary to associate unique scalar variable names with the various values. When the values exist as a family of related data with the same attributes and the number of values in the family is relatively large, it is frequently necessary to reference the entire collection of data items with a single variable name because of the nature of the algorithm or because it would be cumbersome to name each data item because of the number of values involved. An aggregate of homogeneous* values with a single name is known as an *array*. Typical arrays are the vectors and matrices used in mathematics, and the concepts are extended systematically to include structures of higher dimension. The use of arrays does not in general require mathematical concepts, hence the more general term "array" instead of the mathematical terms "vector," "matrix," etc.

Classification. An array is classified by the number of dimensions it possesses and the type of data values it contains. Consider, for example, the monthly sales figures for the following seafood:

Commodity Number	Commodity Name	Units Sold
1	COD	18
2	HALIBUT	65
3	SALMON	36
4	SHRIMP	57
5	TROUT	23

Each sales figure is a scalar value; collectively, the list of sales figures could be stored as a linear array, such as,

$$FSALES = (18, 65, 36, 57, 23)$$

for which the entire list is given a name—the *array name* FSALES. The commodity number serves as the index to a specific value. Clearly, the commodity

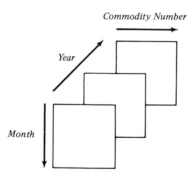

Figure 2.3   Conceptual view of a three-dimensional array. The row index is the month, the column index is the commodity number, and the plane index is the year.

*Homogeneous simply means that an array may consist of all numeric values or all character strings but not a combination of the two types of values.

name list could also be represented as a linear array of character strings, as follows:

FNAME = ('COD', 'HALIBUT', 'SALMON', 'SHRIMP', 'TROUT')

where, as in the sales figures, the commodity number serves as an index to a specific character string.

If the sales data were recorded for each month of a given year, the following two-dimensional array might result:

		Commodity Number				
		1	2	3	4	5
Month	1	18	65	36	57	23
	2	22	70	30	60	19
	3	25	77	25	55	24
	4	31	81	10	58	29
	5	37	93	5	62	35
	6	42	95	6	63	41
	7	34	96	12	60	39
	8	26	92	18	57	40
	9	19	79	27	56	37
	10	13	74	32	62	30
	11	8	66	40	59	29
	12	14	59	39	68	26

The month is identified by row number, and the specific commodity is identified by column number. The concept of a multidimensional array is easily extended to three dimensions. If the above two-dimensional array represented sales figures for a year, other years could be represented by additional two-dimensional arrays, as suggested by Figure 2.3. A pattern exists. A linear (i.e., one dimensional) array is composed of scalars, a two-dimensional array is composed of linear arrays, obviously of the same size, a three-dimensional array is composed of two-dimensional arrays, etc.

Selection. The process of selecting (or referencing) a distinct value in an array is accomplished through the use of the array name and the relative position of the value in the array. The indices necessary to select an element of an array are termed *subscripts* and can exist as constants, variables, or expressions. An index must exist for each dimension of the array. Consider, for example, the linear arrays named FSALES and FNAME given above. Using parentheses to denote a subscript, the value of FSALES(4) is equal to 57, and the value of FNAME(2) is 'HALIBUT.' If the succeeding two-dimensional array were named FLIST, then the values of FLIST(3,4) and FLIST(9,2) are equal to 55 and 79, respectively. Subscripts are enclosed in parentheses because computer input and output devices do not accommodate raised or lowered characters, as in conventional subscripts and superscripts.

Characteristics. The most important characteristics of an array are the number of dimensions, the bounds, and the extent. The number of dimensions governs how values in an array are selected; an index must exist in a subscript for each dimension. Each dimension is further characterized by a bounds and an extent. The *bounds* for a dimension determines the lowest and highest valued indices that apply to that dimension. The *extent* is the number of values along a given dimension—regardless of how they are selected. In the two-dimensional monthly sales figures given above, which were subsequently named FLIST, the row extent is 12, corresponding to each month in a year, and the column extent is 5, corresponding to each of the five types of seafood. In the same array, the row bounds are 1 and 12, and the column bounds are 1 and 5. The BASIC language always uses a lower subscript bound of 1, which simply means that indices run from 1 to n, where n is the corresponding extent. The APL language permits a lower subscript bounds of 0 or 1, so that the user has some flexibility in programming a particular algorithm.

2.4 OPERATORS AND EXPRESSIONS

The concept of a function, as introduced earlier in this chapter, has a well-defined meaning in mathematics and is frequently used in everyday discourse. It is customary to hear, for example, that the cost of a certain product is a function of its weight or its volume. A great many values are a function of several variables, similar to the manner in which the cost of living is a function of the cost of money, the level of unemployment, the amount of government spending, etc. In computer programming, an elementary function, such as addition or division, is termed an operator. It is elementary in the sense that it cannot be constructed from other elementary operators. The term *function* is reserved for a well-defined sequence of calculations, composed of operators and other functions.

Operands

The value upon which a computer operation is performed is termed an *operand*. Consider the following verbal statement of a set of computer operations: "Add B to C and replace A with the result." Another means of expressing the same sequence of calculations is: A=B+C. In both cases, which are equivalent, the variables A, B, and C are operands.

A data value selected through the use of a subscript is used as an operand in the same manner that a nonsubscripted variable is used. Thus, using the array named FSALES, given previously in the chapter, the value of the expression FSALES (4)+1 is equal to 57+1, or the value 58, in the same way that the expression A+1 would be equal to 58 if the value of A were 57.

Types of Operators

Arithmetic, logical, and comparison operators are classed by whether they require one or two operands. Ordinary arithmetic operators, such as addition and multiplication, require two operands, are classed as binary operators,* and are characterized by the fact that the operator symbol separates the operands, as in $x+y$. It follows that if the symbol $\lceil$ denotes the binary maximum operator, as it does in the APL language, then the function $MAX(x,y)$ would be expressed as $x \lceil y$.

Alternately, there are operators, such as negation, that require only one operand. Operators in this class are known as unary operators** and are written with the operator symbol preceding the operand, as in the following definition of negation:

$$-x \equiv 0-x$$

Other examples of unary operators are the logical not operator written as $\sim P$, where P is a logical operand, and the absolute value, ordinarily represented by double bars (i.e., $|x|$), which can be denoted by a single vertical stroke, written and defined as:

$$|x \equiv x \lceil (-x)$$

With the BASIC language, the terms *binary operator* and *unary operator* are usually used. With the APL language, the terms *dyadic* and *monadic* are usually used.

Arithmetic Operators and Expressions

Arithmetic operators in a computer programming language take the form of conventional mathematical notation, so that operators and operands can be combined to form complex sequences of calculations. In the BASIC language, for example, the expression

$$A*B+C$$

means, "multiply the value of A by the value of B and add the value of C to the product." In general, arithmetic operators are used in the conventional fashion, except that the following operator symbols are employed:

Operation	In the BASIC language	In the APL language
Addition	+	+
Subtraction or negation	–	–
Multiplication	*	×
Division	/	÷
Exponentiation	** or ↑	*

*Synonyms for binary operator are *dyadic operator* and *infix operator*.
**Synonyms for unary operator are *monadic operator* and *prefix operator*.

Execution of Operators. The sequence in which operators are executed is also of importance, and either of the two following methods is adopted in the design of a programming language:

1. Establish a hierarchy among the operators and always execute operators in a priority sequence; and
2. Execute the operators on a right-to-left or on a left-to-right basis.

The hierarchy method has been incorporated into the BASIC language, which recognizes the following priority among operators:

Operator	Priority
** (or ↑)	Highest
* and /	
+ and −	Lowest

With the hierarchy method, the expression, for example, 2*3+4 has a value of 10. A right-to-left rule has been adopted for the APL language because a great many operators are involved, and it would be cumbersome establishing a hierarchy. With the right-to-left rule, the expression 2*3+4 has a value of 14.

Arithmetic Expressions. The execution of some expressions requires that the computer deviate from the hierarchy or right-to-left rule. Assume here that the hierarchy method is employed. As an example, consider the representation in a computer program of the following mathematical expression:

$$\frac{3 \times a+b}{c-d} \times e^{x-1}$$

In mathematics, the vertical position of the numerator, denominator, and the exponent have meaning which is not possible with the linear arrangement of characters required for computer input. Therefore, parentheses are used for grouping to alter the sequence in which operators are executed. Expressions enclosed in parentheses are executed before the evaluation of expressions of which they are a part. The above mathematical expression would be represented and evaluated in the BASIC language, using the hierarchy method, as follows:

((3*A+B) / (C−D)) *E↑(X−1)

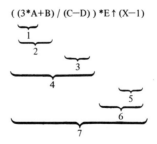

In the APL language, using the right-to-left rule, the same expression would be represented and evaluated as:

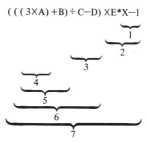

Comparison and Logical Operators

Algorithms frequently include alternatives that permit computations to be based on the value of one or more variables that change dynamically as the procedure is executed. Alternatives are implemented through the use of comparison and logical operators.

Comparison. In the computer representation of an algorithm, an alternative is selected through the use of a comparison operator, as in the following statement in the BASIC language:

$$\text{IF A5+E} > \text{L GOTO 310}$$

The statement means, "if the value of the expression A5+E is greater than the value of L, then make the next statement executed be the one that is numbered 310 and continue processing from there; otherwise, continue with the next statement in sequence." Six comparison operators are defined:

$<$ for *less than*
$\leq$ for *less than or equal to*
$=$ for *equal to*
$\neq$ for *not equal to*
$\geq$ for *greater than or equal to*
$>$ for *greater than*

The comparison operators are summarized in Table 2.1. The result of a comparison operation is always a truth value (i.e., true or false) that is used in a specific statement of a programming language or in a logical or arithmetic expression. In computing, the result of a comparison operation is known as a *condition*, so that it is customary to say that a "condition is true" or a "condition is false."

Logic. Composite conditions can be constructed through the use of logical operators. Some typical composite conditions are:

"Age is greater than 40" *or* "Salary is less than 20,000"   (1)

TABLE 2.1 SUMMARY OF COMPARISON OPERATORS

Operation	Form	Definition (R=result)	Example ($\longleftrightarrow$ denotes equivalence)
Less than	A<B	R is true if A is less than B and is false otherwise	$5<16\longleftrightarrow$true $6<6\longleftrightarrow$false $10<4\longleftrightarrow$false
Less than or equal to	A≤B	R is true if A is less than or equal to B and is false otherwise	$5\leq16\longleftrightarrow$true $6\leq6\longleftrightarrow$true $10\leq4\longleftrightarrow$false
Equal to	A=B	R is true if A is equal to B and is false otherwise	$10=4\longleftrightarrow$false $6=6\longleftrightarrow$true
Not equal to	A≠B	R is true if A is not equal to B and is false otherwise	$10\neq4\longleftrightarrow$true $6\neq6\longleftrightarrow$false
Greater than or equal to	A≥B	R is true if A is greater than or equal to B and is false otherwise	$5\geq16\longleftrightarrow$false $6\geq6\longleftrightarrow$true $10\geq4\longleftrightarrow$true
Greater than	A>B	R is true if A is greater than B and is false otherwise	$5>16\longleftrightarrow$false $6>6\longleftrightarrow$false $10>4\longleftrightarrow$true

$$\text{"Sex is equal to female" } and \text{ "Blood pressure is less than age+100"} \qquad (2)$$

The first composite condition is constructed from two elementary conditions:

"Age is greater than 40"

"Salary is less than 20,000"

each of which could be true or false. The elementary conditions are connected by the logical operator *or*, which denotes that the composite condition is true if either or both elementary conditions are true. If both elementary conditions are false, then the entire composite condition is false. In the second example, the elementary conditions are:

"Sex is equal to female"

"Blood pressure is less than age+100"

each of which can be true or false. In this case, the elementary conditions are connected with the logical operator *and*, which denotes that the composite condition is true if both elementary conditions are true and the composite condition is false, otherwise. Allowing the symbol $\wedge$ to stand for *and* and the symbol $\vee$ to stand for *or*, the above composite conditions could be expressed as:

$$(AGE > 40) \lor (SAL < 20000) \tag{1}$$

$$(SEX = `F') \land (BP < AGE + 100) \tag{2}$$

The *and* and *or* operators are classed as binary because they both require two operands. There is a third logical operator *not* (denoted by the tilde symbol $\sim$) which is unary and requires one operand. The *not* operator corresponds to the following statement:

"It is *not* the case that the temperature is greater than 98.6"

which could be represented symbolically as:

$$\sim(TEMP > 98.6)$$

In general, the truth value of the expression $\sim Q$ is true if Q is false, and it is false if Q is true. If a truth value of true is represented by 1 and a truth value of false is represented by 0, as they are in the APL language, then the following truth tables can be developed:

$\lor$	0	1		$\land$	0	1		$\sim$	0	1
0	0	1		0	0	0			1	0
1	1	1		1	0	1				

| *Or* | *And* | *Not* |

One advantage of using numeric values to represent truth values is that the result of a logical operation can be then used in an arithmetic expression.

Replacement

The process of replacing the value of a variable or the element of an array is called replacement that takes the form:

BASIC	*APL*
LET v=e	v←e

where v is a scalar variable or subscripted array variable and e is an expression. The following are valid examples of replacement statements:

BASIC	*APL*
LET A = (B+C)*D1	A←(B+C)×D1
LET M(I)=(A(J+1)−1)/2	M[I]←(A[J+1]−1)÷2

In general, when a scalar or an array variable is used in an expression, it retains its value. The value of a variable can only be changed through replacement or an input statement.

2.5 DATA MANAGEMENT

Data management is concerned with the form in which data is recorded on a mass storage device and the computer operations used to transfer data between the main storage unit and the mass storage device. Statements are included in programming languages for performing read and write operations to a mass storage device, and system commands are available for transferring complete programs and data files between a mass storage device and the main storage unit without requiring the use of a computer program.

The Byte Concept

The amount of information that can be held in the main storage unit or be recorded on a mass storage medium, such as the magnetic tape cartridge, is measured in terms of bytes. A *byte* is a unit of storage* that can be used to record one character's worth of information. A statement in a program occupies several bytes corresponding to the characters that comprise the statement. On the average, a numeric value occupies four bytes; however, the exact number of bytes is dependent upon the specific type of data. A character is stored in one byte position so that the amount of storage occupied by a character string is dependent upon the number of characters in the string. A logical true/false value requires only one bit of storage so that eight logical values can be stored in one byte location. It follows that the amount of storage necessary to store information (i.e., programs or data) is dependent upon the actual information that is recorded.

Fields

When a numeric value or a character string is recorded on a mass storage device, the data item normally occupies several byte positions. The amount of storage required to record that item is known as a field. More specifically, a *field* is a unit of storage that would lose its meaning if it were broken down further. For example, the string 'TEA FOR TWO' recorded on magnetic tape would be a field. Taken individually, the constituent characters are simply characters in the alphabet. Similarly, the value –123.4 recorded on magnetic tape is also a field, and the constituent digits are again characters of the alphabet.

Data Records

A group of consecutive fields that have some logical relationship to each other is called a *data record*, or more simply a *record*. A typical record might be the

---

*A byte is composed of eight bits, where "bit" is an acronym for binary digit. A bit can be 0 or 1. Combinations of bit patterns are used as codes for the characters in the alphabet recognized by the computer.

entries for a single part in an inventory file and include the following fields: part number, part name, inventory level, reorder point, lot size, unit price, inventory location, weight, delivery period, and primary supplier. The data values that comprise a record are usually recorded with a single output statement, so that the extent of the record can be determined by the computer system.

When programs are placed on a mass storage medium, each statement takes the form of a record, composed of a variable number of characters depending upon the specific statement. Commands for storing programs are covered in a separate section, and language facilities for reading and writing records are covered with the presentation of the respective languages.

Files

A set of related records written to contiguous record positions on a mass storage medium is called a *file*, giving rise to popular terminology such as "payroll file" and "inventory file." In a payroll file, for example, a payroll record would exist for each employee in the organization and the file, as a whole, would represent the organization's payroll activities.

The term *file* is also used to refer to a segment of a magnetic tape cartridge used for a particular application. Prior to being used, a magnetic tape cartridge is preformatted so that sufficient storage space is available in each file to handle the needs of the intended application. When programs, data, or both are subsequently written to a file, facilities are available for assigning a name to the file for identification and for specifying the type of file, i.e., a program file, data file, work area, etc.

SELECTED READINGS

Burch, J. G., Jr., and Strater, F. R., Jr., *Information Systems: Theory and Practice*, Hamilton Publishing Company, Santa Barbara, California, 1974.

Davis, G. B., *Introduction to Electronic Computers*, McGraw-Hill Book Company, New York, 1971.

Katzan, H., *Computer Data Management and Data Base Technology*, Van Nostrand Reinhold Company, 1975.

Mader, C., and R. Hagin, *Information Systems: Technology, Economics, Applications*, Science Research Associates, Inc., 1974.

Wu, M. S., *Introduction to Computer Data Processing*, Harcourt Brace Jovanovich, Inc., 1975.

3 | STRUCTURE OF THE 5100 PORTABLE COMPUTER SYSTEM

The IBM 5100 Portable Computer System is designed to be used for problem solving and data processing without a large investment of time in training and in gaining practical experience. In fact, the 5100 Portable Computer can be used as a desk calculator by a person without any programming knowledge. In order to write programs in either the BASIC or APL languages, a person must be familiar with the programming language and with the operating procedures for the 5100 Portable Computer. Both types of informaton are presented in this book. The language chosen for writing a program, however, must be acceptable to the computer that is used. The 5100 is available in three models: a BASIC machine; and APL machine; and a combined machine that accepts a program written in either language.

3.1 SYSTEM CONFIGURATION

The maximum configuration of a 5100 Portable Computer System is depicted in Figure 3.1 and includes the 5100 Portable Computer, a printer unit, an auxiliary tape unit, and an internal communications adapter. The 5100 Portable Computer is the heart of the system and is required; the other components are optional. Each component has an on/off switch, and the switch must be in an on position before the component can be used.

The 5100 Portable Computer must be operating for any component of the system to operate because the computer controls all functions that are executed. However, the 5100 Portable Computer may be operated when an auxiliary com-

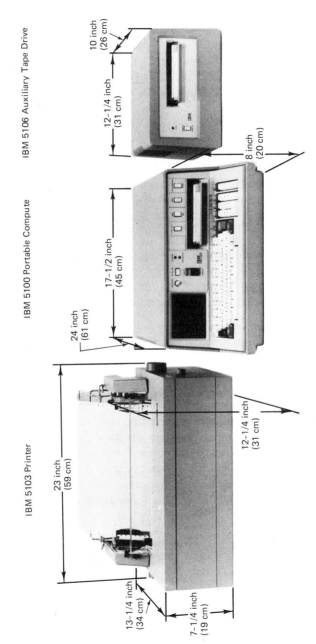

Figure 3.1 Configuration of the 5100 Portable Computer System. (*Courtesy IBM*)

ponent is not turned on—even though it may be physically connected. The 5100 Portable Computer responds to a component that is not turned on as though it were not physically connected.

A component may be turned on and off when the 5100 Portable Computer is executing instructions without disrupting the computer's operation. The only restriction is that a component should not be turned off when it is actively being used by the 5100 Portable Computer.

3.2 THE 5100 PORTABLE COMPUTER

The 5100 Portable Computer is self-contained and weighs 24 kg (approximately 50 pounds). It operates on ordinary 115 volt household current and, except for extreme cases, is insensitive to environmental conditions. No air conditioning is required. The computer includes the following components:

1. A processing unit,
2. A main storage unit,
3. A magnetic tape unit,
4. A keyboard,
5. A display screen, and
6. Various dials, lights, and switches.

The computer also includes an adapter for a black and white TV monitor, which can be used to project the contents of the display screen. The processing unit controls the operation of the 5100 Portable Computer and auxiliary components, performs all computations, and participates in any communication between the computer and the external world. In spite of the importance of the processing unit, its characteristics are transparent to the user—except for the realization that when the computer is operating, it is under the control of the processing unit. The processing unit is not discussed further, as is the case with the TV adapter, which is a straightforward electrical connection. A closer look at the 5100 Portable Computer is given in Figure 3.2 in which the components given above—except for internal components—are labeled. The computer is relatively small in size; the following are its approximate dimensions:

$$\text{Width:} \quad 45 \text{ cm } (17\tfrac{1}{2} \text{ inches})$$
$$\text{Depth:} \quad 61 \text{ cm } (24 \text{ inches})$$
$$\text{Height:} \quad 20 \text{ cm } \quad (8 \text{ inches})$$

The size of the 5100 Portable Computer is not dependent upon the type of machine (i.e., BASIC, APL, or BASIC/APL) or the amount of main storage.

Console

The front of the 5100, which contains the keyboard, display screen, built-in tape unit, and various dials and switches, is called the console. The console of a com-

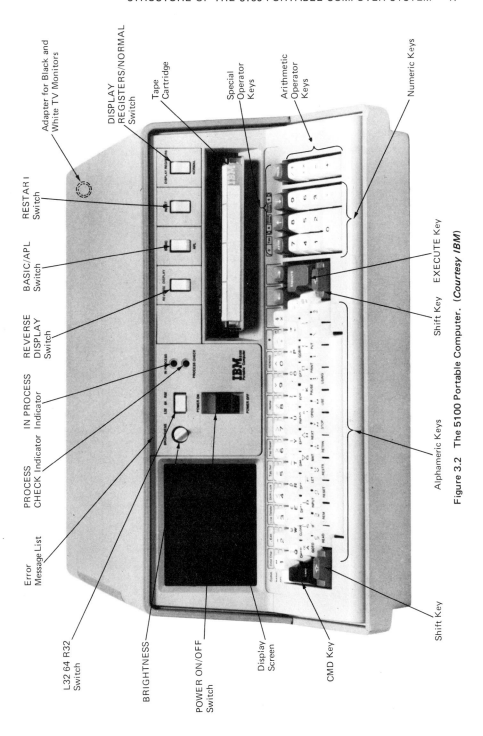

Figure 3.2   The 5100 Portable Computer.   *(Courtesy IBM)*

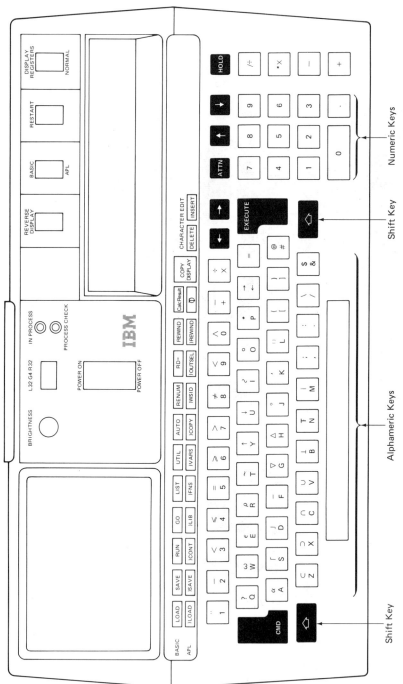

Figure 3.3   Console of a combined BASIC/APL machine.   (*Courtesy IBM*)

bined BASIC/APL machine is shown in Figure 3.3. If a BASIC-only machine is available, then features pertinent to the APL language are not present. Language-dependent features are covered later.

The console is the user's interface with a 5100 Portable Computer System. The keyboard, including several special function keys, is the means by which information, including programs and data, can be entered into the system manually. The keyboard is also used to control the operation of the computer through the use of system commands. Information typed at the keyboard is displayed automatically on the display screen so that it can be inspected prior to entry. The display screen is also used by the computer or the user to display:

1. Error conditions,
2. Computed results,
3. Statements in a program, and
4. Information about the current status of the various components in the computer system.

Above the keyboard is a set of system command words that can be entered by holding down the CMD key and then pressing the key below the desired keyword to be entered. Commands may also be entered on a character-by-character basis.

The dials, switches, indicators, and the built-in tape unit are located in the upper right quadrant of the console. A pull-out card is located at the top of the console; it gives the error conditions that correspond to error codes generated by the 5100 Portable Computer.

Display Screen

The display screen, shown in Figure 3.4, is designed as a visual read-out and is used to display information in character form. With display screen, 16 lines of data can be displayed at a time. Each line may contain up to 64 characters.

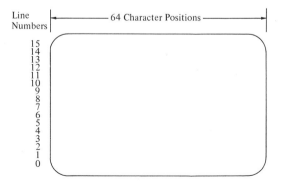

Figure 3.4   5100 display screen.

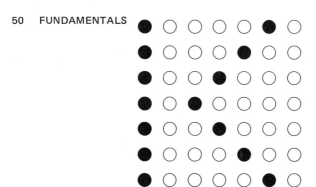

Figure 3.5   Each character is represented on the display screen as an 8 7 matrix of dots. The matrix arrangement permits special and composite characters to be displayed.

The character generator used by the display unit uses an arrangement whereby each character is represented by an 8X7 matrix of dots, as suggested by Figure 3.5. This feature permits the characters shown on the keyboard as well as selected composite characters* to be displayed.

The bottom two lines, numbered 0 and 1, of the display screen are used to display input—for visual verification—and the remaining 14 lines contain a history of previous operations. An input line is entered in line position 1 by typing the desired information and pressing the execute key. As a line is processed, all lines of the display are moved up one position so that information can be entered on the two bottom lines again. The topmost lines of the display are lost as they are moved off the display screen. Input lines are handled slightly differently in BASIC and APL as outlined below.

Cursor. The position in the input line that will be occupied by the next character entered is indicated by a flashing underline character called a *cursor.* When a character is entered, the cursor moves one position to the right. When the cursor is moved to an occupied character position, the character also flashes. Special keys are included in the console for moving the cursor to the right and to the left.

BASIC Input. When the 5100 Portable Computer is in the BASIC mode, input is entered in line position 1, and line position 0 is used to display status information on the state of the computer system, as shown in Figure 3.6. Up to 64 characters of input, corresponding to a line, can be entered at one time. All input and output to the display screen in BASIC begins with the first character position of a line.

---

*A composite character is a character constructed by typing one character, backspacing, and then typing an appropriate overstruck character. For example, the sequence: O, backspace | would give the character ϕ.

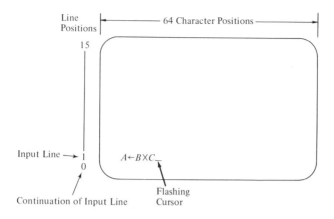

APL Language

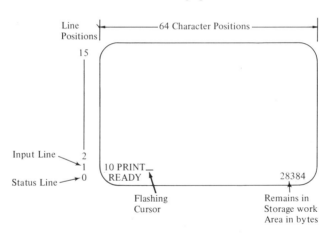

BASIC LANGUAGE

Figure 3.6   Input line positions in the BASIC and APL languages. In BASIC, line 1 is used to enter information; line 0 contains status information. In APL, input line 1 is automatically continued to line 0 if more than 64 characters are entered.

APL Input.   When the 5100 Portable Computer is in the APL mode, input is entered in line positions 1 and 0. After the 64th character position of line 1, the cursor goes automatically to the first character position of line 0. Therefore, up to 128 characters of input, corresponding to two lines, can be entered at one time. APL input is also demonstrated in Figure 3.6. When the keyboard and display screen are readied by the computer for APL input, the cursor is indented six spaces to character position 7 for visual fidelity. All APL output to the display screen begins in the first character position.

Keyboard

The keyboard on the 5100 console consists of three sets of keys:

1. Alphameric keys,*
2. Numeric keys, and
3. Operating keys.

BASIC only and combined BASIC/APL keyboards are shown in Figure 3.7.

Alphameric keys. The alphameric keys are located in the leftmost two-thirds of the keyboard and have a similar arrangement to an office typewriter. All alphabetic characters print as capital letters. As with a typewriter, a character appearing on the lower half of the face of a key is entered by pressing the key— analogous to a lower-case character. A character appearing on the upper half of the face of a key is entered by holding the shift key down and then pressing the key—analogous to an upper-case character. *All 5100 characters may be printed or displayed—regardless of whether they have meaning in a particular language or not.*

Numeric Keys. Numeric keys are located in the top row of the alphameric keys or in the special calculator area at the right of the keyboard. Either set of keys can be used to enter numbers. The rightmost column of the calculator area also contains arithmetic operator symbols for easy access.

With the combined keyboard, the multiplication and division keys in the calculator area show multiple symbols. The symbols * and X are shown for multiplication, and the symbols / and ÷ are shown for division. When either of these keys is used, the computer automatically selects the appropriate symbol, depending on whether the computer is currently in the APL mode or the BASIC mode.

Operating Keys. The grey and black keys on the keyboard are operating keys that are used to perform a variety of editing and control functions. The major function of each key is given here. The manner in which operating keys can be used to facilitate the editing and entry of information is given later. Each operating key has a name that corresponds to the function performed by it; these names are depicted in Figure 3.8 and summarized in the following paragraphs:

The *shift key* is used to enter an upper-shift character displayed on the upper half of the face of a key.

The *attention key* (ATTN) is used to interrupt the execution of a program, to stop the screen from flashing after an error, and to blank the remainder of a line when entering information from the keyboard. More specifically in the latter case, pressing the ATTN key blanks everything to the right of the cursor, including the cursor position, on the input line, which is line position 1 in the BASIC mode and line positions 1 and 0 in the APL mode.

*The term *alphameric* refers to the set of alphabetic, numeric, and special characters.

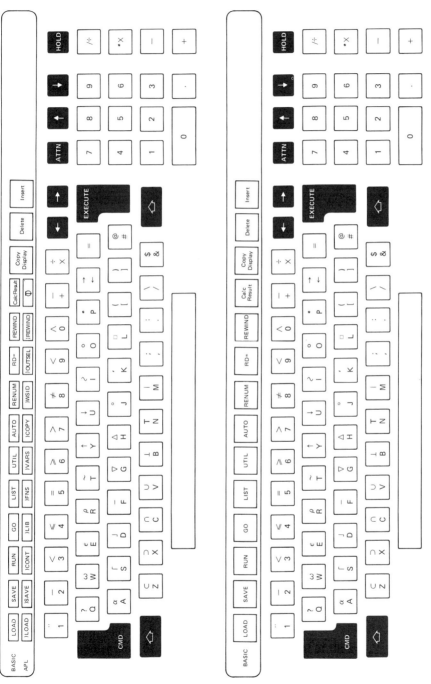

Figure 3.7   BASIC-only and combined BASIC/APL keyboards.

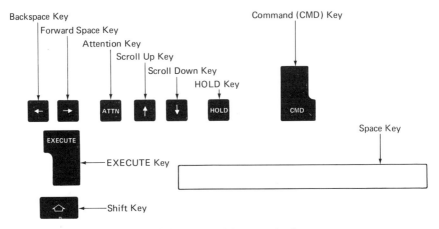

Figure 3.8   Names of the operating keys.

The *backspace key* moves the cursor to the left in the input line. When the cursor is at the first character position of the input line; pressing the backspace key causes the cursor to wrap-around to the rightmost position of the input line. Moving the cursor does not alter the information previously keyed in.

The *forward space key* moves the cursor to the right in the input line. When the cursor is at the rightmost character position of the input line, pressing the forward space key causes the cursor to wrap-around to the first character position of the input line. Moving the cursor does not alter information previously keyed in.

The *scroll up key* moves all displayed lines up one line position, which includes line positions 1 and 0 when the computer is in the APL mode and line position 1 when the system is in the BASIC mode. The topmost line of the display is lost as it is moved off the display screen. As the displayed lines are moved up, a blank line always enters the lowermost line position. In the BASIC mode, pressing the scroll up key causes the cursor to move to the leftmost position of the input line. In the APL mode, the cursor is not moved.

The *scroll down key* moves all displayed lines down one line position. When in the APL mode, the line in line position 1 enters line position 0, and line 0 is lost. When in the BASIC mode, the line in line position 2 enters line position 1, and line 1 is lost; the status line remains unchanged. A blank line always enters the display screen in line position 15. In the BASIC mode, pressing the scroll down key causes the cursor to move to the leftmost position of the input line. In the APL mode, the cursor is not moved.

The *space key,* located at the bottom of the keyboard as in a typewriter, enters a space into the input line and replaces any character previously entered. It should be used to move the cursor only when the insertion of blank characters is desired or when the character positions in the line are blank.

The backspace, forward space, scroll up, scroll down, and space keys have a repeat capability, meaning that the action performed is repeated as long as the key is held down.

The *execute key* initiates the processing of the input line. The execute key must be used to enter any form of input including data, statements, and commands.

The *command key* (CMD) is used to activate the system commands printed above the keyboard. A command is entered into the input line by holding the command key down and then pressing the key in the top row just below the desired system command. The alphameric characters that comprise the command are entered into the input line—as though they were keyed in on a character-by-character basis, which is also permitted. A system command is executed when the execute key is pressed as outlined above. The command key is also used with certain editing functions that permit line-by-line editing of programs and data.

The *hold key* stops the operation of the computer and is used to allow reading of the display screen when output lines are changing rapidly. Pressing the hold key once stops computer processing; pressing the key the second time resumes normal processing. When the operation of the computer is stopped, only the COPY DISPLAY key is active.

The *copy display key* copies the contents of the display screen to the printer. The COPY DISPLAY key is activated by holding down the command key and pressing the appropriate alphameric key. If the printer unit is operatonal, then printing starts immediately. If the printer unit is not operational. an error condition is displayed. The COPY DISPLAY function is the *only* entry that does not require the execute key.

Knowledge of the primary function of the operating keys is fundamental to programming and using the 5100 Portable Computer. Other operational functions are available through the use of various key combinations and are covered under the languages to which they apply.

Switches and Lights

The switches and lights on the 5100 Portable Computer console permit the user to control computer processing and monitor its operation. The intensity of the display screen and the manner in which information is displayed can also be controlled.

Power On/Off Switch. The power on/off switch is red and controls the supply of electrical power to the computer. The computer is operational when this switch is set to the on position; the switch should be turned off when the computer is not in use. When the computer is turned off, all programs and data held in the processing unit and the main storage unit are lost. On dual language machines, the desired language mode should be selected prior to turning the system on; otherwise a restart would be necessary as outlined in the following paragraphs. After turning the switch on, the computer takes 10–15 seconds to perform internal hardware checking and initialization. The computer is ready for use when the READY message is displayed in the BASIC mode or the CLEAR WS message is displayed in the APL mode. (The message CLEAR WS denotes a clear workspace.)

BASIC/APL Switch. The BASIC/APL switch, which is operational on dual-language machines, determines the language that can be used. If the setting of the switch is changed after the computer is turned on, then the restart switch must be pressed to reinitialize the system.

Restart Switch. The restart switch reinitializes the computer and performs the hardware check covered earlier under the on/off switch. This switch is used after the language mode is changed on dual-language machines and to restart the system after a hardward-detected process check, which denotes machine malfunction. After the restart switch is pressed, the contents of the processing unit and the main storage unit are lost.

Display Registers Switch. The display registers switch has two settings: "display registers" and "normal." When the switch is set to "display registers," the first 512 bytes of the main storage are displayed for maintenance purposes. This switch would be set in the "normal" position during ordinary system utilization.

L32-64-R32 Switch. The L32-64-R32 switch governs the extent of information display. When the switch is in the L32 position, the left half of each 64-character line is displayed. Successive characters are displayed with an intervening blank character to facilitate reading. When the switch is in the 64 position, normal 64-character lines are displayed. When the switch is in the R32 position, the right half of each 64-character line is displayed. Successive characters are displayed with an intervening blank to facilitate reading.

Brightness Control Dial. The brightness control dial can be used to vary the intensity of the characters displayed to correspond with lighting conditions.

Reverse Display Switch. The reverse display switch selects one of the following display modes:

1. Light characters on a dark background, or
2. Dark characters on a light background.

Light characters on a dark background gives better visual fidelity because the normal tone of the screen is dark. In the dark-on-light mode, a light rectangle is centered in the display screen upon which dark characters are projected. It is usually necessary to adjust the brightness control when switching between display modes.

Process Lights. There are two process lights: in process and process check. During the execution of a program, expression, or user-defined function—as the case may be in BASIC or APL—the processing may take several seconds or minutes during which time the screen is blank. The IN PROCESS light is turned on to indicate that the computer is operating. When the processing is complete and the display is again turned on, the in process light goes off. The in process light is not turned on when intermittent output is being displayed during a computational process. The action of the hold key pressed when the in process light is on does not take effect until the in process light goes off; however, during that period, the processing may be interrupted with the attention key. The PROCESS CHECK light denotes a hardware detected system malfunction. When this occurs, the restart switch should be pressed to reinitialize the system. If the system cannot be restarted after several attempts, service is required. One word of caution is in order. The case when the screen is blank and the in process light is not on would ordinarily represent an error condition. The in process light is not sensitive to brightness control, but the display screen is. Therefore, it is a good idea to adjust the brightness control dial before calling for service.

Main Storage Capacity

5100 Portable Computers are identified by main storage capacity, in addition to the type of machine (i.e., BASIC, APL, or combined) and system configuration. The following identification scheme is used:

| | *Type of Machine* | | |
Main Storage Capacity	*APL*	*BASIC*	*Combined*
16K	A1	B1	C1
32K	A2	B2	C2
48K	A3	B3	C3
64K	A4	B4	C4

where K is equivalent to 1,024 bytes. (For example, 2K = 2,048 bytes.)

The main storage unit is organized into three major areas (see Figure 3.9):

1. Internal storage requirements,
2. User work area (in BASIC) or active workspace (in APL), and
3. Storage area for internal machine fixes (IMFs).

The *internal storage requirements* include main storage space for control and input/output programs, pointers, and tables. Storage requirements in this category vary depending upon the type of machine but are *approximately* 4,300 bytes for a BASIC machine and 5,800 bytes for an APL machine. The *user work area* (in BASIC) and the *active workspace* (in APL) is used to hold programs, data, and

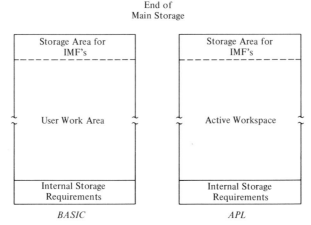

Figure 3.9 Organization of the main storage unit.

associated tables needed to store a program. The *internal machine fix* (IMF) area is used for changes to the control programs that correct anomalous operating conditions. In general, IMF's need not be used unless they apply to the execution of a given program.

The size of the user work area or the active workspace is the most significant from a user's point of view, since it represents the size of programs that can be executed. However, storage space is not commensurate in BASIC and APL, because APL is a more powerful computational language. On the average, more computations can be specified in a single APL statement than in a single BASIC statement.

The number of storage positions available to the user is displayed in the lower right-hand corner of the display screen when the system is in the BASIC mode. For example, with a model C2 computer, which includes both BASIC and APL facilities, this amount is 28,385 bytes before programs or data are entered. In APL, the size of the available workspace is displayed with the □WA system function. With a model C2 computer, this amount is 26,076 bytes with a clear workspace.

3.3 AUXILIARY COMPONENTS

The auxiliary components in a 5100 Portable Computer system are the printer unit, an auxiliary tape unit, and a communications adapter. The built-in tape unit is also covered in this section.

Printer Unit

The 5103 Printer Unit, shown in Figure 3.10, is connected to the 5100 Portable Computer through an ordinary pin connection. Although the printer unit

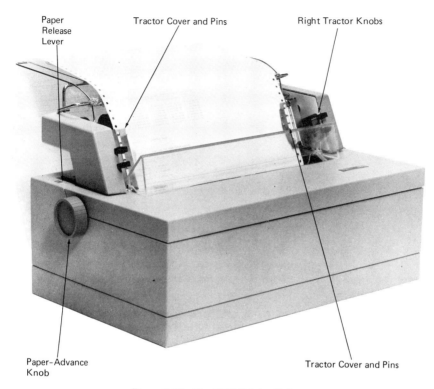

Figure 3.10   The 5103 Printer Unit.

weighs slightly more than the computer at 26 kg (56 pounds) and can be moved easily, it is not regarded as a portable device.

Specifications. The physical dimensions of the printer unit are:

$$\text{Height:}\ \ 31\text{ cm } (12\tfrac{1}{4}\text{ inches})$$
$$\text{Depth:}\ \ \ 34\text{ cm } (13\tfrac{1}{4}\text{ inches})$$
$$\text{Width:}\ \ \ 59\text{ cm } (23\text{ inches})$$

The printer unit can print at a rate of 80 characters per second in a bidirectional mode, which means that the print head can print in a left-to-right or right-to-left direction depending upon the end of the previous line. The unit functions as a matrix printer.

Print Characteristics. The maximum print width is 132 characters and a loss of data occurs if a print line exceeds the width of the form. The spacing of print positions is 10 characters per inch, and the line spacing is 6 lines per inch.

Forms. Individual or continuous multipart forms can be used ranging from 76.2 mm (3 inches) to 368.3 mm (14.5 inches), for individual forms, and 381 mm (for continuous forms). The printer unit permits paper to be fed through

Figure 3.11   A tape cartridge is made available for reading or recording by inserting it into the built-in tape unit of the 5100 Portable Computer.

Figure 3.12   The 5106 Auxiliary Tape Unit.

the printing mechanism with a pin feed forms tractor or with friction feed rollers.

Magnetic Tape Units

The magnetic tape units on the 5100 Portable Computer allow programs and data to be stored on a temporary basis or on a permanent basis through the use of the removable tape cartridge. Two tape units are available: a built-in unit and an auxiliary unit.

Built-in Tape Unit. The built-in tape unit is located in the upper right quadrant of the 5100 console. The built-in unit is standard feature that is included in every 5100 Portable Computer. When the 5100 Portable Computer is turned on, the built-in tape unit is turned on as well. Programs and data are stored on a tape cartridge that is functionally similar to 8-track stereo tape cartridges or tape cassettes in common use for audio recording. The tape cartridge is inserted into the 5100 built-in tape unit as shown in Figure 3.11.

Auxiliary Tape Unit. The 5106 Auxiliary Tape Unit, shown in Figure 3.12, is an optional feature of a 5100 Portable Computer system and provides a second unit for applications that require it. Both units are functionally the same and can be used concurrently. The auxiliary tape unit weights 8 kg (18 pounds) and has the following physical dimensions:

$$\begin{array}{ll} \text{Height:} & \text{19 cm } (7\frac{1}{2} \text{ inches}) \\ \text{Depth:} & \text{26 cm (10 inches)} \\ \text{Width:} & \text{31 cm } (12\frac{1}{2} \text{ inches}) \end{array}$$

The auxiliary unit has an on/off switch that must be turned on before the unit can be used. Magnetic tape cartridges can be read and written interchangeably between the built-in and auxiliary units.

Tape Cartridge. The tape cartridge*, shown in Figure 3.13, contains 91.44 m (300 feet) of 6.35 mm (1/4 inch) magnetic tape and can store a minimum of 200,000 characters of formatted data. The unit operates at the following speeds:

$$\begin{array}{l} \text{Read: 2,850 characters per second} \\ \text{Write: 950 characters per second} \\ \text{Search and rewind: 1.02 m per second (40 inches per second)} \end{array}$$

The magnetic tape is enclosed in a clear plastic case that measures:

$$\begin{array}{ll} \text{Width:} & \text{15.2 cm (6 inches)} \\ \text{Depth:} & \text{10.2 cm (4 inches)} \\ \text{Thickness:} & \text{16 cm (5/8 inch)} \end{array}$$

and is keyed to prevent it from being inserted into the tape unit incorrectly.

*IBM refers to the cartridge as the "IBM Data Cartridge." The term "tape cartridge" is used to communicate the type of storage medium.

Figure 3.13   The tape cartridge.

Each cartridge has a safe switch (Figure 3.14) that is used for file protection. When the arrow is in the safe position, the tape can be read but it cannot be written. When the arrow is not pointing to the safe position, the tape can be read or written.

Formatting the Tape Cartridge.   Before a tape cartridge can be used to store programs or data, it must be formatted. Described briefly, the process of preparing a tape consists of marking the tape so that the space allocated to each file is precisely defined. Files are ordered consecutively on tape and are located and identified by number.

The mark command is used to format a tape cartridge. In the BASIC language, it takes the form:

MARK   3,2,1

and in the APL language, it takes the form:

)MARK   3 2 1

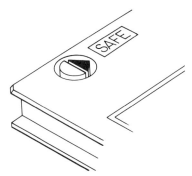

Figure 3.14 Each tape cartridge contains a safe switch that can be used for file protection.

Both commands perform precisely the same function, which in this case marks the tape for two files of 3K characters* each, starting with file numbered 1. The manner in which a marked file can be used is covered with each of the languages.

Communications Adapter

The 5100 Communications Adapter and associated communications programs permit the 5100 Portable Computer to interact with another computer system via telecommunications facilities, through switched or nonswitched lines. With this feature, the 5100 Portable Computer can be a terminal to a larger computer or be used to provide access to a remote data base or program library. Data can be transmitted and received via the 5100.

Communications Keyboard. The communications feature uses the extended keyboard shown in Figure 3.15. Through the use of the command key (CMD) and the keys of the calculator pad, communications-oriented operations and commands can be executed. When the system is in the communications mode, several alphameric keys are used to perform special functions related to a communications environment.

Communications Mode. The 5100 Portable Computer is placed in the communications mode by placing the tape cartridge containing the communications program into the built-in tape unit and then by entering a system command appropriate to the mode of operation. When the system is in the BASIC mode, the user enters:

UTIL MODE CODE

to enter the communications mode and when the system is in the APL mode, the user enters:

)MODE COM

*K is used to indicate 1,024.

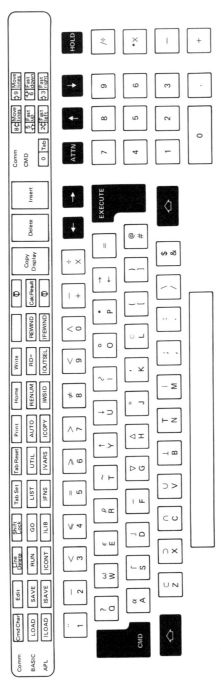

Figure 3.15 Extended keyboard for the communications adapter.

to perform the same function. The communications programs are then loaded, and the various options are presented to the user.

Extended Display. When the 5100 Portable Computer is in the communications mode, the display screen* and the extended display are used to store the transmitted and received data. Line position 0 of the display is used for status information and line position 1, called the *input line*, is used to display data as it is transmitted and received. The remaining 14 lines of the display area plus an extended display store the incoming and outgoing messages on a revolving basis. When the extended display becomes full, the oldest line is deleted. The *extended display* is a storage area in main storage for holding data. The size of the extended display is dependent upon the size of main storage and is approximately the following:

Model	*Size* (of extended display)
A1, B1, C1	1K
A2, B2, C2	17K
A3, B3, C3	33K
A4, B4, C4	49K

Using the scroll keys, covered later, any line of the extended display can be moved to the display screen.

Lines Versus Messages. Information is displayed on the screen and stored in the extended display area as a set of lines, where a *line* is regarded as the data between two line feed characters. A *message* is the data between the start-of-transmission and end-of-transmission codes and may include one or more lines.

Scroll Operations on the Extended Display. Lines are moved between the display screen and the extended display with scroll operations initiated by holding the command key (CMD) down and pressing a calculator key. The *home position* of the extended display is the first 64 characters of the last 14 lines entered into the extended display. The following scroll operations are used only with the extended display and are executed when the system is in the communications mode by holding down the CMD key:

Key		Function
2	Fast left scroll	Moves the data on the display screen 20 positions to the left.
3	Fast right scroll	Moves the data on the display screen 20 positions to the right.

---

*In particular, an area exists in the "internal requirements" section of main storage for lines displayed on the display screen. This is where the information that corresponds to that displayed is stored.

Key		Function
[5]	Fast up scroll	Moves the data on the display screen up 14 lines.
[6]	Fast down scroll	Moves the data on the display screen down 14 lines.
[8]	Scroll left	Moves the data on the display screen one position to the left.
[9]	Scroll right	Moves the data on the display screen one position to the right.

The special function scroll keys for the extended display supplement the BASIC and APL scroll up and scroll down keys, which function only with the display screen.

Editing of the Extended Display. The communications system includes an edit package that permits data in the extended display area to be processed. The functions are executed by holding down the CMD key and pressing one of the following keys:

Key		Function
[2]	Edit	Starts the edit operation.
[3]	Line delete	Deletes all characters on the input line to the right of and at the cursor position.
[7]	Print	Prints the data stored in the extended display from the input line to the end of the extended display.
[8]	Home	Restores the data on the display screen to the home position in the extended display.
[9]	Write (option T only)	Writes the data stored in the extended display on tape from the input line to the end of the extended display.

When a line is edited, it must first be positioned on the input line through the use of the extended display scroll keys. After a series of edit commands, the edit operation can be terminated by pressing execute, attention, or home key (CMD plus alphameric 8).

TABLE 3.1 SUMMARY OF COMMUNICATIONS COMMANDS.

Command	Function
&AUTO	Allows messages to be received that are too long for the extended display.
&CLOSE	Completes tape operations and makes the unit unavailable for further operations.
&OPEN	Prepares a tape file for processing.
&OUTSEL	Controls printing of messages.
&RATE	Specifies bit rate of communications system.
&SYSTEM	Specifies character code translations required between systems.
&TAPEIN	Specifies tape input for transmitted messages.

Commands. System commands are used to establish a particular mode of the communications system. Each command starts with a special character (&) entered by holding the CMD key and pressing the alphameric 1 key. Communications commands are summarized in Table 3.1 and are utilized in a later chapter.

Processing Options. During communications processing, all data transmitted and received is displayed on the display screen. Output data can be transmitted from the tape or the keyboard; input data can be printed or written on tape. Messages can also be composed off-line for later transmission to a remote system. Examples of the various processing options are covered in a later chapter.

REFERENCES

IBM 5100 Portable Computer publications:

a. *IBM 5100 APL Introduction,* Form #SA21-9212
b. *IBM 5100 APL Reference Manual,* Form #SA21-9213
c. *IBM 5100 Communications Reference Manual,* Form #SA21-9215
d. *IBM 5100 BASIC Introduction,* Form #SA21-9216
e. *IBM 5100 BASIC Reference Manual,* Form #SA21-9217
f. *IBM 5100 Maintenance Information Manual,* Form #SY31-0405

IBM Corporation, Rochester, Minnesota, 1975.

PART II:
The BASIC
Language

4

BASIC
ARITHMETIC
AND COMPUTER
OPERATIONS

The IBM 5100 Portable Computer is a full-function computer designed to perform complex as well as simple computations. Elementary computer functions are introduced in this chapter through the BASIC calculator mode. The implementation of complex computer functions involves the development and execution of computer programs, which are introduced accordingly. This chapter also covers operational procedures for using the computer.

4.1 INITIATING A COMPUTER SESSION

The 5100 Portable Computer is started by placing the red power switch in the ON position. Prior to doing this, it is a good idea, but not mandatory, to set the L32-64-R32 switch to the 64 position, and the BASIC/APL switch to BASIC—if appropriate. The DISPLAY REGISTERS/NORMAL switch should already be set to the NORMAL position since the internal registers are usually of interest only to service personnel. If the computer is turned on without the correct BASIC/APL setting, there is no harm in changing the setting and pushing restart before the warm-up process is complete.*

---

*This brings up an important point. Nothing that is done from the keyboard can physically damage the 5100 Portable Computer. The worst thing that can happen from "indiscriminate button pushing" is that the user may alter a program or data in main storage.

Process Check

If the PROCESS CHECK light comes on during the warm-up period, machine operations are suspended and the RESTART switch must be pushed to get any action out of the computer. It is unlikely that a process check condition will be encountered during normal use of the computer and one may wonder whether the lights are functioning properly. (The lights may be tested by holding the RESTART switch in.)   However, if the process check condition occurs repeatedly, then service is necessary.

Ready

After the warm-up process has been completed, the display screen will show a LOAD 0 (zero) message, a flashing *cursor*, and a READY message, as demonstrated in Figure 4.1. The number of available byte positions in the work area is displayed at the right end of the READY line. As the work area is filled with program statements and data, the amount of available storage is decreased.

The messages are meaningful. The LOAD 0 message indicates that the work area is clear. The READY message indicates that the computer is ready to be used and statements may be entered. LOAD 0 is also a command that may be entered by a user to clear the work area, which involves the deletion of *all* program statements *and* data from the main storage unit. The purpose of the LOAD 0 message is to inform the user that the execution of a LOAD 0 command has been initiated and processed internally by the computer. The LOAD 0 command does not alter or involve the use of magnetic tape.

The READY line is strictly a message that serves informational purposes. If the READY message does not appear with LOAD 0, then a machine malfunction

```
LOAD 0
__
  READY                                                          28385
```

Figure 4.1   Contents of the display screen after the warm-up process has been completed. (Example is from a 32K machine.)

has occurred and the RESTART switch should be pushed. However, if the display screen is completely blank, the brightness control probably needs to be adjusted.

4.2 BASIC CALCULATIONS

Prior to the entering of any statements, the flashing cursor is positioned by the computer at the first character position of line position 1 of the display screen. This is where the first character will be entered. The computer is automatically in the calculator mode and any statement entered will be executed immediately.

Two Plus Two

To perform a simple calculation, such as 2+2, data is entered and the execute key is pressed in the following sequence:

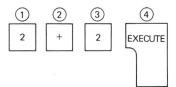

The computer will respond in the following manner:

The answer is indented one position to leave room for the algebraic sign and the contents of the display screen are moved up two lines. The input line, i.e., line position 1, is blank and the cursor is at the leftmost character position for the next entry. Remember, whenever the EXECUTE key is pressed, the contents of the input line are always entered—regardless of whether the characters were placed there by the user or through a scroll up or down operation.

Choice of Calculator Keys

Mathematical information can be entered from the typewriter-like keyboard or the calculator pad and the characters placed in the input line are the same. Consider the following example that uses keys from the keyboard and the calculator pad interchangeably:

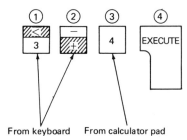

From keyboard   From calculator pad

The computer will respond in the following way:

```
LOAD  0
2+2
    4

3-4
-1

-
  READY
```

The preceding lines on the display screen are moved up accordingly, as indicated.

Simple Expressions

Mathematical computations frequently involve more than one arithmetic operation. With the 5100, a series of calculations is specified in a form that is similar to the manner in which they would be written in mathematics. For example, if it were desired to evaluate the expression 12X15-5, the user would enter:

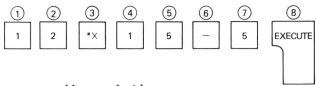

and the computer would respond with:

```
12*15-5
175

-
  READY
```

In this example, the value 5 is subtracted from the product of 12 and 15 and a result of 175 is displayed. The asterisk, (∗), is used to denote multiplication in the BASIC language.

4.3 ERRORS

It is just as easy to correct an error as it is to make one. An error detected before the EXECUTE key is pressed can be corrected by character replacement, deletion, or insertion. An error that is not detected before the EXECUTE key is pressed may or may not be recognized by the computer. If the error results in an incorrect syntactical form, then it will be recognized. Otherwise, the user's intentions may not be specified properly, resulting in invalid computational results. In the latter case, the user would have to analyze the input to identify the source of error.

Syntactical Errors

A syntactical error occurs when an incorrect or unrecognizable sequence of characters is entered. For example, suppose that it were necessary to evaluate the expression 21∗7+13 but that the 7 was inadvertently omitted as the expression was entered and read 21∗+13 when the EXECUTE key was pressed. The fact that two operators appear in succession is incorrect, because it does not make sense. When this occurs, the computer responds by locking the keyboard and causing the screen to flash on and off. The incorrect statement is displayed and the point of error is indicated by an arrow as follows:

```
21∗+13
21∗+13
    ↑                                              ERROR 100
```

The flashing is stopped by pressing the attention key (ATTN). An error code is displayed to the right of the status line and the flashing cursor is returned to the leftmost character position of the input line. In this case it is ERROR 100, which denotes, "Syntax error in statement." When a syntactical error occurs, it is recognized prior to execution of the statement and no computations are performed.

The error condition can be resolved in either of two ways. The most straightforward thing to do is to press the scroll up key once to clear the input line. The correct statement is then entered and the EXECUTE key is pressed to have the statement processed. The second action that can be taken is to scroll down one line so that the original incorrect statement is in the input line and then to edit the statement using the methods given in the following paragraphs. After the incorrect line is edited properly, the EXECUTE key is pressed to initiate computer processing.

Keying Errors

An error in the input line can be corrected prior to pressing the EXECUTE key through one of several editing operations that are implemented as special functions on the 5100 Portable Computer. These functions involve the use of gray special function keys and, in some cases, the command key (CMD).

Scroll Up. When the input line contains errors and the best course of action is to start over, a simple method of clearing the input line is to scroll up once. This operation clears the input line and returns the flashing cursor to the leftmost position. The correct line can then be entered. This method is demonstrated in the following example:

```
21*+13
21*+13
21*7+13
 160

 ‾
 READY
```

The disadvantage of this method is that it fills the display screen with the unnecessary information that would be undesirable in the event that the contents of the display screen were to be "copied to" the printer.

Attention. Another method of correcting the contents of the input line is to press the backspace key until the cursor is positioned below the error and then press the ATTN key. All characters to the right of and including the cursor position in the input line are deleted and the remainder of the line can then be retyped. This method is demonstrated as follows:

```
21*+13_                      (error recognized)
      ↑__flashing cursor

21*+13
      ↑_____+ character is flashing   (backspace to point of error)

21*_
   ↑_____flashing cursor     (press ATTN key)

21*7+13_                      (retype remainder of line)
       ↑_flashing cursor
```

Another frequent error that is easily resolved with the attention key occurs when a system command is entered with a command key but the wrong key is pressed. In this case, several characters are entered into the input line. Suppose a user wanted to enter the RUN command by holding down the CMD key and and pressing the $\boxed{\substack{< \\ 3}}$ key, but pressed the key to the left of it so that SAVE were entered instead of RUN. One of the simplest actions to take here is to backspace until the flashing cursor is under the S in SAVE and press the ATTN key. The line is now blank and the correct command can be entered.

Replace a Character. A character can be replaced in the input line by forward or backward spacing* until the cursor is below the incorrect character and the character is flashing. The incorrect character can then be replaced by keying the correct character over the incorrect character. In the event that the keying action has created a composite character, a space character must be inserted followed by the correct character. The procedure is as follows:

1. Backspace to the incorrect composite character;
2. Press the space key;
3. Backspace one position; and
4. Insert the desired character.

After an editing operation the cursor or flashing character may be in the middle of a line. This does not matter as the cursor character is *not* entered into the computer when the EXECUTE key is pressed.

Delete a Character. A character can easily be deleted from the input line. To delete a character the cursor is positioned, by forward or backward spacing, beneath the character to be deleted so that it is flashing. A character is deleted by holding the CMD key down and pressing the backspace key. The flashing character is deleted and the characters to the right are shifted left, closing up the space created by the deletion. Assume, for example, that 56++73 was entered instead of 56+73, as follows:

```
56++73_          ←──────────────── flashing cursor
READY
```

The cursor is positioned beneath the character to be deleted, i.e.,

```
      ┌──────────────── the + sign
56++73            ,is flashing
READY
```

*Remember, when forward or backward spacing, use the $\boxed{\leftarrow}$ and $\boxed{\rightarrow}$ keys, respectively. Do not use the space key as it always inserts a space character when pressed.

The CMD key is held down, the backspace key is pressed, and the plus sign is deleted as follows:

now the 7
is flashing

56+73
READY

The EXECUTE key is pressed and the sum is computed as follows:

56+73
129

‾
READY

The above procedure for deleting a character from the input line can be applied repetitively to delete successive characters.

Insert a Character. Characters can be inserted into the input line by moving all characters located to the right of the desired position as many places to the right as necessary. To insert one or more characters the cursor is positioned, by forward or backward spacing, beneath the leftmost character that is to be moved, so that the character is flashing. Then, by holding the CMD key down and pressing the forward space key, the flashing character and all characters to the right of it are moved one position to the right. However, the flashing cursor does not move and its position denotes the place where a character can be inserted. As an example, consider the previous case in which an operand was omitted as follows:

21*+13_
READY ⬉
         flashing cursor

(error recognized by user)

The error is corrected through character insertion. First, the cursor is positioned as follows:

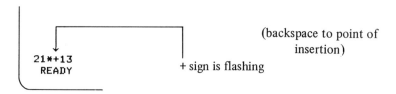

21*+13
READY

+ sign is flashing

(backspace to point of
         insertion)

Next, the CMD key is held down and the forward space key is pressed once:

(CMD key held down: → is pushed once)

```
21*_+13
  ↑
READY ————————————— flashing cursor
```

The needed character can then be inserted as follows:

(insert character)

```
21*7+13
   ↑
READY ————————————— character 7 is flashing
```

The EXECUTE key is pressed and the expression is evaluated as follows:

```
21*7+13
160

READY
```

The above procedure for inserting a character into the input line can be applied repetitively to insert several characters. Normally, the needed spaces are inserted by holding the CMD key down and pressing the forward space key the needed number of times. The flashing cursor will be positioned at the leftmost space. Then the insertion can simply be entered.

An Important Note on Editing

The editing of characters in the input line has been introduced here through the calculator mode of operation. The facilities apply to all keyboard input so that program statements and data can be edited in a similar manner—prior to pressing the EXECUTE key. Once the execute key has been pressed, however, each form of entry is processed in a characteristic manner, relating to the type of input. This topic will be covered in considerable detail as it becomes appropriate.

4.4 ARITHMETIC OPERATIONS

Arithmetic operations in the BASIC language are defined on numeric constants and the values of numeric variables or arrays. Precisely the same arithmetic operations are permitted in the calculator mode and in program statements written in the BASIC language. The only difference is that statements are executed immediately in the calculator mode and are executed in the program mode when a computer program is run.

Summary of Arithmetic Operations

The BASIC arithmetic operations, introduced in chapter two, are summarized in Table 4.1. The primary arithmetic operations of addition, subtraction, multiplication, and division are available through the four-function calculator pad located to the right of the console. The cluster of keys in the calculator pad is designed to facilitate rapid calculations by requiring less hand movement. The sole BASIC arithmetic operation not contained in the calculator pad is exponentiation, which uses the ↑ symbol, (located above the Y symbol), or the double asterisk (∗∗). In the BASIC mode, the meaning of ↑ and ∗∗ are identical. Several elementary calculations are demonstrated in Figure 4.2 which covers binary, but not unary, operators. The use of the positive and negative operations applies primarily to arithmetic expressions, which are covered in subsequent sections of this chapter.

Operands

In general, the form of an arithmetic operation is:

$$operand\ operator\ operand$$

or

$$operator\ operand$$

where an *operand* can be one of the following:

1. Numeric constant,
2. Numeric variable,

TABLE 4.1   SUMMARY OF ARITHMETIC OPERATIONS.

Operation	Operator Symbol	Type	Number of Operands	Example	Result
Addition	+	Binary	2	2+3	5
Positive	+	Unary	1	+9	9
Subtraction	−	Binary	2	6−2	4
Negative	−	Unary	1	−9	−9
Multiplication	∗	Binary	2	2∗3	6
Division	/	Binary	2	10/4	2.5
Exponentiation[†]	↑	Binary	2	3↑2	9

[†]Also known as the power function. The composite symbol ∗∗ can also be used to represent exponentiation.

```
1.23+137
 138.23

450.7123-50
 400.7123

40*3.75
 150

3.14159/2
 1.570795

2.5↑2
 6.25


 READY
```

Figure 4.2   Examples of elementary arithmetic calculations.

3. A subscripted array reference,
4. A function reference, or
5. A subexpression in parentheses.

and the *operator* symbol can be +, -, *, /, or ↑ for binary operations and + or - for unary operations. Thus, for example, if the variable A has been assigned a value, then the expression A+5 represents a valid arithmetic operation, as does the expression - A.

Numeric Constants

In BASIC, a numeric constant can be written as a whole number, a decimal number, or a number expressed in scaled representation.* The following constants, for example, are all numerically equivalent:

$$-5$$
$$-5.0$$
$$-.5E1$$

Similarly, the following constants in decimal and scaled representation are also numerically equivalent:

$$.000123$$
$$.123E-3$$

All numbers in BASIC are expressed to the base 10 for both input and output.

*The forms of numeric representation are covered in the second chapter.

Magnitude. The range of the magnitude* of numbers that can be stored in BASIC extends from .1E-99 to 1E+99. Numbers with very large and very small magnitudes are normally entered in scaled representation, although a number can be entered in any form that is convenient to the user. In the calculator mode, the form of output is selected by the computer. (Output formats are covered under the PRINT statement in the BASIC language.)

Precision. The BASIC language maintains 13 digits of precision for all data formats and for all calculations. Precision is defined as the number of significant digits in a whole or decimal number, and the number of digits to the left of the E in a number in scaled representation. A user may enter more than 13 digits but only the leftmost 13 are retained.

Variables and Replacement

Many of the facilities of the BASIC language are not restricted for use in programs alone. In particular, any language construct that incorporates variables, the replacement operation, and arithmetic operations is both permitted and useful in the calculator mode.

Variables. An arithmetic variable in the BASIC language can be named with a single alphabetic character or an alphabetic character followed by a single digit. Examples of variable names are—R, C2, $2, and @7. An alphabetic character is defined as one of the following: A through Z, @, #, and $; and a digit is defined as 0 through 9.

Replacement. A variable is assigned a value with a statement of the form:

$$v = e$$

where v is a BASIC variable and e is an arithmetic expression. Figure 4.3 depicts several valid expressions and replacement statements. When the 5100 Portable Computer is in the calculator mode, the numeric value of an expression is always displayed, and this philosophy also applies to replacement statements as demonstrated in the preceding figure. When a computer program is being executed, however, the value in a replacement statement is not automatically displayed, and a PRINT statement must be used to display or print a value. (After the result of an expression is displayed by the computer, the contents of the display screen are moved up two lines, as mentioned previously. After the result of a replacement statement is displayed by the computer, the contents of the display screen are moved up one line.)

Undefined Variables. A valid arithmetic BASIC variable that is not assigned a value is automatically initialized to zero. Similarly, arrays are also initialized to zero as demonstrated in Figure 4.4. Arrays and array variables can be used without restriction in the calculator or program modes.

---

*The magnitude of a number is its value without an algebraic sign—or, in other words, its absolute value.

```
D=15.389
  15.389
D+5
  20.389

2*D
  30.778

-D
-15.389

#6=2.718↑2
  7.387524
K4=#6↑.5
  2.718000

-
  READY
```

Figure 4.3   Examples of valid expressions and replacement statements.

Arithmetic Expressions

The use of arithmetic expressions in the BASIC language generally follows the conventions given in chapter two. However, it is important to recognize that an expression is evaluated by being reduced to component sub-expressions, which are in turn evaluated.

Hierarchy. When an arithmetic expression specifies more than one operation, the order of evaluation is governed by the following hierarchy:

1. Expressions enclosed in parentheses,
2. Mathematical functions,

```
LOAD  0
A
  0

B+5
  5

A(7)
  0

139-L(4,3)
  139

-
  READY
```

Figure 4.4   Numeric variables and arrays are always initialized to zero in the BASIC language.

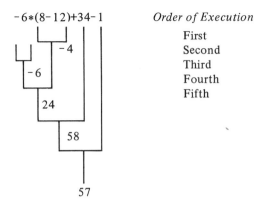

Figure 4.5 In BASIC, operators are executed on a hierarchical basis. Operators with a higher priority are executed before those with a lower priority.

3. Exponentiation,
4. Positive or negative operations,
5. Multiplication and division, and
6. Addition and subtraction.

Thus, operators with a higher priority are executed before those with a lower priority, as shown in Figure 4.5. In general, operands can be constants, variables, subscripted array references, or function references—as covered previously.

Execution. Operations are executed according to the established hierarchy. Higher priority sub-expressions are evaluated before operations of which they are a part, until the complete expression is reduced to a single value. Operations at the same hierarchical level are executed from left to right, as indicated in Figure 4.6. Operations are only defined on numeric values, therefore, all references to symbolic operands must be resolved before the operation is performed.

Evaluation. Some obvious restrictions and operational conventions apply to the values of operands, as depicted in Figure 4.7, where it is assumed that the value of all variables is zero after the LOAD 0 command is entered. The restrictions and operational conventions are summarized in Table 4.2.

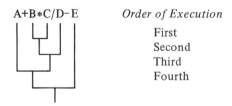

Figure 4.6 Operators at the same hierarchical level are executed from left to right.

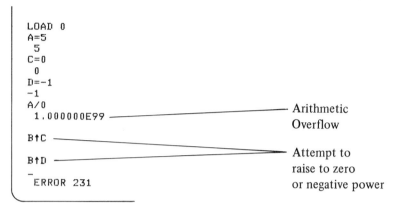

Figure 4.7 Arithmetic operands must have valid values for the operation involved. This figure demonstrates some obvious invalid operands. (After a LOAD 0, all variables are initialized to zero.)

TABLE 4.2 RESTRICTIONS AND OPERATIONAL CONVENTIONS ON THE USE OF ARITHMETIC OPERATORS.

Operation/Condition	*Result*
Exponentiation of the form: $A \uparrow B$	
1) A=0 and B=0	Error
2) A=0 and B<0	Error
3) A<0 and B not an integer	Error
4) A≠0 and B=0	Result is 1
5) A=0 and B>0	Result is 0
Addition of the form: $A+B$	
1) A+B and B+A	Equivalent
2) A+(B+C) and (A+B)+C	Not necessarily equivalent because of rounding
Multiplication of the form: $A*B$	
1) A*B and B*A	Equivalent
2) A*(B*C) and (A*B)*C	Not necessarily equivalent because of rounding
Division of the form: A/B	
1) B=0	Overflow error
Positive/Negative of the form: +A and −A	
1) Must be used following a left parenthesis and preceding an arithmetic expression.	
2) Must be the leftmost character in an expression provided that two operators do not appear in succession.	

An Important Note on Arithmetic Operations

The use of arithmetic operations has been introduced here through the calculator mode of operation. Each and every facility that is available in the calculator mode can also be used in BASIC programs. In addition, it is important to note that the calculator mode can be used any time the 5100 Portable Computer is waiting for keyboard input—except for a couple of minor exceptions noted below. Thus, the execution of a program can be interrupted, the values of variables can be inspected, verified, and possibly changed, and execution can be resumed. This facility is useful for checking and correcting programs that are performing incorrectly.

The calculator mode can be used anytime—except for the following:

1. When an INPUT statement is being executed in a running BASIC program and the user is requested to enter data values; and
2. When the user is constructing a keyboard generated data file and the computer expects data to be entered.

Moreover, there are no restrictions on when the calculator mode may be used. For example, the execution of a payroll program may be stopped for a few mathematical calculations and then be resumed without difficulty of any kind.

4.5 GENERAL FACILITIES AND APPLICATIONS

There are several operational facilities, normally used in BASIC programs, that are also useful in the calculator mode. Two of these facilities are covered here: internal constants and mathematical functions. Another feature, unique to the calculator mode, allows the result of the previous calculation to be recalled.

Previous Calculation Results

The result of the previous calculations can be inserted into the current expression by holding the CMD key down and pressing the $\boxed{\div}$ key. This corresponds to the $\boxed{\text{Calc Result}}$ function printed above the keyboard. Examples of the calc-result function are given in Figure 4.8. Arithmetic results are always enclosed in parentheses to prevent conflict with adjacent arithmetic operators.

Internal Constants

The BASIC language has six built-in constants that are used frequently enough to warrant being included in the language. The incorporation of the constants in the language eliminates having to look up the values in tables and minimizes transcription errors. The internal constants, listed in Table 4.3, are: e (natural log), π (pi), $\sqrt{2}$ (square root of two), and conversion constants for inches to centimeters, pounds to kilograms, and gallons to liters. Figure 4.9 contains

```
T=5
  5
4*2.50
  10

T+( 10)
  15

T=( 15)
  15

--
  READY
```

Figure 4.8 The Calc Result function can be used to insert the result of the previous calculations into the current expression.

TABLE 4.3 INTERNAL CONSTANTS IN THE BASIC LANGUAGE.

Constant	BASIC Symbol	Value
e (natural log)	&E	2.718281828459
π (pi)	&PI	3.141592653590
$\sqrt{2}$ (square root of two)	&SQR2	1.414213562373
Centimeters per inch	&INCM	2.54
Kilograms per pound	&LBKG	0.453592
Liters per gallon	&GALI	3.785412

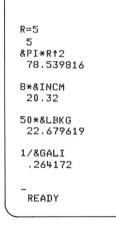

```
R=5
  5
&PI*R↑2
  78.539816

8*&INCM
  20.32

50*&LBKG
  22.679619

1/&GALI
  .264172

--
  READY
```

Figure 4.9 The BASIC language includes several internal constants denoted by the ampersand symbol (&).

several examples of how the BASIC internal constants can be used. Internal constants always begin with the *ampersand* symbol (&).

Mathematical Functions

A mathematical function provides a computational operation that is outside the scope of the BASIC language. Each function is denoted by a unique three-character name followed by an argument, enclosed in parentheses, to which the function is applied. The mathematical functions will be described more fully after the BASIC language is described in detail. Several of the functions, however, are useful in the calculator mode and are mentioned here:

Name	*Function*
SQR (x)	Square root of x.
SIN (x)	Trigonometric sine of x in radians.
COS (x)	Trigonometric cosine of x in radians.
RAD (x)	Converts x in degrees to radians.
ABS (x)	Takes the absolute value (i.e., magnitude only) of x.
LGT (x)	Logarithm of x to the base 10.
EXP (x)	Computes e^x.

Examples of the use of mathematical functions are given in Figure 4.10.

Applications

All applications of the 5100 Portable Computer do not require that a computer program be written—although most applications do involve computer programs. This section gives several applications that require only the calculator mode.

Distance Between Two Points. The distance d between two points (x_1,y_1) and (x_2,y_2) is computed as:

$$d = \sqrt{(x_1-x_2)^2+(y_1-y_2)^2}$$

Figure 4.11 shows calculations for the distance between points (2,4) and (5,8).

Area of Scalene Triangle. The area of a scalene triangle with sides a, b, and c is computed as:

$$\text{Area} = \sqrt{s(s-a)\,(s-b)\,(s-c)}$$

where

$$s = \frac{a+b+c}{2}$$

Figure 4.12 shows calculations for the area of the triangle with sides of 5, 8, and 10.

```
SQR(1296)
 36

SQR(5↑2)
  5

RAD(180)
 3.141593

COS(RAD(45))
 .707107

SIN(RAD(-30))
-.500000

ABS(SIN(RAD(-30)))
 .500000

LGT(100)
  2

EXP(1)
 2.718282

─
 READY
```

Figure 4.10 Mathematical functions in the BASIC language can be used in the calculator mode.

```
D=SQR((2-5)↑2+(4-8)↑2)
 5
─
 READY
```

Figure 4.11 Calculator mode example: distance between points (2,4) and (5,8).

```
S=(5+8+10)/2
 11.5
A=SQR(S*(S-5)*(S-8)*(S-10))
 19.810035
─
 READY
```

Figure 4.12 Calculator mode example: area of scalene triangle with sides of 5, 8, and 10.

```
D1=1.1*50
  55
D2=50↑2/20
  125
D=D1+D2
  180
—
  READY
```

Figure 4.13 Calculator mode example: stopping distance in feet of an automobile traveling 50 miles per hour.

Stopping Distance. The stopping distance of an automobile is a function of reaction time and braking distance. The stopping distance (in feet) is computed as:

$$\text{Stopping distance} = \text{Reaction distance} + \text{Braking distance}$$

where

$$\text{Reaction distance} = 1.1 \text{ times miles per hour}$$

and

$$\text{Braking distance} = \text{miles per hour squared divided by 20}$$

Figure 4.13 calculates the stopping distance in feet for an automobile traveling at the rate of 50 miles per hour.

Volume of a Cylinder. The volume of a cylinder with radius r and length l is computed as:

$$V = \pi r^2 l$$

Figure 4.14 calculates the volume of a cylindrical can with a radius of 3 feet and a length of 4 feet.

Factorial. Stirling's approximation to the factorial function is given as follows:

$$n! = \sqrt{2\pi n}\ n^n e^{-n}$$

```
&PI*3↑2*4
 113.097336

—
 READY
```

Figure 4.14 Calculator mode example: volume of a cylinder with a radius of 3 feet and a length of 4 feet.

```
N=10
 10
F=SQR(2*&PI*N)*N↑N*EXP(-N)
 3598695.618847

‾
 READY
```

Figure 4.15   Calculator mode example: Stirling's approximation to the factorial function.

Figure 4.15 calculates the approximate value of 10 factorial. The true value of 10! is 3,628,800.

Value of Investment. The future value of an investment of p dollars at r percent for n years compounded t times yearly is given as:

$$A = p\left(1 + \frac{r}{t}\right)^{nt}$$

Figure 4.16 calculates the future value of 1000 dollars for 10 years at 7.25 percent compounded daily.

Monthly Payment. The monthly payment on a loan of p dollars for t years at r percent yearly interest is computed as:

$$M = \frac{p \times \frac{r}{12}}{1 - (1 + \frac{r}{12})^{-12t}}$$

Figure 4.17 calculates the monthly payment on a loan of $50,000 at 9% yearly interest for 30 years.

```
P=1000
 1000
R=7.25/100
 7.25E-2
N=10
 10
T=365
 365
A=P*(1+R/T)↑(N*T)
 2064.582443

‾
 READY
```

Figure 4.16   Calculator mode example: future value of an investment of 1000 dollars for 10 years at 7.25 percent compounded daily.

```
P=50000
 50000
R=9/100
 9E-2
T=30
 30
M=(P*R/12)/(1-(1+R/12)↑(-12*T))
 402.311308
 ‾
 READY
```

Figure 4.17 Calculator mode example: monthly payment on a loan of $50,000 at 9% yearly interest for 30 years.

REFERENCES

Edwards, P., and Broadwell, B., *Flowcharting and BASIC*, Harcourt Brace Jovanovich, Inc., New York, 1974.

IBM 5100 Portable Computer Publications:
  a. *IBM 5100 BASIC Introduction*, Form #SA21-9216
  b. *IBM 5100 BASIC Reference Manual*, Form #SA21-9217

IBM Corporation, Rochester, Minnesota, 1975.

5 | BASIC LANGUAGE PROGRAMMING

BASIC is a machine-independent programming language that permits a program to be written without requiring that the user be knowledgeable of the underlying computer. When the computer is in the BASIC mode, it is designed to execute statements in the BASIC language—regardless of whether calculator statements or program statements are entered. This chapter introduces BASIC programming; subsequent chapters cover the statements in the BASIC language, system commands, special computer functions, and matrix operations.

5.1 INTRODUCTION TO THE PROGRAM MODE

The user area of the main storage unit of the 5100 Portable Computer is designed to hold one BASIC program and all statements entered and included as part of that program. The work area is cleared with the LOAD 0 (load zero) command, which also initializes all variables and arrays.

Program Execution

A program is executed by entering the RUN command and then pressing the EXECUTE key. RUN can be entered into the input line on a character-by-character basis or by holding the CMD key down and by pressing the $\left(\begin{smallmatrix} < \\ 3 \end{smallmatrix}\right)$ key, which is below the word RUN above the keyboard. When the RUN command is received by the computer, execution of the BASIC program currently held in the main storage unit is initiated. If a program is stored on tape, it must first be loaded into the main storage unit with the LOAD command before it can be executed.

Statements

Statements in the BASIC language are the same in the calculator and the program modes. A statement that is prefixed with a statement number, such as:

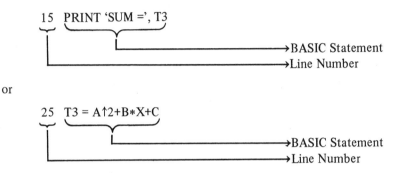

or

is regarded as a statement of a BASIC program and is saved in the user's work area of main storage. A statement entered without a statement number is executed immediately and is *not* saved, since it is regarded as a statement to be processed in the calculator mode. The distinction between the calculator and program modes is the presence or absence of the statement number. Only one statement may be entered on each line and a single statement may not be continued on another line.

Size of a Program

The minimum size of a program is one statement, as shown in Figure 5.1. The maximum size of a program is undetermined and is dependent upon three factors:

1. Size of the work area,
2. Amount of storage used by the program for variables and arrays, and
3. The number and length of statements in the program.

Long statements require more storage than short statements. However, there is a certain amount of overhead associated with each individual statement, so that less storage is required if it is possible to combine two short statements into one long statement. An example of the benefit of combining statements is given in Figure 5.2.

```
LOAD 0

10 PRINT 'TEA FOR TWO'
RUN
TEA FOR TWO
```

READY   28364

Figure 5.1 A BASIC program can be as short as one statement. The maximum length of a program is a function of the storage requirements of the program and the size of the work area.

Statement Numbers

A statement number can be any number between 1 and 9999, inclusive. The numbers 9990 and 9999 are reserved for special purposes.

The computer records each statement number as four digits of the form 0010. Leading zeros need not be supplied by the user as they are supplied automatically by the computer.

Statements are ordered by statement number in the computer and executed in that sequence. This convention permits statements to be entered in any sequence and allows a statement to be placed between two others by choosing an appropriate statement number. Statements are usually numbered $10, 20, 30, \ldots$ to facilitate later insertions.

```
LOAD 0

10 PRINT 'TEA FOR TWO',
20 PRINT 'THIS IS A TEST'
RUN
TEA FOR TWO        THIS IS A TEST
```

READY   28339

(a) Separate statements (note remaining available storage)

```
LOAD 0

10 PRINT 'TEA FOR TWO','THIS IS A TEST'
RUN
TEA FOR TWO        THIS IS A TEST
```

READY   28347

(b) Combined statements (note remaining available storage)

Figure 5.2 Main storage space can be conserved if two short statements are combined into one long statement.

Figure 5.3 gives the script of a program that shows two things:

1. Statement insertion, and
2. Listing of a program by statement number.

All programs are formatted internally by the 5100 Portable Computer to minimize the amount of required storage. This feature eliminates the requirements for storing unneeded blank characters, but may result in a program being listed in a slightly different lexical form from which it was entered. The BASIC statements contained in the program of Figure 5.3 will be described in subsequent sections.

```
LOAD 0

10 READ A,B,C
20 S=A+B+C
30 PRINT A,B,C,S
40 STOP
50 DATA 5,10,-8
60 END
5 PRINT 'A','B','C','SUM'
6 PRINT

   READY                                                    28231
```

(a) Entering of program

```
0005 PRINT 'A','B','C','SUM'
0006 PRINT
0010 READ A,B,C
0020 S=A+B+C
0030 PRINT A,B,C,S
0040 STOP
0050 DATA 5,10,-8
0060 END

  LIST
```

(b) Listing of program

```
RUN
A                 B                 C                 SUM

5                 10                -8                7


   READY                                                    28208
```

(c) Execution of program

Figure 5.3   A sample BASIC program showing statement insertion and the use of the list command.

Blank Characters

Blank characters may be inserted anywhere in a BASIC statement to improve readability and are completely ignored by the computer—except within quote marks. The blank characters are not stored by the computer but are inserted when the program is listed to improve readability. An example of statement re-formatting is given in Figure 5.4.

Statement Format

Each statement in the BASIC language begins with a keyword that denotes the basic function performed by that statement. Consider, for example, the following BASIC statements:

```
  20  PRINT 'ABC CORPORATION'
1175  GO TO 50
 320  LET A=3*I+&PI
6520  READ A,#9,T$,Q,C1
5000  DATA ,123,64E-6,25,'TEA FOR TWO'
```

```
LOAD 0

10 A=          - 10
20PRINT'A     ='; 	  A

  READY                                          28347
```
  (a) Entering program

```
0010 A=-10
0020 PRINT 'A       ='; A

  LIST
```
  (b) Listing of program

```
RUN
A      =-10


  READY                                          28335
```
  (c) Execution

Figure 5.4 Blanks are completely ignored in BASIC statements—except when placed in quote marks. Statements are reformatted by the computer to conserve storage and improve readability.

In each case, the keyword following the statement number readily denotes the intended function as follows:

PRINT—Instructs the computer to output the specified data.

GO TO—Instructs the computer to transfer program control to the statement with the statement number specified in the GOTO statement.

LET—Instructs the computer to evaluate the expression to the right of the equals sign (=) and assign the value to the variable to the left of the equals sign. The LET statement is the only statement for which the keyword can be omitted. Thus, for example, the following statement:

$$A=3*I+\&PI$$

is exactly equivalent to the preceding LET statement.

READ—Instructs the computer to input data from the data set created by one or more DATA statements and to assign the data values to the variables specified in the READ statement.

DATA—Instructs the computer to create a list of data values called a *data set*.

In general, the form of a BASIC statement is

| statement-number [statement-identifier] [statement body] | *Form of a BASIC statement* |

The "statement identifier" is the keyword mentioned above, and the fact that it is enclosed in brackets denotes that it can be omitted—but only in the case of the LET statement. The "statement body" is the remaining characters that comprise the remainder of the statement, and again, the brackets denote that it can sometimes be omitted or it is not always required. The PRINT statement without a statement body, for example, prints a blank line and the END statement simply does not require a statement body.

Program Structure

One of the characteristics of the BASIC mode of operation is that when the RUN command is entered, the statements in the user's work area of main storage are regarded as a complete program. There are no restrictions on the structure of a BASIC program—at least as far as the computer is concerned. From the programmer's viewpoint, however, the statements should represent a meaningful program.

Once the execution of a program is started with the RUN command, the program executes automatically by going from one statement to its successor until one of three possible events occurs:

1. A STOP statement is executed or an END statement is reached;
2. The physically last statement in a program is executed; or
3. A condition arises that prevents further execution.

```
0010 READ A,B
0020 PRINT A;B;A*B
0030 GOTO 0010
0040 DATA 2,3,4,5
RUN
  2     3     6
  4     5     20

ERROR 161                                                    0010
```

Figure 5.5 Example of a condition that prevents further execution of a computer program. (ERROR 161 denotes the following condition: "Too few DATA statements for READs issued." The number 0010 in the lower right-hand corner denotes the number of the statement causing the error.)

The STOP and END statements, discussed in more detail in the next chapter, can be placed anywhere in a program. Figure 5.5 gives an example of a condition that prevents further execution. In the example, the program attempts to read from a data set that is exhausted. An error condition is generated and execution of the program is terminated.

Remarks

A BASIC program can be annotated through the use of the remarks statement, which has the following form:

> statement-number REM [any series of characters] . . .

The following statements are valid remarks lines:

> 45 REM A IS AGE AND P4 IS PAY
> 9214 REMARK PROG ITERATES UNTIL E<.001

A remarks statement can be placed anywhere in a BASIC program and is ignored by the computer during the execution of the program.

5.2 CASE STUDY—INVENTORY PROGRAM

This section describes a sample computer program and is intended to show how the various aspects of a BASIC program fit together and to give illustrative examples of BASIC language statements. Many of the topics presented will be covered again in a different context so that full comprehension is not required. The objective of this section is to introduce four major aspects of a program: input, processing, output, and decision making.

Description of the Inventory Program

A flow chart of the inventory program is given in Figure 5.6. The program is designed to generate an inventory report and to compute the value of inventory

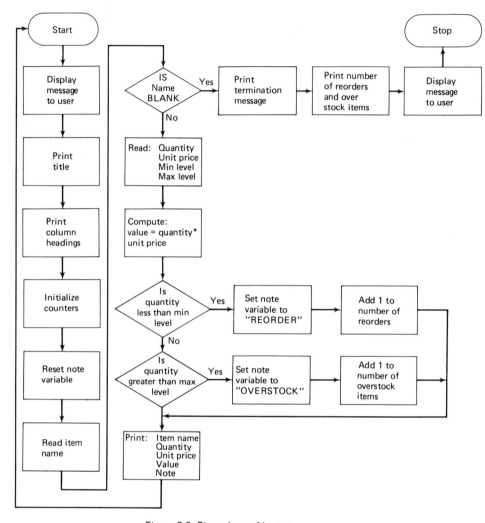

Figure 5.6 Flow chart of inventory program.

items. The program also tests for items that should be reordered and those for which an overstock exists and makes appropriate notes in the report.

The program operates by reading the data for each inventory item separately. The total value is computed by multiplying quantity by unit price, and reorder/ overstock is determined by checking the quantity against given inventory levels. After the calculations are performed, each line of the report is printed separately and program control is returned to the beginning of the program to read the data for the next inventory item. When all the data has been read, the program prints termination messages and halts execution.

Program Listing and Sample Run

A listing of the inventory program is given in Figure 5.7 and the printout from a sample run is given as Figure 5.8. The program is divided for illustrative purposes into four sections:

1. Initialization,
2. Input,
3. Processing and output, and
4. Data.

In this example, the input data is included in the program itself.

```
0010 PRINT 'START OF INVENTORY PROGRAM'
0020 PRINT FLP,TAB(34);'INVENTORY REPORT'
0030 PRINT FLP,'ITEM NAME','QUANTITY','PRICE','VALUE','NOTE'
0040 PRINT FLP,
0050 C1,C2=0
0060 R$=' '
0070 READ N$
0080 IF N$=' ' GOTO 0200
0090 READ Q,P,L1,L2
0100 V=Q*P
0110 IF Q≥L1 GOTO 0150
0120 R$='REORDER'
0130 C1=C1+1
0140 GOTO 0180
0150 IF Q≤L2 GOTO 0180
0160 R$='OVER STOCK'
0170 C2=C2+1
0180 PRINT FLP,N$,Q,P,V,R$
0190 GOTO 0060
0200 PRINT FLP,
0210 PRINT FLP,'END OF INVENTORY REPORT'
0220 PRINT FLP,'NUMBER OF REORDERS =';C1
0230 PRINT FLP,'NUMBER OF OVER STOCK ITEMS =';C2
0240 PRINT 'END OF INVENTORY PROGRAM - REMOVE LISTING FROM '
0250 PRINT 'PRINTER'
0260 DATA 'BOLT  2 INCH'
0270 DATA 512,.13,75,1000
0280 DATA 'COPPER TUBE'
0290 DATA 11,17.52,25,100
0300 DATA 'HOIST CLAMP'
0310 DATA 23,15.81,5,60
0320 DATA 'NAIL  3 PENNY'
0330 DATA 213,11.07,50,200
0340 DATA 'PST JOINT'
0350 DATA 7,62.58,15,65
0360 DATA 'T RACK'
0370 DATA 15,5.45,10,100
0380 DATA ' '
0390 END
```

Figure 5.7   Listing of the inventory program.

```
                              INVENTORY REPORT
ITEM NAME          QUANTITY         PRICE               VALUE            NOTE

BOLT  2 INCH       512               .13                66.56
COPPER TUBE         11              17.52               192.72           REORDER
HOIST CLAMP         23              15.81               363.63
NAIL  3 PENNY      213              11.07              2357.91           OVER STOCK
PST JOINT            7              62.58               438.06           REORDER
T RACK              15               5.45                81.75

END OF INVENTORY REPORT
NUMBER OF REORDERS = 2
NUMBER OF OVER STOCK ITEMS = 1
```

Figure 5.8 Sample run of the inventory program.

Initialization

The section of the flow chart that performs initialization of the program is given as follows:

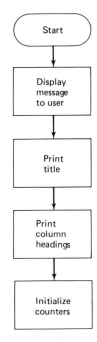

and the corresponding program segment is:

```
0010 PRINT 'START OF INVENTORY PROGRAM'
0020 PRINT FLP,TAB(34);'INVENTORY REPORT'
0030 PRINT FLP,'ITEM NAME','QUANTITY','PRICE','VALUE','NOTE'
0040 PRINT FLP,
0050 C1,C2=0
```

Statement numbered 10 displays a message to the user on the display screen. This is evident from the fact that no unit name follows the PRINT keyword and the specified output is displayed accordingly.

Statements numbered 20 through 40 print a title and column heading on the printer unit, which is specified by the name FLP, which stands for "file line printer." Statement numbered 40 specifies no data so a blank line is printed.

Statement numbered 50 initializes variables C1 and C2 to zero. The variables are used as counters. C1 keeps a running count of the number of reorders and C2 keeps a running count of overstock items.

Input

The input section of the flow chart is given as follows:

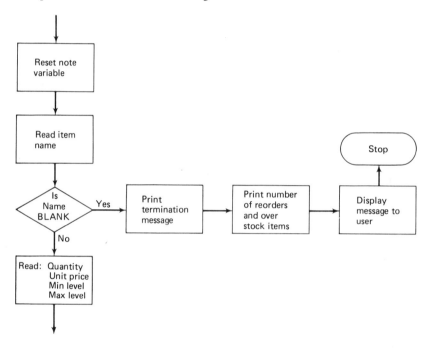

and the corresponding program segment is:

```
0060 R$=' '
0070 READ N$
0080 IF N$=' ' GOTO 0200
0090 READ Q,P,L1,L2

           .
           .
           .

0200 PRINT FLP,
0210 PRINT FLP,'END OF INVENTORY REPORT'
0220 PRINT FLP,'NUMBER OF REORDERS =';C1
0230 PRINT FLP,'NUMBER OF OVER STOCK ITEMS =';C2
0240 PRINT 'END OF INVENTORY PROGRAM - REMOVE LISTING FROM
0250 PRINT 'PRINTER'
```

Statement numbered 60 sets the character variable R$ to a blank value. (A character variable always terminates with a dollar sign and can hold a string of characters in the same way that a numeric variable can hold a numeric value.) If a reorder or over stock note is required, R$ is set to REORDER or OVER STOCK prior to printing. R$ is initialized for each new inventory item.

Statement numbered 70 reads the name of the next inventory item and assigns it to character variable N$. Statement numbered 80 compares the value of N$ with a blank value. If the comparison is true, program control is transformed to statement numbered 200 to terminate the program. The "end of data" condition is denoted by a "blank" item name. A special value used to indicate the end-of-data is known as a *sentinel* value.

If the condition is not true, program control flows to statement numbered 90 which reads in the remainder of the inventory data for the current item. In particular, the following values are read:

Value	Assigned to	Value	Assigned to
Quantity	Q	Low inventory level	L1
Unit price	P	High inventory level	L2

Statement numbered 200 prints a blank line on the printer and statement numbered 210 prints a termination message. Statements numbered 220 and 230 combine descriptive output and variable output. Information in quote marks is printed as given and the value of a variable is printed.

Statements numbered 240 and 250 display a message to the user. Statement numbered 250 is the last executable statement in the program so that execution terminates after it is executed.

Processing and Output

The processing and output section of the flow chart and the corresponding program segment is given on page 105.

Statement numbered 100 computes value (V) as:

$$V=Q*P$$

where Q is quantity, P is unit price, * denotes multiplication, and = denotes replacement.

Statement numbered 110 compares the quantity (Q) with the minimum level (L1). If Q is greater than or equal to L1, denoted by $Q \geq L1$, control is passed to statement numbered 150 to check the max level. If Q is less than L1, program control drops through to statement numbered 120, which sets the note variable R$ to REORDER, and increases the reorder counter (C1) by 1 (statement numbered 130). In the statement:

$$C1=C1+1$$

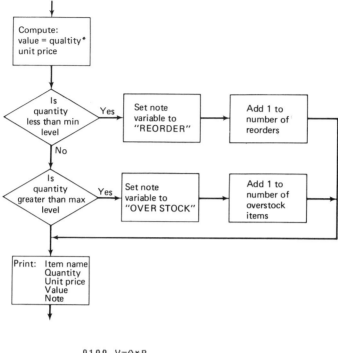

```
0100  V=Q*P
0110  IF Q≥L1 GOTO 0150
0120  R$='REORDER'
0130  C1=C1+1
0140  GOTO 0180
0150  IF Q≤L2 GOTO 0180
0160  R$='OVER STOCK'
0170  C2=C2+1
0180  PRINT FLP,N$,Q,P,V,R$
0190  GOTO 0060
```

the expression C1+1 is evaluated first and the result is assigned to C1, changing its value. Statement numbered 140 branches around the test of the max level and passes control to statement numbered 180 to print the result.

Statement numbered 150 compares the quantity (Q) with the max level (L2). If Q is less than or equal to L2, denoted by Q≤L2, control is passed to statement numbered 180 to print the result. If Q is greater than L2, program control drops through to statement numbered 160, which sets the note variable R$ to OVER STOCK. Statement numbered 170 increases the count (C2) of overstock items by 1. After the execution of statement numbered 170 is complete, program control passes automatically to statement numbered 180.

Statement numbered 180 prints the item name (N$), quantity (Q), unit price (P), value (V), and note variable (R$) on the printer unit in columns on one printed line. The names of data items that are separated by commas in a PRINT statement are printed in columns, and data items separated by semicolons in a PRINT statement are run together. In this case, commas were used as separators so the output data is printed in columns, as shown in Figure 5.8. The column headings printed in statement numbered 30 are also separated by commas and the columns line up in the usual fashion.

Statement numbered 190 passes control to statement numbered 60 to begin processing of the next inventory item.

Data

Statements numbered 250 through 380, listed as follows:

```
0260 DATA 'BOLT  2 INCH'
0270 DATA 512,.13,75,1000
0280 DATA 'COPPER TUBE'
0290 DATA 11,17.52,25,100
0300 DATA 'HOIST CLAMP'
0310 DATA 23,15.81,5,60
0320 DATA 'NAIL  3 PENNY'
0330 DATA 213,11.07,50,200
0340 DATA 'PST JOINT'
0350 DATA 7,62.58,15,65
0360 DATA 'T RACK'
0370 DATA 15,5.45,10,100
0380 DATA ' '
```

supply data to the program through an internal data set created from DATA statements. The DATA statements are ordered by statement number and the values are strung together as one long list of data items. As a data item is read with the READ statement, it is effectively used up.

A DATA statement may contain two kinds of data: character data enclosed in quote marks and numeric data. In a DATA statement, data items are always separated by commas.

5.3 LANGUAGE CHARACTERISTICS

This section covers BASIC language characteristics that were not presented in the introductory chapter on BASIC arithmetic and the calculator mode. A general understanding of BASIC numeric variable names, BASIC arithmetic operators, arithmetic expressions, and BASIC replacement is assumed along with an elementary knowledge of arrays, covered in chapter two.

BASIC Alphabet

Communication with the 5100 Portable Computer is possible through the use of an alphabet along with a set of syntactical and semantical rules. The various characters of the alphabet serve special purposes depending primarily upon how they are used in a statement. These characters are listed in Table 5.1. The letter "A," for example, can be used in a variable or array name, in a statement keyword, in a function name, in a system command, and in a character string enclosed in quote marks. Similarly, a digit can be used in a statement number, numeric variable name, numeric constant, character string enclosed in quote marks, and in a system command. Characters, other than those listed in Table 5.1 but represented on the keyboard, are not part of the language but may be used in character strings enclosed in quote marks.

A character or series of characters that has meaning in its own right is regarded as a *symbol* of the language. The plus sign, for example, denotes the positive

TABLE 5.1 CHARACTERS IN THE BASIC ALPHABET

Alphabetic Characters (29)

A B C D E F G H I J K L M N O P Q R S T U V W X Y Z
@ # $

Digits (10)

0 1 2 3 4 5 6 7 8 9

Name	*Character*
Blank	(no visual representation)
Equal sign	=
Plus sign	+
Minus sign	−
Asterisk	*
Slash	/
Up arrow	↑
Left parenthesis	(
Right parenthesis	)
Comma	,
Point or period	.
Semicolon	;
Colon	:
Question mark	?
Currency symbol (dollar sign)	$
Quotation mark	'
"Less than" symbol	<
"Less than or equal to" symbol	≤
"Greater than or equal to" symbol	≥
"Greater than" symbol	>
"Not equal to" symbol	≠
Vertical stroke character		
And symbol	&

and addition operators and its meaning is not context dependent. Similarly, the composite symbol, **, denotes exponentiation. Symbols of the BASIC language are listed in Table 5.2. An alternate representation of a symbol is always stored in the computer in its primary form. For example, the following statement may be entered without generating a syntax error:

IF A>=B THEN 45

However, when the program is listed, the statement is displayed as:

IF A≥B GOTO 45

Non-BASIC operator symbols that are meaningful to the APL language are not recognized when the computer is in the BASIC mode.

The calculator pad section of the keyboard contains two keys with double symbols: $\boxed{/ \div}$ and $\boxed{* \times}$. When the computer is in the BASIC mode, the / and * characters are operative. When the computer is in the APL mode, the ÷ and × characters are operative.

TABLE 5.2 SYMBOLS OF THE BASIC LANGUAGE

Primary Symbol	Function	Alternate Representation
+	Addition or positive operator	
−	Subtraction or negative operator, minus sign	
*	Multiplication operator	
/	Division operator	
↑	Exponentiation operator	**
>	Greater than operator	
≥	Greater than or equal to operator	>=
=	Equal to operator	
≠	Not equal to operator	<>
≤	Less than or equal to operator	<=
<	Less than operator	
,	Separates elements of lists or subscripts	
.	Decimal point	
;	Separates elements of lists	
=	Replacement symbol	
( )	Enclose list or groups items	
'	Enclose character string data	
		Exponent editing symbol and *or* operator	
#	Numeric or character editing symbol	
&	*And* operator	

```
10  A=5.0
20  B=5
30  C=500000E-5
40  D=.000005E6
50  PRINT A;B;C;D
RUN
 5      5      5      5
```

Figure 5.9 Numeric values, regardless of the form in which they were entered, are stored in floating-point form and are displayed in the most efficient manner.

Data

Two types of data are permitted in the BASIC language: numeric (or arithmetic) data and character string data. The logical result of a comparison operation can not be stored directly; however, logical values can be simulated through the use of numeric values, such as 1 for true and 0 for false.

Numeric Data. A numeric data item is entered in decimal form as an integer, decimal number, as a number in scaled representation in a BASIC statement, or as an input data item. A numeric value is always stored in floating-point form and is printed or displayed in the most efficient representation. All of the numeric values in Figure 5.9, for example, are stored and displayed in the same form—even though each value was entered differently.

Character-String Data. Character-string data are always enclosed in quote marks—in BASIC statements and as input data—and are displayed without the quote marks as demonstrated in Figure 5.10. Statement number 30 in the example of Figure 5.10 requests keyboard input, which is supplied the following character-string data item: 'EARLY TO BED . . .' . (It should be noted that the

```
10  A$='TEA FOR TWO'
20  READ B$
30  INPUT C$
40  PRINT A$
50  PRINT B$
60  PRINT C$
70  DATA 'ALL COWS EAT GRASS'
RUN
'EARLY TO BED ...'
TEA FOR TWO
ALL COWS EAT GRASS
EARLY TO BED ...
```

Figure 5.10 Character-string data are always entered into the computer, in BASIC statements and as input data, enclosed in quote marks and are displayed without quote marks.

```
10 T$='''NORMAL'' IS NORMAL'
20 PRINT T$
30 PRINT 'AND ABNORMAL ISN''T'
RUN
'NORMAL' IS NORMAL
AND ABNORMAL ISN'T
```

READY   28291

Figure 5.11 Within a character string, a quote mark is denoted by two successive quote marks. Composite characters are also permitted in character strings.

output is displayed without quote marks, even though it is entered with quote marks.)

Special Characters. A quote mark, normally used as a delimiter for character strings, may be represented in a character string itself by the occurrence of two successive quote marks, as depicted in Figure 5.11. This is a lexical convention that permits the computer to decipher the programmer's intention. Composite characters, formed by backspacing and overstriking, are permitted in character strings and Figure 5.11 also demonstrates the use of underlined letters, which serve a variety of purposes in tables and reports.

Character Variables

The form of a character-string variable name is a letter followed by a dollar sign—as demonstrated in Figure 5.10. The length of a character-string data item stored by the computer is 18 characters. Shorter character strings are left justified and padded on the right with blanks; longer character strings are truncated after the leftmost 18 characters. Figure 5.12 depicts a program in which the character string assigned to a character-string variable is truncated after 18 characters. Character string literals that are longer than 18 characters can be used in PRINT statements and no truncation takes place when the character string is printed.

Character-String Operations

The operations defined on character strings in BASIC are: replacement, comparison, and selection. Comparison operations apply to both numeric and

```
10 A$='ABCDEFGHIJKLMNOPQRSTUVWXYZ'
20 PRINT A$
30 PRINT 'ABCDEFGHIJKLMNOPQRSTUVWXYZ'
RUN
ABCDEFGHIJKLMNOPQR
ABCDEFGHIJKLMNOPQRSTUVWXYZ
```

READY   28278

Figure 5.12 Character strings are truncated after 18 characters when stored, but a character literal containing more than 18 characters can be placed in a PRINT statement.

character-string data items and will be covered in the next section. The other operations involve the use of the substring functio₁₁ and the notion of a character expression.

Substring Function. The substring function, written as follows:

STR(*n*$,*i*,*l*)

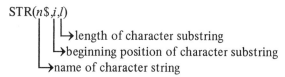

is used to reference a part of a character string—hence the name "substring." Thus, if Q$='5100 PORTABLE COMPUTER', then STR(Q$,6,8) would have a character value of PORTABLE. The beginning position and length of the character substring, denoted by *i* and *l* in the above skeleton, can be numeric constants, variables, or expressions. Their values are truncated to an integer before the substring function is performed, so that from an operational point of view, STR(Q$,6,8) is equivalent to STR(Q$,6.7,8.4).

Character Expressions. A character expression is one of the following:

1. A character-string constant, such as 'INVENTORY REPORT';
2. A character-string variable, such as G$;
3. An element of a character-string array, such as R$(14) (Arrays will be covered later); or
4. A substring function reference, such as STR(G$,I,2∗K+L).

and can be used in a replacement statement, a PRINT statement, and a comparison expression.

Simple Replacement. Several instances of simple character-string replacement were given in previous examples. The general form of simple character-string replacement is similar to numeric replacement and is written as follows:

character-variable = character-expression.

The "character expression" is evaluated and the resulting character string is assigned to the "character variable" using the operational conventions for character variables given previously. Figure 5.13 gives examples of character expressions and simple character-string replacement.

Replacement of a Substring. Characters within a string can be replaced by using the substring function to the left of the equals sign in a replacement statement. In computer terminology this manner of using the substring function is called a *pseudovariable*, which takes the following form:

STR(*n*$,*i*,*l*)=character-expression

and is executed as follows: "The first *l* characters of the *value* of the character expression replace the *l* characters of character-string variable *n*$ beginning with

```
10 Q$='5100 PORTABLE COMPUTER'
20 PRINT Q$
30 R$=Q$
40 PRINT R$
50 PRINT STR(Q$,6,8)
60 Q$='*'
70 PRINT Q$
RUN
5100 PORTABLE COMP
5100 PORTABLE COMP
PORTABLE
*

READY                                    28214
```

Figure 5.13   Examples of character string replacement and the use of the substring function.

character position *i*. Two rules that govern the use of the substring pseudo-variable in a replacement statement are:

1. If the substring function appears to the right of the equals sign, then the substring pseudovariable must be used in that statement.
2. If the substring pseudovariable appears to the left of the equals sign and the substring appears to the right of the equals sign, then the length of the operand to the left of the equals sign must be shorter than or equal to the length of the operand to the right of the equals sign.

Figure 5.14 contains several examples of how the substring pseudovariable is used to replace and combine characters.

```
0010 H$='3415 W. 332ND ST.'
0020 L$='HE LIVES ON 145TH'
0030 STR(H$,9,5)=STR(L$,13,5)
0040 PRINT H$
0050 STR(H$,9,5)='136TH STREET'
0060 PRINT H$
0070 A$='FIRST'
0080 STR(H$,9,5)=A$
0090 PRINT H$
0100 N$='CHAIRPERSON SMITH'
0110 STR(N$,6,6)='MAN'
0120 PRINT N$
0130 P$='MERCEDES '
0140 S$='BENZ'
0150 STR(P$,10,4)=S$
0160 PRINT P$

RUN
3415 W. 145TH ST.
3415 W. 136TH ST.
3415 W. FIRST ST.
CHAIRMAN    SMITH
MERCEDES BENZ
```

Figure 5.14   The substring pseudovariable can be used to replace and combine characters in a character string variable.

Comparison Expressions

Comparison expressions are used for decision making in IF statements and permit two values to be compared. The form of a comparison expression is:

$$e_1 \text{ comparison-operator } e_2$$

where e_1 and e_2 are expressions of the same type (either numeric or character) and "comparison-operator" is one of the following:

Operator	Meaning
$\geq$	Greater than or equal to
$>$	Greater than
$=$	Equal to
$\neq$	Not equal to
$<$	Less than
$\leq$	Less than or equal to

Alternate symbols for the comparison operators are listed in Table 5.2.

Numeric Operands. With numeric expressions, the algebraic value of the expression is used, as in the following example:

        A1=5
        A2=-5
        IF A1>A2+6 GOTO 3120

which would cause program control to be transferred to statement number 3120.

Character Operands. With character operands, the comparison is based on the character collating* sequence for the 5100 Portable Computer, given in the appendices. The comparison is made from left-to-right on a character basis; if character operands of different lengths are compared, the shorter operand is extended on the right with blank characters to the length of the longer operand. The collating sequence is essentially the commonly used alphabetical sequence found in dictionaries and directories. The following examples utilize the 5100 Portable Computer collating sequence given in the appendices:

Expression	Logical Value
'DOG'<'CAT'	False
'AB3T4'≤'ABCT4'	True
'#23'≠'#30'	True
'12R+'≠'-*3P'	True
'34'>'35'	False
'PIbb'='PI'	True
'I'='1'	False

*The ordering among characters in an alphabet based on an established convention is referred to as a *collating sequence*. In computers, the collating sequence is frequently based on the numerical values of the bit representations of the characters.

where ∲ denotes a blank character and the operands are not restricted to character literals. A character operand in a comparison can be any form of a character expression, as defined previously.

5.4 ARRAYS

The BASIC language allows one or two-dimensional arrays defined on numeric or character-string values. An element of a numeric array is a single numeric value; an element of a character-string array is a string of up to 18 characters regarded as a single entity. Only data items of the same type can be grouped to form an array.

Array Names

The name of a numeric array is a single alphabetic character; the name of a character-string array is a single alphabetic character followed by a dollar sign. Scalar variables and arrays with the same name are distinct and may be used in the same program, as demonstrated in Figure 5.15.

Array Reference

Elements of a numeric array are automatically initialized to zero and elements of a character-string array are initialized to a string of 18 blanks. After initialization, values are assigned to an array in three ways:

1. Through the use of a scalar replacement statement in which a specific array element must be identified with a subscript.
2. Through the use of a scalar input/output statement, such as READ or INPUT.
3. Through a matrix statement (MAT statement) in which the array is referenced in aggregate form. (This topic will be covered in a later chapter.)

```
10  A=2
20  A(5)=100
30  A$='PLATO'
40  A$(8)=' ARISTOTLE'
50  B=5
60  B(3,4)=9320
70  B$(7,2)=' KANT'
80  PRINT A;A(5);B;B(3,4)
90  PRINT A$;A$(8);B$(7,2)
RUN
  2       100    5       9320
PLATO ARISTOTLE KANT

READY                                          25153
```

Figure 5.15 Scalar variables and arrays with the same name can be used without ambiguity.

An element of an array is selected as an operand in an expression through the use of a subscript in which the specific element is identified.

Replacement. The form of numeric array replacement is:

$$a(e_1)=e_2 \qquad \text{(One-dimensional numeric array)}$$

and

$$a(e_1,e_2)=e_3 \qquad \text{(Two-dimensional numeric array)}$$

where e_1, e_2, and e_3 are numeric expressions evaluated at the point of reference, and a is a numeric array name. The form of character-string array replacement is:

$$a\$(e_1)=c \qquad \text{(One-dimensional character-string array)}$$

and

$$a\$(e_1,e_2)=c \qquad \text{(Two-dimensional character-string array)}$$

where e_1 and e_2 are numeric expressions evaluated at the point of reference, c is a character expression, and $a\$$ is a character-string array name. Replacement of the value of a one-dimensional array is executed as follows:

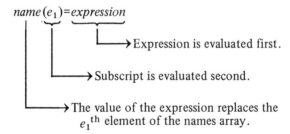

Similarly, replacement of the value of a two-dimensional array is executed as follows:

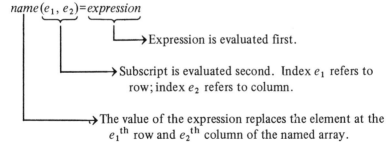

Several examples of array replacement are given in Figure 5.16.

Scalar Array Input. When an element of an array is assigned a value through a scalar input/output statement, the specific element in the array must be identified in the input/output statement. In short, the array reference must include a

```
0010  I=2
0020  J=3
0030  A(4)=I↑5
0040  B(I+4)=100+J
0050  C(I,J-2)=SQR(1296)
0060  PRINT A(4);B(6);C(2,1)
0070  A$(9)='A MINUS B'
0080  A$(I+J)='PRODUCTION CONTROL'
0090  B$(6,I+1)='I'
0100  PRINT A$(9)
0110  PRINT A$(5)
0120  PRINT B$(6,3)
0130  STR(A$(9),3,5)='TIMES'
0140  PRINT A$(9)

RUN
  32     103    36
A MINUS B
PRODUCTION CONTROL
I
A TIMES B




READY
```

Figure 5.16   Examples of array replacement.

subscript. Using the READ statement as an example, scalar array input is executed as follows:

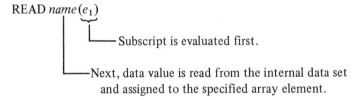

READ *name* (e_1)

—— Subscript is evaluated first.

——Next, data value is read from the internal data set
and assigned to the specified array element.

Figure 5.17 gives examples of scalar array input. More detailed information on array input is given under the specific input/output statements.

Selection. An element of an array is selected by specifying the name of the array followed by a subscript enclosed in parentheses. The value selected can be used in an expression that involves the use of scalar values. The form of array selection is summarized as follows:

	Numeric Array	Character-String Array
One-Dimensional Array	$a(e_1)$	$a\$(e_1)$
Two-Dimensional Array	$a(e_1,e_2)$	$a\$(e_1,e_2)$

```
10 I=8
20 READ A(I),B(2,9),C$(I-3)
30 PRINT A(8);B(2,9);C$(5)
40 DATA 10,20,' TOTAL VALUE'
RUN
 10    20    TOTAL VALUE
```

READY   27120

Figure 5.17 Examples of scalar array input.

where a is the array name and e_1 and e_2 are numeric expressions evaluated at the point of reference. Selection of an element of a one-dimensional array is executed as follows:

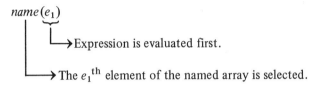

Similarly, the selection of an element of a two-dimensional array is executed as follows:

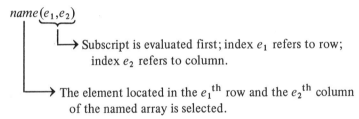

Several examples of array selection are given in Figure 5.18. An expression used in a subscript may include a subscripted variable, so that subscripts can be nested to any level to satisfy the requirements of a given application. Figure 5.18 contains a simple example of a nested subscript and Figure 5.19 contains an example of a multiply-nested subscript.

Array Declaration

The size of an array can be declared explicitly or implicitly. In either case, an array declaration must be made before an array can be used in a matrix (MAT) statement.

Explicit Declaration. An explicit declaration of the extent of an array is made with the dimension (DIM) statement, which is used to give the extent of each dimension of the array. For example, the statement:

DIM A(75),B(10,40),C$(20),D$(50,2)

```
0010  P(5)=25
0020  Q=10
0030  R=Q*P(5)+1
0040  PRINT P(5);Q;R
0050  X=SQR(P(5))
0060  PRINT P(5);X
0070  I(4)=2
0080  K=6
0090  B(3,6)=1234
0100  Y=B(I(4)+1,K)
0110  PRINT B(I(4)+1,K);Y
0120  G$(8)='PHILOSOPHICAL'
0130  L=8
0140  H$=G$(L)
0150  PRINT G$(8),G$(L),H$

RUN
 25      10      251
 25       5
 1234        1234
PHILOSOPHICAL       PHILOSOPHICAL       PHILOSOPHICAL




READY
```

Figure 5.18   Examples of array selection.

defines the following arrays:

1. Numeric array A contains 75 elements. Lower subscript bound is 1; upper subscript bound is 75.
2. Numeric array B has two dimensions and contains 400 elements. The row subscript bounds are 1 and 10, the column subscript bounds are 1 and 40.

```
10  A(1)=5
20  B(5)=6
30  C(6)=2
40  D(2)=4
50  E(4)=5
60  F(5)=9
70  G(9)=3
80  H(3)=1234
90  PRINT H(G(F(E(D(C(B(A(1)))))))))
RUN
 1234


READY
```

Figure 5.19   Subscripts can be nested to any level to meet the needs of a given application.

```
LOAD 0
10 A(7)=1776
20 B(15)=1976
30 PRINT A(7);B(15)
RUN
  ERROR 224                              0020
```

(a) Array error condition in statement numbered 20.

```
5 DIM B(20)
RUN
 1776      1976
```

```
READY                                    28016
```

(b) Resolution of error condition with DIM statement.

Figure 5.20 An array with an extent greater than 10 must be explicitly declared with a DIM statement. (ERROR 224 denotes a subscript that is out of range.)

3. Character-string array C$ contains 20 eighteen-character strings. Lower subscript bound is 1; upper subscript bound is 20.
4. Character-string array D$ has two dimensions and contains 100 character strings. The row subscript bounds are 1 and 50; the column subscript bounds are 1 and 2.

The lower subscript bound for all dimensions in BASIC is always one; the upper subscript bound is the same as the extent given in the DIM statement.

Implicit Declaration. An implicit array declaration is made when an array reference is made to an undefined array. A subscripted array reference with a single index is assigned an extent of 10 with lower and upper subscript bounds of 1 and 10, respectively. A subscripted array reference with a double index is assigned row and column extents of 10; each dimension has lower and upper subscript bounds of 1 and 10, respectively. Figure 5.20 demonstrates the significance of implicit and explicit array declaration.

5.5 OPERATIONAL CONSIDERATIONS

The operational use of the 5100 Portable Computer involves a minimal set of system functions that permit a BASIC program to be executed, saved on tape, loaded from tape, listed, and edited. Additional system functions are covered in a separate chapter.

Replacing and Deleting Lines of a Program

The statements that comprise a program must be in the main storage unit before they can be edited in any way. Normally, a program is placed in the main storage unit on a statement-by-statement basis from the keyboard or loaded into the main storage unit from a tape cartridge.

```
10  N1=0
20  N2=1
30  PRINT N2;
40  N3=N1+N2
50  IF N3>50 GOTO 90
60  PRINT N3;
70  N1=N2
80  N2=N3
90  GOTO 40
100 END
50  IF N3>50 GOTO 100
RUN
 1     1     2     3     5     8     13    21    34

READY
```

Figure 5.21 A statement is replaced by entering another statement with the same statement number.

Replacement. A statement is replaced by entering another statement with the same statement number. Figure 5.21 demonstrates replacement in a program that generates Fibonacci numbers of the sequence:

$$1 \ 1 \ 2 \ 3 \ 5 \ 8 \ 13 \ 21 \ 34 \ \dots$$

wherein each succeeding number is the sum of the previous two numbers. Applications of Fibonacci numbers occur frequently in nature, such as the arrangement of stems on a branch and the growth in rabbit population. It is possible to avoid retyping a complete line by scrolling down until the incorrect statement is in the input line. The statement can then be edited using the methods given in chapter four and entered into the computer with the execute key.

Deletion. A statement from a program can be deleted by entering the statement number of the line to be deleted followed by DEL on the same line, and by pressing the EXECUTE key, as in:

15 DEL

which deletes statement numbered 15 from a program in the main storage unit. Successive lines can be deleted from a program by entering the statement numbers of the first line followed by DEL, followed by the statement number of the last line to be deleted, and by pressing the EXECUTE key. For example, the statement:

45 DEL 280

deletes lines 45 through 280 from the program in the main storage unit.

Files and Tape Preparation

The magnetic tape unit is designed for storing programs and data between runs on the computer. Information is recorded on a tape cartridge, which can be removed from the tape unit and stored in a secure place. To use a program placed on a tape cartridge, the program must first be loaded from the tape cartridge into the main storage unit. Similarly, data recorded on a tape cartridge must be read into the main storage unit with appropriate BASIC statements.

Files. Each program or data file is stored on a tape cartridge as a *file*, which is identified and accessed by number. Files are numbered sequentially on the tape cartridge starting with the number 1.

Size of Files. The approximate size of a program or data file must be known before it can be placed on tape. The size is needed for initializing the tape to hold a program or data file. The size of a program can be determined by inspecting the amount of main storage available, which is displayed in the lower right hand corner of the display screen. The difference between the original amount— displayed with LOAD 0—and the current amount gives the size of a program in bytes. The size of a data file can be estimated on the basis of the type and amount of data, computed as follows:

1. Each character-string datum occupies 18 bytes, and
2. Each numeric datum occupies 8 bytes.

In addition, each file requires an overhead of .5K bytes.*

Marking the Tape Cartridge. Before a program or data file can be placed on the tape cartridge, the tape cartridge must be marked to prepare it for the subsequent save or write operation. The MARK command may only be entered as a system command from the keyboard and takes the following simplified form:

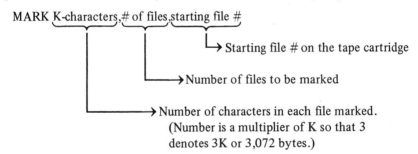

MARK K-characters,# of files,starting file #

⤷ Starting file # on the tape cartridge

→ Number of files to be marked

→ Number of characters in each file marked. (Number is a multiplier of K so that 3 denotes 3K or 3,072 bytes.)

The following command, for example:

MARK 4,2,1

marks the tape cartridge with 2 files, starting with file numbered 1, each containing 4K bytes. The marked files are numbered 1 and 2. Similarly, the command:

MARK 1,3,4

*K denotes 1024.

marks the tape cartridge with 3 files each containing 1K bytes. The files are numbered 4, 5, and 6. Files 1, 2, and 3 on the tape cartridge must have been previously defined. The MARK command can be entered without disturbing a program in the main storage unit. As with other system commands, the MARK command is entered by pressing the EXECUTE key.

Saving a Program on Tape

The SAVE command is used to save the contents of the active work area on the tape cartridge. A simplified form of the SAVE command is:

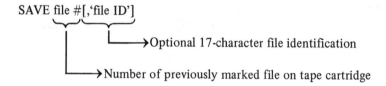

SAVE file #[,'file ID']

└──────→Optional 17-character file identification

└──────→Number of previously marked file on tape cartridge

The following command:

SAVE 4,'LISTPROGRAM'

saves the contents of the work area on the tape cartridge as file numbered 4 with the identification LISTPROGRAM. File numbered 4 must have been previously marked with sufficient capacity to hold the program in the work area.

Other options exist to the SAVE command; they are covered in a later chapter.

Loading a Program from Tape

A program is loaded from tape with the LOAD command that takes the following simplified form:

LOAD file#

The following command:

LOAD 4

loads the program and data from file numbered 4 into the work area of the main storage unit. As with the SAVE command, other options exist to the LOAD command; they are also covered in a later chapter.

Running a Program with Options

A program is executed by keying in the RUN command and pressing EXECUTE. The syntax of the RUN command includes useful options that enable printer

```
LOAD 0
10 PRINT FLP,1/3;1/7;1/11
RUN P=D
 .333333      .142857      9.090909E-2

RUN P=D,RD=2
 .33   .14   9.09E-2
```

READY

Figure 5.22 Parameters to the RUN command permit printed output to be directed to the display and the number of places to the right of the decimal point to be specified.

output to be directed to the display screen and controls the number of digits to the right of the decimal point that cause rounding on printed output. A simplified form of the RUN command is:

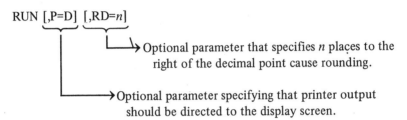

RUN [,P=D] [,RD=n]

→ Optional parameter that specifies n places to the right of the decimal point cause rounding.

→ Optional parameter specifying that printer output should be directed to the display screen.

The value of n for rounding can be from 1 to 13 and is initially set to 6. Figure 5.22 demonstrates a program for which printer output is directed to the display screen and rounding is set at 2 digits to the right of the decimal point.

Listing a Program

As a program is developed, the contents of the display screen frequently become disarranged because of statement editing, insertion, deletion, and error conditions that inevitably arise. A program can be listed by entering LIST and then pressing the EXECUTE key. The first 14 lines of the active program are displayed on the display screen. Additional lines of the program can be displayed by using the scroll up key. The complete active program can be displayed on the printer unit by entering LIST PRINT and then pressing the EXECUTE key.

SELECTED READINGS

Coan, J. S., *Basic BASIC: An Introduction to Computer Programming in BASIC Language*, Hayden Book Company, New York, 1970.

Gately, W. Y., and Bitter, G. G., *BASIC for Beginners*, McGraw-Hill Book Company, New York, 1970.

REFERENCES

IBM 5100 Portable Computer publications:
  a. *IBM 5100 BASIC Introduction*, Form # SA 21-9216.
  b. *IBM 5100 BASIC Reference Manual*, Form #SA 21-9217.
IBM Corporation, Rochester, Minnesota, 1975.

6 | BASIC LANGUAGE STATEMENTS AND PROGRAMMING TECHNIQUES

This chapter describes the statements in the BASIC language that fall into the following classes: *replacement*, *program control*, *looping*, and *elementary input and output*. Programming techniques are given for statements that involve concepts not presented previously, and mathematical functions are introduced briefly. The first section of this chapter covers syntactical conventions used to describe the statement structure.

6.1 SYNTACTICAL CONVENTIONS

In describing the syntactical structure of the statements of the BASIC language, a set of syntactical conventions is used to avoid any ambiguity that may arise in determining how a statement should be written. Careful adherence to the syntax rules normally reduces the number of syntax errors and the need for trial and error procedures. One of the advantages of the 5100 Portable Computer is that an incorrect statement is recognized as soon as it is entered so that it can be corrected immediately.

Syntax Notation

Names are given to the constructs of the BASIC language so that the syntax language can describe a BASIC statement on a general basis. Two concepts are involved: notation variable and notation constant.

Notation Variable. A *notation variable* names a constituent of the BASIC language and takes one of two forms:

(1) Lower-case letters, digits, and hyphens beginning with a letter, such as:

>   constant
>   control-variable
>   array-name

Two or more words separated by hyphens in which one word consists of upper-case letters and one word consists of lower-case letters, such as:

>   K-characters
>   file-ID

A notation variable represents information that must be supplied by the programmer. In the syntactical specification of a BASIC statement, the structure of a notation variable is defined in preceding or adjacent text.

Notation Constant. A *notation constant* stands for itself and is represented by capital letters or special characters. A notation constant must always be written as shown. In the statements:

>   GOSUB statement-number
>   NEXT control-variable

the words GOSUB and NEXT are notation constants.

Syntactical Elements

Three symbols, together with notation variables and constants, are used in a syntax specification to describe a syntactical unit of the BASIC language. The symbols are braces, brackets, and the ellipsis, and are used to denote the syntatical operations of selection, optionality, and repetition.

Braces. A pair of braces { } is used to indicate that a choice is to be made among the syntactical units contained in the braces. For example:

$$\left\{ \begin{array}{l} \text{arith-con} \\ \text{char-con} \end{array} \right\}$$

and

$$\left\{ \begin{array}{l} \text{IN} \\ \text{OUT} \end{array} \right\}$$

In general, the vertical stacking of syntactical units enclosed in braces denotes that a choice should be made of them.

Brackets. A pair of square brackets denotes an option and the enclosed syntatical unit(s) may occur once or not at all. For example,

> END[comment]
> MARK K-characters, files, starting-file [,dev-address]

Ellipsis. The ellipsis (a series of three successive periods) denotes that the preceding syntactical unit may be repeated one or more times. For example,

$$\text{DATA} \begin{Bmatrix} \text{arith-con} \\ \text{char-con} \end{Bmatrix} \left[, \begin{Bmatrix} \text{arith-con} \\ \text{char-con} \end{Bmatrix} \right] \dots$$

> DIM array-name(rows[,columns])) [,array-name(rows[,columns]))] . . .

Juxtaposition. The juxtaposition of two syntactical units means that they should be written in the given order. Not all syntactical units are separated by punctuation characters, which are in themselves syntactical units, as in the following example:

> RESET file-ref[END] [,file-ref[END]] . . .

The syntactical definition of a comparison expression gives another example of juxtaposition:

$$\begin{Bmatrix} \text{arith-exp comp-op arith-exp} \\ \text{char-exp comp-op char-exp} \end{Bmatrix}$$

Examples of Syntactical Specification

Several brief examples serve to clarify the notion of a syntactical specification. The READ statement is defined as:

$$\text{READ} \begin{Bmatrix} \text{arith-var} \\ \text{arith-arr-var} \\ \text{char-var} \\ \text{char-arr-var} \\ \text{str-func} \end{Bmatrix} \left[, \begin{Bmatrix} \text{arith-var} \\ \text{arith-arr-var} \\ \text{char-var} \\ \text{char-arr-var} \\ \text{str-func} \end{Bmatrix} \right] \dots$$

and a typical example is:

> READ A,B$,C(I,J-1),X6,STR(D$,1,4)

The GOTO statement is defined as:

> GOTO line-num [[,line-num]. . .ON arith-exp]]

and a suitable example is:

> GOTO 420

In addition to being accurate, the use of syntactical specifications is also economical since each option need not be listed and explained separately.

6.2 REPLACEMENT STATEMENT

The replacement statement specifies that a data value is to be assigned to a scalar variable or to a subscripted array variable. This section summarizes the simple LET statement, the conventional replacement statement, and multiple replacement. The various forms of scalar replacement are specific instances of the generalized LET statement, defined syntactically as follows:

$$
[LET]
\begin{cases}
\begin{Bmatrix} \text{arith-var} \\ \text{arith-arr-var} \end{Bmatrix}
\left[, \begin{Bmatrix} \text{arith-var} \\ \text{arith-arr-var} \end{Bmatrix} \right] \ldots = \text{arith-exp} \\[3ex]
\begin{Bmatrix} \text{char-var} \\ \text{char-arr-var} \\ \text{str-func} \end{Bmatrix}
\left[, \begin{Bmatrix} \text{char-var} \\ \text{char-arr-var} \\ \text{str-func} \end{Bmatrix} \right] \ldots = \begin{Bmatrix} \text{char-exp} \\ \text{char-con} \end{Bmatrix}
\end{cases}
$$

where the variables (written *var*) are scalar variable names or subscripted array references, *str-func* is a substring reference, the expressions (written *exp*) are arithmetic or character expressions, and *char-con* is a character string enclosed in quotes. The rules governing replacement were covered earlier. Even though they are variations of the same syntactical structures, the three major forms of the replacement statement are covered separately because other versions of the BASIC language offer a more limited capability to which the reader may have been exposed.

Simple LET Statement

The LET statement has the form:

$$\text{LET var=exp}$$

where *var* and *exp* are defined in the generalized LET statement. The keyword LET is optional in 5100 BASIC and is included for compatibility with other versions of the language. The meaning of the simple LET statement is, "Replace the specified variable, array reference, or substring with the value of the given expression evaluated at the point of reference." The following examples depict valid LET statements:

```
LET R7=-13.41
LET W$='ERROR'
LET Y=A*X+B
LET M(4,I↑2-3)=I
LET A$(J)=H$(J+1)
```

In a replacement statement, the operand to the left of the equals sign is replaced only when the statement is executed and no strict equality between that operand and the expression to the right of the equals sign is implied, except at the point of execution when replacement is performed. The keyword LET serves no useful purpose and is not used any further in this book.

Conventional Replacement Statement

The replacement statement used in previous examples does not include the keyword LET and takes the form:

$$var=exp$$

where *var* and *exp* are defined above. This form of the replacement statement is the same as in other programming languages, such as FORTRAN and PL/I. The following examples are exactly equivalent to those given in the preceding section:

$$R7 = -13.41$$
$$W\$ = \text{'ERROR'}$$
$$Y = A*X + B$$
$$M(4, I \uparrow 2 - 3) = I$$
$$A\$(J) = H\$(J+1)$$

The generalized replacement statement is the only statement in the BASIC language that does not require a statement identifier.

Multiple Replacement

The multiple replacement option to the generalized LET statement permits the replacement of two or more operands with the value of a single expression. The general form of multiple replacement is:

$$var[,var]\ldots=exp$$

where, as before, *var* and *exp* are defined above. When the multiple replacement is executed, the expression is evaluated and its value is assigned to the specified variables from left to right. In many instances the use of multiple replacement permits fewer statements to be written. For example, multiple replacement allows the following statements:

$$A1 = 15.34 + SIN(RAD(H6)) \uparrow 2 - I$$
$$A2 = A1$$

to be replaced by:

$$A1, A2 = 15.34 + SIN(RAD(H6)) \uparrow 2 - I$$

Figure 6.1 gives an example of multiple replacement in which the subscript value used in a subsequent replacement in the same statement is replaced. Subscripts

```
10  I=3
20  I,A(I)=I-1
30  PRINT I;A(2);A(3)
RUN
  2      2      0
```

READY   28205

Figure 6.1   In multiple replacement, the expression to the right of the equals sign is evaluated and assigned to the specified variables from left to right. Subscripts are evaluated
when the replacement operation is performed.

are evaluated just prior to replacement so that the value of a subscript may be
altered during the execution of the statement. (This is the case demonstrated
in Figure 6.1.)

Hexadecimal Replacement*

A hexadecimal constant can be assigned to a character variable by enclosing the
hexadecimal constant in quote marks and preceding it with the letter X as follows:

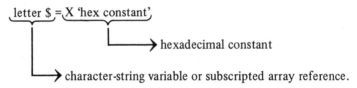

letter $ = X 'hex constant'

→ hexadecimal constant

→ character-string variable or subscripted array reference.

The hexadecimal constant must consist of an even number of hexadecimal
digits.** The hexadecimal equivalents to the 5100 character set are given in Appendix C and Figure 6.2 gives an example of hexadecimal replacement.

```
10  J$=X'010203'
20  A$(4)=X'160F0C0B13'
30  M$(7,2)=X'170107050E'
40  PRINT J$
50  PRINT A$(4),M$(7,2)
60  PRINT A$(4);M$(7,2)
RUN
ABC
VOLKS                WAGEN
VOLKSWAGEN
```

READY   26170

Figure 6.2   A hexadecimal constant can be assigned to a character string variable.

*This section may be omitted without loss of continuity.
**A hexadecimal digit is one of the following: 0 through 9 and A through F.

6.3 PROGRAM CONTROL STATEMENTS

The statements in a BASIC program are executed automatically and program control flows from one statement to the following statement without explicit intervention by the programmer. When program control flows into or is directed to a nonexecutable statement, the first executable statement following the non-executable statement is executed and automatic statement execution continues from there. Six BASIC statements control the manner in which a program is executed: GOTO, IF, FOR, NEXT, STOP, END, and PAUSE. The FOR and NEXT statement fall into the category of program looping, which is presented separately.

The GOTO Statement

The GOTO statement can be used to direct program control to a specified statement in a BASIC program on an unconditional or a selective basis. The generalized form of the GOTO statement is:

> GOTO statement-number [[,statement-number] . . . ON arith-exp]

where *statement-number* is the statement number of an existing statement in the program and *arith-exp* is a numeric expression evaluated at the point of reference.

Simple GOTO Statement. The form of the simple GOTO statement is

> GOTO statement-number

Execution of the GOTO statement causes program control to be transferred to the specified statement, or to the first executable statement following the specified statement in the event that this statement is nonexecutable. An example of a valid GOTO statement is:

> GOTO 3120

After the GOTO statement is executed, automatic program execution continues from the point of the *new* statement and *not* the GOTO statement.

Computed GOTO Statement. The form of the computed GOTO statement is:

> GOTO statement-number [,statement-number] . . . ON arith-exp

where *arith-exp* is an arithmetic expression. The arithmetic expression is evaluated at the point of execution and is then truncated to a positive integer. Program control is then transferred to the statement with the statement number that occupies a position in the GOTO statement equal to the truncated positive integer. For example, if Y3=3.12, then the following statement:

> GOTO 450,75,810,850,630, ON Y3+1

```
0010 REM PROG COMPUTES RAND NUM BETW 1 AND 10 AND BRANCHES
0020 REM TO SPECIFIED STATEMENT.  OUT AT 140.
0030 R=RND(R)
0040 E=INT(10*R)
0050 GOTO 0080,0100,0120,0140 ON E
0060 PRINT 'CONTROL DROPPED THROUGH TO STATMNT 50, E=';E
0070 GOTO 0030
0080 PRINT 'CONTROL AT 80, E=';E
0090 GOTO 0030
0100 PRINT 'CONTROL AT 100, E=';E
0110 GOTO 0030
0120 PRINT 'CONTROL AT 120, E=';E
0130 GOTO 0030
0140 PRINT 'OUT AT 140, E=';E
RUN
CONTROL DROPPED THROUGH TO STATMNT 50, E= 9
CONTROL AT 80, E= 1
CONTROL AT 100, E= 2
CONTROL AT 100, E= 2
CONTROL AT 100, E= 2
CONTROL AT 120, E= 3
OUT AT 140, E= 4


READY                                                         27992
```

Figure 6.3 Example of the use of the GOTO statement. (Function RND computes a random number between 0 and 1 and function INT truncates to an integer.)

would cause program control to be transferred to statement number 850. More specifically, the model statement:

$$\text{GOTO } s_1, s_2, s_3, \ldots s_n \text{ ON } e$$

transfers program control to statement numbered s_1 if $e=1$, to statement numbered s_2 if $e=2, \ldots$, and to statement numbered s_n if $e=n$. If $e<1$ or if $e>n$, then control passes to the next executable statement following the computed GOTO statement. Figure 6.3 demonstrates the use of simple and computed GOTO statements.

The IF Statement

The IF statement permits program control to be altered on a conditional basis and takes the following general form:

$$\text{IF} \begin{Bmatrix} \text{arith-exp comp-op arith-exp} \\ \text{char-exp comp-op char-exp} \end{Bmatrix} \left[\begin{Bmatrix} \& \\ | \end{Bmatrix} \begin{Bmatrix} \text{arith-exp comp-op arith-exp} \\ \text{char-exp comp-op char-exp} \end{Bmatrix} \right] \begin{Bmatrix} \text{THEN} \\ \text{GOTO} \end{Bmatrix} \text{statement-number}$$

where *arith-exp* is an arithmetic expression, *char-exp* is a character expression, and *comp-op* is a comparison operator. The symbolic operators & (and) and

| (or) represent logical operations on the logical result of two comparison operations. In simplified form, the IF statement is:

IF logical-exp GOTO statement-number

If the value of the logical expression is true, then program control is transferred to the statement with the specified statement number. If the logical expression is false, program control drops through to the next statement. The meaning of the keywords GOTO and THEN are synonymous. IF statements are always stored with GOTO in 5100 BASIC.

Comparison. The result of a single comparison expression is a truth value that is computed according to the operational conventions for the comparison operator. Character operands are padded on the right with blanks to a length of 18 characters. Numeric comparisons are based on a precision of 13 digits and values must be equal to 13 digits of accuracy in order to be equal. Numeric operands to a comparison operation may be arithmetic expressions.

Simple IF Statement. A simple IF statement takes the following form:

IF comp-exp GOTO statement-number

where *comp-exp* and *statement-number* are defined above. If the value of the comparison expression is true, then program control is passed to the statement with the specified statement number. The following statements demonstrate the use of the simple IF statement:

IF E<.0001 GOTO 6324

IF ABS(Z↑2-P4)+D1≥FNB(3*Q+1) GOTO 45

IF STR(A$,2,4)='TRUE' GOTO 953

Logical Expressions. A logical expression logically combines two comparison expressions and has either of the following forms:

comp-exp & comp-exp

comp-exp | comp-exp

where *comp-exp* is a comparison expression and the logical symbols & and | stand for the logical operators *and* and *or*, respectively. Logical expressions are processed according to the following truth table:

Logical OR				*Logical AND*		
|	True	False		&	True	False
True	True	True		True	True	False
False	True	False		False	False	False

Two comparison expressions, as introduced above, may be connected with a logical operator in an IF statement.

Execution of the IF Statement. If the logical operator &, denoting AND, is specified in an IF statement, both comparison expressions must be true before program control is passed to the statement with the specified statement number. If the logical operator |, denoting OR, is specified in an IF statement, program control is passed to the statement with the specified statement number if either of the comparison expressions is true. The following statements demonstrate the use of logical expressions:

> IF A+10>L1&S$='F' GOTO 5000
> IF SQR(A*X+B)=10 | ABS(Z↑2-P4)≤523.1 GOTO 3120
> IF Y1≥FNG(X1)&Y1≤FNH(X1) GOTO 170
> IF STR(B$,6,11)>STR(D$,2,11) | STR(B$,6,11)=' ' GOTO 7420
> IF L≠1&L≠0 GOTO 5551

Examples of simple IF statements are given in Figures 5.7 and 5.21. Figure 6.4 contains a simple IF statement in a program that computes the roots x and y of two simultaneous equations of the form:

$$ax+by=c$$
$$dx+ey=f$$

The roots are computed as:

$$x = \frac{ce-bf}{ae-bd} \quad \text{and} \quad y = \frac{af-cd}{ae-bd}$$

However, if the value of ae-bd is equal to zero, the simultaneous equations have no unique solution. The data in Figure 6.3 represents the solution to:

$$4x+5y=20$$
$$4x-5y=0$$

Figures 6.5 and 6.6 give a listing and the output, respectively, of a personnel report program that includes an IF statement with a complex logical expression.

```
0010 READ A,B,C,D,E,F
0020 D1=A*E-B*D
0030 IF D1=0 GOTO 0080
0040 X=(C*E-B*F)/D1
0050 Y=(A*F-C*D)/D1
0060 PRINT 'ROOTS ARE';X;'AND';Y
0070 STOP
0080 PRINT 'NO SOLUTION'
0090 DATA 4,5,20,4,-5,0
RUN
ROOTS ARE 2.5   AND 2
```

READY   28046

Figure 6.4 Program that computes the roots to two simultaneous linear equations. The program demonstrates the use of a simple IF statement.

```
0010 PRINT 'ENTER REQUIRED AGE AND EXPERIENCE'
0020 INPUT A1,E1
0030 PRINT FLP,TAB(19);'PERSONNEL SEARCH'
0040 PRINT FLP,'AGE LIMIT =';A1;'EXPERIENCE LEVEL =';E1;'YEARS'
0050 PRINT FLP,
0060 PRINT FLP,'NAME','AGE','EXPERIENCE','DEGREE'
0070 PRINT FLP,
0080 READ N$,A2,E2,D$
0090 IF N$=' ' GOTO 0130
0100 IF A2>A1|E2≤E1 GOTO 0080
0110 PRINT FLP,N$,A2,E2,D$
0120 GOTO 0080
0130 PRINT FLP,
0140 PRINT FLP,'END OF PERSONNEL REPORT'
0150 PRINT 'END OF PERSONNEL REPORT - REMOVE LISTING'
0160 STOP
0170 DATA 'A. ABLE',35,11,'A.A.'
0180 DATA 'B. BAKER',54,27,'B.S.'
0190 DATA 'C. CHARLY',29,2,'M.A.'
0200 DATA 'D. DAWG',40,15,'NONE'
0210 DATA 'E. EASY',37,12,'B.S.'
0220 DATA 'F. FOXX',41,10,'B.A.'
0230 DATA ' ',0,0,' '
0240 END
```

Figure 6.5 Listing of a personnel program demonstrating an IF statement with a complex logical expression. (Program input and output given in Figure 6.5.)

```
RUN
ENTER REQUIRED AGE AND EXPERIENCE

40,10
END OF PERSONNEL REPORT - REMOVE LISTING


   READY
```

Display Output

```
                 PERSONNEL SEARCH
AGE LIMIT = 40   EXPERIENCE LEVEL = 10   YEARS

NAME              AGE              EXPERIENCE        DEGREE

A. ABLE           35               11               A.A.
D. DAWG           40               15               NONE
E. EASY           37               12               B.S.

END OF PERSONNEL REPORT
```

Printer Output

Figure 6.6 Input and output of the personnel program in Figure 6.5.

The STOP Statement

The STOP statement causes the execution of a program to be terminated and it can be located anywhere in a program. The STOP statement takes the following form:

STOP [comment]

where *comment* is any string of characters in the BASIC alphabet. Execution of the STOP statement causes all open files to be closed prior to the termination of computer processing. The actions of the STOP and END statements are identical.

The END Statement

The END statement is used to specify the logical end of a program and causes program execution to be terminated. The form of the END statement is:

END [comment]

where *comment* is any string of characters in the BASIC alphabet. When the END statement is executed, it causes all open files to be closed and terminates computer processing.

The END statement is not required to be the last statement in a BASIC program. If it is omitted, it is assumed by the computer to follow the highest-numbered statement in the program.

The PAUSE Statement

The PAUSE statement is used to suspend program execution. Processing can subsequently be continued from the point where execution was suspended by entering the GO command.* The PAUSE statement takes the following form:

PAUSE [comment]

where *comment* is any string of characters in the BASIC alphabet. When the PAUSE statement is executed, a message of the form:

$$PAUSE \; n$$

is displayed on line position zero of the display screen. The number n is the line number of the PAUSE statement.

---

*Execution can also be resumed by hitting the EXECUTE key, without entering any command.

Any system command or calculator mode statement can be entered when a program is suspended, except for the following:

1. A renumber statement (RENUM).
2. A statement that alters a user-defined function reference.

One of the most common uses of the PAUSE statement occurs during the execution of a program when a tape cartridge must be marked to hold a new file. The user is given instructions on the display screen from an executing program and the PAUSE statement is then executed until the user has time to enter the needed MARK command. After the tape has been marked, the user enters the GO command and program execution is permitted to continue. (Caution: a tape file cannot be remarked during the execution of a PAUSE statement.)

Looping

A series of statements to be executed repetitively is termed a *loop*. Program loops are needed for a variety of reasons in programming including the following major applications:

1. To avoid repeating the same statements many times in a program.
2. To implement an algorithm for which the exact number of iterations is not known beforehand.

Even though the reasons for using a loop may differ, the characteristics of a loop are similar.

Repetition. A repetitive loop is contained in Figure 6.7. The program computes the square root of integers from 1 to 10 and avoids repeating the same

```
0010 PRINT 'I','SQR(I)'
0020 PRINT
0030 I=1
0040 PRINT I,SQR(I)
0050 I=I+1
0060 IF I≤10 GOTO 0040
RUN
I                   SQR(I)

1                   1
2                   1.414214
3                   1.732051
4                   2
5                   2.236068
6                   2.449490
7                   2.645751
8                   2.828427
9                   3
10                  3.162278

READY                                   28265
```

Figure 6.7   A simple loop that prints the square root of integers from 1 to 10.

statements ten times.   Actually, ten repetitions of the same statements would
not be prohibitive; however, one hundred or one thousand repetitions of the
same statements would be excessive, so that for many applications, looping is a
practical necessity.

Iteration.   An example of an iterative program loop is given in Figures 6.8 and
6.9.   The application uses the method of interval bisection to compute the root

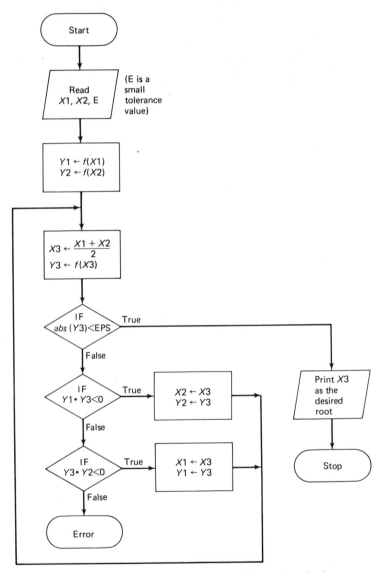

Figure 6.8   Internal bisection algorithm involving an iterative loop.

of an equation. Figure 6.8 gives the algorithm of the iterative procedure and Figure 6.9 gives the BASIC program. The method uses the fact that when a continuous function $f(x)$ has a root in the interval (x_1, x_2), then $f(x_1)$ and $f(x_2)$ have different signs. The interval bisection algorithm involves bisecting the interval and selecting the half that contains the sign change. The iteration continues until the value of the root is approximated to a specified degree of accuracy. The program in Figure 6.9 computes the root of the function:

$$f(x)=9x^3+4x^2+5x-8$$

and shows the following user-defined function:

DEF FNA(X)=9*X↑3+4*X↑2+5*X-8

which calculates the function for any argument X. Defined functions are covered later in this chapter; other statements in the program have been covered previously.

Characteristics of a Loop. The statements that comprise a loop are referred to as the *body of the loop* and the variable used to count the number of iterations is known as the *control* variable. Iterative algorithms do not necessarily use a control variable, but for either type of loop, the body of the loop is executed until either of the following events occurs:

1. The control variable exceeds a limit value.
2. The value of an expression in the program satisfies a given condition.

```
0010 DEF FNA(X)=9*X↑3+4*X↑2+5*X-8
0020 PRINT 'F(X)=9*X↑3+4*X↑2+5*X-8'
0030 READ X1,X2,E
0040 Y1=FNA(X1)
0050 Y2=FNA(X2)
0060 X3=(X1+X2)/2
0070 Y3=FNA(X3)
0080 IF ABS(Y3)<E GOTO 0190
0090 IF Y1*Y3≥0 GOTO 0130
0100 X2=X3
0110 Y2=Y3
0120 GOTO 0060
0130 IF Y3*Y2≥0 GOTO 0170
0140 X1=X3
0150 Y1=Y3
0160 GOTO 0060
0170 PRINT 'ERROR'
0180 STOP
0190 PRINT 'ROOT=';X3
0200 DATA -5,5,.01
RUN
F(X)=9*X↑3+4*X↑2+5*X-8
ROOT= .676270
```

Figure 6.9 Interval bisection program demonstrating an iterative program loop. (Program computes root of $9x^3+4x^2+5x-8$.)

In the program of Figure 6.7, the control variable is I and the loop executes until I>10. In the program of Figure 6.9, there is no control variable and the program executes until ABS(Y3)<E in statement numbered 80.

The FOR and NEXT Statements

The FOR and NEXT statements are used to simplify the programming of repetitive and iterative procedures. Parameters to the FOR statement control the looping process so that explicit computer operations are not needed to program a loop.

Controlled Looping. Controlled looping takes the following general form:

1. The control variable is set to an initial value.
2. The value of the control variable is compared against a limit value. If the limit value is exceeded, then the body of the loop is not executed and the first statement following the loop is executed.
3. The body of the loop is executed.
4. The value of the control variable is incremented by a value established when the loop is entered. This value is known as the *increment* or *step value.* The implication is that the program steps through the loop as the control variable assumes a set of values.
5. The value of the control variable is compared against the limit value. If the limit is exceeded, then the loop is terminated and execution continues with the first statement following the loop. Otherwise, execution of the loop continues with step three.

Although these procedures can be programmed using replacement and IF statements, the frequency with which the general procedure is used warrants the inclusion of the FOR and NEXT statements in the BASIC language.

FOR Statement. The FOR statement initiates a loop by establishing the control variable and the initial, limit, and step values; it takes the following form:

> FOR control-var=arith-exp TO arith-exp[STEP arith-exp]

where *control-var* is a numeric scalar variable and *arith-exp* is a numeric expression. If the STEP is omitted, it is assumed to be +1. Sample FOR statements are:

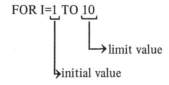

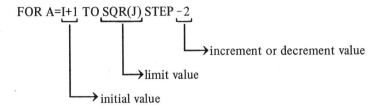

The FOR statement must always be used with a matching NEXT statement.

NEXT Statement. The NEXT statement is used to close a FOR loop and specifies the control variable that should be stepped. The form of the NEXT statement is:

NEXT control-var

where *control-var* is the same numeric scalar variable used in the corresponding FOR statement. A sample NEXT statement is:

NEXT A

Figure 6.10 depicts a simple FOR loop that prints the square root of integers from 1 to 10. Figure 6.11 gives a computer program that uses a FOR/NEXT loop to compute the factorial function.

```
0010  PRINT  'I','SQR(I)'
0020  PRINT
0030  FOR I=1 TO 10
0040  PRINT I,SQR(I)
0050  NEXT I
RUN
I                     SQR(I)

1                     1
2                     1.414214
3                     1.732051
4                     2
5                     2.236068
6                     2.449490
7                     2.645751
8                     2.828427
9                     3
10                    3.162278


READY                                        28270
```

Figure 6.10 A FOR/NEXT loop that prints the square root of integers from 1 to 10. (See Figure 6.7 for an equivalent program without FOR/NEXT statements.)

```
0010 PRINT 'ENTER N';
0020 INPUT N
0030 F=1
0040 FOR K=2 TO N
0050 F=F*K
0060 NEXT K
0070 PRINT N; 'FACTORIAL =';F
RUN
ENTER N
5
 5     FACTORIAL = 120

READY                                          28214
```

Figure 6.11 A program that computes the factorial function, used to demonstrate the use of a FOR/NEXT loop.

Nested Loops. A loop that is contained in the body of an outer loop is called a *nested loop*, which is depicted somewhat as follows:

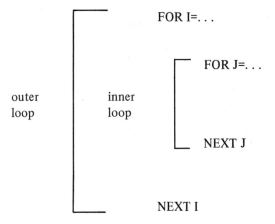

The only restriction on nested loops is that an inner loop must be wholly contained within the outer loop. Figure 6.12 gives a program for computing prime numbers that includes a nested loop. The algorithm used in the program is the Sieve of Eratosthenes that works by isolating a prime number and then eliminates all multiples of it as follows:

```
0010 DIM P(250)
0020 PRINT 'ENTER N';
0030 INPUT N
0040 FOR I=2 TO N
0050 P(I)=I
0060 NEXT I
0070 K=INT(SQR(N))
0080 FOR I=2 TO K
0090 IF P(I)=0 GOTO 0130
0100 FOR J=I+I TO N STEP I
0110 P(J)=0
0120 NEXT J
0130 NEXT I
0140 PRINT 'PRIMES LESS THAN OR EQUAL TO ';N
0150 FOR I=2 TO N
0160 IF P(I)=0 GOTO 0180
0170 PRINT P(I);
0180 NEXT I
RUN
ENTER N
50
PRIMES LESS THAN OR EQUAL TO   50
 2      3      5      7     11     13     17     19     23     29     31
37     41     43     47
```

Figure 6.12   Prime number program showing a nested loop using the sieve of Eratosthenes.

Several features of the program given in Figure 6.12 are: the use of the DIM statement, with increment, limit, and step values that are expressions.

Execution of a FOR/NEXT Loop. In the execution of a FOR/NEXT loop, the control variable takes on successive values beginning with the initial value and ending when the limit value is satisfied. In the loop headed with the statement:

$$FOR\ I = 1\ TO\ 10$$

for example, the control variable I takes on the values $1,2,3,4,5,6,7,8,9$, and 10 for successive iterations of the loop. Similarly, in the loop headed with the statement:

$$FOR\ D = 2\ TO\ 15\ STEP\ 3$$

the control variable D takes on the values $2,5,8,11,14$ for successive iterations of the loop. If the step is positive, execution of the loop ends when the value of the control variable is greater than the limit value. The step can also be negative. In the loop headed by the statement,

$$FOR\ K = 20\ TO\ 1\ STEP\ -5$$

for example, the control variable K takes on the values $20,15,10$, and 5 for successive iterations of the loop. If the step is negative, execution of the loop ends when the value of the control variable is less than the limit value. The program in Figure 6.13 demonstrates a negative step in computing the largest factor of an integer N. The algorithm operates by successively dividing N by the largest possible factors, INT(N/2),INT(N/2)-1,INT(N/2)-2, etc., until either a factor is found or the value 1 is reached for the control variable. A factor is recognized when a factor F divides evenly into N; this is the case when N/F=INT(N/F).

Definition of a FOR/NEXT Loop. The control of program execution in a FOR/NEXT loop is governed by two operational rules:

1. The control parameters (i.e., initial value, limit, and step value) are evaluated when the FOR statement is executed and cannot be changed in the body of the loop.
2. The value of the control variable can be modified from within the body of the loop.

Accordingly, a FOR/NEXT loop of the form:

$$\text{FOR } v=\text{exp1 TO exp2 STEP exp3}$$
$$[\text{body of Loop}]$$
$$\text{NEXT } v$$

is functionally equivalent to the following "pseudo" BASIC statements:

```
10   e₁=exp1
20   e₂=exp2
30   e₃=exp3
35   REMARK IF STEP is omitted, exp3=+1
40   IF e₃<0 THEN 70
50   IF e₁>e₂ THEN 1060
60   GOTO 80
70   IF e₁<e₂ THEN 1060
80   v=e₁
90
  ·
  ·   Body of Loop
  ·
999
1000   v=v+e₃
1010   IF e₃ ≥ 0 THEN 1040
1020   IF v<e₂ THEN 1050
1030   GOTO 90
1040   IF v≤e₂ THEN 90
1050   v=v-e₃
1060   REMARK upon exit v contains last loop value
```

```
0010 INPUT N
0020 FOR F=INT(N/2) TO 1 STEP -1
0030 IF N/F=INT(N/F) GOTO 0050
0040 NEXT F
0050 PRINT 'LARGEST FACTOR OF';N;'IS';F
RUN
537
LARGEST FACTOR OF 537  IS 179


READY                                                           28214
```

Figure 6.13 Program that computes the largest factor of an integer N, demonstrating a FOR/NEXT loop with a negative step.

In this set of model statements, v is the control variable and e_1, e_2, and e_3 are dummy variables. Two additional points warrant brief mention. A transfer of control out of a loop is permitted, but a transfer into the body of a loop is not. Also, a loop is reinitialized each time program execution passes through the FOR statement.

6.4 USER INPUT AND OUTPUT

Input and output data is conveniently classified by whether it is "user readable" or "machine readable." Keyboard and printer operations are user readable. File operations to the tape units are machine readable. This section covers the former category and presents the PRINT, READ, DATA, and RESTORE statements. File input and output are covered in the next chapter.

The PRINT Statement

The PRINT statement is used to display readable information on the display screen and the printer unit. Alternately, the same information can be written to a tape file. The syntactical form of the PRINT statement is:

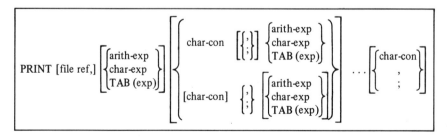

where the *file ref* can be FLP for the printer or the designations FL0 through FL9 for tape files 0 through 9. The specifications *arith-exp*, *char-exp*, and *char-con* stand for arithmetic expression, character expression, and character constant respectively, as introduced earlier. The *TAB(exp)* construct denotes a

TAB function as covered below. It is used for indentation and positioning. The PRINT statement requires a certain amount of detailed explanation.

Display vs. Printer Output. A PRINT statement without the file reference causes printed output to be displayed on the display screen. If the FLP file reference is specified in a PRINT statement, then printed output is sent to the printer unit. If the FLP option is specified and the printer unit is not connected or turned on, then the program will not execute. The problem can be circumvented by using the RUN command with the P=D option (printer=display) as follows:

RUN P=D

In the latter case, the BASIC program will execute and all printed output will be displayed on the display screen. The P=D option is also a good means of verifying that a program is correct before generating printer output.

Full vs. Packed Print Zones. The manner in which printed information is laid out across a page is known as a print zone. Two types are available in BASIC: a full print zone and a packed print zone. A *full print zone* occupies 18 characters and is used to arrange output data in columns. The page is divided into columns that are 18 characters wide. When a comma is used between output expressions, as in the following PRINT statement:

PRINT A,A↑2, SQR(A)

a "position pointer" is simply advanced to the next column after an item is printed or displayed. The size of a *packed print zone* is determined by the data to be printed or displayed. With character output, the width of the packed print zone is simply the length of the character string. With numeric data, the width of the packed print zone is given by Table 6.1. In general, the first position is always reserved for the algebraic sign and the last position always contains a

TABLE 6.1   WIDTH OF THE PACKED PRINT ZONE FOR NUMERIC OUTPUT

*Length of Numeric Data Value**	*Width of Packed Print Zone*	*Example (b=blank)*
2–4	6	b1.23b
5–7	9	-12.345bb
8–10	12	b753.62148bb
11–13	15	-2.12345E-15bbb
14–16	18	b1.2345678912345bb
17–19	21	-2.3456789123456E-10b

*The number of digits printed or displayed is controlled by the RD= parameter to the RUN command.

blank character that serves as a separator. A packed print zone is specified when a semicolon is used between output expressions, as in the following example:

$$PRINT\ A;A\uparrow 2;SQR(A)$$

The difference between full and packed print zones is demonstrated in Figure 6.14. When character output is generated, the computer does not place blank characters between character strings, as shown in the preceding figure.

Combining Character and Numeric Data. There is no restriction on combining character and numeric output on the same line, as demonstrated in Figure 6.15. Each expression in the body of a PRINT statement is handled separately, depending upon the data involved and the delimiter immediately following the output expression.

```
0010 REM FULL PRINT ZONES
0020 PRINT FLP,'A','A↑2','SQR(A)'
0030 PRINT FLP,
0040 FOR A=1 TO 10
0050 PRINT FLP,A,A↑2,SQR(A)
0060 NEXT A
0070 PRINT FLP,
0080 REM PACKED PRINT ZONES
0090 PRINT FLP,' A  ';'   A↑2  ';' SQR(A)'
0100 PRINT FLP,
0110 FOR A=1 TO 10
0120 PRINT FLP,A;A↑2;SQR(A)
0130 NEXT A
```

A	A↑2	SQR(A)
1	1	1
2	4	1.414214
3	9	1.732051
4	16	2
5	25	2.236068
6	36	2.449490
7	49	2.645751
8	64	2.828427
9	81	3
10	100	3.162278

A	A↑2	SQR(A)
1	1	1
2	4	1.414214
3	9	1.732051
4	16	2
5	25	2.236068
6	36	2.449490
7	49	2.645751
8	64	2.828427
9	81	3
10	100	3.162278

Figure 6.14 Difference between full and packed print zones.

```
0010 N=1296
0020 R=SQR(N)
0030 PRINT 'THE SQUARE ROOT OF',N,'IS',R
0040 PRINT 'THE SQUARE ROOT OF';N;'IS';R
RUN
THE SQUARE ROOT OF 1296              IS              36
THE SQUARE ROOT OF 1296      IS 36

READY                                                        28252
```

Figure 6.15   Numeric and character output can be combined on the same line.

Decision Rules for Numeric Output Formats

The computer chooses the format for numeric output with the PRINT statement based on three rules:

1. An *integer format,* consisting of a sign (blank or minus) and up to 13 significant digits is selected if the numeric value is an integer with an absolute value of less than 1E+14.
2. An *exponent format,* consisting of a sign (blank or minus) and up to 13 significant digits, with a decimal point following the first digit, and the letter E, followed by a two-digit signed exponent, is selected if the absolute value is less than 1E-1 or greater than or equal to 1E+14.
3. A *fixed format,* consisting of a sign (blank or minus) and up to 13 significant digits, with a decimal point in the appropriate place, is selected for numeric values that do not satisfy the requirements of the integer or exponent formats.

Numeric output formats are selected automatically, based on the numeric value and the RD=parameter. The only means of overriding these conventions is to use the PRINT USING statement, covered in the following chapter.

Line Spacing. When the execution of a PRINT statement is completed, the carriage (or cursor, as the case may be) is moved up to the next line. The user can prevent the carriage (or cursor) from moving up by ending the PRINT statement with a comma or semicolon. This case is demonstrated in Figure 6.16.

Blank Line vs. Blank Column. A PRINT statement without a statement body causes the carriage or cursor to move up one line. This can serve either of two purposes. If the preceding PRINT statement executed did not end with a delimiter, then a blank line is printed. However, if the preceding PRINT statement executed did end with a delimiter, then the carriage or cursor is simply moved to the next line. Two delimiters placed in succession in a PRINT statement cause a null field to be generated. With a full print zone, an entire column of 18 characters is skipped over. With a packed print zone, three blank characters are inserted in the output line after a numeric value and no characters are inserted after a character-string value. Figures 6.17 and 6.18 depict the null field for numeric and character data, respectively.

```
0010 FOR I=1 TO 5              0010 FOR I=1 TO 5
0020 PRINT I                   0020 PRINT I;
0030 NEXT I                    0030 NEXT I
RUN                            RUN
 1                              1     2     3     4     5
 2
 3
 4
 5


0010 A$='MISSISSIPPI'           0010 A$='MISSISSIPPI'
0020 FOR I=1 TO 11              0020 FOR I=1 TO 11
0030 PRINT STR(A$,I,1)          0030 PRINT STR(A$,I,1);
0040 NEXT I                     0040 NEXT I
RUN                             RUN
M                               MISSISSIPPI
I
S
S
I
S
S
I
P
P
I
```

Figure 6.16 The user can prevent the carriage (or cursor) from moving up by ending a PRINT statement with a comma or semicolon.

Trailing Blanks. When a character-string constant is placed in a PRINT statement, the entire character string including preceding, imbedded, or trailing blanks is printed—without the enclosing quotation marks. When a character expression* is printed or displayed, trailing blanks are excluded. The case with trailing blanks is demonstrated in Figure 6.19.

```
0010 A=5
0020 B=10
0030 PRINT A+B,A*B
0040 PRINT A+B,,A*B
0050 PRINT A+B,;A*B
0060 PRINT A+B;,A*B
0070 PRINT A+B;;A*B
RUN
 15                 50
 15                                   50
 15                      50
 15                         50
 15           50
```

READY   28244

Figure 6.17 The "null field" for numeric data.

*Recall that a character-string expression is a character-string variable or a substring reference.

```
0010 C$='TEA FOR TWO'
0020 PRINT C$,STR(C$,5,3)
0030 PRINT C$,,STR(C$,5,3)
0040 PRINT C$,;STR(C$,5,3)
0050 PRINT C$;,STR(C$,5,3)
0060 PRINT C$;;STR(C$,5,3)
RUN
TEA FOR TWO          FOR
TEA FOR TWO                              FOR
TEA FOR TWO          FOR
TEA FOR TWO                    FOR
TEA FOR TWOFOR
```

READY   28145

Figure 6.18 The "null field" for character data.

TAB Function. The TAB function permits the next print position in an output line to be specified, so that columns of data can be aligned. The TAB function also allows precision printing, usually found on monthly billing statements and computer-generated bank checks. The function, TAB(n), specifies that the next output field starts in column n of the output line. If position n is greater than the line length L, then the output field is placed at character position x of the next line; when $x=n-L*INT((n-1)/L)$. The format of the TAB function is:

$$TAB(exp)$$

where *exp* is an arithmetic expression evaluated at the point of reference. The following statement:

$$PRINT\ TAB(30),A,B$$

would indent 29 spaces before printing the value of A.

Omitted Delimiter. Careful attention to the syntax of the PRINT statement indicates that the separating comma or semicolon can be omitted in some cases. This variation is allowed when the construct to be printed includes natural de-

```
0010 N$='JOHN SMITH'
0020 A$='HIS NAME IS
0030 PRINT 'HIS NAME IS     ';N$
0040 PRINT A$;N$
RUN
HIS NAME IS     JOHN SMITH
HIS NAME ISJOHN SMITH
```

READY   28247

Figure 6.19 Trailing blanks are excluded when character-string expressions are printed or displayed. However, trailing blanks are *not* excluded when character-string constants are printed or displayed.

```
0010 PRINT 'ENTER N';
0020 INPUT N
0030 F=1
0040 FOR K=2 TO N
0050 F=F*K
0060 NEXT K
0070 PRINT N;'FACTORIAL=';F
0080 PRINT N'FACTORIAL='F
RUN
ENTER N
5
   5    FACTORIAL= 120
   5    FACTORIAL= 120


READY                                            28191
```

Figure 6.20 The delimiter can be omitted between expressions in a PRINT statement if the constructs contain natural delimiters.

limiters, as in the case of character-string constants and the TAB function. Figure 6.20 shows the uses of omitted delimiters as a variation to the factorial program in Figure 6.11.

File Option. The file option in the PRINT statement alternately permits an output line to be written to a tape file. This operation requires a knowledge of file operations covered in the next chapter.

Internal Data Sets—The DATA, READ, and RESTORE Statements

The BASIC language allows an internal data set to be created that is logically a part of a BASIC program. The internal data set is created with the DATA statement and is accessed with the READ statement. The RESTORE statement is used to reposition the internal data set for reprocessing of the data.

DATA Statement. The DATA statement is a nonexecutable statement that builds a data set that is internal to the program. The statement takes the following form:

$$\text{DATA} \begin{Bmatrix} \text{arith-con} \\ \text{char-con} \end{Bmatrix} \left[, \begin{Bmatrix} \text{arith-con} \\ \text{char-con} \end{Bmatrix} \right] \cdots$$

where *arith-con* is a numeric constant and *char-con* is a series of characters enclosed in quotes. DATA statements can be placed anywhere in a BASIC program. Prior to execution of a program, after the RUN command is entered, all data values specified in DATA statements are collected to form the internal data set. The order of data values is determined by the relative physical order of the DATA statements in the program. After the internal data set is created, a pointer is set to the first constant in the data set. As data values from the internal data set are supplied to READ statements, the pointer is advanced through the data set.

READ Statement. The READ statement is used to assign values to scalar variables and to elements of an array. The statement takes the following form:

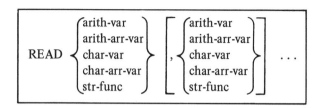

where, as defined previously, the following definitions exist for the notation variables:

arith-var is a scalar numeric variable.

arith-arr-var is an element of a numeric array, specified as a subscripted numeric array variable.

char-var is a scalar character-string variable.

char-arr-var is an element of a character-string array, specified as a subscripted character-string array variable.

str-func is a substring function used to replace a substring of a scalar or subscripted array variable.

During the execution of a READ statement, data values are assigned to variables in the READ statement from left to right from the list of values in the internal data set. Subscripts are evaluated as they are encountered from left-to-right so that a value can be assigned to a subscript variable in a READ statement and that subscript variable can be used in a subscript computation in the same statement, as follows:

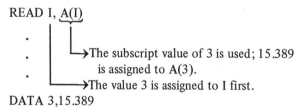

As values are used from the internal data set, the pointer is advanced through the list of values. A data value in the internal data set must be of the same type as the variable to which it is assigned. For example:

READ A,B,C$ READ A,B$,C

$\bullet$ $\bullet$

$\bullet$ $\bullet$

$\bullet$ $\bullet$

DATA 17.1,0, 'RECEIVABLE'   DATA 51,-13.2,'FINI'

Valid Combination   *Invalid Combination*

Several examples of the READ and DATA statements are given in Figure 6.21. If insufficient values exist in the internal data set to satisfy a READ statement, an error condition will occur.

RESTORE Statement. The RESTORE statement resets the pointer to the first value in the internal data set created from DATA statements. The form of the RESTORE statement is:

> RESTORE [comment]

where *comment* is any string of characters from the BASIC alphabet. An example of the use of the RESTORE statement is given in Figure 6.22. The comment serves informational purposes and has no affect on the execution of the RESTORE statement. If the pointer is currently pointing to the first value in the internal data set when the RESTORE statement is encountered during normal processing, its execution is suppressed. A RESTORE statement in a program with no DATA statements is ignored.

Keyboard Input—The INPUT Statement

In many applications, data must be entered into a program on a dynamic basis. In these cases, use of the READ and DATA statements is inappropriate because

```
0010 I=3
0020 C$='JOHN BAKER JONES'
0030 READ I,A(I),B$,STR(C$,6,5)
0040 PRINT I,A(3),A(5)
0050 PRINT B$
0060 PRINT C$
0070 DATA 5
0080 DATA -17.991,'IBM 5100'
0090 DATA 'SMITH'
RUN
 5                  0              -17.991
IBM 5100
JOHN SMITH JONES

READY                                        28033
```

Figure 6.21 READ and DATA statements. Data values are assigned to variables in the READ statement from left to right.

```
0010 READ N
0020 FOR I=1 TO N
0030 READ A
0040 S=S+A
0050 NEXT I
0060 PRINT 'SUM=';S
0070 RESTORE
0080 READ N
0090 P=1
0100 FOR I=1 TO N
0110 READ A
0120 P=P*A
0130 NEXT I
0140 PRINT 'PRODUCT=';P
0150 DATA 5,-9,-1.5,2,13,163.5
RUN
SUM= 168
PRODUCT= 57388.5
```

Figure 6.22 The RESTORE repositions the pointer to the first value in an internal data set.

they require that the input be preplanned. The INPUT statement functions exactly the same as the READ statement except for the fact that the user is prompted for input at the keyboard. The INPUT statement is placed in a program at a point where input is needed. Execution of the INPUT statement causes a question mark to be displayed in line position 1 of the display screen, and the user must enter the required data on the same line. If insufficient data is entered, the user is prompted for the remainder of the required input. If too much data is entered, the excess is ignored.

```
0010 DIM N$(100),Q(100),P(100)
0020 READ N
0030 FOR I=1 TO N
0040 READ N$(I),Q(I),P(I)
0050 NEXT I
0060 PRINT 'RETRIEVAL PROGRAM'
0070 PRINT 'ENTER PART NAME.  ''DONE'' WHEN FINISHED.';
0080 INPUT A$
0090 IF A$='DONE' GOTO 0170
0100 FOR I=1 TO N
0110 IF A$=N$(I) GOTO 0150
0120 NEXT I
0130 PRINT 'NOT FOUND';
0140 GOTO 0080
0150 PRINT 'PART=';N$(I);' QUANTITY=';Q(I);'PRICE=';P(I);
0160 GOTO 0080
0170 PRINT 'FINI'
0180 DATA 4
0190 DATA 'WRENCH',50,12.98
0200 DATA 'SCREW DRIVER',125,4.39
0210 DATA 'BP HAMMER',103,7.95
0220 DATA 'LADDER - 6 FT',14,21.98
```

Figure 6.23 Simple query program containing an INPUT statement.

```
RUN
RETRIEVAL PROGRAM
ENTER PART NAME.   'DONE' WHEN FINISHED.
'BP HAMMER'
PART=BP HAMMER QUANTITY= 103   PRICE= 7.95
'WRENCH'
PART=WRENCH QUANTITY= 50    PRICE= 12.98
'LADDER'
NOT FOUND
'LADDER - 6 FT'
PART=LADDER - 6 FT QUANTITY= 14    PRICE= 21.98
'DONE'
FINI
```

READY   24317

Figure 6.24   Sample script for the query program in Figure 6.22.

The form of the INPUT statement is:

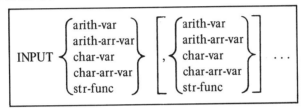

where the notation variables have exactly the same meaning as given for the READ statement. The same operational rules exist for the INPUT statement as for the READ statement: (1) input variables are processed from left to right; (2) subscripts are evaluated when they are encountered during left-to-right processing; and (3) the variable type must match the data type. Figure 6.23 contains an example of an INPUT statement in a simple retrieval program, and Figure 6.24 gives a sample script of a series of query operations.

6.5 FUNCTIONS AND INTERNAL CONSTANTS

Mathematical functions and internal constants were presented earlier with regard to the BASIC calculator mode. The internal constants are listed in their entirety in Table 4.3. The mathematical functions were only partially presented and a complete listing of them is given here.

Mathematical Functions

The mathematical functions are defined on numeric expressions and can only be used in a numeric expression. Table 6.2 gives a complete list of the mathematical functions available in the 5100 BASIC language. Three functions in the list require special attention: the substring (STR) function, the random number (RND) function, and the determinant (DET) function. The substring function was

TABLE 6.2 MATHEMATICAL FUNCTIONS IN THE 5100 BASIC LANGUAGE

Function-Reference	Description
ABS(x)	Absolute value of x
ACS(x)	Arc cosine (in radians) of x
ASN(x)	Arc sine (in radians) of x
ATN(x)	Arc tangent (in radians) of x
COS(x)	Cosine of x (in radians)
COT(x)	Cotangent of x (in radians)
CSC(x)	Cosecant of x (in radians)
DEG(x)	Degrees in x radians
DET(x)	Determinant of a numeric array x
EXP(x)	Natural exponent of x
HCS(x)	Hyperbolic cosine of x
HSN(x)	Hyperbolic sine of x
HTN(x)	Hyperbolic tangent of x
INT(x)	Integral part of x
LGT(x)	Logarithm of x to base 10
LOG(x)	Logarithm of x to base e
LTW(x)	Logarithm of x to base 2
RAD(x)	Radians in x degrees
RND[(x)]	Random number between 0 and 1
SEC(x)	Secant of x (in radians)
SGN(x)	Sign of x (-1 if $x<0$, 0 if $x=0$, 1 if $x>0$)
SIN(x)	Sine of x (in radians)
SQR(x)	Square root of x
STR($n\$,i.j$)	Substring of length j from string $n\$$ starting at character position i
TAN(x)	Tangent of x (in radians)

covered earlier. The random number function is covered below. The determinant function will be covered under matrices, in the next chapter. The following list gives BASIC equivalents to some common mathematical expressions involving functions:

Mathematical Expression	BASIC Expression
$\sqrt{1-\sin^2 x}$	SQR(1-SIN(X)↑2)
$\cos 30°$	COS(RAD(30))
$\sqrt{a^2+b^2-2ab\cos c}$	SQR(A↑2+B↑2-2*A*B*COS(C))
$\dfrac{e^x-e^{-x}}{2}$	(EXP(X)-EXP(-X))/2
$(\lvert x \rvert)^5$	ABS(X)↑5

```
0010 N=RND(1234)
0020 FOR I=1 TO 100
0030 N=RND
0040 PRINT FLP,INT(100*N);
0050 K=INT(10*N)+1
0060 C(K)=C(K)+1
0070 NEXT I
0080 PRINT FLP,
0090 PRINT FLP,
0100 PRINT FLP,        CLASS','NUMBER'
0110 PRINT FLP,
0120 FOR I=1 TO 10
0130 PRINT FLP,10*(I-1);'TO ';10*I-1;'    ';C(I)
0140 NEXT I
```

```
45  33  17  80  47  54  31  74  98  51  71  95  57  74  18  17  65   2  17   7  70  81
83  83   0  34  53  10  14  12  79  10  71  54  34   5  69  88  88  10  73  66  65   5
74  32  95  62  43  69  31  13  89  51  84  13  32  88  85  68  81  53  18  78  65  85
46  16  58  11  14  21  96  71  52  15  60  20  36  94  19  58  70  36  41  62  86   2
26  47  77  25  31  16  52  86  48   8  48  72
```

```
CLASS       NUMBER

 0 TO   9      7
10 TO  19     18
20 TO  29      4
30 TO  39     10
40 TO  49      8
50 TO  59     11
60 TO  69     10
70 TO  79     13
80 TO  89     14
90 TO  99      5
```

Figure 6.25 Generation of 100 random numbers and their distribution.

In the evaluation of an arithmetic-expression that includes mathematical functions, functions are executed first, followed by the operations in the expression in accordance with the established hierarchy among operators.

Random Numbers

The random number function generates a pseudo-random number in the interval 0 to 1. The function is unique because it can be invoked with or without an argument. If the argument is included, it is used to initialize the random number generator so that computed results can be *rerun* exactly. If the function is referenced without an argument, the random number is computed from the previous number generated. Figure 6.25 gives a sample program that includes a random number function. If the RND function is initially referenced without

(Power up)

```
LOAD 0
RND
  9.208743E-2

RND
 .318803

LOAD 0
RND
 .928633

RND(1)
 .108837

RND
 .369051

RND(1)
 .108837

RND
 .369051
```

(Power down)
(Power up)

```
LOAD 0
RND
  9.208743E-2

RND
 .318803


READY                                              28385
```

Figure 6.26 The LOAD 0 command does not cause the random number generator to be reinitialized, but the power up sequence does.

an argument, it is programmed to initialize itself, so the first random number generated after the power up sequence will always be the same. However, a LOAD 0 command does not cause the random number generator to be re-initialized as shown in Figure 6.26.

Single-Line User-Defined Function

The DEF statement allows a user to define a mathematical function that is not provided in the 5100 BASIC language. The DEF statement for a single-line user-defined function is:

> DEF FNfunction-name [(arith-var [,arith-var]. . .)] =arith-exp

where:

function-name is a single alphabetic character identifying the function.

arith-var is a scalar numeric variable name used as a dummy variable.

arith-exp is a numeric expression involving the dummy variables and possibly other program variables.

As an example, consider the computation of the largest roots of a quadratic equation using the following formula:

$$\text{root}(a,b,c) = \frac{-b+\sqrt{b^2-4ac}}{2a}$$

The following DEF statement is a single-line user-defined function that computes the root:

DEF FNR(A,B,C)=(-B+SQR(B↑2-4*A*C))/(2*A)

→dummy variables

→name of function

A defined function is referenced in the same way that a built-in function is referenced. As an example, assume that it were desired to compute the largest root of the following quadratic equation:

$$f(x)=x^2+5x-14$$

so that $a=1$, $b=5$, and $c=-14$. Figure 6.27 gives the printout for this example. The function is referenced as FNR(A,B,C) after variables A, B, and C are assigned values. Another example of a defined function is contained in the interval bi-section program given earlier in the chapter.

```
0010 DEF FNR(A,B,C)=(-B+SQR(B↑2-4*A*C))/(2*A)
0020 READ A,B,C
0030 PRINT 'A','B','C','ROOT'
0040 PRINT A,B,C,FNR(A,B,C)
0050 DATA 1,5,-14
RUN
A                    B                   C                   ROOT
1                    5                  -14                  2


READY                                                       28152
```

Figure 6.27 Single-line user defined function to compute the root of the quadratic equation $x^2 + 5x - 14$.

The following operational conventions apply to single-line user-defined functions:

1. The DEF statement is non-executable so that the single-line function definition can appear anywhere in a program.
2. A function-name consists of 3 letters so the prefix FN must always be used. Thus, 29 different functions can be defined.
3. Use of a variable name as a dummy variable does not conflict with other use of that variable name in a program.
4. Dummy variables serve as parameters that are assigned values when the function is referenced.
5. A defined function always returns a value to the point of reference so that it may be used in an arithmetic expression.
6. Other variables appearing in the arithmetic expression of a function definition are "global variables" and assume whatever values they have at the point of reference in the program.
7. A defined function cannot refer to itself or to any other function that refers to itself, directly or indirectly. This is known as a *recursive function definition*, which is not permitted in 5100 BASIC. However, a function-definition may refer to other user-defined or built-in functions, within the above restrictions.

One of the options available with a user-defined function is that it need not use parameters, as in the following function definitions for generating random numbers between 0 and 10, 0 and 100, and 0 and 1000, respectively:

$$DEF \ FNA = INT(10*RND)$$
$$DEF \ FNB = INT(100*RND)$$
$$DEF \ FNC = INT(1000*RND)$$

Multiple-line user-defined functions are also permitted in 5100 BASIC. This topic is more advanced and is covered in the next chapter.

SELECTED READING

Nolan, R. L., *Introduction to Computing through the BASIC Language*, Holt, Rinehart, and Winston, Inc., New York, 1974.

Sass, C. J., *BASIC Programming and Applications*, Allyn and Bacon, Inc., Boston, 1976.

REFERENCES

Katzan, H., *Introduction to Programming Languages*, Auerbach Publishers Inc., Philadelphia, 1973.

IBM 5100 Portable Computer publications:
  a. *IBM 5100 BASIC Introduction*, Form #SA 21-9216
  b. *IBM 5100 BASIC Reference Manual*, Form #SA 21-9217

IBM Corporation, Rochester, Minnesota, 1975.

7 | ADVANCED TOPICS IN BASIC PROGRAMMING

This chapter covers five important topics: *files, formatted printing, subprograms, matrices,* and *chaining.* Knowledge of file concepts is necessary for storing data on tape and for accessing stored information. The objective of formatted printing is to allow data editing and precision printing to be done in a convenient manner. The objective of a subprogram is to modularize a program to avoid duplicate statements and minimize main storage requirements. Matrix operations facilitate programming by subordinating the detail normally associated with the programming of matrix operations to the computer. Lastly, the chaining facility permits one BASIC program to pass control to another BASIC program, which is independent of the calling program. Comprehension of the material presented in this chapter requires a familiarity with the introductory material on the BASIC language presented in preceding chapters.

7.1 FILES

There are two ways of saving data on tape. The first method is straightforward. Simply save the entire user area—both program and data—with the SAVE command, covered earlier. The second method is to create a tape file that only contains data. The first method is satisfactory if used infrequently with small amounts of data. Otherwise, multiple copies of the same program will exist, which is undesirable when program changes are required. In addition, the size of a data file is limited by the size of main storage. Therefore, when large amounts of data are involved, the use of tape files is necessary.

File Processing

A tape cartridge has the capacity for holding many tape files. Each file has an overhead of .5K bytes so that 200K byte capacity of the tape cartridge can hold 132 1K byte files, 80 2K byte files, 44 4K byte files, etc., or any combination thereof. Before a file can be accessed, it is necessary to inform the computer which file to process. This is known as activating a file; it is performed with the OPEN statement, covered below. When a file process is complete, the file is deactivated with the CLOSE statement to insure that all records have been completely processed. File input is performed with the GET statement and file output is performed with the PUT statement, so that typical sequences of file processing statements might exist as follows:

Writing a File	*Reading a File*
OPEN file for output	OPEN file for input
———	———
———	———
———	———
PUT data to file	GET data from file
.	.
.	.
.	.
———	———
———	———
PUT data to file	GET data from file
.	.
.	.
.	.
———	———
———	———
CLOSE file	CLOSE file

The GET statement is analogous to the READ statement—they both perform input functions. The PUT statement is analogous to the PRINT statement—they both perform output functions.

When a tape file is activated for a GET statement, it is said to be "opened for input." Similarly, when a tape file is activated for a PUT statement, it is said to be "opened for output." A file cannot be opened for input and output at the same time. If, for example, a file is opened for input and it is necessary to write to the file, then the file must first be closed and then opened for output. The same operational convention exists for input when a file is opened for output.

Activation

A file is activated with the OPEN statement and the following example shows what it looks like:

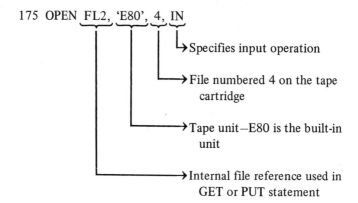

175 OPEN FL2, 'E80', 4, IN

→ Specifies input operation

→ File numbered 4 on the tape cartridge

→ Tape unit—E80 is the built-in unit

→ Internal file reference used in GET or PUT statement

A sample OPEN statement for an output operation might be:

380 OPEN FL8, 'E80', 103, OUT

In this case, the internal file reference is FL8, the tape unit is E80, (the built-in unit), file number 103 is to be written, and the file is opened for an output operation.

The general format of the OPEN statement is:

$$\text{OPEN file-ref, 'dev-address'[,file-num]} \left[, \begin{Bmatrix} \text{'user ID'} \\ \text{char-var} \end{Bmatrix} \right] \begin{Bmatrix} \text{IN} \\ \text{'OUT} \end{Bmatrix}$$

where:

file-ref specifies the internal reference to the file that must be used in a corresponding input or output statement. The file reference can be FL0 (FL'zero') through FL9.

dev-address is a hexadecimal device address enclosed in quote marks. The following device assignments exist:

E80 for the built-in tape unit.
E40 for the auxiliary tape unit.
500 for the printer.

file-num is an integer constant or numeric variable specifying the file number on the tape cartridge.

user-ID is a file identification stored with the file. The identifier can be up to 17 characters. For input, this parameter serves no purpose. For output, this parameter causes the identification to be written on the file header record.

char-var is a character-string variable that serves the same function for output as the *user-ID* above. For input, the file identification is read from the tape file and placed in the specified character-string variable for use by the program.

IN or *OUT* specifies whether the file is to be opened for input or output.

A file is always positioned at its beginning when it is opened.

Some obvious restrictions apply to opened files. First, the tape cartridge should not be removed for an opened file before the file has been closed. Second, once a file is opened, it cannot be opened again unless an intervening close is executed. Lastly, the tape cartridge should be inserted in the tape unit before the OPEN statement is executed.

Deactivation

A file is deactivated with the CLOSE statement and the following example shows what it looks like:

3110 CLOSE FL2

→ File reference used in corresponding
OPEN statement

In this case, the file reference is FL2, which should have been opened earlier in the program. The general format of the CLOSE statement is:

```
CLOSE file-ref[,file-ref] . . .
```

where *file-ref* is an internal reference to the file that can be FL0 (FL'zero') through FL9. If the specified file reference is not active when the CLOSE statement is executed, the close operation is ignored.

If a file is not closed, it may be unusable for later file processing. Therefore, when a program comes to a normal termination, all open files are closed automatically. A normal termination occurs when a STOP or END statement is executed. Recall here that if a program does not contain an END statement, it is supplied automatically by the computer and placed physically after the last statement in the program. An instance of an abnormal termination occurs when the execution of a program is interrupted by pressing the ATTN key or because of an error condition. In this case, a system command, namely, GO END, can be entered to close all files.

Output

A tape file is created with the OPEN/PUT/CLOSE statements together with any intermediate processing that is required. The following example shows what a PUT statement looks like:

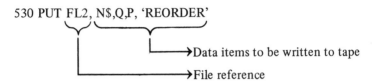

530 PUT FL2, N$,Q,P, 'REORDER'

→Data items to be written to tape

→File reference

Data are written to tape in blocks of 512 bytes. As PUT statements are executed, specified data items are placed in a 512 byte buffer. When the buffer is full, its contents are written to tape as one record.

The format of the PUT statement is:

$$\text{PUT file-ref,}\begin{Bmatrix}\text{arith-exp}\\\text{char-exp}\end{Bmatrix}\begin{bmatrix},\begin{Bmatrix}\text{arith-exp}\\\text{char-exp}\end{Bmatrix}\end{bmatrix}\cdots$$

```
0010 PRINT 'INVENTORY PROGRAM'
0020 PRINT 'ENTER FILE NUMBER AND NAME IN QUOTES'
0030 INPUT F,F$
0040 OPEN FL5,'E80',F ,F$,OUT
0050 PRINT 'ENTER INVENTORY DATA IN THE FOLLOWING ORDER:'
0060 PRINT 'NAME,QUANTITY,PRICE,REORDER LEVEL,OVERSTOCK LEVEL'
0070 PRINT 'ENTER NAME IN QUOTES - OTHER DATA W/O QUOTES'
0080 PRINT 'ENTER '' '',0,0,0,0 WHEN FINISHED'
0090 INPUT N$,Q,P,L1,L2
0100 IF N$=' ' GOTO 0130
0110 PUT FL5,N$,Q,P,L1,L2
0120 GOTO 0090
0130 CLOSE FL5
0140 PRINT 'END OF PROCESSING'
```

(A) Program

```
'BOLT  2 INCH',512,.13,75,1000
'COPPER TUBE',11,17.52,25,100
'HOIST CLAMP',23,15.81,5,60
'NAIL  3 PENNY',213,11.07,50,200
'PST JOINT',7,62.58,15,65
'T RACK',15,5.45,10,100
' ',0,0,0,0


READY                                          27315
```

(B) Input Data

Figure 7.1 Sample program that uses OPEN/PUT/CLOSE statements to create an inventory file.

```
0001 DATA 'BOLT  2 INCH', 512, .13, 75, 1000
0002 DATA 'COPPER TUBE', 11, 17.52, 25, 100
0003 DATA 'HOIST CLAMP', 23, 15.81, 5, 60
0004 DATA 'NAIL  3 PENNY', 213, 11.07, 50, 200
0005 DATA 'PST JOINT', 7, 62.58, 15, 65
0006 DATA 'T RACK', 15, 5.45, 10, 100
```

(A) Loaded with the LOAD 15, DATA command and listed with the LIST command

```
'BOLT  2 INCH', 512, .13, 75, 1000'COPPER TUBE', 11, 17.52, 25, 100'HOIST CLAMP', 23, 15.81, 5, 60'NAIL  3 PENNY', 213, 11.07, 50
, 200'PST JOINT', 7, 62.58, 15, 65'T RACK', 15, 5.45, 10, 100
```

(B) As stored on the tape cartridge

Figure 7.2 Structure of the file created in Figure 7.1.

where *file-ref* is the internal reference to a file previously opened for output and *arith-exp* and *char-exp* are numeric or character string expressions. The statement must specify at least one output value. Data items are placed in the output buffer in the order given, so that the initial value written by the PUT statement executed first is the initial value read by the first GET statement.

A sample program that creates an inventory file is given in Figure 7.1 Data values are written to the file as a long list of items separated by commas; character strings are enclosed in quote marks. Figure 7.2 shows what the file created in Figure 7.1 looks like.

Input

A tape file is read with the OPEN/GET/CLOSE statements together with any intermediate processing that is required. The following example shows what a GET statement looks like:

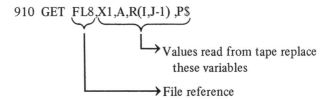

Data values from tape are read sequentially in the order written. The list of variable references in the GET statement is processed from left to right, so that a subscript value can be assigned and used in the same statement. The READ, INPUT, and GET statements are the same in this regard. Another consideration is that the data value *must* match the variable type. Otherwise, the resulting error condition will cause execution to be terminated.

The format of the GET statement is:

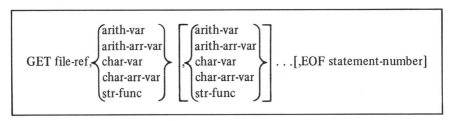

where *file-ref* is the internal reference to a file previously opened for input and the input list is the same set of constructs that was defined previously. The "EOF statement-number" option applies when a GET statement is executed and all the values in the file are exhausted. In this case, program control is transferred to the specified statement number. The EOF option is useful because it usually is not known how many values are in a file.

```
0010 OPEN FL2,'E80',015,IN
0020 PRINT FLP,'NAME','QUANTITY','PRICE','REORDER LEVEL',
0030 PRINT FLP,'OVERSTOCK LEVEL'
0040 PRINT FLP,
0050 GET FL2,N$,Q,P,L1,L2,EOF 0080
0060 PRINT FLP,N$,Q,P,L1,L2
0070 GOTO 0050
0080 CLOSE FL2
0090 PRINT FLP,
0100 PRINT FLP,'END OF INVENTORY'
```

NAME	QUANTITY	PRICE	REORDER LEVEL	OVERSTOCK LEVEL
BOLT 2 INCH	512	.13	75	1000
COPPER TUBE	11	17.52	25	100
HOIST CLAMP	23	15.81	5	60
NAIL 3 PENNY	213	11.07	50	200
PST JOINT	7	62.58	15	65
T RACK	15	5.45	10	100

END OF INVENTORY

Figure 7.3

As GET statements are executed, values from the referenced file are assigned to the specified variables in sequence. As values are read, the "current" file position moves through the file in the same manner that values from an internal data set are "used up" through the execution of successive READ statements.

A sample program that reads the inventory file created with GET statements in Figure 7.1 is given in Figure 7.3.

Repositioning

The RESET statement permits a tape file to be repositioned—either at its beginning or at its end. The format of the RESET statement is:

RESET file-ref [END] [,file-ref[END]   ...]

where *file-ref* is the internal file reference, which must be FL0 (FL0"zero") through FL9, to a previously opened file. Two general options to the statement are available: with or without the END option.

Without the END option, the RESET statement repositions the file so that the next GET or PUT statement to the file will refer to the first item in the file. However, this option does not change the mode of the file from input to output or from output to input.

With the END option, the RESET statement causes the file to be closed and reopened for output. The file is repositioned at its end so that the writing of new data will begin at the end of existing data. Figure 7.4 uses the RESET statement in adding an inventory item to the end of the inventory file. As a special case, a series of system commands are entered in Figure 7.5 to "look at"

```
0010 PRINT 'INVENTORY FILE UPDATE'
0020 PRINT 'ENTER FILE NUMBER'
0030 INPUT F
0040 OPEN FL6,'E80',F ,G$,IN
0050 PRINT 'FILE = ';G$;' --- OK?'
0060 PRINT 'HIT EXEC TO CONTINUE - OTHERWISE ENTER GO END'
0070 PAUSE
0080 RESET FL6END
0090 PRINT 'ENTER INVENTORY IN THE FOLLOWING ORDER:'
0100 PRINT 'NAME,QUANTITY,PRICE,REORDER LEVEL,OVERSTOCK LEVEL'
0110 PRINT 'ENTER '' '',0,0,0,0 WHEN FINISHED'
0120 INPUT N$,Q,P,L1,L2
0130 IF N$=' ' GOTO 0160
0140 PUT FL6,N$,Q,P,L1,L2
0150 GOTO 0120
0160 CLOSE FL6
0170 PRINT 'END OF UPDATE'
```

(A) Program

```
'L. BRACE',150,1.98,100,200
'G. PIN',38,124.50,15,30
' ',0,0,0,0
```

READY   28385

(B) Input Data

Figure 7.4 Sample program that uses the RESET statement to add data to the end of a file.

the inventory file after the program in Figure 7.4 is executed. Full comprehension is not expected here because system commands have not been covered. For completeness, however, the commands are:

LOAD 15 ,DATA
LIST PRINT

```
LOAD 15,DATA

DATA        JUNE INVENTORY   ,002,001,                       28081
0001 DATA 'BOLT  2 INCH', 512, .13, 75, 1000
0002 DATA 'COPPER TUBE', 11, 17.52, 25, 100
0003 DATA 'HOIST CLAMP', 23, 15.81, 5, 60
0004 DATA 'NAIL  3 PENNY', 213, 11.07, 50, 200
0005 DATA 'PST JOINT', 7, 62.58, 15, 65
0006 DATA 'T RACK', 15, 5.45, 10, 100
0007 DATA 'L. BRACE', 150, 1.98, 100, 200
0008 DATA 'G. PIN', 38, 124.5, 15, 30
```

Figure 7.5 Loading and listing of the data file resulting from the execution of the programs in Figures 7.1 and 7.4.

The LOAD command loads a data file into the main storage unit and the LIST PRINT command lists it on the printer unit.

Print Files

Aside from operational details, the basic difference between the PUT and PRINT statements is that the PUT statement outputs data values separated by commas with character strings enclosed in quote marks and the PRINT statement outputs information without commas and quote marks. In general, the difference is not significant since each statement is designed for use in a particular manner: the PRINT statement for readable output and the PUT statement for file output. In communicating with other systems via the communications feature, it is sometimes desirable to have tape files with readable characteristics. Therefore, it is possible to generate a print file with the following sequence of statements:

OPEN file ref for output
.
.
.
PRINT file ref
.
.
.
CLOSE file ref

A file is created, as with the PUT statement, except that it is not formatted for subsequent input to the 5100 Portable Computer. However, it can be listed with the following sequence of commands:

LOAD file#,DATA
LIST or LIST PRINT

There is one problem with tape files. Each PRINT statement causes a record to be written, as in printing. In the case of files, it is 512 bytes long, which cannot be read—even with the LOAD file#,DATA command. The way of alleviating the problem is to end each line written to the print file with the "end of line character," as follows:

```
10  A$=X'E3'
20  OPEN FL3,'E80',2,OUT
30  FOR I=1 TO 10
40  PRINT FL3,I;I↑2;'TEST PROG';A$;
50  NEXT I
60  CLOSE FL3
```

```
0010 A$=X'E3'
0020 OPEN FL3,'E80',002,OUT
0030 FOR I=1 TO 10
0040 PRINT FL3,I;I†2;'TEST PROGRAM';A$;
0050 NEXT I
0060 CLOSE FL3
RUN

READY                                                      27663
```

Figure 7.6 Creation of a print file.

The hexadecimal E3 assigned to A\$ in statement 10 and appended to each record in statement 40 does the job. This program is listed and executed in Figure 7.6 and the print file is listed with system commands in Figure 7.7.

Types of Files

The following types of files are permitted on the 5100 Portable Computer:

Type	File Description
0	Marked but unused file
1	Data exchange file
2	General exchange file
3	BASIC source file
4	BASIC work area file
5	BASIC keys file
6	APL continued file
7	APL save file
8	APL internal data file
16	Patch/tape recovery/tape copy file
17	Diagnostic file
18	IMF file (Internal Machine Fix)
72	Tape storage dump

```
LOAD 2,DATA

DATA                           ,016,015,                  28075
0001 DATA   1      1      TEST PROGRAM
0002 DATA   2      4      TEST PROGRAM
0003 DATA   3      9      TEST PROGRAM
0004 DATA   4     16      TEST PROGRAM
0005 DATA   5     25      TEST PROGRAM
0006 DATA   6     36      TEST PROGRAM
0007 DATA   7     49      TEST PROGRAM
0008 DATA   8     64      TEST PROGRAM
0009 DATA   9     81      TEST PROGRAM
0010 DATA  10    100      TEST PROGRAM
```

Figure 7.7 Listing of the print file created in Figure 7.6 with system commands.

Each type of file is described in appropriate portions of the book. Thus far, however, file types 0, 1, and 4 have been covered. A file that has been initialized with the MARK command but not used is a type 0 file. A tape file created with the PUT statement is a type 1 file. A print file is a type 1 file also. These files can be read by BASIC or APL. When a work area is saved, a type 4 file is created. A work area file contains a BASIC program in internal form ready for execution. To save a BASIC program in the form it was entered, the following command would be used:

SAVE file#,SOURCE

This command creates a type 3 file. A considerable amount of file space on tape can be conserved by saving a BASIC program in source form.

General Interchange File

A type 2 general interchange file may contain either programs or data and can be read by BASIC or APL. This type of file is created with a negative file number— as in the following example:

```
10  F=-2
20  A$=X'E3'
30  OPEN FL9, 'E80',F,OUT
40  PRINT FL9,'0010 FOR I=1 TO 5';A$;
50  PRINT FL9,'0020 PRINT I;';A$;
60  PRINT FL9,'0030 NEXT I';A$;
70  CLOSE FL9
```

This program creates a general interchange file that can be loaded as a BASIC source file. The program contained therein is listed as follows:

```
0010  FOR I=1 TO 5
0020  PRINT I;
0030  NEXT I
```

```
0010 F=-2
0020 A$=X'E3'
0030 OPEN FL9,'E80',F ,OUT
0040 PRINT FL9,'0010 FOR I=1 TO 5',A$;
0050 PRINT FL9,'0020 PRINT I;',A$;
0060 PRINT FL9,'0030 NEXT I',A$;
0070 CLOSE FL9
RUN
```

READY   27653

Figure 7.8 Sample program that creates a type 2 general interchange file.

```
LOAD 2,SOURCE
0010 FOR I=1 TO 5
0020 PRINT I;
0030 NEXT I
RUN
 1    2    3    4    5
READY                                    28304
```

Figure 7.9   This script loads the general interchange file created in Figure 7.8, and then lists and executes it.

The sample program that creates the type 2 general interchange file is listed and executed in Figure 7.8. The file is loaded as a BASIC source file, listed, and executed in Figure 7.9.

7.2 FORMATTED PRINTING

Even though the PRINT statement, together with packed and zoned output and the RD=parameter, is a convenient and flexible facility for generating readable output, there are many instances when a user would gladly sacrifice convenience for direct control over the printing process. This capability is available through the use of the PRINT USING statement and an associated "image" of the line to be printed.

Basic Concepts

The line *image* is a line, which has a statement number for identification, that contains the exact characters that comprise the line to be displayed or printed. Numeric fields to be replaced during the output process are denoted by special characters, as in the following example:

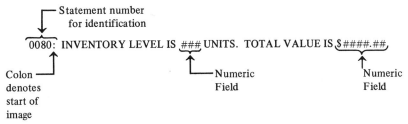

The image line could be used in a PRINT USING statement, such as:

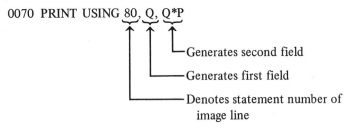

so that if the variable Q contained the value 125 and variable P contained the value 8.73, then execution of the above PRINT USING statement with the associated image line would generate the following output line:

INVENTORY LEVEL IS 125 UNITS. TOTAL VALUE IS $1091.25

The PRINT USING statement permits character-string and numeric data to be displayed or printed and allows the implicit formatting rules, covered earlier with the PRINT statement, to be overridden. Numeric output data can be generated in integer, fixed-point, and floating-point formats.

The PRINT USING Statement

The format of the PRINT USING and associated image statement is given as follows:

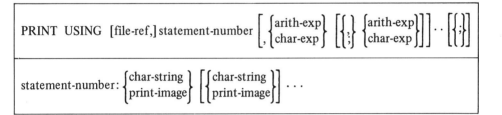

where *file-ref* refers to FL0 (FL"zero") through FL9 or FLP, as in the PRINT statement, and *arith-exp* and *char-exp* denote an arithmetic or character expression, as covered earlier. If FL0 through FL9 is specified, that file must have been previously opened since this option generates a print file. If no file reference is specified, the output data is displayed on the display screen. The *statement-number* in the PRINT USING statement refers to the statement number of the associated image line. In the image line, *char-string* denotes a string of characters, *not* enclosed in quote marks, and *print-image* denotes a format specification. Some operational conventions apply to the use of the PRINT USING statement and the image line:

1. The same image line may be specified in more than one PRINT USING statement.
2. If the PRINT USING statement includes at least one arithmetic or character expression, then the associated image line must specify at least one print image (i.e., format specification).
3. If the PRINT USING statement does not include an arithmetic or character expression, then the image line need not contain a print image.
4. The *char-string* in an image line may be comprised of any characters—including spaces. Therefore, the image line may be blank except for the statement number and the colon character.

```
0010 PRINT USING 0020
0020 :            ABC CORPORATION
0030 P=1
0040 PRINT USING 0050,P
0050 :      INVENTORY REPORT (CONTINUED)        PAGE ###
0060 PRINT USING 0050,P+1
0070 A=123
0080 B=-456
0090 C=78
0100 PRINT USING 0110,A,B,C
0110 :   ABC  ###     EFG   ####
0120 PRINT USING 0130
0130 :-----------------------------------------------
0140 PRINT USING 0110,A;B;C
0150 PRINT USING 0130
0160 PRINT USING 0110,2+2
RUN
        ABC CORPORATION
     INVENTORY REPORT (CONTINUED)        PAGE   1
     INVENTORY REPORT (CONTINUED)        PAGE   2
   ABC   123     EFG    -456
   ABC    78     EFG
------------------------------------------------------
   ABC   123     EFG    -456   ABC    78    EFG
------------------------------------------------------
   ABC    4      EFG
```

Figure 7.10 Sample PRINT USING statements and image lines depicting a variety of conditions, including the use of a continued image line.

During the execution of a PRINT USING statement, the specified expressions are evaluated in the order of appearance in the statement and are edited into the corresponding format specifications in the specified image line. The following conventions apply:

1. If there are more expressions than format specifications, then the image line is used repetitively.

2. If there are fewer expressions than format specifications, then display or printing of the image line is terminated just prior to the first unused format specifications.

Several examples of the preceding concepts are given in Figure 7.10.

Format Types

Four format types are permitted through the use of the PRINT USING statement and an image line: character, integer, fixed-point, and floating-point.

The *character format* is used for displaying the value of a character expression. Character strings are moved into the field position on a left to right basis.

The *integer format* is used to convert the value of an arithmetic expression to an integer number. Rounding is performed on the fractional part of the value.

The *fixed-point format* is used to convert the value of an arithmetic expression to a fixed-point number. The value is rounded or extended with zeros to satisfy the format specification.

The *floating-point format* is used to convert the value of an arithmetic expression to a floating-point number. The value is rounded or extended with zeros and the exponent is adjusted to satisfy the format specification. Numeric values are always aligned by decimal point, where the decimal point of an integer value is assumed to be to the right of the rightmost digit.

Print Image

The print image construct in the image line permits the following format specifications:

1. Character format, consisting of one or more # characters of the form:

$$\#[\#]\ldots$$

The number of # characters determines the length of the edited field. Character-string values longer than the field size are truncated on the right. Examples:

$$\#$$
$$\#\#\#\#\#$$

2. Integer format, consisting of an optional sign and one or more # characters of the form:

$$[\{\pm\}]\,\#[\#]\ldots$$

The implied decimal point is to the right of the format field. The width of the field is the number of characters in the format specification. Examples:

$$-\#\#$$
$$+\#\#\#$$
$$\#$$
$$\#\#\#\#\#\#\#\#\#\#$$

3. Fixed-point format, consisting of an optional sign, a decimal point, and one or more # characters of the form:

$$[\{\pm\}]\,\left\{\begin{array}{l}\#[\#]\ldots.[\#]\ldots\\ [\#]\ldots.\#[\#]\ldots\end{array}\right\}$$

The width of the field is the number of characters in the format specification. Examples:

$$-\#\#\#.\#\#$$
$$\#\#.$$
$$+.\#\#\#\#\#$$

4. Floating-point format, consisting of an integer or fixed-point format followed by four | characters of the form:

$$[\{\pm\}] \begin{cases} \#[\#] \dots \\ \#[\#] \dots .[\#] \dots \\ [\#] \dots .\#[\#] \dots \end{cases} | | | |$$

where the four | characters denote an exponent of the form: E±xx. Examples:

$$-\#.\#\#\#\#\#| | | |$$
$$\#\#| | | |$$
$$+.\#\#\#\#\#\#\#\#\#\#| | | |$$

The character string in an image line may include any sequence of characters. Therefore, a set of rules is applied by the computer in the recognition of the start and end of a format specification. The image line is scanned from left to right. The start of a format specification is recognized as follows:

1. A # character is encountered during the scan and the preceding character is not a # character, plus sign, minus sign, or decimal point.
2. A plus or minus sign is encountered during the scan and it is followed by a # character or a decimal point that precedes a # character.
3. A decimal point is encountered during the scan and it is followed by a # character, and the following is true: the preceding character is not a # character, plus sign, or minus sign, or the preceding character string is not a fixed-point format specification. For example,

$$\#\#.\#\#\#.\#\#$$

→2nd specification

→1st specification

Similarly, the end of a format specification is recognized as follows:

1. A # character is encountered during the scan and the following character is not a # character, a decimal point, or four consecutive | characters. Alternately, if a decimal point has already been encountered, another decimal point after a # sign ends the format specification.

TABLE 7.1 EXAMPLES OF CASES IN WHICH FORMAT SPECIFICATIONS ARE JUXTAPOSED.

Segment of Image Line	Format Specification
++##.###-	+##.###
-##..##	-##. and .##
## ###	## and ###
-#.#### | | | |	-#.####
- #.##	#.##
-#.##	-#.##
RATE=$+####.##	+####.##
-###.##CR	-###.##
##| | | |##	##| | | | and ##

2. A decimal point is encountered during the scan and it is not followed by a # character or four consecutive | characters. Alternately, a decimal point followed by another decimal point ends the leftmost format specification after the first decimal point.

In general, the above rules serve primarily to remove the ambiguity concerning "borderline" cases in which format specifications are juxtaposed. Several examples of borderline cases are given in Table 7.1.

Conversion

During conversion, characters from the data value being transferred to the external medium are edited into the output line, replacing all characters in the format specification. The length of the output field is always equal to the number of characters in the format specification.

Editing. When character-string data is edited, the character data type overrides the sense of the format descriptor, so, for example, the following statements generate equivalent results:

```
10   PRINT USING 11,A$
11 :  ##########

20   PRINT USING 21,A$
21 :  +#.###| | | |
```

When numeric data is edited, the following conventions apply:

1. If the format specification contains a plus sign and the value is positive, then a plus sign is edited into the output field. If the value is negative, then a minus sign is edited into the output field.
2. If the format specification contains a minus sign and the value is positive, then a blank is edited into the output field in the sign position. If the value is negative, then a minus sign is edited into the output field.
3. If the value is negative and the format specification does not contain a sign, a minus sign is edited into the output field in its leftmost position. If a signed negative number or a positive number is too large for the output field, then it is replaced with asterisks.

Several examples of output editing are listed in Table 7.2.

Line Positioning. If there are more expressions in the PRINT USING statement than there are format specifications in the specified image line, a decision must be made by the computer whether to place the repeated line image on the same or the next line. Line positioning is effectively controlled by the PRINT USING statement. For the first PRINT USING statement, output always begins with a new line. If the number of expressions in the PRINT USING statement exceeds the number of format specifications in the line image, then line positioning is controlled by the delimiter immediately following the last expression

TABLE 7.2 EXAMPLES OF OUTPUT EDITING.

Value	*Format Specification*	*Edited Result*
'INVENTORY REPORT'	###############	INVENTORY REPO
'FINI'	######	FINIƀƀ
−34.12	#####	−ƀƀ34
+6.3814	+##.###	+ƀ6.381
−6.3814	+##.###	−ƀ6.381
+6.3814	−##.###	ƀƀ6.381
−6.3814	−##.###	−ƀ6.381
−.123	##.##	−ƀ.12
−1.23	##.##	−1.23
−12.3	##.##	*****
12345	####	****
789	##.#||||	78.9E+01
7.89	###||||	789E-02
7894	#.#####||||	7.89400E+03
−.3456	+#.#####||||	−ƀ.34560E+00
12	#####||||	12000E-03
−12	−#####||||	−12000E-03
.789412345	###.#####||||	789.41235E-03

formatted according to the line image. If it is a comma, then the current line is displayed or printed, and the output of the remaining expressions begins on a new line. If it is a semicolon, then the output of the remaining expressions continues on the same line. If the width of the display or print line is exceeded, then the remaining data is continued on the next line. Consider the following example:

```
10  A=5
20  B=1.234
30  C=13.789
40  PRINT USING 50,A,B,C
50   : FIRST VALUE=##.###,SECOND VALUE=##.###
```

```
0010 FOR I=1 TO 10
0020 PRINT I;I†2;SQR(I);I†(3/2)
0030 NEXT I
RUN
  1      1      1       1
  2      4      1.414214      2.828427
  3      9      1.732051      5.196152
  4     16      2      8.000000
  5     25      2.236068     11.180340
  6     36      2.449490     14.696938
  7     49      2.645751     18.520259
  8     64      2.828427     22.627417
  9     81      3      27.000000
 10    100      3.162278     31.622777


READY                                                    28262
```

(A) Without formatted printing

```
0010 FOR I=1 TO 10
0020 PRINT USING 0030,I;I†2;SQR(I);I†(3/2)
0030 :   ##.#####
0040 NEXT I
RUN
   1.00000      1.00000      1.00000      1.00000
   2.00000      4.00000      1.41421      2.82843
   3.00000      9.00000      1.73205      5.19615
   4.00000     16.00000      2.00000      8.00000
   5.00000     25.00000      2.23607     11.18034
   6.00000     36.00000      2.44949     14.69694
   7.00000     49.00000      2.64575     18.52026
   8.00000     64.00000      2.82843     22.62742
   9.00000     81.00000      3.00000     27.00000
  10.00000     ********      3.16228     31.62278


READY                                                    28241
```

(B) With formatted printing

Figure 7.11 Examples of line positioning with the PRINT USING statement.

There are three expressions and two format specifications. Therefore, the comma following the variable B controls the line positioning after the first line image is printed and the following output is generated:

> FIRST VALUE= 5.000,SECOND VALUE= 1.234
> FIRST VALUE=13.789,SECOND VALUE=

As mentioned earlier, editing stops with the first unused format specification. On the other hand, if a semicolon were placed after the variable B, as follows:

> 10 A=5
> 20 B=1.234
> 30 C=13.789
> 40 PRINT USING A,B;C
> 50   : FIRST VALUE=##.###,SECOND VALUE=##.###

then the two output lines would be juxtaposed, as follows:

FIRST VALUE= 5.000,SECOND VALUE= 1.234 FIRST VALUE=13.789,SECOND VALUE=

The delimiter following the last expression in a PRINT USING statement controls the printing after execution of the statement has been completed. If the final delimiter is a comma or a blank, then the current line is displayed or printed so that the next output will start a new line. If the delimiter is a semicolon, then the current line is not displayed or printed and the next output is added to the current line. Examples of the preceding are given in Figure 7.11.

7.3 SUBPROGRAMS

A function is an instance of a more general concept known as a subprogram. In the previous chapter, two kinds of functions were covered: built-in functions and single-line user-defined functions. The common characteristic between them is that they are included once in a program and are referenced whenever they are needed. The subprogram concept is depicted in Figure 7.12. A subprogram may perform a mathematical function, a data processing operation, or a routine procedure, such as the printing of a title and a page number. There are two kinds of subprograms: functions and subroutines. A *function* always returns a value and can be used in an expression. Functions covered previously, such as the trigonometric sine function, the square root function, and the user-defined root function fall into this category. A *subroutine* is a more general procedure that does not return a value and cannot be used in an expression. A subroutine is referenced with the GOSUB statement.

Multiple-Line User-Defined Functions

Multiple-line user-defined functions are used when a computational procedure cannot be programmed in a single expression. The general form of a multiple-

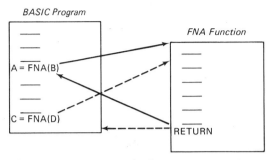

(a) Conceptual view of subprogram execution.

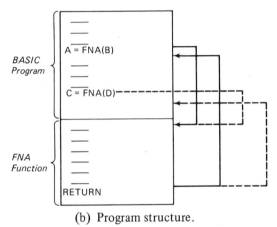

(b) Program structure.

Figure 7.12   Concept and structural view of a subprogram.

line user-defined function is:

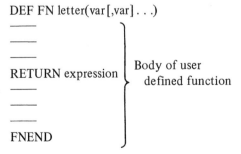

The DEF and FNEND statements denote the beginning and the end of the function definition, respectively. The RETURN statement causes program control to be returned to the calling statement with the value of the specified expression.

DEF Statement. The form of the DEF statement for a multiple-line user-defined function is:

> DEF FNfunction-name [(arith-var [,arith-var] . . .)]

where:

function-name is a single alphabetic character identifying the function.
arith-var is a scalar numeric variable used as a dummy variable.

A dummy variable is replaced when the function is invoked with the value of an expression used as an argument. The form of the function reference is:

> FNfunction-name [(arith-exp [,arith-exp] . . .)

Where *function-name* is the single alphabetic character that identifies the function and *arith-exp* is an arithmetic expression evaluated at the point of reference. The number of arithmetic expressions in a function reference must be equivalent to the number of dummy variables in the corresponding DEF statement.

FNEND Statement. The FNEND statement has the following form:

> FNEND [comment]

where *comment* is any string of characters that is ignored by the computer. The FNEND statement denotes the physical end of a function and is a non-executable statement. Program control must not flow into the FNEND statement, so it must be preceded by a program control statement.

RETURN Statement. The RETURN statement used with defined functions has the following form:

> RETURN arith-exp

where *arith-exp* is an arithmetic expression evaluated at the point of reference. Execution of the RETURN statement causes program control to be returned to the calling statement with the value of the specified expression.

Example. A commonly used function in probability theory and other areas of mathematics is the factorial function, demonstrated earlier, and defined as follows:

$$n! = n \times (n-1) \times (n-2) \times \ldots \times 3 \times 2 \times 1$$

```
0010 REM FACTORIAL FUNCTION
0020 DEF FNF(N)
0030 IF N≠0&N≠1 GOTO 0050
0040 RETURN 1
0050 K=1
0060 FOR J=2 TO N
0070 K=K*J
0080 NEXT J
0090 RETURN K
0100 FNEND
0110 REM MAIN PROGRAM THAT USES FNF
0120 PRINT 'N','N!'
0130 FOR M=0 TO 10
0140 PRINT M,FNF(M)
0150 NEXT M
RUN
N                   N!
 0                   1
 1                   1
 2                   2
 3                   6
 4                   24
 5                   120
 6                   720
 7                   5040
 8                   40320
 9                   362880
10                   3628800

READY                                        28018
```

Figure 7.13 Multiple-line user-defined function for computing factorials.

Figure 7.13 gives a multiple-line user-defined function for computing the factorial function. The factorial function is used in computing permutations. The number of ways that four objects can be arranged is given as 4! or 4X3X2X1. Its meaning is determined as follows:

1. The first object can be arranged in four ways.
2. After the first object is fixed, the second object can be arranged in three ways—since there are only three objects remaining.
3. After the first two objects are fixed, the third object can be arranged in two ways.
4. After the first three objects are fixed, the last object can only be arranged one way.

Using similar reasoning, five objects taken two at a time, can be arranged in 5X4 number of ways. The mathematical formula for computing permutations of N things taken K at a time is:

$$\binom{N}{K} = \frac{N!}{(N-K)!}$$

```
0010 REM PERMUTATION N THINGS K AT A TIME
0020 PRINT 'N','K','PERM'
0030 READ N,K
0040 IF N=0 GOTO 0240
0050 PRINT N,K,FNP(N,K)
0060 GOTO 0030
0070 DEF FNP(A,B)
0080 X=FNF(A)
0090 RETURN X/FNF(A-B)
0100 FNEND
0110 DEF FNF(U)
0120 IF U≠0&U≠1 GOTO 0140
0130 RETURN 1
0140 V=1
0150 FOR W=2 TO U
0160 V=V*W
0170 NEXT W
0180 RETURN V
0190 FNEND
0200 DATA 7,3
0210 DATA 8,2
0220 DATA 6,3
0230 DATA 0,0
0240 END
RUN
N                    K                    PERM
 7                   3                    210
 8                   2                     56
 6                   3                    120
```

Figure 7.14   Permutation program computing N things taken K at a time. Program demonstrates nested multiple-line functions, wherein one function references another function.

Figure 7.14 contains a permutation program, which uses the factorial program as a function, for computing permutations. The program in Figure 7.14 demonstrates the case wherein a multiple-line user-defined function references another multiple-line user-defined function. The program also depicts a branch to the END statement (in statement numbered 40) to terminate execution of the program.

Operational Conventions. The operational conventions governing multiple-line user-defined functions are the same as those given earlier for single-line functions, with extensions for the use of multiple lines. A multiple-line user-defined function can be placed anywhere in a BASIC program and the only way that it can be executed is with an appropriate function reference. When program

control flows into a function definition, the computer goes to the first executable statement following the FNEND statement. One user-defined function may
reference another user-defined function through a normal function reference;
however, function definitions cannot be nested. A multiple-line user-defined
function that is referenced in an input or output statement may not itself perform input and output operations. Lastly, if the parameter to a function reference is a variable, such as K in:

$$\text{PRINT FNF(K)}$$

and that variable is altered from within the function, unpredictable results may
occur. In this case, the variable is *not* a dummy variable since dummy variables
only occur in function definitions.

Subroutines

A subroutine in the BASIC language has the following general structure:

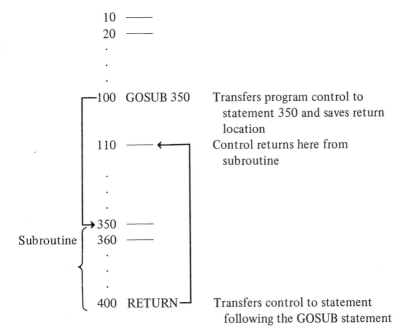

Since a subroutine does not return an explicit result, as is the case with a function, it must be invoked with a special statement in the BASIC language. The
GOSUB statement is used for this purpose. Control is always returned to the
calling program with the RETURN statement.

Example. An example of a subroutine is given in Figure 7.15. This program
uses the GOSUB statement to branch to a subroutine that maintains a line

```
0010 REM PRINT PAGE TITLE
0020 GOSUB 7600
0030 REM GENERATE DUMMY REPORT
0040 FOR I=1 TO 500
0050 PRINT USING FLP,0060,I,I*I
0060 :     ####    ########
0070 REM MAINTAIN LINE AND PAGE COUNTER
0080 GOSUB 7500
0090 NEXT I
0100 STOP
7460 REM *******************************************************
7470 REM TITLE, PAGE, AND LINE SUBROUTINE
7480 REM Y1=LINE COUNTER,  Z1=PAGE COUNTER
7490 REM ADD TO LINE COUNT
7500 Y1=Y1+1
7510 IF Y1≥51 GOTO 7540
7520 RETURN
7530 REM NEXT PAGE - ADD TO PAGE COUNT
7540 Z1=Z1+1
7550 REM SPACE TO TOP OF PAGE
7560 FOR I9=1 TO 15
7570 PRINT FLP,
7580 NEXT I9
7590 REM PRINT TITLE AND RESET LINE COUNTER
7600 IF Z1≠0 GOTO 7620
7610 Z1=1
7620 PRINT USING FLP,7630,Z1
7630 :            ABC CORPORATION               PAGE ###
7640 REM INITIALIZE LINE COUNTER
7650 Y1=1
7660 RETURN
7670 REM *******************************************************
7680 END
```

Figure 7.15 Example of a subroutine used to print a title and page number and to control the number of lines printed on each page.

counter. When the desired number of lines per page is exceeded, the subroutine spaces to the top of the next page and prints a title and page number. The subroutine can be entered at two points. Initially, the subroutine is entered at statement number 7600 to print only the title and initialize the line counter. Thereafter, the subroutine is entered at statement number 7500 to perform the above functions.

GOSUB Statement. The form of the GOSUB statement is given as follows:

> GOSUB statement-number [[,statement-number]...ON arith-exp]

where *statement-number* denotes the number of the initial statement of a subroutine and *arith-exp* is an arithmetic expression evaluated at the point of reference and truncated to an integer. The GOSUB statement is functionally similar to the GOTO statement. Execution of the GOSUB statement without the ON option causes program control to be transferred to the specified statement or to the first executable statement following the specified statement in the event that the specified statement is nonexecutable. When the ON option is specified with the GOSUB statement, program control is transferred to the statement with the statement number that occupies a position in the GOSUB statement equal to the truncated positive integer. More specifically, the statement:

$$\text{GOSUB } s_1, s_2, s_3, \ldots, s_n \text{ ON } e$$

transfers program control to statement numbered s_1 if $e=1$, to statement numbered s_2 if $e=2$, ..., and to statement numbered s_n if $e=n$. If $e<1$ or if $e>n$, then control passes to the next executable statement following the GOSUB statement.

RETURN Statement. The form of the RETURN statement used with subroutines is:

> RETURN

The RETURN statement returns program control to the first executable statement following the last active GOSUB statement. If no active GOSUB statement exists, then an error condition is generated.

Operational Conventions. Subroutines may be nested, such as in the following skeleton:

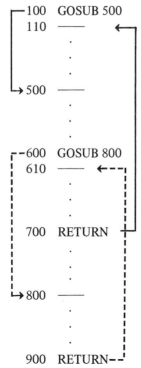

and may be "flowed into," as in the following case:

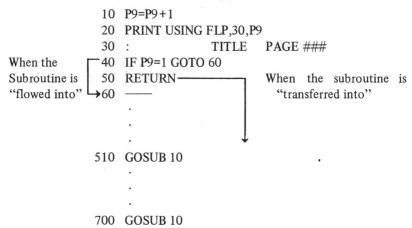

```
10   P9=P9+1
20   PRINT USING FLP,30,P9
30   :              TITLE   PAGE ###
40   IF P9=1 GOTO 60
50   RETURN
60   ─────
```

When the Subroutine is "flowed into"

When the subroutine is "transferred into"

```
510   GOSUB 10

700   GOSUB 10
```

When a subroutine is both flowed into and transferred into, a branch should be made around the RETURN statement in the former case.

7.4 MATRIX OPERATIONS

Matrix (MAT) statements in the BASIC language permit operations that deal with complete arrays, thereby subordinating the detail normally associated with programming to the computer. Each matrix statement begins with the prefix MAT and requires that constituent arrays be declared explicitly or implicitly beforehand. Matrix arithmetic operations are defined only on numeric arrays; matrix assignment and input/output statements are additionally defined on character-string arrays.

The DIM Statement

The DIM statement is used to explicitly declare an array and thereby assign it a name and its row and column bounds. The form of the DIM statement is:

DIM array-name (rows[,columns]) [,array-name(rows[,columns])] ...

where *array-name* is the name of the numeric or character-string array being declared, and the entries *rows* and *columns* are non-zero positive integer constants specifying the dimensions of the array. The rows entry gives the length of a one-dimensional array and both the *rows* and *columns* entries must be used for two-dimensional arrays. Each element of a numeric array is initialized to zero and each element of a character-string array is initialized to 18 blank characters. The maximum size of an array dimension is 255. The following DIM statement

DIM A(11,23),B(3,4),C(15,1),D(50),E(1,6)

for example, establishes the following numeric arrays:

> A has 11 rows and 23 columns
> B has 3 rows and 4 columns
> C has 15 rows and 1 column
> D has 50 elements
> E has 1 row and 6 columns

Similarly, the following DIM statement:

> DIM F$(3,4),G$(50) ,H$(100,5)

establishes the following character-string arrays:

> F$ has 3 rows and 4 columns
> G$ has 50 elements
> H$ has 100 rows and 5 columns

Numeric and character-string array declarations can be made in the same DIM statement, which must be placed in the program prior to the first reference to the array. Otherwise, there are no restrictions on where a DIM statement must be placed in a program.

Array Replacement

All MAT operations result in the replacement of the elements of an array. A few operations pertain to both numeric and character-string arrays and are referred to as array operations, and use operands denoted as *"array-name."* Operations defined only on numeric arrays are referred to as matrix operations, and use operands denoted as *"matrix-name."* The array replacement operations take the following form:

$$\text{MAT array-name}\,[(\text{rows}\,[,\text{columns}]\,)] = \begin{Bmatrix} (\text{scalar-exp}) \\ \text{array-name} \end{Bmatrix}$$

where *array-name* is a previously defined numeric or character-string array and *scalar-exp* is an expression of the same type. The *rows* and *columns* options refer to redimensioning, covered below.

Scalar Replacement. Replacement of the elements of an array with the value of a scalar expression takes the following simplified form:

$$\text{MAT } \underbrace{A} = \underbrace{(e)}$$

→Evaluated first
→Scalar value is assigned to *each* element of A

If the dimension of A is A(k), then the scalar replacement statement is equivalent to A(i)=e, for i=1,2,...,k. If the dimension of A is A (m,n), then the scalar replacement statement is equivalent to A(i,j)=e, for i=1,2,...,m and j=1,2,...,n. The following statements demonstrate scalar replacement:

$$MAT\ B = (-5.341)$$
$$MAT\ C = (3*A2\uparrow2+6*A2-17.1)$$
$$MAT\ D\$ = ('ABCD')$$
$$MAT\ E\$ = (STR(D\$,7,2))$$

In scalar replacement, the scalar expression must be enclosed in parentheses. Redimensioning may also apply to scalar replacement. Figures 7.16 and 7.17 give examples of scalar replacement. In several of the figures that follow, the MAT PRINT statement is used. This statement is introduced later in the chapter. At this stage, it is sufficient to know that it can be used to print or display a complete array, without having to explicitly print or display each item of the array.

Array Replacement. Replacement of the elements of an array with the elements of another array on an element-by-element basis takes the following simplified form:

$$MAT\ A=B$$

where the two arrays *A* and *B* must have the same dimensions, possibly after redimensioning, if specified. If the dimensions of A and B are A(k) and B(k), respectively, then the array replacement statement is equivalent to A(i)=B(i), for

```
0010 DIM A(13),B(2,3)
0020 MAT A=(5.31)
0030 MAT B=(INT(10*RND(123)))
0040 MAT PRINT A;
0050 MAT PRINT B;
RUN


  5.31      5.31      5.31      5.31      5.31      5.31      5.31
  5.31      5.31      5.31      5.31      5.31      5.31



  1       1       1

  1       1       1


READY                                                      28092
```

Figure 7.16 Replacement of the elements of a numeric array with the value of a numberic scalar expression. Note the required parentheses around the expressions.

```
0010 DIM A$(3),B$(2,3)
0020 MAT A$=('TEA FOR TWO')
0030 MAT B$=(STR(A$(2),5,3))
0040 MAT PRINT A$
0050 MAT PRINT B$
RUN
```

TEA FOR TWO   TEA FOR TWO   TEA FOR TWO

FOR   FOR   FOR

FOR   FOR   FOR

READY   28065

Figure 7.17 Replacement of the elements of a character-string array with the value of a character-string expression. Note the required parentheses around the scalar expressions.

i=.,2,...,k. If the dimensions of A and B are A(m,n) and B (m,n), respectively, then the array replacement statement is equivalent to A(i,j)=B(i,j), for i=1,2,...,m and j=1,2,...,n. The following statements demonstrate array replacement:

$$MAT\ P=Q$$
$$MAT\ T\$=V\$$$

```
0010 DIM X(13),Y(13),U(2,3),V(2,3)
0020 MAT Y=(&PI)
0030 MAT V=(&PI+1)
0040 MAT X=Y
0050 MAT U=V
0060 MAT PRINT X;
0070 MAT PRINT U;
RUN RD=3
```

```
3.142    3.142    3.142    3.142    3.142    3.142    3.142
3.142    3.142    3.142    3.142    3.142    3.142


4.142    4.142    4.142

4.142    4.142    4.142
```

READY   27888

Figure 7.18 Numeric array replacement.

```
0010 DIM A$(4),B$(4),C$(2,3),D$(2,3)
0020 MAT B$=('AUDIT')
0030 MAT D$=('CONTROL')
0040 MAT A$=B$
0050 MAT C$=D$
0060 MAT PRINT A$
0070 MAT PRINT C$
RUN
```

```
AUDIT             AUDIT            AUDIT            AUDIT



CONTROL           CONTROL          CONTROL

CONTROL           CONTROL          CONTROL



READY                                                      27822
```

Figure 7.19   Character-string array replacement.

Redimensioning may also apply to array replacement.   Figures 7.18 and 7.19 give examples of array replacement.

Redimensioning.   An array can be redimensioned in any MAT statement that assigns a value to its elements.   Replacement and input statements fall into this category.   Redimensioning is achieved by following the replaced array with the new dimensions enclosed in parentheses, as follows:

$$\text{MAT } a(e) = \ldots$$

⟶ The value of this expression determines
the number of elements in the
redimensioned array.

or

$$\text{MAT } a(e_1, e_2) = \ldots$$

⟶ The value of these expressions determine
the number of rows and columns,
respectively, in the redimensioned
array.

A dimension of the redimensioned array can be specified as a scalar numeric expression which is evaluated at the point of reference and truncated to an

```
0010 DIM A(10),B(8),C(3,4),D(2,3)
0020 MAT B=(180/&PI)
0030 MAT D=(&PI/180)
0040 MAT A(8)=B
0050 MAT C(2,3)=D
0060 MAT PRINT A;
0070 MAT PRINT C;
RUN RD=4
```

```
57.2958       57.2958       57.2958       57.2958       57.2958
57.2958       57.2958       57.2958
```

```
1.7453E-2    1.7453E-2    1.7453E-2

1.7453E-2    1.7453E-2    1.7453E-2
```

```
READY                                                        27862
```

Figure 7.20   Redimensioning of a numeric array.

integer.   Redimensioning applies to numeric and character-string arrays and is governed by the following rules:

1. The total number of elements in the redimensioned array may not exceed the number of elements in the original array.

```
0010 DIM E$(10),F$(3),G$(5,4),H$(2,3)
0020 MAT F$=('INVENTORY')
0030 MAT H$=('CONTROL')
0040 MAT E$(3)=F$
0050 MAT G$(2,3)=H$
0060 MAT PRINT E$
0070 MAT PRINT G$
RUN
```

```
INVENTORY            INVENTORY            INVENTORY


CONTROL              CONTROL              CONTROL

CONTROL              CONTROL              CONTROL
```

```
READY                                                        27444
```

Figure 7-21   Redimensioning of a character-string array.

2. Redimensioning applies to both one-dimensional and two-dimensional arrays.
3. The number of dimensions in an array can be changed with redimensioning.

The following statements demonstrate redimensioning:

$$\text{MAT A(3,4)=(\&PI)}$$
$$\text{MAT B\$(15)=(STR(P\$,4,10))}$$

Redimensioning also applies to other MAT statements in the same manner. Figures 7.20 and 7.21 give examples of redimensioning.

Matrix Arithmetic

Matrix arithmetic statements permit arithmetic operations to be performed on the elements of a numeric array on an element-by-element basis. Since the operations are numerical, the arrays are referred to as matrices. Matrix arithmetic statements have the following form:

$$\text{MAT matrix-name } [(\text{rows }[,\text{columns}])] = \begin{cases} \text{matrix-name} \{\pm\} \text{matrix-name} \\ (\text{arith-exp}) * \text{matrix-name} \end{cases}$$

where *matrix-name* denotes a numeric array. In the matrix addition and subtraction operations, all three matrices must have the same dimensions after redimensioning, if specified. *Arith-exp* is a numeric scalar expression.

Matrix Addition. Matrix addition takes the following simplified form:

$$\text{MAT C=A+B}$$

and adds matrix B to matrix A on an element-by-element basis and replaces matrix C with the result. If the dimension of A,B, and C is (k) then the matrix addition statement is equivalent to $C(i)=A(i)+B(i)$, for $i=1,2,\ldots,k$. If the dimensions of A,B, and C are (m,n), then the matrix addition statement is equivalent to $C(i,j)=A(i,j)+B(i,j)$, for $i=1,2,\ldots,m$ and $j=1,2,\ldots,n$.

Matrix Subtraction. Matrix subtraction takes the following simplified form:

$$\text{MAT C=A-B}$$

and subtracts matrix B from matrix A on an element-by-element basis and replaces matrix C with the result. If the dimension of A,B, and C is (k), then the matrix subtraction statement is equivalent to $C(i)=A(i)-B(i)$, for $i=1,2,\ldots,k$. If the dimensions of A,B, and C are (m,n), then the matrix subtraction statement is equivalent to $C(i,j)=A(i,j)-B(i,j)$, for $i=1,2,\ldots,m$ and $j=1,2,\ldots,n$.

Scalar Multiplication. Scalar multiplication takes the following simplified form:

$$\text{MAT C} = (e) *B$$

where matrices B and C have the same dimensions and e is a numeric scalar ex-expression evaluated at the point of reference. The statement multiplies matrix B by expression e on an element-by-element basis and replaces matrix C with the result. If the dimension of matrices C and B is (k), then the scalar multiplication statement is equivalent to C(i)=e*B(i), for i=1,2,...,k. If the dimensions of C and B are (m,n), then the scalar multiplication statement is equivalent to C(i,j)= e*B(i,j), for i=1,2,...,m and j=1,2,...,n.

Examples. The following statements demonstrate the use of matrix arithmetic:

> MAT Q=F-R
> MAT W(6,24)=(&P1*R↑2)*D
> MAT P=(14.731)*N
> MAT D(9,1)=I+J

Figure 7.22 gives the computer printout for several examples of matrix arithmetic.

Significant Characteristic. One significant characteristic of matrix arithmetic statements is that the same matrix can appear on both sides of the equals sign, as follows:

$$\text{MAT A=A+B}$$

Therefore, if it were desired to add a constant, such as 5 to every element of a matrix, then a sequence of statements, such as the following would be used:

> DIM A(20,30),B(20,30)
> .
> .
> .
> MAT B=(5)
> MAT A=A+B

Similarly, if it were desired to multiply every element of matrix A by 10, one could write:

$$\text{MAT A=(10)*A}$$

Logically, a matrix arithmetic operation, such as:

$$\text{MAT A=A+B}$$

```
0010 DIM A(10),B(2,3),C(2,3),D(2,3)
0020 MAT A=(5)
0030 MAT C=(6)
0040 MAT D=(2)
0050 MAT A=(2)*A
0060 MAT PRINT FLP,A;
0070 MAT B=C+D
0080 MAT PRINT FLP,B;
0090 MAT B=C-D
0100 MAT PRINT FLP,B;
0110 MAT A(2,3)=(-1)*D
0120 MAT PRINT FLP,A;
```

(A) Program

```
10     10     10     10     10     10     10     10     10     10



 8      8      8

 8      8      8



 4      4      4

 4      4      4



-2     -2     -2

-2     -2     -2
```

(B) Input

Figure 7.22 Matrix arithmetic demonstrating matrix addition, matrix subtraction, scalar multiplication, and redimensioning.

is interpreted as follows, "Add matrix B to matrix A and replace matrix A with the result." In reality, the operation is performed on an element-by-element basis, equivalent to the following nested FOR loop:

$$\text{FOR I=1 TO M}$$
$$\text{FOR J=1 TO N}$$
$$A(I,J)=A(I,J)+B(I,J)$$
$$\text{NEXT J}$$
$$\text{NEXT I}$$

where M and N are the row and column bounds, respectively. Similarly, the statement

$$\text{MAT A} = (3*X+B)*A$$

is equivalent to the following nested FOR loop:

```
T=3*X+B
FOR I=1 TO M
   FOR J=1 TO N
      A(I,J)=T*A(I,J)
   NEXT J
NEXT I
```

where again, M and N are the row and column bounds, respectively. The scalar expression in matrix arithmetic is *always* evaluated first and its *value does not change* during the matrix operation. The following example demonstrates this point. In the statement:

$$MAT\ A=(A(2,3))*A$$

which is equivalent to the following nested FOR loops:

```
T=A(2,3)
FOR I=1 TO M
   FOR J=1 TO N
      A(I,J)=T*A(I,J)
   NEXT J
NEXT I
```

the elements of matrix A are each multiplied by the same value, namely, the initial value of $A(2,3)$, even though the value of $A(2,3)$ in the resulting matrix is changed part way through the computation. The above concepts also apply to one-dimensional numeric arrays in an analogous fashion.

Matrix Mathematics

Matrix mathematical operations are permitted on previously declared matrices. This facility allows an identity matrix to be established and includes facilities for the transpose, inverse, and matrix multiplication functions.

Identity Function. The identity function permits an identity matrix to be assigned to a square matrix and has the following format:

$$\boxed{MAT\ matrix\text{-}name\,[(rows,columns)]=IDN}$$

where *matrix-name* is a square numeric matrix and *rows* and *columns* are arithmetic expressions evaluated at the point of reference, as explained above, and specify redimensioning. The following statements, for example:

$$\text{DIM A(50),B(3,3)}$$

$$\cdot$$
$$\cdot$$
$$\cdot$$

$$\text{MAT B=IDN}$$
$$\text{MAT A(7,7)=IDN}$$

would create the following matrices:

$$A = \begin{vmatrix} 1 & 0 & 0 & 0 & 0 & 0 & 0 \\ 0 & 1 & 0 & 0 & 0 & 0 & 0 \\ 0 & 0 & 1 & 0 & 0 & 0 & 0 \\ 0 & 0 & 0 & 1 & 0 & 0 & 0 \\ 0 & 0 & 0 & 0 & 1 & 0 & 0 \\ 0 & 0 & 0 & 0 & 0 & 1 & 0 \\ 0 & 0 & 0 & 0 & 0 & 0 & 1 \end{vmatrix} \quad B = \begin{vmatrix} 1 & 0 & 0 \\ 0 & 1 & 0 \\ 0 & 0 & 1 \end{vmatrix}$$

Transpose.   The mathematical transpose B of matrix A is defined as:

$$B(j,i)=A(i,j), \text{ for } i=1,2,\ldots,m \text{ and } j=1,2,\ldots,n$$

where the dimensions of A are (m,n) and the dimensions of B are (n,m). The fact that the number of rows of B is equal to the number of columns of A and that the number of columns of B is equal to the number of rows of A is significant, and must be true for the matrix transpose statement that has the following form:

MAT array-name [(rows,columns)] =TRN(array-name)

where *array-name* is a numeric or character-string array and the (rows, columns) option specifies redimensioning. Since no arithmetic is required in the transpose function, the operation applies to both numeric and character-string arrays. Sample transpose statements are:

$$\text{MAT Q=TRN(R)}$$
$$\text{MAT F(4,3)=TRN(H)}$$
$$\text{MAT B\$=TRN(W\$)}$$

and the printout of a computer program that uses the transpose is given next under "matrix multiplication." The matrix transpose statement:

$$\text{MAT B=TRN(A)}$$

is equivalent to the following nested FOR loops:

```
FOR I=1 TO M
   FOR J=1 TO N
      B(J,I)=A(I,J)
   NEXT J
NEXT I
```

where the M and N are the row and column bounds, respectively, of matrix A and are the column and row bounds, respectively, of matrix B. The same array *cannot* appear on both sides of the equal signs in a matrix transpose statement.

Matrix Multiplication. The multiplication of two matrices A and B is defined as:

$$C(i,j)= \sum_{k=1}^{n} A(i,k)*B(k,j)$$

for i=1,2, . . . ,m and j=1,2, . . . ,p. The dimensions of the matrices are: $A(m,n)$, $B(n,p)$, and $C(m,p)$. The number of columns in matrix A must equal the number of rows in matrix B. For example,

$$\begin{pmatrix} 1 & 2 & 3 \\ 4 & 5 & 6 \end{pmatrix} * \begin{pmatrix} 5 & 6 \\ 7 & 8 \\ 9 & 10 \end{pmatrix} = \begin{pmatrix} 46 & 52 \\ 109 & 124 \end{pmatrix}$$

The matrix multiplication statement has the form:

MAT matrix-name [(rows, columns)] =matrix-name*matrix-name

where *matrix-name* is a numeric matrix and the (rows, columns) option denotes redimensioning. The matrices specified in the matrix multiplication statement must all be two-dimensional and the same matrix must not appear on both sides of the equals sign; however, the same matrix may appear twice to the right of the equals sign, as follows:

Mat A=A*B	MAT B=A*A
Illegal	*Legal*

The mathematical requirement of conformality of operands also applies to the matrix multiplication statement. As stated above, in a statement of the form:

MAT A=B*C

the following dimensions must hold:

DIM A(M,N),B(M,P),C(P,N)

which is summarized as follows:

1. The number of columns in B must equal the number of rows in C.
2. The number of rows in A must equal the number of rows in B.
3. The number of columns in A must equal the number of columns in C.

Moreover, if the above dimensions are true, then the MAT statement of the form:

$$\text{MAT A=B*C}$$

is equivalent to the following nested FOR loops:

```
FOR I=1 TO M
  FOR J=1 TO N
    S=0
    FOR K=1 TO P
      S=S+B(I,K)*C(K,J)
    NEXT K
    A(I,J)=S
  NEXT J
NEXT I
```

As an example of matrix multiplication, consider the theorem in mathematics that states:

$$(AB)^T = B^T A^T$$

where A and B are matrices and the T denotes transpose. The program in Figure 7.23 gives an example of the theorem.

Matrix Inverse. The inverse of a matrix A is a matrix B that satisfies the following identity:

$$A*B=B*A=I$$

where I is the identity matrix. The notion of the inverse of a matrix is easily demonstrated. To compute the inverse of the matrix $\begin{pmatrix} 1 & 2 \\ 3 & 4 \end{pmatrix}$, a matrix of the form $\begin{pmatrix} a & b \\ c & d \end{pmatrix}$ is needed such that:

$$\begin{pmatrix} a & b \\ c & d \end{pmatrix} * \begin{pmatrix} 1 & 2 \\ 3 & 4 \end{pmatrix} = \begin{pmatrix} 1 & 0 \\ 0 & 1 \end{pmatrix}$$

After performing the matrix multiplication symbolically and equating elements to the identity matrix, the following simultaneous equations are obtained:

$$a+3b=1 \qquad 2a+4b=0$$
$$c+3d=0 \qquad 2c+4d=1$$

```
0010 DIM A(3,2),B(2,3),C(3,3),D(3,3)
0020 DIM E(2,3),F(3,2),G(3,3)
0030 MAT READ A,B
0040 MAT C=A*B
0050 MAT D=TRN(C)
0060 PRINT FLP,'TRANSPOSE (A*B)'
0070 MAT PRINT FLP,D;
0080 MAT E=TRN(A)
0090 MAT F=TRN(B)
0100 MAT G=F*E
0110 PRINT FLP,'TRANSPOSE(B)*TRANSPOSE(A)'
0120 MAT PRINT FLP,G;
0130 DATA 1,2,3,4,2,1
0140 DATA 3,1,1,2,4,3
```

TRANSPOSE (A*B)

```
7       17      8

9       19      6

7       15      5
```

TRANSPOSE(B)*TRANSPOSE(A)

```
7       17      8

9       19      6

7       15      5
```

Figure 7.23 An instance of the mathematical theorem $(AB)^T = B^T A^T$ demonstrating matrix transpose and matrix multiplication.

The solution to the simultaneous equations is a=-2, b=1, c=1.5, and d=$-.5$, so that the inverse matrix is $\begin{pmatrix} -2 & 1 \\ 1.5 & -.5 \end{pmatrix}$.* The form of the matrix inverse statement is:

MAT matrix-name [(rows,columns)] =INV(matrix-name)

where *matrix-name* is a numeric square** matrix, and the (rows, columns) option denotes redimensioning. In the execution of the matrix inverse statement, the

*The reader can verify that $\begin{pmatrix} -2 & 1 \\ 1.5 & -.5 \end{pmatrix} * \begin{pmatrix} 1 & 2 \\ 3 & 4 \end{pmatrix} = \begin{pmatrix} 1 & 0 \\ 0 & 1 \end{pmatrix}$.

**In a square matrix, the number of rows equals the number of columns.

inverse is taken of the matrix to the right of the equals sign, which must be non-singular,* and the inverse is assigned to the matrix to the left of the equals sign. The matrix inverse is frequently used in the solution of simultaneous linear equations. For example, consider the system of equations:

$$x_1+x_2+2x_3=3$$
$$x_1+2x_2+3x_3=4$$
$$x_1-x_2-x_3=2$$

If $A=\begin{pmatrix} 1 & 1 & 2 \\ 1 & 2 & 3 \\ 1 & -1 & -1 \end{pmatrix}$, $X=\begin{pmatrix} x_1 \\ x_2 \\ x_3 \end{pmatrix}$, and $B=\begin{pmatrix} 3 \\ 4 \\ 2 \end{pmatrix}$, then the system of equations can be expressed as:

$$AX=B$$

Multiplying each side of the matrix equation by the inverse of A (expressed as A^{-1}) and simplifying as follows:

$$A^{-1}AX=A^{-1}B$$
$$IX=A^{-1}B$$
$$X=A^{-1}B$$

the solution X is obtained. Figure 7.24 gives a BASIC program that solves the system of equations that has the following solution: $X=\begin{pmatrix} 3 \\ 2 \\ -1 \end{pmatrix}$.

User-Oriented Input and Output

User-oriented array input and output facilities closely parallel those given earlier for single data values. Four statements are involved: READ, INPUT, PRINT, and PRINT USING. The matrix forms of the statements are prefixed with the keyword MAT.

The MAT READ Statement. The MAT READ statement is used to read data values from the internal data set created from DATA statements and assigns those values to specified arrays. The statement has the following form:

MAT READ array-name $\left[(\text{rows}[,\text{columns}])\right]\left[,\text{array-name}\left[(\text{rows}[,\text{columns}])\right]\right]$ ...

---

*A matrix is singular if its determinant is zero. This is determined with the DET function. Therefore, a matrix A is non-singular if DET(A)=0. The DET function can be used on matrices up to 50×50; and a determinant is considered to be zero if its value is 1E-20 or less.

```
0010 DIM A(3,3),B(3,1),X(3,1),Q(3,3)
0020 MAT READ A,B
0030 IF DET(A)=0 GOTO 0090
0040 MAT Q=INV(A)
0050 MAT X=Q*B
0060 MAT PRINT X;
0070 STOP
0080 PRINT 'A IS SINGULAR'
0090 DATA 1,1,2,1,2,3,1,-1,-1
0100 DATA 3,4,2
RUN


 3.000000

 2.000000

-1.000000



READY                                                    27818
```

Figure 7.24 Solution to a system of simultaneous linear equations demonstrating the use of the matrix inverse.

where *array-name* is a previously declared numeric or character-string array that may have one or two dimensions and the (rows, columns) option denotes re-dimensioning. If redimensioning is not specified, then the dimension of the specified array is taken from its declaration, and the appropriate number of values are read from the internal data set and assigned to the array in a row-wise order. For example, the statements:

$$DIM\ R(3,4)$$
$$MAT\ READ\ R$$
$$DATA\ -7,3,9,6,5,1,4,2,8,-9,0,3$$

would cause the following matrix to be formed in the main storage unit:

$$R = \begin{pmatrix} -7 & 3 & 9 & 6 \\ 5 & 1 & 4 & 2 \\ 8 & -9 & 0 & 3 \end{pmatrix}$$

and the statements:

$$DIM\ K(15)$$
$$MAT\ READ\ K$$
$$DATA\ -7,3,9,6,5,1,4,2,8,-9,0,3,-6,7,-1$$

would cause the following one-dimensional array to be constructed:

$$K = (-7\ 3\ 9\ 6\ 5\ 1\ 4\ 2\ 8\ -9\ 0\ 3\ -6\ 7\ -1)$$

The concepts also apply to character-string arrays, as in the following statements:

DIM D$(2,3)
MAT READ D$
DATA 'PINTO', 'VEGA', 'ARROW'
DATA 'STARFIRE', 'SKYHAWK', 'MONZA'

that cause the following two-dimensional character-string array to be constructed:

$$D\$ = \begin{pmatrix} \text{'PINTO'} & \text{'VEGA'} & \text{'ARROW'} \\ \text{'STARFIRE'} & \text{'SKYHAWK'} & \text{'MONZA'} \end{pmatrix}$$

Figure 7.25 contains several examples of MAT READ statements as well as corresponding MAT PRINT statements, covered below.

```
0010 DIM C$(15,15),H(20),T(5,12),W(1,1),D$(6)
0020 READ I,J,K,M,N
0030 MAT READ C$(I,J),H(K),T(M,N),W,D$
0040 MAT PRINT FLP,C$,H;T;W;D$;
0050 DATA 2,3,7,4,3
0060 DATA 'PINTO','VEGA','ARROW','STARFIRE','SKYHAWK','MONZA'
0070 DATA -7,3,9,6,5,1,4
0080 DATA 1,1,2,3,5,8,13,21,34,55,89,144
0090 DATA -713.4385
0100 DATA 'A','B','C','D','E','G'
```

```
PINTO          VEGA          ARROW

STARFIRE       SKYHAWK       MONZA


 -7     3     9     6     5     1     4


  1     1     2

  3     5     8

 13    21    34

 55    89   144


-713.4385

ABCDEG
```

Figure 7.25 Examples of the use of the MAT READ and MAT PRINT statements.

The MAT INPUT Statement.   The function MAT INPUT statement is identical to the MAT READ statement, except that input is requested from the keyboard instead of being read from the internal data set.   The form of the MAT INPUT statement is:

MAT INPUT array-name $\left[(\text{rows}[,\text{columns}])\right]\left[,\text{array-name}\left[(\text{rows}[,\text{columns}])\right]\right]$ ...

where *array-name* is a previously declared numeric or character-string array, having either one or two dimensions, and the (rows, columns) option denotes redimensioning.   If redimensioning is not specified, then the dimension of the specified array is taken from its declaration, and the appropriate number of values are requested from the keyboard and assigned to the array in a row-wise order.   An example of a valid MAT INPUT statement is:

MAT INPUT Q,R(2,N+5)

When the MAT INPUT statement is executed, the user at the keyboard is prompted with a question mark.   Values are placed into the input line separated by commas.   As each line is filled, it is entered into the computer by pressing the EXECUTE key.   If the array is not filled, then the question mark is displayed again.   This process is continued until all arrays specified in the MAT INPUT statement have been assigned values.   Moreover, the input is assigned successively; after one array is filled, the next value entered is assigned to the next array in the input list.   Excess values, after the last array in the list has been filled, are ignored.   All values entered must match the corresponding type of variable in the input list.   Figure 7.26 includes examples of matrix input.

The MAT PRINT Statement.   The MAT PRINT statement is used to print or display a complete array without referring to specific array elements.   The statement has the following form:

MAT PRINT [file-ref,] array-name $\left[\begin{Bmatrix}, \\ ;\end{Bmatrix}\text{array-name}\right]\dots\left[\begin{Bmatrix}; \\ ;\end{Bmatrix}\right]$

where *file-ref* can be FLP for the printer or the designations FL0 through FL9 for tape files 0 through 9.[*]   *Array-name* is a previously declared one- or two-dimensional array that contains either numeric or character-string elements.   If the file reference is omitted, then the arrays are displayed on the display screen.

---

[*]If a file is specified in a MAT PRINT statement, the file must be opened before the statement is executed.

```
0010 DIM A(4),B$(3),C(2,1)
0020 MAT INPUT A,B$,C
0025 PRINT FLP,TAB(10),'OUTPUT'
0030 MAT PRINT FLP,A;B$,C;
RUN
-7,3,9,6
'BOLT','HAMMER','WRENCH'
3,14,2.72
```

                                                              0020
                    (A) Program and input

        OUTPUT

    -7   3   9   6

    BOLT   HAMMER   WRENCH

    3,14

    2,72

                         (B) Output

                  Figure 7.26 Matrix input.

An example of valid MAT PRINT statements are:

                    MAT PRINT FLP, A;B;C
                    MAT PRINT W;

Each array is printed or displayed by rows with each row starting on a new line. The first row is preceded by two blank lines and succeeding rows are separated from the preceding row by one blank line. If the array reference is followed by a comma,* the array elements are printed or displayed using full print zones. If the array reference is followed by a semicolon, the array elements are printed or displayed using packed print zones. Values are displayed using the same formatting conventions as were given for the PRINT statement. Examples of the use of the MAT PRINT statement were given in Figure 7.25.

The MAT PRINT USING Statement. The MAT PRINT USING statement is used to print or display complete arrays using a specified line image. The form of the line is the same as with the PRINT USING statement. The form of the

---

*For the last array in an output list, a blank character following the array name is equivalent to a comma.

MAT PRINT statement is:

MAT PRINT USING [file-ref,] statement-number, array-name $\left[\left\{{; \atop ,}\right\} \text{[array-name]}\right] \dots \left[\left\{{; \atop ,}\right\}\right]$

where:

file-ref is FLP or FL0 through FL9, as specified above,
statement-number is the statement number of the corresponding line image
statement, and
array-name is a previously declared one or two-dimensional array that contains either numeric or character-string elements.

An example of a valid print using statement is:

$$100 \quad \text{PRINT USING } 101, A, B$$
$$101 \quad : \#\#\#\#.\#\# \quad \#.\#\#\#\#\#| \, | \, | \, |$$

Each array reference is edited and then printed or displayed in row order according to the specified line image. As with the MAT PRINT statement, the first
row of each array begins on a new line, preceded by two blank lines. Each
succeeding row begins on a new line and is separated from the preceding row by
one blank line. The beginning of each row is printed or displayed according to
the start of the line image. If the line image contains more format specifications
than the number of elements in the row, then the excess format specifications
are ignored. If the number of format specifications is less than the number of
elements in the row, then the spacing is controlled by the delimiter following the
array reference, as follows:

1. If the delimiter is a comma or a blank and the end of the line image is
   reached, the current line is printed or displayed and output continues on a
   line with the start of the line image.
2. If the delimiter is a semicolon and the end of the line image is reached, the
   output continues on the same line with the start of the line image.

Figure 7.27 gives several examples of the use of the MAT PRINT USING statement. The last row of the last array in a MAT PRINT USING statement, as
demonstrated in Figure 7.28, requires special attention. If the trailing delimiter
is a comma or a blank character, the line containing the last row is printed or
displayed so that the next output will begin on a new line. If the trailing delimiter is a semicolon, then the current line is not printed or displayed so that
the next output will be on the same line. The concept is analogous to that of
ending a simple PRINT statement with a semicolon.

```
0010 DIM A(5),B(4,3),C(2,6),D$(4)
0020 MAT READ A,B,C,D$
0030 MAT PRINT USING FLP,0040,A
0040 :  ###.##    ####.##
0050 MAT PRINT USING FLP,0060,B,C
0060 :  ###    ####.##    .####||||    #.##||||
0070 MAT PRINT USING FLP,0060,B;C;
0080 MAT PRINT USING FLP,0090,D$
0090 :  #####    #####    #####    #####    #####
0100 DATA 1.23,2.34,3.45,4.56,5.67
0110 DATA 1,2,3,4,5,6,7,8,9,10,11,12
0120 DATA 10,20,30,40,50,60,70,80,90,100,110,120
0130 DATA 'ABLE','BAKER','CHARLY','DAWG'
```

```
1.23       2.34
3.45       4.56
5.67

  1        2.00    .3000E+01

  4        5.00    .6000E+01

  7        8.00    .9000E+01

 10       11.00    .1200E+02

 10       20.00    .3000E+02    4.00E+01
 50       60.00

 70       80.00    .9000E+02    1.00E+02
110      120.00

  1        2.00    .3000E+01

  4        5.00    .6000E+01

  7        8.00    .9000E+01

 10       11.00    .1200E+02

 10       20.00    .3000E+02    4.00E+01    50    60.00

 70       80.00    .9000E+02    1.00E+02   110   120.00

ABLE     BAKER     CHARL     DAWG
```

Figure 7.27 Examples of the use of the MAT PRINT USING statement.

File-Oriented Input and Output

The facilities for file-oriented input and output of complete arrays closely resembles those given earlier for single data values. Two statements are involved: GET and PUT. The matrix forms of the statements are prefixed with the key-

```
0010 DIM A(2,3)
0020 MAT READ A
0030 MAT PRINT USING 0040,A;
0040 :  ##  ##  ##
0050 PRINT 'ALL DONE'
0060 DATA 1,2,3,4,5,6
RUN

   1   2   3

   4   5   6ALL DONE


READY                                        28172
```

Figure 7.28 If the MAT PRINT USING a statement contains a trailing semicolon, then the next output is printed or displayed on the last line of array output.

word MAT. All files referenced with the MAT GET and MAT PUT statements require the use of OPEN and CLOSE statements, as previously introduced, and input and output processing is the same—except for the fact that entire arrays are being transmitted instead of single values.

The MAT GET Statement. The MAT GET statement is used to read data values from the specified file and assign them in row order to the specified array. The statement has the following form:

MAT GET file-ref,array-name$\left[(\text{rows}[,\text{columns}])\right]$ $\left[,\text{array-name}\left[(\text{rows}[,\text{columns}])\right]\right]$ ...[EOF statement-number]

where *file-ref, array-name*, and *(rows, columns)* have the same definitions as given previously. The *EOF statement-number* option specifies the statement number to which program control should be directed if the values in the data file are exhausted before the input list is satisfied. An example of a valid MAT GET statement is:

MAT GET FL2,H,K(15,25)

When the MAT GET statement is executed, data values are read from the specified file until the declared or redimensioned size of the specified array is satisfied. Figure 7.29 demonstrates the case wherein an array is written to a file as single data values and read back as a complete array. The fact that a data file exists as a list of discrete data values is clearly evident with the input and output of complete arrays.

The MAT PUT Statement. The MAT PUT statement is used to write a complete array to a specified data file. The elements of the array are written in row order and exist in the data file as a list of discrete values. The statement has the

```
0010 DIM A(3,4)
0020 MAT READ A
0030 OPEN FL8,'E80',003,OUT
0040 FOR I=1 TO 3
0050 FOR J=1 TO 4
0060 PUT FL8,A(I,J)
0070 NEXT J
0080 NEXT I
0090 CLOSE FL8
0100 MAT A=(0)
0110 OPEN FL8,'E80',003,IN
0120 MAT GET FL8,A
0130 MAT PRINT A;
0140 CLOSE FL8
0150 DATA 1,2,3,4,5,6,7,8,9,10,11,12
RUN
```

```
1     2     3     4

5     6     7     8

9     10    11    12
```

READY   27317

Figure 7.29   Example of the use of the MAT GET statement in which an array is written to a file as single data values and read back as an array.

following form:

> MAT PUT file-ref, array-name [, array-name] . . .

where *file-ref* and *array-name* have the same definitions as given previously. An example of a valid MAT PUT statement is:

$$MAT\ PUT\ FL4,U,V,W$$

Data files are written so that the first value written with a MAT PUT statement is the first value read by a subsequent MAT PUT (or GET) statement. This case is demonstrated in Figure 7.30 that gives the combined use of MAT PUT and MAT GET statements.

7.5 PROGRAM CHAINING AND COMMON STORAGE

Program chaining is a computer facility that permits one program to call another program, and common storage is a special area in the main storage unit that is

```
0010 DIM V(5),M(4,4)
0020 MAT V=(1)
0030 MAT M=(25)
0040 PRINT FLP,'VECTOR - MATRIX'
0050 MAT PRINT FLP,V;M;
0060 OPEN FL5,'E80',002,OUT
0070 MAT PUT FL5,V,M
0080 CLOSE FL5
0090 OPEN FL5,'E80',002,IN
0100 MAT GET FL5,M,V
0110 PRINT FLP,'MATRIX - VECTOR'
0120 MAT PRINT FLP,M;V;
0130 CLOSE FL5
```

VECTOR - MATRIX

1	1	1	1	1
25	25	25	25	
25	25	25	25	
25	25	25	25	
25	25	25	25	

MATRIX - VECTOR

1	1	1	1	
1	25	25	25	
25	25	25	25	
25	25	25	25	
25	25	25	25	25

Figure 7.30 Example of the use of MAT PUT and MAT GET statements. The first value written to a data file with the MAT PUT statement is the first value read in a subsequent MAT GET (or GET) statement.

effectively used to exchange data betweeen programs that are executed successively. The need for program chaining and common storage facilities is a direct consequence of the fact that the effective use of the main storage unit is dependent upon the size of both programs and data.

Storage Organization

The organization of the main storage unit, as given earlier in chapter three, consisted of three major areas:

1. Internal storage area,
2. User work area, and
3. Internal machine fix area.

An item of information related to a program is always stored in the user work area, which can be delineated further. The user work area is further subdivided into the following subareas:

1. BASIC statements
2. Variable area and buffers
3. Variable table
4. Common area.

The organization of the user work area is given in Figure 7.31. The exact size of each subarea is dependent upon the characteristics of the program being executed.

Statement Area. The statements that comprise the BASIC program are stored in a condensed form to preserve storage space. This is the reason that a program is always listed in a form that is slightly different from the form in which it was entered. An entry exists in this area for each BASIC statement.

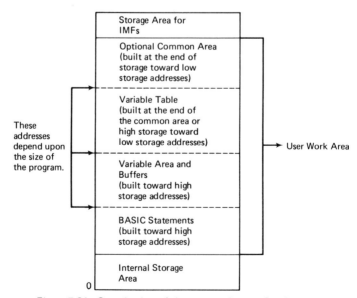

Figure 7.31   Organization of the user work area of main storage.

Variable Area. The variable area and buffers contain the physical storage for holding variables, arrays, and input/output buffers. Each item of data is stored in this area.

Table Area. The variable table contains an entry for each variable name and each array name used in a BASIC program. Each entry contains the name and a pointer to the corresponding storage in the variable area.

Common Area. The common area holds data that is shared between programs. When a BASIC program is loaded, the statement, variable and buffer, and variable table areas are overlaid so that the old program is wiped out. The common area is left untouched so that it can be used for passing data between programs.

Example. As an example, consider the following statements:

$$10 \quad \text{DIM A(50)}$$
$$20 \quad \text{READ B,C,D}$$
$$30 \quad \text{A(10)=B*C+D}$$

Each statement is stored in the statement area in condensed form. The names A,B,C, and D are contained in the variable table and the associated storage for array A and scalar variables B,C, and D is in the variable area. When the program segment is executed, the computer interprets the BASIC statements and uses the variable table to determine the location of the data values, which are then used in the respective computations.

Program Chaining

There are two main reasons for using program chaining:

1. To allow one program to call another program as directed by the user, and
2. To allow a program that is too large for the user area to be broken up and executed in pieces.

The computer facilities used in either case are the same.

Example. Assume a set of programs and a program directory established on tape as follows:

File 1: Directory program (given below)
File 2: Accounts receivable program
File 3: General ledger program
File 4: Personnel management program
File 5: Inventory control program

The directory is of primary concern here because it is used to call the other programs. The user is presented with a directory of available programs, as shown in Figure 7.32. The number of the desired program is entered and the directory

DIRECTORY

```
CHOOSE THE DESIRED PROGRAM AND ENTER THE ITS NUMBER
         1 - ACCOUNTS RECEIVABLE
         2 - GENERAL LEDGER
         3 - PERSONNEL MANAGEMENT
         4 - INVENTORY CONTROL
         5 - TERMINATE PROCESSING


  ?
```

0110

Figure 7.32   A directory.

program causes the desired program to be executed with the CHAIN statement. An appropriate directory program is given in Figure 7.33. In addition to presenting a directory and including a CHAIN statement, this program contains a subroutine for clearing the screen.

The CHAIN Statement. The CHAIN statement is used to terminate execution of the program currently being executed, close all files, load a new program, and

```
0010 GOSUB 0250
0020 PRINT TAB(25),'DIRECTORY'
0030 PRINT
0040 PRINT 'CHOOSE THE DESIRED PROGRAM AND ENTER THE ITS NUMBER'
0050 PRINT TAB(10),'1 - ACCOUNTS RECEIVABLE'
0060 PRINT TAB(10),'2 - GENERAL LEDGER'
0070 PRINT TAB(10),'3 - PERSONNEL MANAGEMENT'
0080 PRINT TAB(10),'4 - INVENTORY CONTROL'
0090 PRINT TAB(10),'5 - TERMINATE PROCESSING'
0100 PRINT
0110 INPUT N
0120 GOTO 0150,0170,0190,0210,0230 ON N
0130 PRINT 'NUMBER OUT OF RANGE - REENTER IT'
0140 GOTO 0110
0150 PRINT 'ACCOUNTS RECEIVABLE PROGRAM CALLED'
0160 CHAIN 'E80',N+1
0170 PRINT 'GENERAL LEDGER PROGRAM CALLED'
0180 CHAIN 'E80',N+2
0190 PRINT 'PERSONNEL MANAGEMENT PROGRAM CALLED'
0200 CHAIN 'E80',N+3
0210 PRINT 'INVENTORY CONTROL PROGRAM CALLED'
0220 CHAIN 'E80',N+4
0230 PRINT 'PROCESSING TERMINATED'
0240 STOP
0250 REM CLEAR SCREEN
0260 FOR I=1 TO 14
0270 PRINT
0280 NEXT I
0290 RETURN
```

Figure 7.33   Directory program.

initiate execution of the new program. The statement has the following form:

> CHAIN 'dev-address', arith-exp

where *dev-address* is the device address of the tape unit containing the next program to be loaded and executed, and *arith-exp* is a numeric expression that is evaluated at the point of reference and truncated to an integer. The program contained in the file denoted by the arithmetic expression is then loaded from the specified device and executed. Execution always begins with the lowest numbered statement in the new program. The following is a valid CHAIN statement:

CHAIN 'E80',N+1

The address of the built-in tape unit is E80; the address of the auxiliary tape unit (if present) is E40.

Common Storage

The common storage area is a repository for data that can be exchanged between BASIC programs. Each BASIC program addresses the common area directly and it is the user's responsibility to put the right data in the right place in the common area at the right time.

The USE Statement. The USE statement can be used to place the storage required by a variable or an array in the common storage area. Storage is assigned to variables in the order given in the USE statement. The statement has the following form:

$$
\text{USE} \left\{ \begin{array}{l} \text{arith-var} \\ \text{arith-arr-var(rows[,columns])} \\ \text{char-var} \\ \text{char-arr-var(rows[,columns])} \end{array} \right\} \left[, \left\{ \begin{array}{l} \text{arith-var} \\ \text{arith-arr-var(rows[,columns])} \\ \text{char-var} \\ \text{char-arr-var(rows[,columns])} \end{array} \right\} \right] \ldots
$$

where the various constructs denote arithmetic variables, arithmetic arrays, character-string variables, and character-string arrays, respectively. *All variables to be placed in common storage must be declared in a USE statement.* An example of a valid USE statement is:

USE A,B(5,30),C$,D$(50),E,F,G(2),H$(3,3)

An array specification in a USE statement serves as an array declaration and must not be included in an additional DIM statement. A program must contain

```
LOAD 13
0010 USE A,B(5),C$(2),D$
0020 READ A,D$
0030 MAT READ B,C$
0040 CHAIN 'E80',14
0050 DATA -7,'CHARLY'
0060 DATA 3,9,6,5,1,'ABLE','BAKER'


READY      CHAIN-1          ,001,000,0010,0060          28203



RUN
0010 USE M(6),N$(3)
0020 MAT PRINT M;N$



-7    3    9    6    5    1


ABLE            BAKER            CHARLY


READY      CHAIN-2          ,001,000,0010,0020      0020 28219
```

Figure 7.34   Example of the use of common storage and program chaining.

only one USE statement and that statement must precede any statement in the program that contains a variable reference. A USE statement must be included in the program chained from and in the program chained to. This is the method by which the correspondence between the respective variables is made.

Example. Figure 7.34 contains two programs that contain the following common storage areas:

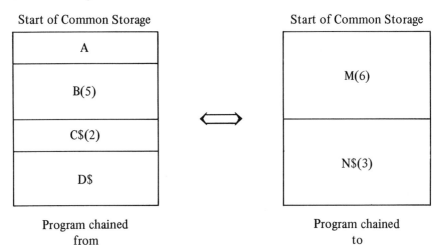

Start of Common Storage   Start of Common Storage

Program chained   Program chained
from   to

Correspondence between the data values is based on their relative position in the common storage area.

The programs have been placed on a tape cartridge as files 13 and 14. The first program, which places data values in the common area, is loaded with the following command:

LOAD 13

and is executed with the RUN command. This program chains to the second program with the following statement:

CHAIN 'E80', 14

At this point, the computer loads the second program, which prints the data values that were placed in common storage by the first program.

REFERENCES

Katzan, H., *Introduction to Programming Languages*, Auerbach Publishers, Inc. Philadelphia, 1973.

IBM 5100 Portable Computer publications:
  a. *IBM 5100 BASIC Introduction*, Form #SA 21-9216
  b. *IBM 5100 BASIC Reference Manual*, Form #SA 21-9217

IBM Corporation, Rochester, Minnesota, 1975.

8 | BASIC SYSTEM COMMANDS

The IBM 5100 Portable Computer system provides a comprehensive set of operational functions that are outside the scope of the BASIC language. These functions are available through system commands, grouped into the following categories:

1. Program control,
2. Tape control,
3. Execution control, and
4. Program management.

Program control commands involve the statements that comprise a program and encompass functions such as statement numbering and listing. Tape control commands involve the manipulation of complete data files and the placement of files on a tape cartridge. Execution control commands involve the initiation and continuation of program execution. Program management commands allow programs and data to be loaded from tape and saved on tape, and include special 5100 capabilities such as keyboard generated data files and the creation and use of function keys.

8.1 GENERAL CONSIDERATIONS

Each system command begins with a keyword denoting the function performed by that command, followed by additional parameters as required. The following list gives the keyword and major function performed by each command:

Keyword	*Major Function*
AUTO	Permits BASIC statements to be numbered automatically by the computer.
GO	Causes execution of a program or a system command to be resumed.
LIST	Commands the computer to display or print the contents—either program or data file—of the user work area of main storage.
LOAD	Initiates the loading of the user work area of main storage with either a program or a data file from tape or a data file from the keyboard.
MARK	Initializes a tape cartridge for subsequent storing of program or data.
MERGE	Causes a program or data file from tape to be combined with the same type of entity (i.e., program or data) in the user work area of main storage.
PATCH	Invokes execution of a special 5100 system program that permits system modifications, tape recovery, or tape copying.
RD=	Allows the number of decimal digits of printing precision to be specified.
RENUM	Causes the numbers of the statements of a program in the user work area of main storage to be renumbered.
REWIND	Initiates a rewind of the tape cartridge.
RUN	Initiates execution of the BASIC program currently held in the user work area of main storage.
SAVE	Saves the contents of the user work area of main storage on tape.
UTIL	Displays or prints a directory of the contents of a tape cartridge or puts the IBM 5100 computer system into the communications mode.

Each command is described separately.

Entering of Commands

A command keyword may be entered on a character-by-character basis from the keyboard or by holding down the CMD key and pressing the number key below the name of the function placed above the keyboard. The result in either case is exactly the same. Three keywords cannot be entered with the CMD key: MARK, MERGE, and PATCH. These keywords, which are infrequently used, must always be entered on a character-by-character basis. Depending upon the particular command, the keyword is followed by appropriate parameters for that command.

After a system command is entered into line position 1 of the display screen, it is executed by pressing the EXECUTE key. A system command is always processed immediately by the computer.

Rules for Entering Commands

Five rules govern the manner in which system commands are entered:

1. A system command always begins with the appropriate keyword. No statement number is required and will cause an error if it is present.
2. Each command must begin on a new line.
3. The maximum length of a command, including keyword, parameters, and spaces is 64 characters.
4. Blank characters are ignored—except within quote marks.
5. All parameters must be separated by commas.

The following examples demonstrate these rules:

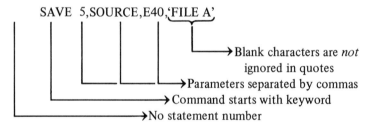

Errors

When a command is entered, it is immediately checked for syntax errors.* If an error is detected, the up arrow denotes the portion of the command that is in error and the display screen flashes. At this point, the keyboard is locked and the only active keys are ATTN and HOLD. Pressing ATTN stops the flashing. The error can then be corrected in one of two ways:

1. By scrolling up so that the input line is clear and entering the command correctly.
2. By scrolling down so that the incorrect statement is in the input line, editing it, and then pressing the EXECUTE key.

It is also possible to generate an error during the execution of a system command. These errors are corrected in a manner specific to a particular command.

---

*This is true of BASIC statements as well. All statements entered from the keyboard are immediately checked for syntax errors.

8.2 PROGRAM CONTROL COMMANDS

The set of program control commands provides four functions that involve the statements that comprise a program:

1. Automatic statement numbering,
2. Statement renumbering,
3. A means of obtaining a listing of a program, and
4. A means of merging programs and data.

Each command is described independently of other commands and may involve the use of facilities available through other system commands.

The AUTO Command

The AUTO command provides automatic statement numbering. After the AUTO command is entered, the first statement number is supplied by the computer. After the BASIC statement is entered and the EXECUTE key is pressed, the computer automatically supplies the next statement number, and so forth. Use of this command simplifies the task of entering a program. The form of the AUTO command is:

> AUTO [statement-number[,increment]]

where *statement-number* is the initial statement number and *increment* is the positive difference between successive statement numbers. The default value for the initial statement number is 0010 and the default value for the increment is also 0010. The initial statement number and increment, if specified, must be between 1 and 9,999.

Once the computer is placed in the AUTO mode, it continues to operate in that mode until one of two events occurs:

1. A statement number other than the one displayed is entered. This can result from line editing.
2. A system command or a calculator mode statement is entered. This is accomplished by scrolling up so that the computer generated statement number is no longer in the input line and any form of input can be entered.*

After automatic statement numbering has been discontinued, it can be reinstituted by entering an AUTO command with an appropriate initial statement number and increment.

---

*Recall that when the system is in the BASIC mode, a scroll up operation causes the flashing cursor to return to the leftmost position in the input line.

```
AUTO 100,20
0100 DIM A(50)
0120 READ N
0140 _
READY                                                    28356
```

Figure 8.1   AUTO command.

Figure 8.1 gives an example of the use of the AUTO command. When this command is entered, the current contents of the user work area are not altered in any way.

The RENUM Command

The RENUM command can be used to renumber the statements in the user work area. The form of this command is:

RENUM [KEY x] [,statement-number,increment]

```
5 PRINT USING FLP,6,'NUMBER','FACTOR'
6 : ######  ######
7 :  ####    ####
10 READ N
11 IF N=0 GOTO 500
20 FOR F=INT(N/2) TO 1 STEP -1
21 IF N/F=INT(N/F) GOTO 80
22 NEXT F
80 PRINT USING FLP,7,N,F
100 GOTO 10
150 DATA 1234,47,0
500 END
9 PRINT FLP
RENUM

  READY                                                  28089
```

(A)   Original program entry and the RENUM command

```
0010 PRINT USING FLP,0020,'NUMBER','FACTOR'
0020 : ######  ######
0030 :  ####    ####
0040 PRINT FLP,
0050 READ N
0060 IF N=0 GOTO 0130
0070 FOR F=INT(N/2) TO 1 STEP -1
0080 IF N/F=INT(N/F) GOTO 0100
0090 NEXT F
0100 PRINT USING FLP,0030,N,F
0110 GOTO 0050
0120 DATA 1234,47,0
0130 END

  LIST
```

(B)   Listing after the program was renumbered.

Figure 8.2   RENUM and LIST commands.

where *statement-number* is the statement number to be assigned to the first statement in the BASIC program and *increment* is the positive difference to be used between successive statement numbers. In addition to renumbering statement numbers, the RENUM command also adjusts all references to statement numbers appropriately. Figure 8.2 contains a listing of a program before and after renumbering.

The KEY *x* option specifies that a key group should be renumbered, where *x*=0 to 9. A key group is renumbered as though it were a separate program. Because of the existence of key groups, however, statement numbers greater than 9989 cannot be renumbered, since they implicitly denote key group header statements. (Key groups are covered later in this chapter.)

The LIST Command

The LIST command is used to display or print the statements in the user work area, and has the following form:

$$\text{LIST [PRINT]} \left[, \left\{ \begin{array}{l} \text{KEY } x \\ \text{statement-number} \end{array} \right\} \right]$$

where the keyword PRINT denotes that listing should be printed on the printer unit. If PRINT is not specified, the listing is displayed on the display screen. If no options are specified with the LIST command, the first 14 lines are displayed and the scroll up and scroll down keys can be used to arrive at a particular line. If *statement-number* is specified without the PRINT option, the statement corresponding to the given statement number is displayed in line position 2 of the display screen and the preceding 13 lines of the program are displayed above it. The scroll up and scroll down keys can also be used here to display a particular line. If *statement-number* is specified with the PRINT option, all statements in the user work area, starting with the specified statement number, are printed on the printer. Figure 8.3 gives an example of a program listing.

If KEY *x* is specified, where *x*=0 to 9, then the corresponding key group is displayed or printed.

```
0010 PRINT USING FLP,0020,'NUMBER','FACTOR'
0020 :  ######  ######
0030 :   ####    ####
0040 PRINT FLP,
0050 READ N

LIST
```

Figure 8.3 LIST command. (Program of 8.2 was listed with the following command: LIST 50.)

The MERGE Command

The MERGE command is used to merge all or part of a saved file with the contents of the user work area. The work area and the file must have the same type. That is, they both must be a BASIC program or both be a keyboard generated data file.* The form of the MERGE command is:

MERGE file-num [,[from-statement-number] ,[through-statement-number] ,[new-statement-number] [,dev-address]]

where:

file-num is the file number of the saved file.

from-statement-number is the statement number of the first statement in the saved file to be merged.

through-statement-number is the statement number of the last statement in the saved file to be merged.

new-statement-number is the initial statement number to be used in renumbering the statements from the saved file. The default increment is 10.

dev-address is the number of the tape unit on which the saved file resides. The default is the built-in unit number E80.

Operation of the MERGE command is based on the value of the respective statement numbers. If a line from the saved file and a statement in the user work area have the same number, the line from the saved file replaces the statement in the user work area.

The MERGE command can be used to load a portion of a saved file, which is the example demonstrated in Figure 8.4.

```
MERGE 1,20,90

   READY                                                    28192
```
(A) MERGE command.
```
0020 :  ######   ######
0030 :   ####     ####
0040 PRINT FLP,
0050 READ N
0060 IF N=0 GOTO 0130
0070 FOR F=INT(N/2) TO 1 STEP -1
0080 IF N/F=INT(N/F) GOTO 0100
0090 NEXT F

   LIST
```
(B) Listing of loaded program.

Figure 8.4 Example of the MERGE command used to load a portion of a saved file.

*More specifically, both files must be either type 4 BASIC files or type 1 data interchange files.

8.3 TAPE CONTROL COMMANDS

The set of tape control commands provides four functions that involve tape manipulation without dealing with specific files or the data items that comprise a file. The PATCH command additionally provides serviceability features for use with the IBM 5100 Portable Computer.

The REWIND Command

The REWIND command is used to rewind the tape cartridge on the specified tape unit and has the following form:

REWIND [dev-address]

where *dev-address* specifies the address of the tape unit on which the tape cartridge to be rewound has been inserted. The device address may be one of the following:

1. E80 for the built-in tape unit, and
2. E40 for the auxiliary tape unit.

If the device address is omitted, then the default address is E80. The following are valid REWIND commands:

REWIND
REWIND E80
REWIND E40

The UTIL command without the file option lists a directory of the contents of a tape cartridge—starting at its current position. (This is covered later.) The REWIND command can be used prior to the UTIL command so that the directory begins with the first file on the cartridge, as follows:

REWIND
UTIL

This sequence of commands may be more convenient than using

UTIL DIR1

which gives equivalent results.

It is not necessary to rewind a tape cartridge before removing it from a tape unit. Moreover, *all* file operations require that files be referenced by number and the computer is designed to search for a needed file—regardless of the current position of the tape cartridge. During "normal" operations, therefore, the REWIND command is not needed.

The REWIND command can be used, however, as a convenience. If, for example, a work session normally starts with a LOAD 1 command, then the tape cartridge can be rewound prior to the end of the previous session so as to minimize subsequent startup time.

The MARK Command

The MARK command is used to initialize a tape cartridge for storing tape files. If a tape cartridge has not been previously marked to hold a file, an attempt to save a work area or write a file will result in an error condition. A tape cartridge is always marked in increments of 1,024 characters of storage. The form of the command is:

MARK K-characters,files,starting-file [,dev-address]

where:

K-characters is the number of increments of 1,024 character positions (bytes) to be reserved for each file.
files is the number of files to be marked.
starting-file is the lowest-numbered file to be marked.
dev-address is the address of the tape unit, i.e., E80 or E40, in which the tape cartridge has been inserted. (The default address is E80.)

A sample MARK command is:

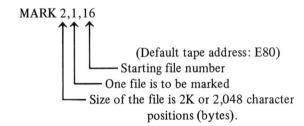

MARK 2,1,16

(Default tape address: E80)
Starting file number
One file is to be marked
Size of the file is 2K or 2,048 character
positions (bytes).

If the file number specified in the MARK command has already been marked, an error is generated. To continue with the operation and re-mark the file, the keyword GO should be entered. If an existing file is re-marked, then that file on the tape and all succeeding files are inaccessible. *This means that the storage positions occupied by those files has been reformatted and the previous data cannot be read.* However, old files preceding the newly marked files continue to be accessible. In this respect, the tape cartridge is similar to recorder tape since information is always stored sequentially.

Before a data file can be marked to hold a program, data file, or user work area, the required amount of storage must be estimated. In general, this is not a problem since an educated guess is usually satisfactory. The size of a program or the user work area can be determined by inspecting the amount of main storage available, which is displayed in the lower right-hand corner of the display screen. The difference between this value and the original amount—displayed with LOAD 0—gives the size of a program or the user work area in bytes. The size of a data file can be estimated from the type and amount of data, computed as follows:

1. Each character-string datum occupies 18 bytes.
2. Each numeric datum occupies 8 bytes.

In addition, each file has an overhead of .5K (i.e., 512) bytes.

The UTIL Command

The UTIL command is used to perform two functions:

1. Display or print a directory of a tape cartridge,
2. Change the operating mode of the computer from BASIC to communications.

The communications mode will be covered in a later chapter and is invoked with the following command:

UTIL MODE COM

Form of the UTIL Command. The form of the UTIL command for listing the directory of a tape cartridge is given as follows:

UTIL [PRINT,] [DIR [integer]] [,dev-address]

The PRINT option specifies that the directory should be printed on the line printer. Otherwise, the directory is displayed on the display screen. The DIR [integer] option specifies the number of the file with which the directory should begin. If the [integer] option is omitted, then the directory begins with the current tape position. If the DIR option is omitted altogether, then the directory also begins with the current tape position. The *dev-address* option denotes the address of the tape unit in which the tape cartridge has been inserted—E80 for the built-in tape unit and E40 for the auxiliary tape unit. The default address is E80. The following are valid UTIL commands:

Command	*Meaning*
UTIL	Directory starting with current position of tape unit; unit E80; directory listed on display screen.
UTIL PRINT	Directory starting with current position of tape unit; unit E80; directory listed on printer unit.

| UTIL DIR4 | Directory starting with file 4; unit E80; directory listed on display screen. |
| UTIL PRINT,DIR1,E40 | Directory starting with file 1; unit E40; directory listed on printer unit. |

Execution of the UTIL command requires space in the user work area for internal operation. If insufficient space is available, a diagnostic message is generated. In this case, the user work area should be cleared with the LOAD 0 command and the UTIL command should be reentered. Execution of the UTIL command can be interrupted with the ATTN key.

The Directory. The directory consists of one line for each file; it consists of the following information:

File number
File identification
File type
Number of contiguous 1,024 byte segments assigned to the file
Number of contiguous 1,024 byte segments unused in the file
Number of defective 512 byte areas in the file (If the number of defective areas is greater than 9, an asterisk is printed.)
First and last statement numbers for BASIC user work area and SOURCE files
Key numbers saved for KEYS or KEY (0–9) files

The file types are listed in Table 8.1 and Figure 8.5 gives a sample annotated directory.

TABLE 8.1   FILE TYPES.

Type	*File*
0	Marked or unused file
1	Data exchange file
2	General exchange file
3	BASIC source file
4	BASIC user work area file
5	BASIC KEYS file
6	APL continued file
7	APL SAVE file
8	APL internal data
16	Customer Support File (Patch/recovery/copy)
17	Diagnostic file
18	IMF file
72	Tape storage dump

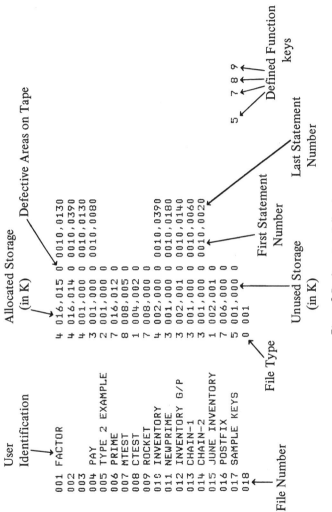

Figure 8.5 Annotated directory.

The PATCH Command

The PATCH command is used to invoke an IBM supplied serviceability program or to copy a tape. More specifically, the PATCH command permits the following options:

1. Copy IMF tape
2. Load IMFs
3. Display EC version
4. Key enter an IMF
5. End of job
6. Tape recovery
7. Tape copy program

The PATCH command does not require parameters and has the following form:

PATCH

The command is used by placing an IBM supplied "Customer Support Cartridge" into the built-in tape unit and then entering the keyword PATCH on a character-by-character basis. After the EXECUTE key is pressed, the computer responds with the options given in Figure 8.6. Three of the options deal with Internal Machine Fixes (IMFs) that rectify system-based errors. In general, it is only necessary to apply an IMF if the user encounters a corresponding system problem. The directory of a customer support cartridge is given in Figure 8.7.

Copy IMF Tape. The copy IMF option is used to copy the first two files of the "Customer Support Cartridge." The remaining files cannot be copied—

```
ENTER OPTION NO.
1. COPY IMF TAPE
2. LOAD IMF'S
3. DISP EC VER.
4. KEY ENTER IMF
5. END OF JOB
6. TAPE RECOVERY
7. TAPE COPY PGM
```

Figure 8.6   Options available with the PATCH command.

```
UTIL

001 IMF COPY/LOAD    16 008,000 0
002 IMF FILE         19 008,000 0
003 TAPE RECOVERY    16 014,000 0
004 TAPE COPY        16 005,000 0
005 APLAIDS           7 008,000 0


READY                                        28385
```

Figure 8.7   Directory of the customer support cartridge.

except by service personnel. When this option is selected, the copy IMF program directs the user on the action that should be taken. Before files 1 and 2 can be copied, the tape cartridge onto which they will be copied must be marked with the MARK command for two files of the correct size. The required sizes can be determined by issuing the UTIL command for the "Customer Support Cartridge." (An example of this directory was given in Figure 8.7.)

Load IMFs. The load IMFs option loads the applicable internal machine fixes (IMFs) from the Customer Support Cartridge into the computer. The IMFs occupy space in the user work area and utilize processing time—as required. Therefore, IMFs should only be used when they affect the user's task. The load IMFs program directs the user on the action that should be taken.

Display EC Version. This option is used by service personnel to display the latest engineering change (EC) level of the computer.

Key Enter IMF. This option is used by service personnel to enter an IMF from the keyboard into the computer. After the IMF is loaded, it is written onto the Customer Support Cartridge so that it can be loaded with the "Load IMFs" option, covered above.

End of Job. This option terminates processing of the PATCH command and returns the computer to normal operation. This is the option that permits the user to escape from the PATCH command. After the processing of the other options, the computer always displays the PATCH options in preparation for another operation.

Tape Recovery. This option permits data to be recovered from a tape cartridge on which errors are occurring and from which, as a result, the data cannot be read. The following file types can be recovered:

> Type 01—Data exchange file
> Type 02—General exchange file
> Type 03—BASIC source file
> Type 08—APL internal data file

The tape recovery program is used by inserting the tape cartridge containing the errors into the built-in tape unit. The program then directs the user on the action that should be taken.

Tape Copy. This option permits a tape to be copied and can operate with or without the auxiliary tape unit. The program also marks the tape onto which the copy is made. The program directs the user on the action that should be taken.

8.4 EXECUTION CONTROL COMMANDS

The set of execution control commands is used to specify execution-time-options and to initiate program execution initially or after the execution of a program has been interrupted.

RD Command

The RD command is used to specify the number of digits to the right of the decimal point that should be displayed or printed. Rounding always takes place before a number is truncated. The form of the RD command is:

$$RD=n$$

where n is an integer between 1 and 13. Rounding is initially set to 6 digits when the computer is turned on. The RD parameter can be changed with the RD or RUN command and that setting is not affected by a LOAD 0 command.

RUN Command

The RUN command is used to initiate execution of the BASIC program currently active in the user work area. The program can be executed in three modes:

1. *Normal mode*, in which the program is executed without interruption.
2. *Step mode*, in which the computer pauses before the execution of *each* statement and prints out the word STEP, followed by the statement number of the next statement to be executed. The number of the statement previously executed is in the lower right-hand corner of the display screen.
3. *Trace mode*, in which the number of each statement executed is displayed or printed.

The form of the RUN command is:

$$RUN \left[\left\{ \begin{matrix} STEP \\ TRACE[,PRINT] \end{matrix} \right\} \right] [,P=D] [,RD=n]$$

The STEP option denotes the step mode. The TRACE option specifies the trace mode and the PRINT option denotes that the trace of statement numbers should be printed instead of being displayed. If neither the STEP nor the TRACE option is selected, then the program is run in the normal mode. If the P=D option is selected, all printer output is directed to the display screen. The RD parameter specifies rounding. The following are valid examples of the RUN command:

        RUN RD=2
        RUN STEP,P=D
        RUN TRACE,PRINT,P=D

In the last example, printed output as well as the program trace information is displayed on the display screen. Trace information is additionally listed on the printer.

Program execution always begins with the first executable statement in the BASIC program and all variables and arrays are initialized to zero or blanks, depending upon the type of variable.

When the computer pauses between statements in the step mode, execution is resumed by pressing the EXECUTE key or by entering the GO command, described next. If the EXECUTE key is used, execution resumes with the next statement in the step mode.

GO Command

The GO command is used to resume processing after the computer has been interrupted for any of the following reasons:

1. Error condition,
2. During processing of a MARK command,
3. Interrupted processing in the step mode,
4. Pressing of the ATTN key, or
5. Interrupted processing after a PAUSE statement is executed.

With the GO command, the following options are available:

1. Resume normal processing,
2. Resume processing in the step mode,
3. Resume processing in the trace mode,
4. Specify rounding,
5. Continue processing with a specified statement number, and
6. Terminate program or command execution.

The form of the GO command is:

$$
\text{GO [statement-number]} \left[, \left\{ \begin{array}{l} \text{RUN} \\ \text{STEP} \\ \text{TRACE [,PRINT]} \end{array} \right\} \right] [,\text{RD}=n]
$$

The *statement-number* specifies the number of the statement with which execution of a BASIC program should continue. If the statement number is not specified, execution of the program continues with the next executable statement. The $\left\{ \begin{array}{l} \text{RUN} \\ \text{STEP} \\ \text{TRACE [,PRINT]} \end{array} \right\}$ option specifies the mode under which program execution should continue. If this option is not specified, execution continues in the same mode that was in operation when processing was interrupted. The RUN, STEP, and TRACE keywords denote the normal, step, and trace modes, respectively. This option operates in the same manner as the RUN command.

The RD parameter specifies rounding. The following are valid examples of the GO command:

GO 80,RD=8
GO RUN
GO STEP
GO 150,STEP,RD=4
GO TRACE

In the last example, trace information is displayed on the display screen, but is not printed, regardless of whether program output is to be printed or displayed.

To terminate execution of a program or a command after an interruption, the following variation to the GO command should be entered:

GO END

In the case of a BASIC program, the END option serves to close all files.

If the input line is blank, pressing the EXECUTE key is equivalent to entering a GO command without parameters. The only exception to this convenience is with the MARK command, for which the word GO must be entered to remark a marked file.

8.5   PROGRAM MANAGEMENT COMMANDS

The set of program management commands include LOAD and SAVE, which are collectively the most comprehensive of the system commands. The LOAD command is used to clear the user work area and to load a previously saved file into the user work area. The SAVE command is used to save the contents of the user work area as a file on a tape cartridge. Because of the large number of options, however, the commands are extensive in both scope and complexity.

Form of the LOAD Command

The form of the LOAD command is:

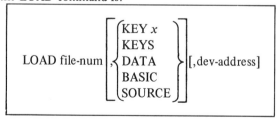

where:

   file-num is an integer value.
   KEY *x*, KEYS, DATA, BASIC, or SOURCE specifies the type of file to be loaded.

dev-address is the address from which the file is to be loaded. The default value is E80 for the built-in tape unit. If the device address is specified, E40 denotes the auxiliary tape unit and E80 denotes the built-in tape unit.

All combinations of the above options are not valid, as described in the following sections.

Operation of the LOAD Command

When a saved file is loaded from tape, status information is displayed on the display screen summarizing the operation performed. In general, the following information is displayed as it applies to a particular option:

User file identification (stored with the file),
Number of contiguous 1,024 byte segments in the file,
Number of contiguous 1,024 byte segments of unused storage in the file,
First statement number, if a BASIC program is loaded,
Last statement number, if a BASIC program is loaded,
KEY *x* numbers for KEY files, and
Amount of unused storage in the user work area.

Figure 8.8 gives a sample of this information for a type 4 file, which contains a BASIC user work area.

```
LOAD 10,BASIC

READY       INVENTORY          ,002,000,0010,0390                    27354
```
Figure 8.8 Sample of information that is displayed when a file is loaded. (This is an example of a type 4 file.)

Load Zero. The "load zero" command takes the following form:

LOAD 0

and clears the entire work area, including all key functions. The zero parameter denotes that a new file will be entered from the keyboard.

Load File. The "load file" command takes the following form:

LOAD file-num[,dev-address]

and is used to load a BASIC or SOURCE file from tape. If the file is any other type, such as a data file or key group, an error condition is generated. The following are valid instances of the load file command:

LOAD 5
LOAD 23,E40

With this form of the LOAD command, the program is loaded from the saved file into the user work area without altering existing key functions. A general exchange file (type 2) is loaded as though it were a SOURCE file. (See "Load Source" below.) Thus, this form of the command can be used to load type 2 (General exchange), type 3 (BASIC source), and type 4 (BASIC work area) files.

Load BASIC. The "load BASIC" command takes the following form:

LOAD file-num,BASIC [,dev-address]

and is used to load a BASIC file from tape or clear the user work area. If a zero file is specified, then the user work area, except for the keys, is cleared, and the computer prepares for the keyboard entry of a BASIC program. If the specified file is not a type 4 BASIC file, then an error condition is generated by the computer. The following are valid instances of the "load BASIC" command:

LOAD 10,BASIC,E40
LOAD 2,BASIC

The program is loaded into the user work area after eliminating its prior contents—except for key functions which are unaltered.

Load SOURCE. The "load SOURCE" command takes the following form:

LOAD file-num, SOURCE [,dev-address]

and is used to load a BASIC source file from tape. The BASIC source file can be a type 2 (general exchange) or a type 3 (BASIC source) file. A zero file cannot be specified as the file number. The following are valid instances of the "load SOURCE" command:

LOAD 2,SOURCE
LOAD 41,SOURCE,E80

As each line is read from a BASIC source file, its syntax is checked. When a syntax error condition occurs, it must be resolved in one of the following ways:

1. By correcting the statement and pressing the EXECUTE key. Loading will then continue.
2. By scrolling up to ignore the statement. Loading continues as soon as the scroll up key is pressed. The incorrect statement is not loaded in the user work area, even though it is displayed on the display screen.

Lines longer than 64 characters cannot be loaded. When loading is completed using this form of the load command, the program is displayed and the READY message appears. An example of the use of the "load SOURCE" command is given in Figure 8.9.

Load DATA. The "load DATA" command takes the following form:

LOAD file-num,DATA [,dev-address]

```
LOAD 4,SOURCE
0010 INPUT H,R
0015 IF H=0 GOTO 0080
0020 IF H>40 GOTO 0060
0030 P=H*R
0040 PRINT 'HOURS=';H;'RATE=';R;'PAY=';P
0050 GOTO 0010
0060 P=40*R+(H-40)*R*1.5
0070 GOTO 0040
0080 STOP


   READY        PAY              ,001,000,0010,0080                28201
```

Figure 8.9   Example of the use of the "load SOURCE" command.

and is used to load a type 1 (data exchange) or a type 2 (general exchange) file, if the file number is not zero and the file is one of the specified types. The following are valid instances of the "load DATA" command:

LOAD 12,DATA

LOAD 2,DATA,E40

When a data file is loaded, each line is automatically prefixed with a statement number and the keyword, DATA. This case is demonstrated in Figure 8.10, which gives the result of the "load DATA" command for a type 1 file and a type 2 file that contains a source program. It should be noted in the latter case that each statement is prefixed with a statement number and the keyword DATA. (When the same file is loaded as a BASIC source file, the lines are not prefixed with the statement number and the keyword DATA.) When a zero file number is specified, a keyboard generated data file is created, as covered in a subsequent section. During the execution of a "load DATA" command, calculator statements are not valid, and the computer is placed in the data entry mode.

Load KEYS. The "load KEYS" command takes the following form:

LOAD file-num,KEYS [,dev-address]

and is used to load all key functions from the specified type 5 (BASIC KEYS) file into the user work area. The following are valid instances of the "load KEYS" command:

LOAD 17,KEYS

LOAD 9,KEYS,E40

If key functions with the same number exist in the user work area, they are replaced with the key functions loaded. Otherwise, the contents of the user work area are unaltered. Figure 8.11 gives an example of the use of the "load KEYS" command. When the key functions are loaded, line position 0 of the display screen gives the numbers of the loaded key functions. With this form of the load command, the file number cannot be zero.

```
LOAD 15,DATA

DATA        JUNE INVENTORY   ,002,001,                    28081




0001 DATA 'BOLT   2 INCH', 512, .13, 75, 1000
0002 DATA 'COPPER TUBE', 11, 17.52, 25, 100
0003 DATA 'HOIST CLAMP', 23, 15.81, 5, 60
0004 DATA 'NAIL   3 PENNY', 213, 11.07, 50, 200
0005 DATA 'PST JOINT', 7, 62.58, 15, 65
0006 DATA 'T RACK', 15, 5.45, 10, 100
0007 DATA 'L. BRACE', 150, 1.98, 100, 200
0008 DATA 'G. PIN', 38, 124.5, 15, 30

  LIST
```

(A)   Type 1 (data exchange) file.

```
LOAD 5,DATA

DATA        TYPE 2 EXAMPLE   ,001,000,                    28323
```

```
0001 DATA 0010 FOR I=1 TO 5
0002 DATA 0020 PRINT I;
0003 DATA 0030 NEXT I

  LIST
```

(B)   Type 2 (general exchange) file.

Figure 8.10   Examples of the "load DATA" command.

```
LOAD 17,KEYS

READY       SAMPLE KEYS      ,001,000,          5    7 8 9  28129
```

Figure 8.11   An example of the "load KEYS" command. (Key functions numbered 5, 7, 8, and 9 are loaded.)

LOAD KEY x.   The "load Key *x*" command takes the following form:

LOAD file-num,KEY *x* [,dev-address]

where *x* is the number of a key function in the specified type 5 (BASIC KEYS) file. The following are valid instances of the "load KEY *x*" command:

```
LOAD 17,KEY9
```

```
READY        SAMPLE KEYS      ,001,000,        5    7 8 9   28129
```
Figure 8.12 Example of the "load KEY*x*" command. (Key function number 9 is loaded.)

LOAD 10,KEY2
LOAD 4,KEY9,E40

The specified key function is loaded from the specified file into the user work area. If a key function with the same number exists in the user work area, it is replaced with the key function loaded. Otherwise, the contents of the user work area are unaltered. Figure 8.12 gives an example of the use of the "load KEY *x*" command. When the key function is loaded, line position 0 of the display screen gives the number of the loaded key function. When a zero file number is specified, the definition of a key function is initiated, as covered in a subsequent section.

Keyboard Data Files

Through the use of a system command, a data file can be created that has a type 1 (data exchange) file type and can be accessed with the GET or MAT GET statements. Data can be entered through the use of the LOAD 0,DATA command and data entry is the same as with the DATA statement. Using this facility is more convenient than writing a short program to input values with an INPUT or MAT INPUT statement and then write them out to a file with a PUT or MAT PUT statement. After a keyboard generated data file is created, it can be saved as a type 1 tape file with the SAVE command.

Load Zero DATA Command. The "load zero DATA" command takes the following form:

LOAD 0,DATA

and is used to create a keyboard generated data file in the user work area. This form of the command puts the system in the data entry mode, which means that input is restricted to data values as outlined below.

Data Entry. The "load zero DATA" command automatically provides automatic statement numbering and the keyword DATA for each line. The beginning line number is 0010 and the increment is 10—the same default parameters that exist with the AUTO command. Data values are entered on each line separated by commas and character string values must be enclosed in quote marks, as shown in the following example:

0020 DATA 147,'PICKUP TRUCK',3749.95,4895.50,'FLINT','DK. BLUE'

After the EXECUTE key is pressed, the line is placed in the user work area and the computer responds by moving the contents of the display screen up by one

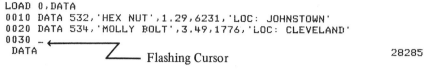

```
LOAD 0,DATA
0010 DATA 532,'HEX NUT',1,29,6231,'LOC: JOHNSTOWN'
0020 DATA 534,'MOLLY BOLT',3,49,1776,'LOC: CLEVELAND'
0030 _
DATA                          Flashing Cursor                    28285
```

Figure 8.13 Operation of the "load zero DATA" command.

line and by displaying the next statement number in sequence. Figure 8.13 demonstrates the data entry mode.

Exit from the Data Entry Mode. The only exit from the data entry mode to the normal BASIC mode is with the LOAD command or by pressing the restart switch. However, it is possible to initiate or to discontinue automatic statement numbering. Discontinuation of automatic statement numbering is performed in the same way as exiting from the AUTO mode—covered earlier. The computer continues to operate in the automatic mode until one of two events occurs:

1. A statement number other than the one displayed by the computer is entered. This can result from line editing.
2. A system command is entered.* This is accomplished by scrolling up until the input line is cleared, so that any form of input can be entered.

After "automatic" data entry has been discontinued, it can be reinstated with the AUTO command without losing previously entered data. It cannot be reinstated with the LOAD 0, DATA command without losing previously entered data, because the LOAD 0, DATA command automatically clears the user work area. However, additional DATA statements can be entered and statement editing can be performed even though automatic statement numbering has been discontinued.

Errors. A keying error will cause the display screen to flash and the keyboard to lock; the incorrect entry is in the input line—ready for editing. The flashing is stopped by pressing the ATTN key. After the correction is made, data entry is continued by pressing the EXECUTE key.

Storage. After construction of the data file has been completed, it can be saved on tape with the SAVE command. As the file is written to tape, the statement numbers and the DATA keywords are removed, so that the file logically exists as a continuous stream of values. This form is consistent with the requirements of the GET and MAT GET statements. The following command demonstrates how a keyboard generated data file might be saved:

SAVE 18

---

*The system commands that can be used in the data entry mode are restricted to those that do not explicitly control program execution. Thus, the only facilities that *cannot* be used are the RUN and GO commands, and the "Calc Result" key.

The mode of the user work area is DATA so the file type is implicitly specified as a type 1 (data exchange) file.

Loading. A keyboard generated file must be loaded with the "load data" command, as outlined previously. When the contents of the file are loaded, a statement number and the keyword DATA is placed before each line of the file, so that it may be edited in the user work area. However, it should be noted that the "load DATA" command places the computer in the data entry mode and BASIC statements cannot be executed.

Key Functions

A key function is a computer operation that is performed by holding down the CMD key and pressing one of the digits on the calculator pad. Key functions numbered 0 through 9 can be defined.

Definition. A key function is defined with the following form of the LOAD command:

LOAD 0,KEY*x*

where x is the number of the key function to be defined. Example:

LOAD 0,KEY 2

After pressing the EXECUTE key, a header statement of one of the following forms *must* be entered:

999*x* CMD system-command or calculator-statement
999*x* TXT 'Character string'
999*x* REM [comment]
999*x* NULL

where x is the number of the key function and the keywords CMD, TXT, REM, and NULL denote specific types of key functions.

Command Key Function. The command key function is denoted with the CMD keyword and specifies a system command or calculator statement that is to be executed immediately. The following statements give valid examples of this type of key function:

9994 CMD UTIL PRINT,DIR1
9998 CMD K*&INCM

In either case, the statement is executed immediately after holding down the CMD key and pressing the appropriate number key on the calculator pad. It is not necessary to press the EXECUTE key. In the latter example, which converts from inches to centimeters, the value to be converted must first be assigned to variable K with a previous calculator mode statement. Only one system command or calculator statement can be executed with a command key function.

Text Key Function. The text key function is denoted with the TXT keyword and specifies a string of characters that is to be inserted into the input line at the current cursor position. The following statements give valid examples of this type of key function:

9996 TXT 'PRINT USING'
9997 TXT 'ABC CORPORATION'
9998 TXT 'MARK,2,1,'

The character string enclosed in quote marks is entered into the input line immediately when the CMD key is held down and the appropriate number key from the calculator pad is pressed. It is not necessary to press the EXECUTE key.

BASIC Key Function. The BASIC key function is denoted with the REM keyword and specifies that a series of BASIC statements follows. The following statements give an example of this type of key function:

```
LOAD 0,KEY2
9992 REM CLEAR SCREEN
10 PRINT TAB(20),'(CLEAR SCREEN)'
20 FOR I=1 TO 12
30 PRINT
40 NEXT I
50 RETURN

READY                                              28005
```

The statements that comprise a BASIC key function are independent of other BASIC statements, except that variables with the same name occupy the same storage locations. The following example demonstrates this concept:

A=35   [Calculator mode statement]
LOAD 0,KEY6   [Definition of KEY6]
9996 REM
10 PRINT A
20 RETURN

Then, if the CMD key is held down and the number 6 key on the calculator pad is pressed, the value 35 is printed. The following rules apply to BASIC key functions:

1. The statements DATA, END, STOP, DEF, FNEND, READ, and MAT READ may not be used in a key function definition.
2. The last statement must be CHAIN or RETURN, (without an expression).
3. The statements in a BASIC key function definition may not reference a user-defined function.

```
LOAD 0,KEY7
9997 REM VERIFY PASSWORD AND CHAIN
10 PRINT 'ENTER PASSWORD'
20 FOR I=1 TO 5
30 INPUT A$
40 IF A$='ALPINE' GOTO 90
50 PRINT 'INCORRECT PASSWORD'
60 NEXT I
70 PRINT 'LIMIT EXCEEDED - ENTER GO END'
80 PAUSE
90 CHAIN 'E80',14
```

READY   28140

Figure 8.14 BASIC key function definition.

4. A BASIC key function may be referenced in a GOSUB statement with a statement of the form GOSUB 999*x*.

Figure 8.14 demonstrates a BASIC key function definition.

Null Key Function. The null key function is denoted with the NULL keyword and serves to delete the key functions with the specified number. The following statements, for example, delete key function number 4:

LOAD 0,KEY4
9994 NULL

After a key function has been deleted, an attempt to invoke it results in an error condition.

Key Function Editing. The statements in a BASIC key function (specified with the REM keyword) can be deleted with the DEL function by preceding the deletion statement with the number of the key function, as follows:

KEY7, 60 DEL 90
KEY8, 121 DEL

The first statement deletes statements numbered 60 through 90 in key function 7. The second statement deletes statement number 121 in key function 8. In a similar manner, a statement can be replaced or inserted by preceding the insertion with the number of the key function, as follows:

KEY3, 45 INPUT N$

This statement replaces or inserts the statement

45 INPUT N$

into key function 3. Header statements cannot be edited. In order to change a header statement, the key function must first be deleted entirely and then it may be redefined.

Form of the SAVE Command

The form of the SAVE command is:

$$
\text{SAVE file-num} \left[, \left\{ \begin{array}{l} \text{KEY}x \\ \text{KEYS} \\ \text{SOURCE} \end{array} \right\} \right] [, \text{dev-address}] \, [, \text{'file-ID'}]
$$

where:

file-num is an integer value specifying the number of the file in which the keys or user work area is to be stored.

KEYx specifies a key function, where x is a digit 0 through 9, is to be stored in the specified file.

KEYS specifies that all defined key functions are to be stored in the specified file.

SOURCE specifies that the BASIC program in the user work area is to be stored in its original form.*

dev-address is the address of the tape unit in which the tape cartridge has been inserted. E80 denotes the built-in tape unit and E40 denotes the auxiliary tape unit. The default address is E80.

file-ID is a character string of up to 17 characters enclosed in quote marks used to identify the file. The file-ID is listed in the file directory and can be referenced with an OPEN statement.

The following statement is a valid example of the SAVE command:

SAVE 12,SOURCE,E40,'JULY 76 TRNS FILE'

The SAVE command is complimentary to the LOAD command; a user work area or key function must be saved before it can be loaded.

Operation of the SAVE Command

The completion of the processing of a SAVE command is denoted by a READY message in line position zero of the display screen along with the following status information:

Number of contiguous 1,024 byte segments allocated to the file.
Number of contiguous 1,024 byte segments of unused storage in the file.

Figure 8.15 gives an example of a SAVE command and a corresponding LOAD command.

---

*When a BASIC user work area is stored as a type 4 (BASIC) file, the program is stored in an internal form.

```
SAVE 1,'FACTOR'
READY      016,015                                          27907
```
(A) SAVE Command
```
LOAD 1
READY      FACTOR           ,016,015,0010,0130             28089
```
(B) Corresponding LOAD Command

Figure 8.15   Example of a SAVE command and a corresponding LOAD command.

If the KEYx, KEYS, or SOURCE option is not specified in a SAVE command, the contents of the user work area are stored as either a BASIC program (type 4 file) or as a DATA file (type 1 file), depending on whether the computer is operating in the normal BASIC mode or the data entry mode.

Internal machine fixes (IMFs), if any, are not stored with the SAVE command. If an IMF is required for the execution of a particular program or system command, then the required IMF must be applied with the PATCH command before the program is loaded or the command is entered.

REFERENCE

IBM 5100 Portable Computer publication:
IBM 5100 BASIC Reference Manual, Form #SA 21-9217, IBM Corporation, Rochester, Minnesota, 1975.

PART III:
The APL Language

9 | APL ARITHMETIC AND COMPUTER OPERATIONS

The IBM 5100 Portable Computer is a full-function computer designed to perform complex as well as simple computations. Elementary computer functions are introduced in this chapter through the APL interactive mode. The implementation of complex computer procedures involves the development and execution of defined functions, the use of arrays, functions defined on arrays, and the use of a large set of primitive scalar functions extended to arrays on an element-by-element basis. APL is a powerful language and many computational procedures requiring several statements in other programming languages can be represented in APL with a single operator or statement. This chapter also covers operational procedures for using the computer.

9.1 INITIATING A COMPUTER SESSION

The 5100 Portable Computer is started by placing the power switch in the On position. Prior to doing this, it is a good idea, but not mandatory, to set the L32–64–R32 switch to the 64 position, and the BASIC/APL switch to APL—if appropriate. The DISPLAY REGISTERS/NORMAL switch should already be set to the NORMAL position since the internal registers are usually of interest only to service personnel. If the computer is turned on without the correct BASIC/APL setting, there is no harm in changing the setting and pushing restart before the warm-up process is complete.

Process Check

If the PROCESS CHECK light comes on during the warm-up period, machine operations are suspended and the RESTART switch must be pushed to get any action out of the computer. It is unlikely that a process check condition will be encountered during normal use of the computer and one may wonder whether the lights are functioning properly. (The lights may be tested by holding the RESTART switch in.) However, if the process check condition occurs repeatedly, then service is necessary.

Ready

After the warm-up process has been completed, the display screen will show a CLEAR WS message and a flashing cursor indented six spaces, as demonstrated in Figure 9.1. The message indicates that the workspace is clear.

The amount of available storage in the workspace can be displayed with the system variable ⎕WA, as demonstrated in Figure 9.2. As information is entered into the workspace, the amount of available storage is decreased.

The CLEAR WS message serves informational purposes only. It is not a command to the user. If this message does not appear in approximately 20–30 seconds* after power has been turned on or after the RESTART switch has been pushed, then a machine malfunction has occurred and the RESTART switch should be pushed. However, if the display screen is completely blank, the brightness control probably needs to be adjusted.

Figure 9.1   Contents of the display screen after the warm-up process has been completed.

---

*On the author's machine, initial warm-up takes 12.0 seconds and restart takes 11.4 seconds.

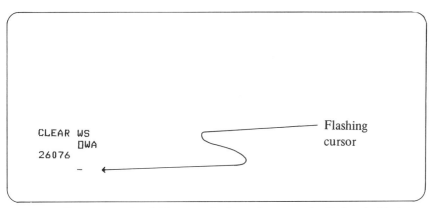

Figure 9.2   The amount of available storage in the workspace can be displayed with the system variable ☐WA. (Example is from a 32K machine with the clear workspace.)

Clearing the Workspace

The workspace can be cleared at any time by entering the)CLEAR system command, entered as follows:

$$)CLEAR$$

The operation of this command clears the workspace of all data values, variables, and defined functions, and the previous contents of the workspace are lost. If it is desired to retain the contents of a workspace, then the)SAVE command should be used to place the workspace on tape. The save command will be covered later.

The)CLEAR command does not involve or alter the contents of a magnetic tape cartridge.

Operation of the Computer in the APL Mode

It is customary to refer to the computer in the APL mode as the APL system or simply, the *system*. In general, the terms "computer" and "system" will be used interchangeably. From the user's point of view, the system operates in two modes: the execution mode and the definition mode. In the *execution mode*, the system responds immediately to the user's input by performing calculations or by taking the specified system action. In Figure 9.3, for example, the com-

```
        2+3x4
14
        )LOAD 16 POSTFIX
LOADED 1016 POSTFIX
```

Figure 9.3   APL statements entered and executed in the *execution mode*.

puter responds to the first line of input (i.e., $2+3\times4$) by carrying out the required computation and by displaying the result, which is 14. The computer responds to the second input line [i.e.,)LOAD 16 POSTFIX] by taking the requested action and by responding to the user with an appropriate message. *All computations*, regardless of whether they are trivial arithmetic, such as the example given, or an involved series of calculations, are initiated in the execution mode.

Programs are synthesized in APL through the *definition mode*, in which statements are not executed immediately, as in the execution mode, but are saved as part of a defined function. A defined function can be invoked from a statement entered when the system is in the execution mode, or it can be used in a statement being executed as part of another defined function. In other words, one defined function can reference one or more defined functions, including itself,* and this process can be extended to as many levels as necessary. Figure 9.4 gives an example of defined functions. The subject of defined functions will be covered in considerable detail in later chapters, and full comprehension of the sample functions in the figure should not be expected this early in the presentation of the APL language.

Hard Copy

As a user interacts with the system in either the execution or the definition mode, results are shown on the display screen, giving a history of previous computations. When a new line is displayed, the preceding lines are moved up one position. If the printer unit is attached and turned on, all input and output is automatically printed, in addition to being displayed. Automatic printing can be turned off with the following command:

)OUTSEL OFF

```
        ∇L←LITIN G
[1] L←3.785412×G
[2] ∇

        ∇G←GALIN L
[1] G←L÷3.785412
[2] ∇

        LITIN 2
7.5708
        GALIN 3
0.79252
```

Figure 9.4   A defined function LITIN that converts gallons to liters and a second defined function GALIN that converts liters to gallons. (The ∇ character denotes the definition mode.)

---

*A defined function that references itself is known as a *recursive function*.

If it is desired to print only the computer output and not the keyboard input, the following command should be entered:

)OUTSEL OUT

Finally, if it is desired to reinstate automatic printing, the following command should be entered:

)OUTSEL ALL

Independently of the)OUTSEL options, data can be printed through APL output facilities, covered in a later chapter.

Since information that is displayed on the display screen is printed automatically with the ALL option, the term "displaying" also refers implicitly to "printing." With regard to output, henceforth, only the term "display" is used, with the knowledge that it refers collectively to printing as well, when the appropriate option is set.

9.2 APL FUNDAMENTALS

After the CLEAR WS message is displayed, the flashing cursor is indented six character positions in the input line.* This is where the first character of keyboard input will be entered. The system is automatically in the execution mode and any statement entered will be executed immediately.

Two Plus Two

A statement to perform a simple calculation, such as $2+2$, is entered in the following manner:

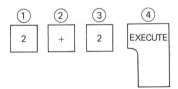

The computer responds as follows:

---

*Recall that an APL statement can be 128 characters long. It starts in line position one and can be continued to line position zero, as covered in chapter three.

The answer is printed starting in the first character position of the output line and the contents of the display screen are moved up one line. The input line, i.e., line positions 1 and 0, is blank and the cursor is again indented six character positions for the next entry. When it is desired to enter information into the computer, the appropriate keyboard characters are pressed to enter the characters into the input line. The EXECUTE key must then be pressed to indicate to the computer that the input line is complete and processing may begin. Remember that whenever the EXECUTE key is pressed, the contents of the input line are always entered—regardless of whether the characters were placed there by the user or through a scroll up or down operation.

Choice of Keyboard Characters

Numeric and arithmetic symbols can be entered from the typewriter-like keyboard or from the calculator pad and the characters placed in the input line are the same. Consider the following example that uses keys from the keyboard and the calculator pad interchangeably:

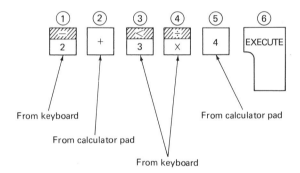

The computer responds in the following manner:

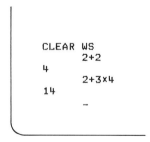

The preceding lines on the display screen are moved up appropriately, as shown above.

TABLE 9.1 REPRESENTATIVE SET OF PRIMITIVE SCALAR FUNCTIONS
USED IN ARITHMETIC CALCULATIONS.

Function	Function Symbol	Type	Number of Operands	Example	Result
Addition	+	Dyadic	2	2+3	5
Positive	+	Monadic	1	+9	9
Subtraction	−	Dyadic	2	6−2	4
Negative	−	Monadic	1	−9	⁻9
Multiplication	×	Dyadic	2	3×⁻5	⁻15
Division	÷	Dyadic	2	10÷4	2.5
Reciprocal	÷	Monadic	1	÷2	0.5
Exponentiation	*	Dyadic	2	3*2	9

Functions

The APL language includes an extensive assortment of arithmetic operations
and mathematical functions collectively termed *primitive functions* because
they are incorporated into the language and need not be defined by the user.
These primitive functions are further characterized as "primitive scalar functions" because they are defined on scalar values and are extended to arrays
on an element-by-element basis. Each primitive scalar function is denoted
by a special symbol, such as +, ×, ∧, or ⌊. Most function symbols have two
meanings, depending upon whether they are used as dyadic functions or as
monadic functions. When a function symbol is used with two operands, as in
134.61-100, it is classed as a dyadic function. When a function symbol is used
with one operand, as in ⁻97.83, it is classed as a monadic function. When a
dyadic function is written, the function symbol is always placed between the
operands, as in $x+y$. When a monadic function is written, the function symbol
is always placed before the operands, as in ÷r. Table 9.1 lists a representative

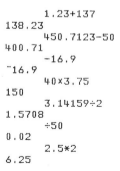

Figure 9.5 Examples of arithmetic calculations on scalar operands.

set of primitive functions normally used in arithmetic calculations, and Figure 9.5 gives several examples of arithmetic calculations in which the operands are restricted to numeric constants. Depending upon how it is used, an operand can be one of the following:

1. A constant,
2. A variable,
3. A subscripted array reference,
4. A function reference,
5. An expression, or
6. An expression in parentheses.

Operands are also discussed under "APL Expressions" in this chapter.

Numeric Constants

In APL, a numeric constant can be written as a whole number, a decimal number, or a number expressed in scaled representation.* The following constants, for example, are all numerically equivalent:

$$^-5$$
$$^-5.0$$
$$^-.5E1$$

as are the following constants in decimal and scaled representation, respectively:

$$.000123$$
$$1.23E^-4$$

All numeric values in APL are expressed to the base 10 for both input and output. Figure 9.6 gives several examples of numeric constants.

```
              5+5.0+.005E3
        15
              10.0×1.2
        12
              123÷1E3
        0.123
```

Figure 9.6 Examples of APL numeric constants entered as whole numbers, decimal numbers, and numbers in scaled representation.

Representation. The thirteen characters 0 1 2 3 4 5 6 7 8 9 . ‾ E are used to represent numeric data in APL. The digits are keyboard or calculator pad digits and the decimal point is used interchangeably with the period. The negative symbol should be distinguished from the minus symbol, which denotes subtraction. The number "minus seven," for example, is entered as ‾7. Close observation will detect that the negative symbol, found over the digit 2 in the APL key-

*The forms of numeric representation are covered in the second chapter.

```
            ¯2+4
      2
            ¯2-¯5
      3
            ¯5-¯2
     ¯3
          1000E¯2-5
      5
```

Figure 9.7 Examples of the use of the negative symbol. (The negative symbol is located over the 2 on the APL keyboard and should be distinguished from the minus sign located over the + sign.)

board, is raised to a superior position. The minus symbol, found over the + symbol, is never used in APL to represent an algebraic sign. The negative symbol is also used to denote a negative exponent in scaled representation. Figure 9.7 gives several examples of the use of the negative symbol.

Magnitude. The range of the magnitude* of numbers that can be stored in APL extends from approximately 5E¯79 to approximately 7E75.** Numbers with very large and very small magnitudes are normally entered in scaled representation, although a number can be entered in any form that is convenient to the user. The upper limit on the external representation of a numeric constant is 128 characters—the maximum size of an APL statement. In actual practice, however, the number of digits in a numeric constant is usually considerably less since the internal precision of a number is fixed in size. Numbers entered that are larger in absolute value than the maximum value are stored as the maximum value; numbers entered that are smaller in absolute value than the minimum value are stored as zero. Both cases are demonstrated in Figure 9.8.

```
            4E85
     7.237E75
            4E¯85
      0
```

Figure 9.8 Numbers entered that are larger or smaller in absolute value than the limits of APL are stored as the maximum value and zero, respectively.

Precision. The APL system maintains up to 16 digits of precision for all numbers and for all calculations. Precision is defined as the number of significant digits in a whole or decimal number, and the number of digits to the left of the E in scaled representation. A user may enter more than 16 digits but only the leftmost 16 of them are retained by the system. Several examples of the limits of precision are given in the next section.

---

*The magnitude of a number is its value without an algebraic sign—or in other words, its absolute value.

**The magnitude of the largest number that can be represented in APL is precisely 7.237005577332262E75; the magnitude of the smallest number that can be represented in APL is precisely 5.397604346934028E¯79.

```
        1÷9
0.11111
        5÷4
1.25
        1E3÷9
111.11
```

Figure 9.9 Display of numeric values. (With a clear workspace, the number of significant digits displayed is 5 and trailing zeros after the decimal point are suppressed.)

Accuracy and the Display of Numeric Values

Even though a number may be entered in any form, the computer chooses the output representation for numeric values according to a well-defined algorithm. In general, the 5 most significant digits for non-integer values are displayed and trailing zeros after the decimal point are suppressed. This case is demonstrated in Figure 9.9. With integer values, up to ten digits are displayed.

Printing Precision. The number of significant digits to be displayed is initially set to 5 with a clear workspace. The system variable $\Box$PP allows this value to be changed and can range from 1 to 16. Figure 9.10 gives an example of printing precision. Rounding always occurs in the rightmost digit displayed.

```
CLEAR WS
        □PP
5
        1.23456
1.2346
        □PP←6
        1.23456
1.23456
```

Figure 9.10 The number of significant digits is controlled by the system variable $\Box$PP. (Rounding always occurs in the rightmost significant digit.)

Integer Values. The number of significant digits displayed for integer values is approximately equal to 10, or the value of $\Box$PP, whichever is greater. When the value of system variable $\Box$PP is equal to 10 or less, the largest value that is printed in integer format is $2^{31}-1$, which is equal to 2147483647. Integer values are not restricted to those entered as integers and can result from some arithmetic calculations, as shown in Figure 9.11, which also demonstrates how the system variable $\Box$PP affects the display of integer values.

Fractional Values. A fractional value that is greater than or equal to $1E^-4$ is always printed as a decimal number with one leading zero—regardless of the input representation. Figure 9.12 gives several examples of the display of fractional values.

Scaled Representation. If a number is less than $1E^-4$, greater than or equal to $1EN$ (where N is the number of significant digits displayed—initially set to 5), or is an integer greater than $2^{31}-1$, then scaled representation is used. Otherwise, decimal form is used to display a value. With scaled representation, a number is always displayed as a value with a magnitude between 1 and 10 followed by a base-10 exponential multiplier, as demonstrated in Figure 9.13.

```
        )CLEAR
CLEAR  WS
        12340000+5678
12345678
        12345678×10
123456780
        100.341-.341
100
        L(2*31)-1
2147483647
        □PP←12
        2*36
68719476736
```

Figure 9.11 Integer values containing up to 10 digits are displayed in integer format. Larger values can be displayed in integer format by resetting the print precision. (The L function, known as the *floor function*, gives the largest integer not exceeding the value of the expression to its right.)

```
        2.5E⁻1+.5
0.75
        1E⁻4+1E⁻3
0.0011
        .00005+.00005
0.0001
        ÷3
0.33333
```

Figure 9.12 Fractional values less than or equal to 1E⁻4 are always displayed as a decimal number with one leading zero.

```
        3×10*6
3E6
        2*36
6.8719E10
        .0000000123×2
2.46E⁻8
        3×10*⁻6
3E⁻6
```

Figure 9.13 Display of numeric values in scaled representation.

Storage. When a numeric constant is entered into the APL system, the number of digits retained by the system may be less than the number of digits entered. However, the APL system usually retains more digits than are printed, which may be significant as far as tests of equality are concerned.

Names and Variables

Names, as introduced in chapter two, are used to identify variables, workspaces, functions, and statements. A variable may refer to a scalar value or an array of values. Data files are also assigned a file identification, but the lexical conventions that apply to names need not be observed when identifying files. This section is concerned primarily with variable names; function names, workspace names, and statement labels are covered when needed in the presentation of related material.

Naming Conventions. A name is a sequence of the letters A through Z, the digits 0 through 9, or the Δ character. A letter may additionally be underscored for clarity or to indicate a data value of special interest. The first character of a name must not be a digit and the beginning sequences SΔ and TΔ are not permitted. Operators, punctuation characters, and spaces delimit names so that the use of an embedded space specifies a different construct than the name intended. The maximum length of a variable, function name, or statement label is 77 characters; the maximum length of a workspace name and a file identification is 17 characters. The following list gives several examples of valid and invalid names:

Valid Names	*Invalid Names*
AB12	1B18
X	M_N
M44	SΔABC
YPLUSΔY	TΔX2
PRIME	BA.CD
XTΔT	2E11
ΔZ	X,Y
A	3A
TOTALOFRESIDUALVALUES	)QRS
E4	E4.1

Although lengthy variable names can be used in APL, their use requires extra space in the active workshop. The optimum size for variable names is three characters or less. This is discussed further.

Simple Variables. A name assigned to a scalar value is known as a simple variable, a scalar variable, or simply a *variable*. More specifically, a variable has two components: a name and a value. The correspondence between the name and the value is established through a symbol table stored in the active workspace. The statement label, discussed later, is a scalar variable to which is assigned the number of a statement in a defined function.

Array Variables. A name assigned to an array of values is known as an array variable or simply an *array*. There are no restrictions on array names or on the number of dimensions that an array may possess.

Workspace Names. A workspace name is assigned to a workspace when it is stored on tape with the)SAVE or)CONTINUE command. The workspace name is used for identifying a file on tape and must be used with a subsequent)LOAD command that loads the saved workspace back into the main storage unit.

Using a Variable

Before a variable can be used, it must be assigned a value through a replacement operation or through an input statement. In APL, a variable name is not restricted to a given type (i.e., a scalar variable, an array variable, a statement label, etc.) and the context in which a variable name is used may change during the execution of a program. Variable names can be assigned and used dynamically— at one point in a function a given name can be used as a scalar variable and, later in the same function, it can be used as an array variable name.

Specification. The specification* function, denoted by a left-pointing arrow, is used to assign a value to a variable. For example, the statement

$$CHI \leftarrow 13.847$$

assigns a value of 13.847 to the variable CHI. Both the name CHI and the value 13.847 are stored in the active workspace. In this case, CHI is a scalar variable because a single value is assigned to it.

Operands. Once a variable has been assigned a value, it may be used as an operand in an expression. In fact, a variable can be used in any context in which a constant can be used. Figure 9.14 gives some examples of specification and the use of specified variables. In the first statement in Figure 9.14, a value of 2 is assigned to variable X. In the second statement, a value of 1 is added to X and the value of the expression is displayed. In the third and fourth statements, the values 4 and 3 are assigned to variables H and B, respectively. In the final statement, the expression B×H is evaluated and its value is assigned to AREA.

```
                    X←2
                    X+1
         3
                    H←4
                    B←3
                    AREA←B×H
```

Figure 9.14 A variable is assigned a value with the specification function denoted by the left-pointing arrow.

Respecification. After a variable had been assigned a value, it may be re-specified without difficulty through the execution of an APL statement in which it is placed directly to the left of the specification function. Figure 9.15 demon-strates respecification. When the value of a variable is replaced, the previously assigned value is lost. In Figure 9.15, the variable RAD is assigned a value of 1 and AREA is computed as 3.1416 in the first series of calculations. In the second set of statements, RAD is respecified as 3 and AREA is computed as 28.274. The first value for RAD, which was 1, was replaced by the second value, which was 3. The variable AREA is also respecified in an analogous manner. If it were desired to retain the first value assigned to RAD, then its value would

---

*In other programming languages, the specification function may be referred to as the *replacement operation* and the statement as a whole is known as the *assignment statement.*

```
        RAD←1
        AREA←3.14159×RAD*2
        AREA
3.1416
        RAD←3
        AREA←3.14159×RAD*2
        AREA
28.274
        C←1
        C←C+2
        C
3
        C←C-1
        C
2
```

Figure 9.15 The value of a variable may be specified and the same variable may appear to the right and to the left of the specification symbol.

have to be assigned to a temporary variable, as follows:

$$TEMPRAD \leftarrow RAD$$

Scalar variables are frequently used to keep a count of the number of occurrences of a particular event. Each time the event occurs, the counter is increased or decreased by a fixed amount. (This case is also shown in Figure 9.15.) The following skeleton of a series of statements demonstrates a situation in which a variable QT is initially assigned a limit value, specified elsewhere; each time a particular event occurs, the value of QT is decreased by one and the value of an index I is increased by one:

$$QT \leftarrow LIMIT$$
$$I \leftarrow 0$$
.

.

.

$$I \leftarrow I + 1$$
.

.

.

$$QT \leftarrow QT - 1$$

The statements I←I+1 and QT←QT-1 exhibit the case in which the same variable appears on either side of the specification symbol. In each case, the calculation is executed and then the respecification is performed.

Undefined Variables. A variable must be assigned a value before any functions or computer operations that use it can be executed. Thus, no variables are pre-initialized—such as to zero as they may be in other programming languages.

```
        CLEAR WS
              A+1
        VALUE ERROR
              A+1
              ^
              A←100
              A+1
        101
              )ERASE A
              A+1
        VALUE ERROR
              A+1
              ^
              )ERASE A
        NOT FOUND: A
```

Figure 9.16   A variable must be defined before it can be used in an APL statement.

Figure 9.16 demonstrates an attempt to reference an undefined variable. The)ERASE command used in Figure 9.16 deletes a variable or a defined function from the active workspace.

Display. Knowledge of the criteria used by the APL system for deciding whether or not to display a result is needed for writing effective APL statements. Recall in Figure 9.16 that the value of the expression A+1 was displayed, whereas in the specification statement A←100 nothing was displayed. After a calculation or a series of calculations, two possibilities exist for displaying or storing the result:

1. *The specification function is specified as the last function to be executed.* The computed result is assigned to the indicated variable and no value is displayed.
2. *The specification function is not specified as the last function to be performed.* The system assumes that the user would like to see the result— otherwise, why do the calculations?—and displays it on the display screen.

The latter statement implies that the specification function need not be the last statement performed in an APL statement. This is indeed the case, and specification is regarded like any other dyadic function. This topic will be discussed further with respect to APL expressions.

APL Expressions

In the APL language, complex expressions denoting a series of calculations can be specified in one statement. In order to avoid problems relating to the structure of expressions and to the order in which functions are executed, most examples given thus far have included only one or two operations, even though the topic was introduced in chapter two. Functions were classed as being monadic or dyadic; this section goes into more detail on the subject in preparation for the study of compound expressions and primitive scalar functions.

Monadic vs. Dyadic. The structure of a function has two general forms, appropriately termed monadic and dyadic. If m denotes a monadic function and d denotes a dyadic function, then the structure of the two forms is depicted as follows:

Monadic Function	Dyadic Function
m*R*	*L*d*R*

where L represents a constant, a variable, or an expression in parentheses, and R represents a constant, a variable, or the value of an expression. These notions are further introduced through examples. The operational distinction between a monadic and a dyadic function is obvious. Given a function symbol, such as minus, which can represent either a monadic or dyadic function, the monadic form is assumed if the symbol directly to its left is another function symbol. Otherwise, the function symbol is interpreted as a dyadic function. For example, consider the following expressions:

$$A+-B \qquad (1)$$
$$A-B \qquad (2)$$

In expression (1), the minus symbol denotes a monadic function since the symbol to its immediate left is another function symbol. In expression (2), the minus symbol denotes a dyadic function, because it is preceded by an operand. (In this example, expressions (1) and (2) are mathematically equivalent.) The following examples give valid and invalid expressions:

Valid	Invalid	Reason
A+B	X¯5	Illegal use of negative symbol.
(A+1)×2	(¯10+N)T	Implied multiplication not allowed.
-Z*W	¯X*Y	Illegal use of negative symbol.

The APL language includes a multiplicity of functions and corresponding function symbols and most of them have monadic and dyadic interpretations.

Order of Execution. Because APL includes a multiplicity of functions, it would be cumbersome to establish a hierarchy among the operations and then to use the established hierarchy in an effective manner. Therefore, the APL system uses no precedence relations and executes all expressions in a strict right-to-left order. Thus, any function assumes as its rightmost operand the value of the entire expression to its right. The expression 2×3+4, for example, evaluates to 14 and the expression 2*4-1 evaluates to 8, remembering that the * symbol denotes exponentiation in APL. The right-to-left rule is demonstrated in Figure 9.17 and Figure 9.18 gives some typical examples.

Imbedded Specification. The following statement is included in Figure 9.18:

$$A \times B \leftarrow B \div 2$$

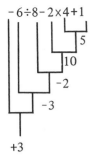

$$-6 \div 8 - 2 \times 4 + 1$$

Order of Execution
First
Second
Third
Fourth
Fifth

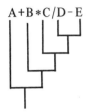

$$A + B * C / D - E$$

Order of Execution
First
Second
Third
Fourth

Figure 9.17 In APL, functions are executed from right-to-left. The rightmost argument to a function is the value of the expression to its right.

```
              A←11
              B←6
              100÷B-A
       ¯20
              C←2
              A-B-C
        7
              8÷4÷2
        4
              2*3*2
      512
              2*3×2
       64
              A×B←B÷2
       33
              B
        3
              +C←-A-B
       ¯8
```

Figure 9.18 Examples of the right-to-left rule for the execution of APL expressions.

where the variables A and B have the values 11 and 6, respectively. Recall that specification is an ordinary dyadic function that assigns the value of the expression to the right of the arrow to the variable to its left. Thus, in the execution of the above statement, B is divided by 2 and then respecified as the quotient; the result of 3 is then multiplied by A, which is 11, and the product is displayed.

Special Cases [to be Aware Of. The fact that expressions are read and entered from left to right gives rise to some simple errors. The expression

$$A-B-C$$

included in Figure 9.18, which is effectively 11-6-2, gives a correct result of 7, whereas using a left-to-right convention for functions of equal precedence, the result is 3. In general, repeated subtraction is the difference of the sum of alternating arguments—for example:*

$$A-B-C-D \leftrightarrow (A+C)-(B+D)$$

and repeated division is the quotient of the product of alternating arguments—that is:

$$A \div B \div C \div D \leftrightarrow (A \times C) \div (B \times D)$$

As experience is gained with the APL language, using the right-to-left rule becomes a definite convenience because it eliminates the necessity of determining which operation comes first.

Parentheses. Parentheses are used for grouping and can be used to deviate from the right-to-left rule for execution. Expressions within parentheses are evaluated before the expressions of which they are a part and the use of parentheses can be nested to as many levels as is necessary. Table 9.2 lists examples of correct APL expressions, and Figure 9.19 gives a computer display of other examples.

TABLE 9.2 EXAMPLES OF APL EXPRESSIONS.

Mathematical Notation	APL Expression	Alternate Form of APL Expression
$a \cdot b$	$A \times B$	
$a \cdot (^- b)$	$A \times (-B)$	$A \times -B$
$\dfrac{a+b}{c+d}$	$(A+B) \div (C+D)$	$(A+B) \div C+D$
a^{i-1}	$A * (I-1)$	$A * I-1$
$a \cdot y - 1$	$(A \times Y)-1$	$^-1+A \times Y$
$a+b \cdot y+c \cdot y^2$ or	$A+(B \times Y)+(C \times Y * 2)$	$A+(B \times Y)+C \times Y * 2$
$a+y(b+c \cdot y)$	$A+Y \times (B+(C \times Y))$	$A+Y \times B+C \times Y$
$\dfrac{x}{1-\dfrac{x}{1-x}}$	$X \div 1 - X \div (1-X))$	$X \div 1 - X \div 1 - X$
$\left(1+\dfrac{1}{n}\right)^n$	$(1+1 \div N) * N$	$(1+ \div N) * N$

*The symbol $\leftrightarrow$ should be read "is equivalent to."

```
        (2×3)+4
10
        A←5+B←2×3
        A,B
11  6
        C←2
        (A-B)-C
3
        (99÷A)+B
15
        Z←(2×X)+Y←1+X←-W← ̄2
        X,Y,Z,W
2  3  7   ̄2
        (X+Y)×Z+W
25
        (3×X*2)+(2×X)+1
17
```

Figure 9.19   Parentheses can be used for grouping in APL expressions.

Multiple Specification.   In several of the examples, more than one specification symbol was included in a single statement. This is termed *multiple specification*, which also adheres to the right-to-left rule. Extreme care should be
exercised when using multiple specification, especially in cases where a specified
variable is also a constituent part of an expression. Figure 9.20 contains three
illustrative examples. In the first case, the specification in parentheses is executed
first so that the expression is computed as 3×3 and B assumes a value of 9. In
the second case, the monadic function $- A$ is executed prior to the respecification of A so that the expression is computed as $3 \times - 2$ and B assumes a value of
 ̄6. In the third case, the dyadic function $5 + A$ is executed prior to the respecification of A so that the expression is computed as $3 \times 5 + 2$ and B assumes a value
of 21. In general, it is best to avoid expressions of this type.

```
            A←2
            B←(A←3)×A
            B
    9
            A←2
            B←(A←3)×-A
            B
    ̄6
            A←2
            B←(A←3)×5+A
            B
    21
```

Figure 9.20   Multiple specification (extreme care should be taken when using a variable that
has been specified in the same statement).

Error Detection and Specification.   The execution of a statement containing
an error is terminated as soon as the error is detected during right-to-left execution and any partial result is lost. If the statement in error contains an imbedded

```
            A←B←10
            B←5÷A←0
      DOMAIN ERROR
            B←5÷A←0
               ^
            A
   0
            B
   10
```

Figure 9.21 Error in a statement containing an imbedded specification (specification to the right of the carat is completed).

specification, then any specification to the right of the error (denoted by a carat) will have been completed before the error is detected. Figure 9.21 gives an example of an error situation of this type.

9.3 ERRORS

It is just as easy to correct an error as it is to make one. An error detected before the EXECUTE key is pressed can be corrected by character replacement, deletion, or insertion. An error that is not detected before the EXECUTE key is pressed may or may not be recognized by the computer. If the error results in an incorrect syntactical form, then it will be recognized. Otherwise, the user's intentions may not be specified properly, resulting in invalid computational results. In the latter case, the user would have to analyze the input to identify the source of error.

Syntactical Errors

A syntactical error occurs when an incorrect or unrecognizable sequence of characters is entered. For example, suppose that it were necessary to evaluate the expression A+(C−D)× E but that the rightmost parenthesis was omitted when the EXECUTE key was pressed. The unbalanced parenthesis is a syntax error, so the system responds by typing the message SYNTAX ERROR, the incorrect statement, and a carat denoting the cause of the error as follows:

The input line is clear and the flashing cursor denotes that the system is ready to receive another input line. When a syntax error occurs, as mentioned previously under "Error detection and specification," all computations to the right of the point of error are lost but specification functions to the right of the point of error will have been completed.

The error condition can be resolved in either of two ways. The most straightforward thing to do is to re-enter the APL statement and press the EXECUTE key. The second action that can be taken is to scroll down until the original statement is in the input line and then edit the statement using the methods given in the following paragraphs. It is important that the original statement be edited and not the copied statement, for the reason implied by the following script:

```
         A+(C-DxE
   SYNTAX ERROR
         A+(C-D)xE
           ^
   SYNTAX ERROR
         A+(C-D)xE^
                  ^
```

The problem emanates from the fact that the carat, which is also a logical "and" symbol in APL is also in the input line, remembering that it includes line positions 0 and 1. Spaces are ignored between function symbols and arguments so that the carat (∧) is logically placed after the E—hence the error. If the original statement had been used for editing, then the second error condition would not have occurred.

Keying Errors

An error in the input line can be corrected prior to pressing the EXECUTE key through one of several editing operations that are implemented as special functions on the 5100 Portable Computer. These functions involve the use of gray special function keys and, in some cases, the command key (CMD).

Scroll Up. When the input line contains errors and the best course of action is to start over, a simple method of clearing the input line is to press the scroll up key once or twice, depending upon whether line position 1 or line positions 1 and 0 of the display screen contain information. This operation clears the input line and the correct line can then be entered. This method is demonstrated in the following example:

```
         A+(C-DxE
         A+(C-D)xE
   10
```

The disadvantage of this method is that it fills the display screen with unnecessary information that would be undesirable in the event that the contents of the display screen were to be "copied to" the printer. If the automatic printing option were on [i.e., the) OUTSEL ALL command], then only information that is actually entered with the EXECUTE key is printed, as well as system output.

Attention. Another method of correcting the contents of the input line is to press the backspace key until the cursor is positioned below the error and then press the ATTN key. All characters to the right and including the cursor position in the input line, which include line positions 1 and 0, are deleted and the remainder of the line can then be retyped. This method is conceptualized as follows:

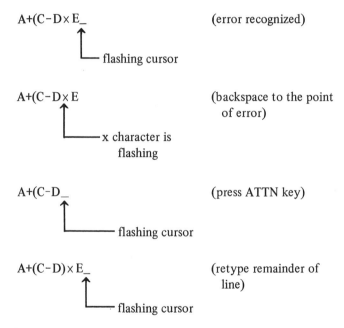

A+(C-D×E_   (error recognized)

⌐ flashing cursor

A+(C-D×E   (backspace to the point
                                    of error)

x character is
flashing

A+(C-D_   (press ATTN key)

flashing cursor

A+(C-D)×E_   (retype remainder of
                                    line)

flashing cursor

Another frequent error that is easily resolved with the attention key occurs when a system command is entered with a command key but the wrong key is pressed. In this case, several characters are entered into the input line. Suppose, for example, that a user wanted to enter the) SAVE command by holding down the CMD key and pressing the $\bar{2}$ key, but pressed the key to the right of it so that) CONTINUE were entered into the input line instead of) SAVE. One of the simplest actions to take here is to backspace until the) in) CONTINUE is flashing and press the ATTN key. The input line is now blank and the correct command can be entered.

Replace a Character. A character can be replaced in the input line by forward or backward spacing* until the incorrect character is flashing. The incorrect character can then be replaced by keying the correct character over the incorrect character. In the event that the keying action has created a composite character,** a space character must be entered to clear the character position, followed by a backspace and the correct character. After an editing operation, the cursor or flashing character may be in the middle of a line. This does not matter, as the cursor character is *not* entered into the computer when the EXECUTE key is pressed.

Delete a Character. A character in the input line can be deleted by positioning the cursor by forward or backward spacing until the character to be deleted is flashing. The character is deleted by holding the CMD key down and pressing the backspace key. The flashing character is deleted, and the characters to the right are shifted left, closing up the space created by the deletion. Assume, for example, that A+(C−−D)×E was entered instead of A+(C−D)×E, as follows:

The cursor is moved to the character to be deleted, i.e.,

```
A+(C--D)×E                    – sign is
        ↑                     flashing
```

The CMD key is held down and the backspace key is pressed, and the minus sign is deleted as follows:

```
A+(C-D)×E                     the D is
        ↑                     flashing
```

*Remember, when forward or backward spacing, use the → and ← keys, respectively. Do not use the space key, as it always inserts a space character when pressed.

**A *composite character* is an APL symbol formed by typing one symbol, backspacing, and then typing another symbol. For example, the character φ is formed by typing o, followed by ← , followed by |.

The EXECUTE key is pressed and the expression is evaluated as follows:

The procedure for deleting a character from the input line can be applied repetitively to delete successive characters.

Insert a Character.   Characters can be inserted into the input line by moving all characters located to the right of the desired position as many places as necessary to the right. To insert one or more characters, the cursor is moved, by forward or backward spacing, to the leftmost character that is to be moved, so that the character is flashing or, in the case of a blank position, the cursor is flashing. Then, by holding the CMD key down and pressing the forward space key, the flashing character and all characters to the right of it are moved one position to the right. However, the flashing cursor does not move and its position denotes the place where a character can be inserted.   As an example, consider the previous case in which a right parenthesis was omitted as follows:

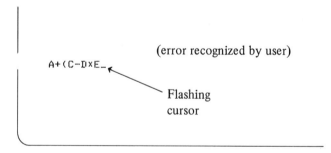

The keying error is corrected through character insertion. First, the cursor is positioned as follows:

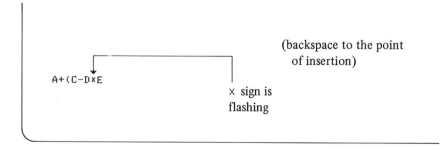

Next, the CMD key is held down and the forward space key is pressed once:

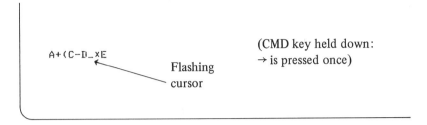

The needed character can then be inserted as follows:

The EXECUTE key is pressed and the expression is evaluated as follows:

The above procedure for inserting a character into the input line can be applied repetitively to insert several characters. Normally, the number of needed spaces is inserted by holding the CMD key down and pressing the forward space key the needed number of times. The flashing cursor will be positioned at the leftmost space and the insertion can simply be keyed into the input line.

An Important Note on Editing

The editing facilities introduced here apply to all keyboard input so the APL statements and data can be edited in a similar manner—prior to pressing the EXECUTE key. Once the EXECUTE key has been pressed, however, each form of entry is processed in a characteristic manner, relating to the type of input. This topic will be covered in detail as it becomes appropriate.

9.4 GENERAL FACILITIES AND APPLICATIONS

Thus far, the characteristics of the APL language and facilities for using the computer have been introduced, but most of the mathematical functions—built into APL—have not been covered. These mathematical functions, referred to as primitive scalar functions, will be covered completely in chapter ten. This chapter covers a few functions commonly used in everyday calculations and shows some typical applications that utilize them.

Elementary Mathematical Functions

The APL language does not include special internal constants or functions that are not formally defined into the language. Any facility available to the user is provided as a standard APL function.

Roots. The root of a value, such as the square or cube root, is available through the exponential function in APL. The square root of a variable x is commonly represented in mathematics as $\sqrt{x}$ or $x^{1/2}$. Similarly, the cube root is written $\sqrt[3]{x}$ or $x^{1/3}$. In APL, the square root of X is specified as X*.5 or alternately as X*1÷2 (obviously, the first form is preferred), and the cube root of X is specified as X*1÷3. In general, the Nth root of X is specified as X*1÷N.

Pi. The mathematical constant π is provided through the "Pi times" function in APL. "Pi times" is a monadic function that uses the circle symbol ○ found over the letter O on the APL keyboard. The expression "Pi times Y," therefore, is specified as ○Y.

Mathematical Constant e. The monadic form of the exponential symbol * is used to raise the mathematical constant e to a given power. Thus the expression e^P is specified in APL as *P.

Radians. Most trigonometric functions utilize an argument in radians, where π radians is equal to 180 degrees. Thus, one radian is equivalent to $\dfrac{180}{\pi}$ or 57.27577951308232, computed in APL as follows:

```
      □PP←16
      180÷○1
57.29577951308232
```

If D represents degrees and R represents radians, the forumula to convert degrees to radians is given as follows:

$$R = \frac{D \cdot \pi}{180}$$

The expression $\dfrac{D \cdot \pi}{180}$ is specified in APL as ○D÷180.

Trigonometric Functions. The dyadic form of the circle symbol ○ is used to compute trigonometric functions. The form of a trigonometric function is:

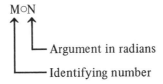

The left argument identifies the trigonometric function to be computed, and the following list gives the most commonly used functions:

$$\text{sin } X:\quad 1 \circ X$$
$$\text{cos } X:\quad 2 \circ X$$
$$\text{tan } X:\quad 3 \circ X$$

For example, the trigonometric sine of 30 degrees would be specified as:

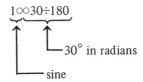

Obviously, no one would write the above expression in the above form and would enter 1○○÷6. Other trigonometric functions are covered in chapter ten. Examples of the use of elementary mathematical functions are given in Figure 9.22.

Applications

All applications of the 5100 Portable Computer do not require that an APL function be written—although most applications do involve function develop-

```
            1296*.5
      36
            (5*2)*.5
      5
            27*1÷3
      3
            o1
      3.1416
            *1
      2.7183
            100÷6
      0.5
            300÷4
      1
```

Figure 9.22 Examples of the use of elementary mathematical functions in the APL language.

ment. This section gives several simple applications that demonstrate how APL can be used in the execution mode without the use of defined functions.

Distance Between Two Points. The distance *d* between two points (x_1, y_1) and (x_2, y_2) is computed as:

$$d = \sqrt{(x_1 - x_2)^2 + (y_1 - y_2)^2}$$

Figure 9.23 shows calculations for the distance between points (2,4) and (5,8).

```
D←(((2-5)*2)+(4-8)*2)*.5
D
```
```
        5
```

Figure 9.23   APL execution mode example: distance between points (2, 4) and (5, 8).

Area of a Scalene Triangle. The area of a scalene triangle with sides *a*, *b*, and *c* is computed as:

$$\text{Area} = \sqrt{s(s-a)\,(s-b)\,(s-c)}$$

where

$$s = \frac{a+b+c}{2}$$

Figure 9.24 shows calculations for the area of the triangle with sides of 5, 8, and 10.

```
S←(5+8+10)÷2
A←(S×(S-5)×(S-8)×S-10)*.5
A
```
```
     19.81
```

Figure 9.24   APL execution mode example: area of a scalene triangle with sides 5, 8, and 10.

Stopping Distance. The stopping distance of an automobile is a function of reaction time and braking distance. The stopping distance (in feet) is computed as:

Stopping distance = Reaction distance+Braking distance

where

Reaction distance = 1.1 times miles per hour

and

Braking distance = miles per hour squared divided by 20

Figure 9.25 calculates the stopping distance in feet for an automobile traveling at the rate of 50 miles per hour.

```
D1←1.1×50
D2←(50*2)+20
D1+D2
```
    180

Figure 9.25   APL execution mode example: stopping distance in feet of an automobile traveling 50 miles per hour.

Volume of a Cylinder.   The volume of a cylinder with radius r and length l is computed as:

$$v = \pi r^2 l$$

Figure 9.26 calculates the volume of a cylindrical can with a radius of 3 feet and a height of 4 feet.

```
        o4×3*2
```
    113.1

Figure 9.26   APL execution mode example: volume of a cylinder with a radius of 3 feet and a length of 4 feet.

Factorial.   Stirling's approximation to the factorial function is given as follows:

$$n! = \sqrt{2\pi n}\, n^n e^{-n}$$

Figure 9.27 calculates the approximate value of 10 factorial.   The true value of 10! is 3628800.

```
        N←10
        F←((o2×N)*.5)×(N*N)×*-N
        F
3.5987E6
        □PP←7
        F
3598696
```

Figure 9.27   APL execution mode example: Stirling's approximation to the factorial function.

Value of Investment.   The future value of an investment of p dollars at r percent for n years compounded t times yearly is given as:

$$A = p\left(1+\frac{r}{t}\right)^{nt}$$

Figure 9.28 calculates the future value of 1000 dollars for 10 years at 7.25 percent compounded daily.

```
P←1000
R←7.25÷100
N←10
T←365
A←P×(1+R÷T)*N×T
A
2064.6
⎕PP←6
A
2064.58
```

Figure 9.28 APL execution mode example: future value of an investment of 1000 dollars for 10 years at 7.25 percent compounded daily.

Monthly payment. The monthly payment on a loan of *p* dollars for *t* years at *r* percent yearly interest is computed as:

$$M = \frac{p \times \dfrac{r}{12}}{1 - \left(1 + \dfrac{r}{12}\right)^{-12t}}$$

Figure 9.29 calculates the monthly payment on a loan of $50,000 at 9% yearly interest for 30 years.

```
P←50000
R←9÷100
T←30
M←(P×R÷12)÷1-(1+R÷12)*-12×T
M
402.31
```

Figure 9.29 APL execution mode example: monthly payment on a loan of $50,000 at 9% yearly interest for 30 years.

REFERENCES

Katzan, H., *APL Programming and Computer Techniques,* Van Nostrand Reinhold Company, New York, 1970.
IBM 5100 Portable Computer Publications:
  a. *IBM 5100 APL Introduction*, Form #SA21-9212
  b. *IBM 5100 APL Reference Manual*, Form #SA21-9123
IBM Corporation, Rochester, Minnesota, 1975.

APL PROGRAMMING I:

Primitive Scalar Functions, Vectors and Vector Functions

This chapter covers three major topics that are fundamental to APL programming: primitive scalar functions, vectors, and vector functions. In APL, operands are not restricted to scalars and vectors, but may additionally include *n*-dimensional arrays, referred to here as *matrices*. Matrices are covered in a later chapter in line with the philosophy that a person need only read far enough in the book to solve problems of particular interest. APL facilities also include the use of character data, which is covered in this chapter. Several topics relevant to using APL effectively are also summarized in this chapter for the convenience of the reader.

10.1 APL CONVENTIONS AND OPERATIONAL TECHNIQUES

The power of the APL system is not only a result of the language, but also of the special keyboard and the manner in which the system operates in response to statements and commands. Although the APL functions would indeed be useful without the special keyboard and the APL system, the various constituents collectively permit APL to be a computing facility that combines the convenience of a desk calculator with the power and flexibility of an automatic computer.

The APL Typeface and Keyboard Arrangement

The APL typeface and keyboard arrangement is given in Figure 10.1. The letters are capitalized and are included, along with the digits and most punctuation

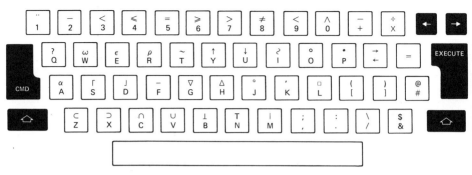

Figure 10.1   APL typeface and keyboard arrangement.

TABLE 10.1   APL Symbols for some Frequently Confused Characters

Digit	Letter	Function Symbol
0	O	◯ (circle symbol)
1	I	| (vertical stroke)
2	Z	

Special attention:

‾ (negative symbol found over the 2)

_ (underline symbol found over the F)

– (minus symbol found over the + sign)

characters, as lower-case keyboard characters. Table 10.1 gives APL symbols for some characters that are frequently confused in other programming systems. The special symbols of the APL language are primarily included as upper-case characters and generally have some apparent relationship to their alphabetic or numeric correspondents. For example, ω is over W, ϵ over E, ρ (rho) over R, $*$ (for power) over P, ◯ (circle symbol over O, α over A, $\lceil$ (for ceiling over S, ' (for Kwote) over K, ? (for question) over Q, $\sim$ (tilde) over T, and ι (iota) over I. The additive functions ($+$ and $-$) are on the same key as are the multiplicative functions ($\times$ and $\div$). Lastly, the colon (:) is over the period (.), the semicolon (;) is over the comma (,), the reverse solidus ($\backslash$) is over the solidus ($/$), and the parentheses are over the brackets. The meanings of the various function symbols will become apparent as the respective functions are introduced.

Discourse with the APL System

The keyboard/display unit serves as an input device or an output device, depending upon whether it is the user's turn to enter information or the computer's turn to display information. If the cursor is flashing, the user may enter a statement. When the user has finished typing an input line, the EXECUTE key is pressed so that the computer knows that it is time to process the line. The display unit is driven by the computer which maintains a buffer, in the main storage unit, containing a byte position for each character displayed. Thus, for example, when the user enters a character, the computer reads the character pressed—which is one step—and displays it in the appropriate character position—which is another step, and then moves the cursor to the next position. All of this happens so fast that the user is given the illusion that each character typed is displayed automatically. As far as the user is concerned this is true, but the computer is doing a lot of work under the cover to support the interactive mode of operation. Therefore, when the EXECUTE key is pressed, the computer automatically goes to the buffer for the input line and begins processing.

Internal to the computer, the *scroll up* and *scroll down* operations simply move information in the character buffer. This is precisely the reason that information entered into the input line through the keyboard or by a scroll down operation can be interpreted in exactly the same way by the computer.

Three events take place when the EXECUTE key is pressed:

1. The computer recognizes that the statement has been completed and can initiate processing it.
2. The display screen is blank.
3. The IN PROCESS light is turned on.

In many cases, the above events do not appear to take place because the computer operates very quickly. When the computer is processing one statement, additional statements cannot be entered, because the computer is simply not ready to accept another statement. When the required calculations have been completed, the computer responds by displaying the result (if any) beginning in the left-hand margin. When the display is complete, the contents of the display screen are moved up one position and the cursor is indented six spaces and begins to flash. The computer is then ready to accept another statement.

It is important to remember when reading the display screen or printed output that computer output always begins in the left-hand margin and that user input is indented six spaces. However, the entire input line may be used for input. The user may backspace the cursor to the left-hand margin prior to entering a statement and the result will be exactly the same as when no backspacing is performed.

Interrupting the Computer

In this and later chapters, procedures for defining functions and for constructing sophisticated statements using structured arguments—such as vectors, matrices, and higher-dimensional arrays—are given. Through these facilities,

```
          A←((\1000)*2)*.5
INTERRUPT
          A←((\1000)*2)*0.5
          ∧
```

Figure 10.2 When the ATTN key is pressed twice during the execution of a statement, execution stops as soon as possible; an INTERRUPT message and the statement are displayed and the caret (∧) denotes where the execution of the statement was interrupted. (When the ATTN key is pressed once, execution is interrupted at the statement currently being processed.)

lengthy series of computations can be specified. In other situations, the computer may initiate the display of an obvious error message or several output lines. In any case, it may be desirable or necessary to interrupt what the computer is doing. The processing of the computer can be interrupted at any time by pressing the attention (ATTN) key.

When the ATTN key is pressed during the execution of an expression or a user-defined function, execution stops at the end of the statement currently being processed. All output is terminated and the contents of the display screen are moved up until the input line is clear. The cursor is indented six spaces and begins to flash, indicating that the user may enter another statement.

When the ATTN key is pressed twice during the execution of a statement, execution of that statement stops as soon as possible. An INTERRUPT message and the statement are displayed and the caret (∧) indicates where the execution of the statement was interrupted. (Figure 10.2 gives an example of statement execution that was interrupted by pressing ATTN twice.)

The HOLD key is an On/Off switch that can be used to stop all processing; when the key is pressed again, processing resumes. The HOLD key is used primarily to permit reading of the display screen during an output operation in which the contents of the display screen are changing rapidly. When the HOLD key is in effect, the entire keyboard is deactivated, except for the COPY DISPLAY key which can be used to copy the contents of the display screen to the printer.

Typing Conventions

When an APL statement or system command is entered, spaces (i.e., blank characters) may appear anywhere except within a constant or a name. Thus, spaces can be included at will to improve readability. A space is inserted by pressing the space bar on the keyboard. The space bar should not be used for forward spacing over characters that have been previously inserted into the input line. Although most statements and commands are usually typed in order, this is not necessary. For example, spaces can be left in a line and filled in by backspacing and insertion of the required characters. A good rule, termed *visual fidelity*, is that the input line is processed by the computer in exactly the same form that the user can see it.

The position of the cursor is not significant when the EXECUTE key is pressed, because the cursor is not read by the computer.

Numeric Output and Input

A sequence of operations frequently encountered is that of specification followed by a display of the variable specified. That is, for example, a series of statements of the form:

$$A \leftarrow 131 * 2$$
$$A$$

Using the concept of multiple specification and the *quad symbol*, ☐, the two statements can be combined into one statement. The quad symbol, sometimes called the *window function*, is used as follows:

$$☐ \leftarrow A \leftarrow 3$$

and indicates that the value specified is to be displayed. In this case, the value 3 is displayed on the screen. Statements containing the quad symbol also adhere to the right-to-left convention. For example, the statement:

$$☐ \leftarrow 5 + A \leftarrow 2$$

assigns the value 2 to A and displays the value 7 for the user. The quad symbol is frequently embedded in lengthy statements to display intermediate values. The statement:

$$C1 \leftarrow {}^{-}1 + ☐ \leftarrow 2 \times 3$$

for example, displays the intermediate result 6 and assigns the value 5 to the variable C1. Figure 10.3 gives some examples of how the quad symbols can be used in APL statements. During the checkout* of a program, it is often useful to display partial results to determine the location of programming errors.

```
        []←A←131*2
17161
        R←4+[]←PP←1296*.5
36
        R
40
        WOW←[]←([]←1296*.5)*.5
36
6
        WOW
6
```

Figure 10.3 Specification using the quad symbol for output.

Checkout refers to the process of verifying the correctness of a program and eliminating logical and grammatical errors.

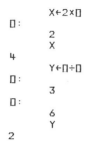

Figure 10.4   Numeric input using the quad symbol.

The quad symbol ⎕ is used in a statement to denote numeric input. In this context, it can appear anywhere that a constant or variable can be used, except directly to the left of a specification arrow. The computer halts execution of the statement containing the quad symbol and makes an input request to the terminal as shown in Figure 10.4. After the desired value is entered, execution continues as though that value were actually a part of the statement.

The computer displays the symbols ⎕: to indicate that it is time to enter a value, moves the contents of the screen up one line, indents six spaces, and unlocks the keyboard. The user follows by typing the value that he wants entered and presses the EXECUTE key. The computer then continues with the execution of that statement.

10.2 PRIMITIVE SCALAR FUNCTIONS

A *primitive function* is a function that is defined as a part of the APL programming language and is available to the user without having to define it. Addition (+), subtraction (−), multiplication (×), and division (÷) are common examples. A primitive function is always denoted by a special symbol or a composite symbol, from the set of APL symbols, and requires either one or two arguments. A *primitive scalar function* always yields a result which is a scalar value.

One of the powerful features of APL is that the scalar functions presented in this chapter are extended to arrays on an element-by-element basis. The extension of functions to arrays is divided into two parts: *Vectors and Vector Functions and Matrices and Arrays of Higher Dimension*, which are covered in this chapter and the next chapter, respectively. Since addition, subtraction, multiplication, and division are commonly known, they are not covered further. Otherwise, this chapter can be used as an introduction to the primitive scalar functions.

Monadic Arithmetic Functions

The monadic *negation function* was introduced earlier as a means of changing the sign of an argument. Figure 10.5 depicts some illustrative examples.

```
            A←-B←2
            A
    ‾2
            B
    2
            -B
    ‾2
            ‾B
    SYNTAX ERROR
            ‾B
            ∧
```

Figure 10.5   The negative function.

```
            +10
    10
            A←‾5
            +A
    ‾5
            +‾15
    ‾15
```

Figure 10.6   The identity function.

Formally, the result R of the negation function applied to an argument B is defined as:

$$R \equiv 0-B$$

where the symbol $\equiv$ should be read "is defined as." At this point, it should be noted that formal definitions use other functions in the language. Formal definitions are normally used for reference purposes and the reader, in his first reading of the material, can effectively branch around them.

The monadic use of the symbol $+$ denotes the *identity function* which returns the value of the given argument. Examples of the identity function are given in Figure 10.6. It may be used to display the result of a specification such as +A←B+C instead of writing ⎕←A←B+C.

Formally, the result R of the identity function applied to an argument B is defined as:

$$R \equiv 0+B$$

The monadic use of the symbol $\times$ denotes the *signum function* and returns the value -1, 0, or 1, depending upon whether the argument is negative, zero, or positive, respectively. Figure 10.7 indicates some uses of the signum function.

Formally, the result R of the signum function applied to an argument B is defined as:

$$R \equiv (0<B)-0>B$$

```
              A← ¯5
              ×A
     ¯1
              ×5
     1
              ×A+5
     0
```

Figure 10.7   The signum function.

```
              ÷5
     0.2
              ÷÷5
     5
              1÷÷5
     5
```

Figure 10.8   The reciprocal function.

The monadic use of the symbol ÷ is a convenient way of finding the reciprocal of a value and is more convenient than using a division into 1. It is appropriately named the *reciprocal function* and is exhibited in Figure 10.8.

Formally, the result R of the reciprocal function applied to an argument B is defined as:

$$R \equiv 1 \div B$$

As evidenced by the formal definitions, the monadic arithmetic functions are a convenience rather than a necessity. However, the relevance of an interactive system is directly related to the amount of typing required to get the job done.

Exponentiation and the Exponential Function

The dyadic *exponentiation function* is commonly regarded as raising a number to a given power. The function uses the power symbol * and the arguments are not restricted to integers so that exponentiation can be used for taking square roots, cube roots, etc. Figure 10.9 gives some typical ways of using the power function.

Formally, the result R of the exponentiation (power) function, A*B, is defined as:

$$R \equiv A^B$$

The definition holds for the following cases:

1. $A > 0$ and B any value;
2. $A = 0$ and $B \geqslant 0$; and
3. $A < 0$ and B equivalent to an expression of the form $M \div N$ where M is an integer and N is an odd integer.

```
                5*2
      25
                25*.5
      5
                25*÷2
      5
                (3*3)*÷3
      3
                A←1.5
                I←4
                □←Y←A*I-2
      2.25
```

Figure 10.9   The power function (exponentiation).

```
                FIVE←5
                ZERO←0
                0*FIVE
      0
                ZERO*ZERO
      1
                FIVE*0
      1
                5*¯2
      0.04
                0*5-FIVE
      1
```

Figure 10.10   Special cases of the power function.

Moreover, $(A*0)=1$ and $(0*0)=1$ but $(0*B)=0$, when $B \neq 0$. Figure 10.10 gives special cases of the power function.

The monadic *exponential* symbol * raises the mathematical value e to a given power and thus eliminates inaccuracies resulting from entering that value at different times. Figure 10.11 gives brief examples of the way that e^1 and e^{-1} can be computed.

Formally, the result R of the exponential function applied to an argument B is defined as:

$$R \equiv e^B$$

where e is stored as 2.718281828459045.

Applications. The mathematical formula:

$$y = \frac{e^x - e^{-x}}{2}$$

```
                *1
      2.7183
                *¯1
      0.36788
```

Figure 10.11   The exponential function.

can be expressed in APL as:

$$Y \leftarrow ((*X) - * - X) \div 2$$

and the formula:

$$y = e^{-x^2/2}$$

can be expressed in APL as:

$$Y \leftarrow *(-X*2) \div 2$$

Maximum and Minimum

Many algorithmic procedures require that the maximum or the minimum of two values be selected. APL includes two primitive dyadic functions which perform these operations. The *maximum* function uses the symbol ⌈ and selects the algebraically largest of the two arguments, while the *minimum* function, which uses the symbol ⌊, selects the algebraically smallest of its arguments. Figure 10.12 gives some examples of the use of the maximum and minimum functions.

Formally, the result R of the maximum function applied to arguments A and B is defined as:

$$R \equiv A, if A > B$$
$$R \equiv B, if A \leqslant B$$

Similarly, the result R of the minimum function applied to arguments A and B is defined as:

$$R \equiv A, if A \leqslant B$$
$$R \equiv B, if A > B$$

Floor, Ceiling, and Rounding

Many computer applications involve computations in the neighborhood of a given value. In addition, it is frequently desirable to limit the resulting values

```
            A←.25
            B←.3
            A⌈B
   0.3
            (÷A)⌈÷B
   4
            A⌊-B
   ⁻0.3
            -B⌊A
   ⁻0.25
```

Figure 10.12 The maximum and minimum functions.

$$
\begin{array}{c}
3 \\
\lfloor 3.14 \\
\\
^-4 \\
\lfloor\ ^-3.14 \\
\\
4 \\
\lceil 3.14 \\
\\
^-3 \\
\lceil\ ^-3.14 \\
\\
5 \\
\lfloor 5 \\
\\
5 \\
\lceil 5
\end{array}
$$

Figure 10.13   The floor and ceiling functions.

to integers. The monadic use of the symbol $\lfloor$ is termed the *floor* function and gives the largest integer not exceeding the single argument. Similarly, the monadic use of the symbol $\lceil$ is termed the *ceiling* function and provides the smallest integer not exceeded by the given argument. Examples of both functions are given in Figure 10.13.

Formally, the result R of the floor function applied to the argument B is defined as:*

$$R \equiv B - 1 | B$$

Similarly, the result R of the ceiling function applied to the argument B is defined as:

$$R \equiv B + 1 | - B$$

The floor function can be used to conveniently round a number to the nearest integer or to a given number of decimal places. The accepted practice for rounding a number to the nearest integer is to add one half and to retain only the integral part of the result. In APL, this process applied to the value B is expressed as:

$$\lfloor B + .5$$

A similar expression for rounding the value B to N decimal places is given as:

$$(10 * - N) \times \lfloor 0.5 + B \times 10 * N$$

Figure 10.14 gives additional examples of rounding.

Application.   Yearly FICA tax is computed as 5.85% of gross income up to $15,300. A one-statement program to compute this tax is given as:

```
FICA←.0585×15300⌊GROSS
```

The statement gives the correct tax, regardless of the income of the taxpayer.

---

*The meaning of the | operator is given later; formal definitions are included for reference purposes.

```
        B←33.3
        ⌊B+.5
33
        C←77.7
        ⌊C+.5
78
        N←3
        ⎕←B←2÷3
0.66667
        (10*-N)×⌊.5+B×10*N
0.667
        (10*-N)×⌊.5+(÷3)×10*N
0.333
```

Figure 10.14   Rounding using the floor function.

```
        D← ¯5
        |D
5
        | ¯8*÷3
2
        |÷ ¯3
0.33333
```

Figure 10.15   The absolute value function.

Absolute Value

The absolute value function in mathematics is identified by vertical strokes enclosing a single argument. For example, the expression

$$|x|$$

denotes the magnitude of x, regardless of its original sign. In APL, the absolute value function is indicated by the monadic use of the symbol |, which is placed in its usual position, and is defined on the expression to its right—just as any other monadic function. The examples in Figure 10.15 show how absolute value is used.

Formally, the result R of the absolute value function on an argument B is defined as:

$$R≡B⌈-B$$

or as

$$R≡B××B$$

Comparison Functions

When the values of A and B are known and posed with the question, "Is A greater than B?" one can usually respond with the answer *yes* or *no*. In a computer, the truth values *true* for yes and *false* for no must be represented by symbolic values, and the values chosen can be of major significance. In APL, the

TABLE 10.2 Comparison Functions

Expression	Truth Value If A Is Less Than B	Truth Value If A Is Equal To B	Truth Value If A is Greater Than B
A<B	1	0	0
A≤B	1	1	0
A = B	0	1	0
A≥B	0	1	1
A>B	0	0	1
A≠B	1	0	1

truth value *true* is represented by the scalar value 1 and the truth value *false* is represented by the scalar value 0. Thus, the result of a comparison can be used in arithmetic calculations much like any other numeric value. Six comparison operations are incorporated into APL as primitive dyadic functions:

Function Symbol	Meaning
<	less than
≤	less than or equal to
=	equal to
≥	greater than or equal to
>	greater than
≠	not equal to

In fact, the six symbols are conveniently located, in sequence, over the numeric characters 3 through 8 on the APL keyboard. The six comparison functions are further defined in Table 10.2. Like any other dyadic function, a comparison function adheres to the right-to-left convention for arithmetic. Figure 10.16 gives some examples of how the comparison functions can be used. It should be noted in that figure that the right-to-left convention significantly affects the result in the last two interactions of the user with the computer.

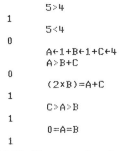

```
        5>4
1
        5<4
0
        A←1+B←1+C←4
        A>B+C
0
        (2×B)=A+C
1
        C>A>B
1
        0=A=B
1
```

Figure 10.16   The comparison functions.

```
        0.3333333333333333=0.3333333333333333999
    1
        ⌈5+10*¯12
    6
        ⌈5+10*¯13
    5
```

Figure 10.17 Equality of arguments.

When dealing with numbers stored in scaled representation, the question of how close is equal is of importance. The *comparison functions*, as well as *floor* and *ceiling*, are dependent, to some extent, on how close in magnitude numeric values have to be before they are regarded as equal. This tolerance is termed *comparison tolerance*, (⎕CT), and in APL it is set, approximately, to 1.0E¯13 with a clear workspace. When computing with only a few significant digits, as in integer arithmetic, tests of equality are of little concern. On the other hand, the examples in Figure 10.17 indicate cases where equality and the value of ⎕CT are important. In statement (1), it should be remembered that only 16 digits of accuracy are maintained in the computer—regardless of how many are entered. Thus, the values are equal. In statement (2), the expression 5+10*¯12 is greater than 5+⎕CT, so that its ceiling is the value 6. In statement (3), the expression 5+10*¯13 is less than or equal to 5+⎕CT so that its ceiling is the value 5. The system variable ⎕CT can be changed with a statement of the form:

$$⎕CT←n$$

where n is the desired comparison tolerance. Comparison tolerance is used in the formal definition of the comparison functions.

Formally, the result R of a comparison function applied to arguments A and B is defined as:

	R≡1 *if*	R≡0 *if*
A<B	(A-B)≤-⎕CT×|B	otherwise
A≤B	(A-B)≤⎕CT×|B	otherwise
A=B	(|A-B)≤⎕CT×|B	otherwise[a]
A≥B	(A-B)>-⎕CT×|B	otherwise
A>B	(|A-B)>⎕CT×|B	otherwise
A≠B	(|A-B)>⎕CT×|B	otherwise[a]
	⎕CT←1.0E¯13	

[a] If arguments A and B are characters (see Section 5.9), then R≡1 if the relationship holds; otherwise R≡0.

```
        1∧1
  1
        1∧0
  0
        (3<2)∧5>4
  0
```

Figure 10.18   The and function.

```
        0∨0
  0
        1∨0
  1
        (3<2)∨5>4
  1
```

Figure 10.19   The or function.

```
        ~1
  0
        ~0
  1
        ~(3<2)∨5>4
  0
        ~(3<2)∧5>4
  1
```

Figure 10.20   The not function.

Logical Functions

Logical functions are ordinarily used to form complex expressions from the truth values of one or more logical events. In APL, a logical event can take the form of a scalar data item which has the value 0 or 1 or be the result of a logical or comparison function. A 0 or 1 truth value can additionally result from arithmetic computation. The APL language contains five logical functions defined on the values of 0 and 1: *and, or, not, nand*, and *nor. And, or, nand*, and *nor* are frequently referred to as *connectives* and are dyadic functions. *Not* is a monadic function.

The connective *and* is represented by the symbol ∧, and returns the value 1 if both arguments are 1 and returns the value 0 otherwise (e.g., Figure 10.18).

The connective *or* is represented by the symbol ∨ and returns the value 1 if either or both of the arguments is 1 (e.g., Figure 10.19).

The monadic form of the symbol ~ (tilde symbol) denotes the *not* function, and returns the value 0 if its argument is 1 and returns 1 if its argument is 0 (e.g., Figure 10.20).

The dyadic *nand* function, commonly referred to as *not and*, uses the composite symbol ⍲, formed by overstriking the symbol ∧ with the symbol ~. *Nand* returns the value 0 if both arguments are 0 and returns 1 otherwise (e.g., Figure 10.21).

```
        (3<2)⍲5>4
1
        1⍲1
0
        (100<1)⍲2>200
1
```

Figure 10.21 The nand function.

```
        0⍱0
1
        (3<2)⍱5>4
0
        (100<1)⍱2>200
1
```

Figure 10.22 The nor function.

```
            (3<2)∨1-2
    DOMAIN ERROR
            (3<2)∨1-2
            ^
            2∨1
    DOMAIN ERROR
            2∨1
            ^
            1∧1∨1∧1∧0
1
```

Figure 10.23 Arguments of logical functions are restricted to the values 0 and 1.

The dyadic *nor* function, commonly referred to as *not or*, uses the composite symbol ⍱, formed by overstriking the symbol ∨ with the symbol ~. *Nor* returns the value 1 if both arguments are 0 and returns a 0 otherwise (e.g., Figure 10.22).

Since the arguments of logical functions are limited to the values 0 and 1, the result of the dyadic functions can be formally defined by truth tables. They are given as follows:

∧	0	1		∨	0	1		⍲	0	1		⍱	0	1
0	0	0		0	0	1		0	1	1		0	1	0
1	0	1		1	1	1		1	1	0		1	0	0

The result R of the *not* function applied to argument B is defined as:

$$R \equiv 1 \neq B$$

where B must be a 0 or 1.

Arguments are restricted to 0 or 1 values as depicted in Figure 10.23).

Application. A one-statement program to compute the value y of the following step function:

$$y=0, \text{if } x \leqslant 0$$
$$y=3.51, \text{if } 0 < x \leqslant 50$$
$$y=134.138, \text{if } x > 50$$

is given as follows:

$$Y \leftarrow(((X>0) \wedge X \leqslant 50) \times 3.51) + (X>50) \times 134.138$$

Residue

In many computational procedures, it is necessary to compute the residue R of a numeric value B modulus another value A; that is:

$$R \equiv B(\bmod A)$$

If A and B are both integers, then R is the remainder after dividing B by A. APL extends this facility by allowing the arguments to be nonintegral and non-negative. The dyadic residue function uses the symbol |, the vertical stroke, and has the following form:

$$A|B$$

where the letters A and B correspond to the arguments in the above definition. Figure 10.24 gives some examples of the residue function applied to integral and nonintegral arguments. As evidenced in the above examples and described in the formal definitions below, the result of the residue function is always *positive*. The order of the arguments is of particular interest. Because of the right-to-left rule and the fact that a function interprets the expression to its right as its rightmost argument, the residue function can be applied to a compound expression without requiring parentheses. The value of the expressions

```
        B←5+A←2
        A I B
1
        A I 6
0
        A I 13.4
1.4
        5 I ¯13.4
1.6
        1.5 I 3.4
0.4
        ¯5 I 13
¯2
```

Figure 10.24 The residue function.

$$X \leftarrow 3$$
$$0 = 2 \mid 1 + X * 3$$

1

$$X \leftarrow 2$$
$$0 = 2 \mid 1 + X * 3$$

0

Figure 10.25   Use of the residue function to test if an argument is divisible by two.

in statements (1) and (2) in Figure 10.25 is 1 (for true) if the value of the expression to the right of the residue function is divisible by 2; it assumes the value 0 otherwise.

Formally, the result R of the expression $A \mid B$ is defined as follows:

$$R \equiv B - A \times \lfloor B \div A$$
$$R \equiv B, \text{ if } A = 0$$

Application. An APL statement that computes $z = x^2$ if x is odd and $z = x^3$ if x is even is given as follows:

$$Z \leftarrow ((X * 2) \times 1 = 2 \mid X) + (X * 3) \times 0 = 2 \mid X$$

Generalized Combination and Factorial

One of the fundamental identities in mathematics and statistics is the binomial theorem, frequently expressed as:

$$(a + b)^n = \sum_{k=0}^{n} \frac{n!}{k!(n-k)!} a^k b^{n-k}$$

The coefficient $\dfrac{n!}{k!(n-k)!}$ is commonly known as the binomial coefficient and is usually abbreviated as $\binom{n}{k}$ or C_k^n. In the latter case, C_k^n in usually interpreted as the number of combinations of n things taken k at a time. For example, $C_2^3 = 3$. In mathematics, n is not restricted to integers and the function is known as the complete beta function. The APL system contains a dyadic function to compute the binomial coefficient* which uses the symbol !, a composite symbol formed by overstriking the quote symbol with a period. Thus, the binomial coefficient $\binom{N}{K}$ is represented in APL as $K ! N$. Figure 10.26 gives some examples of the generalized combination function.

Formally, the result R of the generalized combination of N things taken K at a time is defined as:

$$R \equiv (!N) \div (!K) \times !N - K$$

---

*Called the *generalized combination* because of its extension to nonintegral values.

```
        N←6
        3!N
20
        (7-2)!10-2
56
        1.3!8.9
14.369
```

Figure 10.26   The generalized combination function.

```
        !3
6
        !2×5
3628800
        !1.5
1.329340388
        !¯1.5
¯3.544907702
        !¯2
DOMAIN ERROR
        !¯2
        ∧
```

Figure 10.27   The factorial function.

and is related to the complete beta function as follows:

$$\text{Beta } (K,N) = \div N \times (K-1)\,!\,K+N-1$$

The definition of the generalized combination function uses another mathematical function, which is also widely known. Usually called the *factorial*, it gives the number of arrangements of n distinct objects in a row. In APL, the monadic factorial function also uses the composite symbol ! and gives the product of the first N positive integers, that is, $N \times (N-1) \times (N-2) \ldots 1$. For a non-integral argument, the factorial function is equivalent to the gamma function of $N+1$. The statements in Fig. 10.27 also demonstrate an obvious restriction.

Formally, the result R of the factorial function on an argument N is defined as:

$$R \equiv N \times (N-1) \times (N-2) \ldots 2 \times 1, \text{ for } 0=1|N;$$
$$R \equiv \text{undefined, for } (0=1|N) \wedge (^-1 = \times N); \text{ and}$$
$$R \equiv \Gamma N+1, \text{ otherwise.}$$

Applications. An APL expression for the mathematical expression:

$$x - \frac{x^3}{3!} + \frac{x^5}{5!} - \frac{x^7}{7!} + \frac{x^9}{9!}$$

can be computed easily by rewriting the expression as:

$$x\left(1 - x^2\left(\frac{1}{3!} - x^2\left(\frac{1}{5!} - x^2\left(\frac{1}{7!} - \frac{x^2}{9!}\right)\right)\right)\right)$$

```
                            ?5
                1
                            ?10
                8
                            ?7
                4
```

Figure 10.28 The roll function (?N) which selects an integer pseudo-randomly from the first N positive integers.

and is given as follows:

$$X \times 1 - XP \times (\div !3) - XP \times (\div !5) - XP \times (\div !7) - (XP \leftarrow X * 2) \div !9$$

Random Number Generation

The APL system contains two functions for generating pseudo-random numbers and both appropriately use the symbol *?*. The monadic interpretation, called *roll*— that is, ?N—selects an integer pseudo randomly from the first N positive integers. The dyadic version called *deal*, that is M?N, creates a vector of M components selected pseudo-randomly from the first N positive integers without replacement. A discussion of the *deal* function, which uses the concept of a vector, is covered later in this chapter. With the monadic roll function, any integer in the range 1 to N has an equal chance of being selected. Some examples of the roll function are given in Figure 10.28. The roll function uses a starting number for generating the random result, termed the *random link* ($\Box RL$), which is initially set to $7*5$ or 16807 with a clear workspace. The random link is modified each time a random number is generated. The random link can be changed with a statement of the form:

$$\Box RL \leftarrow n$$

where *n* is a seed value for a new set of random numbers.

Logarithms. The age-old definition, "A logarithm is an exponent," is useful for remembering the symbol for the logarithm functions, which is the composite symbol ⊛ formed from the circle symbol ○ and the exponentiation (or power) symbol *.

The monadic form of the symbol is defined as the *natural logarithm*. It is written as ⊛N and computes the expression: $\log_e N$. The dyadic version of the function computes the *common logarithm* so that M⊛N is defined as the $\log_M N$. Figure 10.29 gives some examples of both types of logarithms.

Antilogarithms can be computed by exponentiation using the familiar relations:

(1) If $L = \ln N$, then $\text{antilog}_e(L) = e^L = N$.
(2) If $L = \log_b N$, then $\text{antilog}_b(L) = b^L = N$.

Figure 10.30 demonstrates how an antilogarithm can be computed.

```
      ⍟2
0.69315
        ⍟*1
1
        (*1)⍟2
0.69315
        10⍟1
0
        10⍟2
0.30103
        10⍟2+2
0.60206
        10⍟2+3
0.69897
```

Figure 10.29   The natural and common logarithm functions.

```
        X←10⍟3
        Y←10⍟4
        10*X+Y
    12
```

Figure 10.30   Computing the antilogarithm.

Formally, the result R of the natural logarithm applied to argument N is defined as:

$$R \equiv \ln N$$

or

$$N = {*} R$$

Similarly, the result R of the common logarithm applied to arguments M and N is defined as:

$$R \equiv \log_M N$$

or

$$R \equiv (\circledast N) \div \circledast M$$

Pi Times.   A familiar problem to most computer users, doing scientific work, involves the exact value of π. The first problem usually requires a secondary decision regarding how many places to include once the value has been looked up in a table. APL contains a monadic function, which uses the circle symbol ○, and is defined as pi times the argument; that is $\pi \times N$ is written ○N. Figure 10.31 applied the *pi times* function to some sample arguments.

```
        ○1
3.1416
        R←2
        ○R*2
12.566
```

Figure 10.31   Pi times the argument.

Formally, the result R of the monadic pi times function applied to argument N is defined as:

$$R \equiv \pi \times N$$

where

$$\pi = 3.141592653589793$$

Circular Functions

The circular functions, commonly known as the trigonometric functions, are defined in APL as the dyadic interpretation of the circle symbol ○. Each of the circular functions, defined in terms of radian measure, is assigned an identifying number which serves as the left argument. The right argument is the value to which the function is applied. The functions are identified in Table 10.3. Thus, 1○○÷6 is the sine of $\pi/6$ radians, which is one half. Other examples are given in Figure 10.32.

The following list presents the frequently used circular functions:

sin X:	1○X	arcsin X:	‾1○X
cos X:	2○X	arccos X:	‾2○X
tan X:	3○X	arctan X:	‾3○X

TABLE 10.3   CIRCULAR FUNCTIONS (M○N)

M	Function	Domain of N
7	Tanh N	
6	Cosh N	
5	Sinh N	
4	$(1 + N*2)*.5$	
3	Tan N	
2	Cos N	
1	Sin N	
0	$(1 - N*2)*.5$	$N \leq 1$
‾1	Arcsin N	$1 \geq \vert N$
‾2	Arccos N	$1 \geq \vert N$
‾3	Arctan N	$1 \geq \vert N$
‾4	$(‾1 + N*2)*.5$	$N \geq 1$
‾5	Arcsinh N	
‾6	Arccosh N	$N \geq 1$
‾7	Arctanh N	$1 > \vert N$

```
            THIRTY←o÷6
            1oTHIRTY
    0.5
            FORTY5←o÷4
            1oFORTY5
    0.70711
            X←(100÷4)÷200÷4
            X
    1
            Y←¯3oX
            (o1)÷Y
    4
```

Figure 10.32   Circular functions.

Order of Arguments

In spite of the fact that functions in a statement are executed in a right-to-left sequence, the established *order of arguments* is maintained in most cases. For functions that are commutative, such as addition and multiplication, the order is not significant. In noncommutative functions, such as division or exponentiation, the defined order must be maintained; for example,

$$A \div B \text{ means A divided by B}$$

and

$$A * B \text{ means A raised to the power B.}$$

In other functions, such as residue and the circular functions, no formal order of arguments has been established. In fact, B (mod A) is expressed in APL as A|B. It is here that the right-to-left order of execution is of prime significance. Clearly, a function, regardless of whether it is monadic or dyadic, is defined on the entire expression to its right, except when grouping indicates a departure from the established order of execution. In the residue function, denoted as A|B, the right argument B is more likely to be the result of a series of computations than the left argument A. Similarly, with the circular functions, for example, sin X, written as 1oX, the right argument X is more likely to be the result of an expression than the left argument 1. In fact, the left argument is nothing more than a function designator. Thus, the convention of placing the argument that is more likely to be computed on the right is consistent with the right-to-left convention for the execution of functions.

Summary of Primitive Scalar Functions

A brief summary of primitive scalar functions is included as Table 10.4 for reference and review.

TABLE 10.4 SUMMARY OF PRIMITIVE SCALAR FUNCTIONS

Function	Meaning	Example[a]
A+B	A plus B	$5 \leftrightarrow 2+3$
+B	0 plus B	$10 \leftrightarrow +10$
A−B	A minus B	$4 \leftrightarrow 10-6$
−B	Minus B	$^-5 \leftrightarrow -5$
A×B	A times B	$6 \leftrightarrow 2 \times 3$
×B	Sign of B	$^-1 \leftrightarrow \times \, ^-3$
A÷B	A divided by B	$2 \leftrightarrow 6 \div 3$
÷B	Reciprocal of B	$0.5 \leftrightarrow \div 2$
A∗B	A to the Bth power	$9 \leftrightarrow 3 \ast 2$
∗B	e to the Bth power	$2.718281828 \ldots \leftrightarrow \ast 1$
A⌈B	Maximum of A and B	$^-3 \leftrightarrow ^-4 \lceil \, ^-3$
⌈B	Ceiling of B	$4 \leftrightarrow \lceil 3.14$
A⌊B	Minimum of A and B	$3 \leftrightarrow 3 \lfloor 4$
⌊B	Floor of B	$3 \leftrightarrow \lfloor 3.14$
A|B	B (modulus A)	$1 \leftrightarrow 2 \mid 7$
|B	Absolute value of B	$3.14 \leftrightarrow \mid ^-3.14$
A<B	A less than B	$0 \leftrightarrow 10 < 5$
A≤B	A less than or equal to B	$1 \leftrightarrow 5 \leq 5$
A=B	A equals B	$0 \leftrightarrow 10 = 5$
A≥B	A greater than or equal to B	$1 \leftrightarrow 10 \geq 5$
A>B	A greater than B	$1 \leftrightarrow 10 > 5$
A≠B	A not equal to B	$0 \leftrightarrow 5 \neq 5$
A∧B	A and B	$1 \leftrightarrow 1 \wedge 1$
A⍲B	A nand B	$0 \leftrightarrow 1 ⍲ 1$
A∨B	A or B	$1 \leftrightarrow 1 \vee 0$
A⍱B	A nor B	$0 \leftrightarrow 1 ⍱ 0$
~B	Not B	$1 \leftrightarrow \sim 0$
A!B	Number of combinations of B things taken A at a time	$35 \leftrightarrow 3!7$
!B	B factorial	$24 \leftrightarrow !4$
?B	Random selection of an integer from 1, 2, . . . , B	$1 \leftrightarrow ?5$
A⍟B	Log$_A$ B	$0.3010299957 \leftrightarrow 10 ⍟ 2$
⍟B	Ln B	$0.6931471806 \leftrightarrow ⍟2$
A○B	Circular functions	$0.5 \leftrightarrow 1 \circ \circ \div 6$
○B	Pi times	$3.141592654 \leftrightarrow \circ 1$

[a] $\leftrightarrow$ denotes "is equilvalent to."

10.3 VECTORS

A *vector* is a linear aggregate of data, referred to in computer terminology as a one-dimensional *array*. Arrays were introduced briefly in chapter 2 in the discussion of data organization. This chapter expands upon the concepts presented previously, as they pertain to the APL language. Some of the basic concepts are restated to provide supplementary material at the introductory level.

Fundamental Concepts

Most computations deal with single data values called scalars. This is so, perhaps, because most people are accustomed to thinking in terms of single values—regardless of whether they lend themselves to the physical situation at hand. Suppose, for example, that a market researcher stands on a street corner for a period of time, and counts sporty automobiles of various makes. He might come up with the following list:

Category Number	Name	Total Number Observed
1	Riviera	7
2	Toronado	4
3	Thunderbird	6
4	Eldorado	5
5	Mark V	2

Clearly, the total of observations for a given category is a scalar value. Yet, the scalar values collectively form a *family* of related items. In this case, each value is a count giving a number of automobiles. The list of totals can also be interpreted as a linear sequence of values called a *vector*. Each value has an *index* given by the category number. The index can be used to select a value from the vector. For example, the index 4 would denote the value 5, which is said to be the fourth *element* of the vector. The concept is easily extended to other dimensions. If the above observations were repeated for each of five days, then the following collection of data might result:

	Day				
	1	2	3	4	5
1	7	5	7	6	9
2	4	3	2	5	3
Category 3	6	8	8	7	6
4	5	2	3	4	5
5	2	0	3	1	4

where the total observations for category 2 on day 3 is the value 2; here, the value 2 is selected by two indices: the row index and the column index. A two-dimensional collection of values is termed a *matrix*. A vector or a matrix is a special case of a collection of related data called an *array*, which is extended to as many dimensions as are required by a given application. In the above example, a three-dimensional array of data values would be created if observations were taken on several street corners, that is,

Corner	Day				
1	1	2	3	4	5

	Category		Day				
		1	7	5	7	6	9
		2	4	3	2	5	3
Category		3	6	8	8	7	6
		4	5	2	3	4	5
		5	2	0	3	1	4

Corner	Day				
2	1	2	3	4	5

	Category		Day				
		1	10	5	8	3	9
		2	2	5	4	6	2
Category		3	8	5	9	4	5
		4	0	3	2	4	5
		5	1	4	2	1	3

The total of observations corresponding to the indices (2,4,1), denoting corner 2, category 4, and day 1, is the value 0. An array with more than two dimensions is called, appropriately, a three-dimensional array, or a four-dimensional array, etc. If an element of an array can be denoted by an index, it is not necessary to give a unique name to each individual value, and only the array, as a whole, need be named.

Thus, a variable name is given to an entire array of data items and an element within the array is selected by an appropriate number of indices. If the three-dimensional array, given above, were assigned the name AUTO, for example, then the indexed variable AUTO[1;1;5] would denote the value 9. (In computer terminology, an index is frequently termed a subscript, so a vector array needs one subscript, a matrix needs two subscripts, a three-dimensional array needs three subscripts, etc. In APL, an index may also be an array, making the concept of a subscript inappropriate. The term subscript will not be used further.)

It is not difficult to imagine situations where it is more convenient to regard an array as a whole rather than as distinct elements. If one wanted to display every element of a vector, for example, it would be more convenient, and economical as well, to simply give the name of the vector and let the computer print the elements, regardless of how many there were. This is where APL achieves its power as a programming language and as a means for describing the functional characteristics of discrete systems. Primitive scalar functions are extended to accept arrays as arguments and additional functions are defined, primarily, for use on arrays. In treating entire arrays, two items are of significance: the *name* of the array and the *dimension* of the array. A vector has one dimension, which is the number of elements. Similarly, a matrix has two dimensions: the number of rows and the number of columns. It follows that a three-dimensional array has three dimensions, a four-dimensional array has four dimensions, etc. The dimensions of an array are conveniently referred to as its size. For some functions on arrays, the size of the arguments must agree. In others, it is necessary that the size be known and functions are available for obtaining this value.

The remainder of this chapter is concerned with vectors and vector functions. The material is self-contained and covers all functions applicable to vectors. Matrices and arrays of higher dimension will be presented in Chapter 12.

Entering a Constant Vector

In APL, a vector of numeric values (called a *constant vector*) is created by typing the numbers with at least one intervening space between elements. The vector can be used in an expression, much like a scalar argument, and the result is stored in the active workspace by using the specification function. When a vector is created in this way, the elements must be constants and may not be scalar variables. Later, methods are presented for forming vectors (and arrays) from scalar variables and from arrays which already exist. For example, consider Figure 10.33. V is specified as a vector of five elements. The dimension of V is determined and saved automatically by the APL system, and the user need not be concerned with the bookkeeping aspects of array processing. The conventions that govern the display of scalar data also apply to vectors.

Extension of Scalar Functions to Arrays

The primitive scalar functions, defined for scalars, are extended to vectors on an element-by-element basis for arguments of the same dimensions. It is important to note that a constant vector is regarded as a single argument and need not be enclosed in parentheses when used in an expression. Thus, the vector expression 1 2 3+4 5 6 is permitted and has the value 5 7 9. Compound expressions can be constructed with vectors as arguments similar to the manner in which scalar expressions are formed. Figure 10.34 gives numerous examples of statements containing these concepts. The last two statements of that example should be

```
        V←3 .5 ¯16 7.4 10
        V
3 0.5 ¯16 7.4 10
```

Figure 10.33   Entering and displaying a vector.

```
            1 2 3+4 5 6
5 7 9
            A←1 2 3 4 5
            B←6 7 8 9 10
            A+B
7 9 11 13 15
            ☐←C←A+1 2 3 4 5
2 4 6 8 10
            1 2 3 4 5-A
0 0 0 0 0
            A×A
1 4 9 16 25
            -A
¯1 ¯2 ¯3 ¯4 ¯5
            ÷A
1 0.5 0.33333 0.25 0.2
            !A
1 2 6 24 120
            A÷2 2 2 2 2
0.5 1 1.5 2 2.5
            A*3 3 3 3 3
1 8 27 64 125
            A<B
1 1 1 1 1
            A>B
0 0 0 0 0
            D←¯27 12 16.8 6E25 0
            E←0 12 ¯123.4 13 99.873
            D≥E
0 1 1 1 0
            F←1 0 0 1 0
            F∧D≥E
0 0 0 1 0
            D⌈E
0 12 16.8 6E25 99.873
            A←2 3 4
            A*3
8 27 64
```

Figure 10.34 Extension of scalar functions to vectors.

noted. In the statement A ← 2 3 4, A is respecified. Although it previously existed in the active workspace with a dimension of 5, it now has a dimension of 3 with elements 2, 3, and 4. This leads to an important fact. Computer storage is maintained dynamically in APL. The user need not explicitly reserve storage for an array, and the system uses whatever storage is necessary. In the statement A*3, each element of the vector A is raised to the third power. The function uses a vector *and* a scalar as arguments. This demonstrates another important point. If a scalar value is used as an argument in a scalar function along with an array, then it is used with each element of that array. The examples in Figure 10.35 clarify this point.

Three final remarks on the extension of scalar functions on an element-by-element basis to arrays are in order. First, the concept applies to arrays of higher dimension—even though methods for their generation have not been

```
            A←13 ¯256 59.67 0
            A>0
1  0  1  0
            2|1 2 3 4 5 6
1  0  1  0  1  0
            A←6 7 8
            A+1
7  8  9
            B←1 2 3
            C←B+2×A
            C
13 16 19
            A←2 4 6 8 10
            A×A>5
0  0  6  8 10
            A←1 2 3 4 5 6 7 8 9 10 11 12
            A×0=3|A
0  0  3  0  0  6  0  0  9  0  0 12
            ANGL←○÷6 4 3 2
            1○ANGL
0.5 0.70711 0.86603 1
```

Figure 10.35   Extension of a scalar argument to all elements of a vector.

introduced. Second, when a function is executed using two arrays or an array and a scalar as arguments, it applies uniformly to all elements of that structure. Third, the right-to-left conversion applies to functions with array arguments just as it does when the arguments are scalars.

Indexing

Given a vector, regardless of how it was formed, a specific element is selected for display or for use in computation with an index, denoted by square brackets. For example, the element A_i is represented in APL as A[I] and is interpreted to be the Ith element of the vector A. The square brackets must follow the vector name or vector expression, and an index may be a constant, a variable, or an expression. An index may even be an array, as noted later. Figure 10.36 gives examples of these concepts. The statement

$$(2\ 3\ 4\ 5+6\ 7\ 8\ 9)[3]$$

```
            I←2
            V←2 4 6 8 10
            V[1]
2
            V[I]+V[I+2]
12
            2 3 4 5+6 7 8 9
8 10 12 14
            (2 3 4 5+6 7 8 9)[3]
12
```

Figure 10.36   Vector indexing.

```
        V←¯12 13.768 .4E¯13 6
        V[2]←113.768
        V
¯12 113.77 4E¯14 6
```

Figure 10.37   Indexed variable to the left of a specification symbol.

```
            )CLEAR
    CLEAR WS
            V←2 4 6 8
            V[I+1]
    VALUE ERROR
            V[I+1]
             ^
            I←2
            V[I+7]
    INDEX ERROR
            V[I+7]
            ^
            V[I+1]
    6
```

Figure 10.38   Protection against selecting nonexistent values.

requires further explanation. Indexing is regarded as a dyadic function and applies to the argument on its immediate left. Most of the time, the left argument will be a vector name. Occasionally, however, it is a vector expression, as shown. An indexed variable can also appear on the left-hand side of the specification symbol or in any context in which a scalar variable can be used (Figure 10.37).

The APL system offers protection against referencing nonexistent values. If an attempt is made to select an element not in the range of an array, the system responds with an appropriate error message, as shown in Figure 10.38.

Vector indices are not limited to scalar values and may be vectors, matrices, or arrays of higher dimension. Thus, if $V \leftarrow ¯7\ 3\ 1\ 8\ 4$, then $V[1\ 3\ 5]$ is equal to the vector $¯7\ 1\ 4$. Similarly, $V[5\ 1\ 2]$ is equal to the vector $4\ ¯7\ 3$. The concept also applies to arrays, in general, and is covered further in Chapter 12. The result R of the indexing function $V[N]$, where V is a vector, has the following properties:

1. R is formed by selecting from vector V those components whose indices are the argument N.
2. $(\rho R) = \rho N$.

If the index is omitted, then $V[\ ] = V$.

Index Origin

Ordinarily, the lower bound for an index is 1 and the upper bound is the number of elements in the vector. The lower bound for an index can be changed to 0 with a statement of the form:

$$\square IO \leftarrow n$$

```
            )CLEAR
      CLEAR WS
            T←¯7 3 9 6 5
            T[1]
  ¯7
            T[3]
  9
            ⎕IO←0
            T[1]
  3
            T[3]
  6
            T[0]
  ¯7
            ⎕IO←1
            T[0]
INDEX ERROR
            T[0]
            ^
```

Figure 10.39   The index origin is governed by the system variable ⎕IO.

where *n* can be 1 or 0.   The system variable ⎕IO, which stands for *index origin*, governs whether the first element of a vector is indexed with a 1 or a 0, depending upon the setting.   ⎕IO is set to 1 with a clear workspace.   Figure 10.39 gives examples of the index origin.   The following functions are also affected by the index origin:

Index generator (ι)
Index of (ι)
Roll (?)
Deal (?)
Grade up (⍋)
Grade down (⍒)

Each of these functions is described in subsequent paragraphs.

Generating a Vector

One of the difficulties in dealing with arrays is the typing of long sequences of numbers.   When the numbers represent distinct data values, no alternative method for entering the information exists.   But, when the numbers are the same or are consecutive integers, something can be done.   The monadic use of the symbol *iota*, that is, ιN, generates a vector of length N which contains the positive integers 1 through N.   (When the index origin is 0, the function ιN generates a vector of length N that contains the positive integers 0 through N - 1.

The iota function has several names of which *index generator* is perhaps the best known.   Here, N must be a positive integer.   Figure 10.40 depicts some examples containing the iota function.   The above definition permits a vector of zero length to be created.   The expression ι0 creates a vector of zero length,

```
      N←5
      ιN
1 2 3 4 5
      ι4
1 2 3 4
      ι2×N
1 2 3 4 5 6 7 8 9 10
      []←V←ι6
1 2 3 4 5 6
      (ι6)*2
1 4 9 16 25 36
      []IO←0
      []←N←ι5
0 1 2 3 4
```

Figure 10.40 The iota function (index generator).

```
      ι0
```
                    (blank line)
```
      V←ι0
      V
```
                    (blank line)

Figure 10.41 The empty vector.

termed an *empty vector*, and if a specification function is involved, assigns it to the given variable. Consider, for example, Figure 10.41. An empty vector is generated and is assigned to the variable V; it prints as a blank line, which is reasonable for a variable that is regarded as null (or nonexistent). A scalar variable, on the other hand, may not have a null value, and the language contains no facility for making that specification.

Another method of generating an array is through the dyadic version of the symbol ρ, called *rho*. The function is commonly known as the *reshape function*, although the precise meaning of that particular terminology will not become evident until matrices are discussed in Chapter 12. When M is a scalar, the function M ρ N generates a vector of length M using the argument N. If N is a scalar, it is repeated M times in the generated vector. If N is a vector and its size is less than M, it is repeated cyclically. If the size of N is greater than M, the first M elements are used. Figure 10.42 gives some examples of the reshape function.

When M is equal to zero in the reshape function M ρ N, an empty vector is created. The result of the reshape function is always an array.

Size of a Vector

The monadic interpretation of the symbol ρ gives the *size* of a vector, although the precise definition is also more general and applies to arrays of higher dimension. Applied to a vector V, ρV gives the number of elements in V. Applied to a scalar N, ρN generates a null value which prints as a blank line. Figure 10.43 gives several examples of the size function.

```
      5ρ2
2 2 2 2 2
      ⎕←V←¯2 3 18.4 639 ¯9.2
¯2 3 18.4 639 ¯9.2
      W←3ρV
      W
¯2 3 18.4
      10ρι3
1 2 3 1 2 3 1 2 3 1
      V←0ρ1
      V
```
                                        (blank line)

Figure 10.42   The reshape function.

```
      V←3 5 45E12 100 67 ¯.00123 8
      ρV
7
      ρV[2 3 6]
3
      V×0=3|ιρV
0 0 4.5E13 0 0 ¯0.00123 0
      W←ι0
      ρW
0
      ρι0
0
      ρ0ρ100
0
      ρ3×4
                                        (blank line)
      ⎕←A←1ρ4
4
      ρA
1
```

Figure 10.43   The size function.

The monadic ρ function always gives a vector as a result. The number of elements in the result is equal to the number of dimensions* in the argument. Thus, a scalar has no dimension, a vector has one dimension, a matrix has two dimensions, etc.

Forming a Vector

Methods are available for creating arrays (although the present discussion is limited to vectors) from scalar and array variables that already exist in the active workspace. The comma is used as the function symbol in either of two ways: (1) As a monadic symbol it denotes the *ravel function*, which is a means of creating a vector from either a scalar or an array of higher dimension. It is useful for functions which require that an argument be a vector. (2) As a dyadic function,

---

*Later, the dimensions of an array will be referred to as the *coordinates* of an array.

```
        V←5
        ρV                      (blank line)
        []←V←,5
 5
        ρV
 1
        W←ι3
        ρW[2]                   (blank line)
        ρW[,2]
 1
```

Figure 10.44   The ravel function.

```
        V←10 20
        W←30 40 50
        []←X←V,W
 10  20 30 40 50
        V,2E13
 10  20 2E13
        []←Y←13,W
 13 30 40 50
        A←3+B←2
        []←C←(A*2),(B*3),0
 25  8 0
        ¯6,2 3
 ¯6  2 3
        ¯6 2,3
 ¯6  2 3
```

Figure 10.45   The catenation function.

the symbol denotes *catenation*, and chains scalars or vectors together in the usual fashion. After a catenation function, the dimension of the resultant vector is the sum of the number of elements in the two arguments. Figures 10.44 and 10.45 give examples of ravel and catenation, respectively.

When scalar constants are catenated, it is only necessary to separate them with one or more spaces. When variables are catenated, the dyadic catenation symbol must be used. The concept also applies to expressions—although the right-to-left rule applies and the user should exercise caution. Consider the statements in Figure 10.46. In the first example, the value of the expressions $A*2$ and $2 \times B-1$ were computed and then catenated. In the latter case, $2 \times B-1$ is computed, catenated to the scalar 2, and A is raised to the power indicated by

```
        A←2
        B←3
        (A*2),2×B−1
 4  4
        A*2,2×B−1
 4 16
```

Figure 10.46   Catenation of compound expressions.

```
            )CLEAR
      CLEAR WS
            V←1  2  3
            W,V
      VALUE ERROR
            W,V
            ^
            W←ι0
            W,V
      1  2  3
```

Figure 10.47 A variable must be specified before it can be used as an argument in any function.

```
      FIB←0  1  2  3  5  8
      FIB←FIB,FIB[(ρFIB)-1]+FIB[ρFIB]
      FIB
0  1  2  3  5  8  13
```

Figure 10.48 The Fibonacci series—an example of catenation.

```
            A←2+B←1+C←2
            A,B,C
      5  3  2
```

Figure 10.49 Using catenation to display results on the same line.

the catenated vector. Parentheses are useful for avoiding ambiguity—even if it is only on the part of the user.

It was mentioned earlier that a variable must be specified before it can be used. The rule applies in all functions of the language including catenation. This is demonstrated in Figure 10.47.

Catenation provides a convenient method of accumulating values, once the process has been started, as in Figure 10.47. A familiar example is the Fibonacci sequence where the ith term is the sum of the $(i-1)$st and $(i-2)$nd terms, for $i \geq 3$. A one-line expression to add a term to the sequence is given in Figure 10.48.

Catenation explains the form of output used in Figure 10.49. It is evident now that a vector is formed by catenation, and then and only then is the result printed.

Applications. Given a vector P, where $(\rho P) > 100$, and another vector T, a single statment to insert the vector T between the 73rd and 74th elements of P is given as follows:

$$P \leftarrow P[\iota 73], T, P[73+\iota(\rho P)-73]$$

Given a vector W and scalars I and J, where $(\rho W) > I+J$, a single statement to delete the (I+1)st through the (I+J)th elements of W is given as follows:

$$W \leftarrow W[(\iota I), I+J+\iota(\rho W)-I+J]$$

Character Data

A great many interesting and useful applications of computers involve data that are not strictly numeric. Text editing, information retrieval, message dissemination, formula manipulation and theorem proving, record keeping, and data processing are only a few examples. APL permits character data to be entered, processed, and output—as required by a particular application. Character data are enclosed in quote symbols in APL to distinguish them from the name of something or a construct in the language. One character is interpreted as a scalar element, so sequences of characters form an array, as shown in Figure 10.50. A series of characters enclosed in quote symbols is termed a *literal*, which can contain any keyboard character *including composite symbols* and the space character. Since elements of a literal array are restricted to single characters, there is no need to distinguish between them and they are printed without intervening spaces. The quote character, used as a delimiter for literals, is a special case. If it is to be used in a literal, then it must be represented by a double quote. The use of composite and quote symbols in literals is depicted in Figure 10.51.

It should be noticed that literals are printed without the enclosing quote symbols.

In general, arrays with characters as components can be processed as numeric arrays except for the following cases:

1. A function whose domain is strictly a numeric value is not permitted.
2. Numeric and character arrays may not be intermixed.

```
              A←'ABCD25+'
              ρA
        7
              A[3]
        C
              A[ρA]
        +
              B←'12345'
              B[4]←'T'
              B
        123T5
              C←'ABCDEFGHIJKLMNOPQRSTUVWXYZ '
              C[20 5 1 27 6 15 18 27 20 23 15]
        TEA FOR TWO
```

Figure 10.50   Character data.

```
              A←'BE CAREFUL OF THE SYMBOL ''Φ'''
              A
        BE CAREFUL OF THE SYMBOL 'Φ'
              ρA
        28
```

Figure 10.51   Composite symbols and the quote symbol are permitted in a literal.

```
      5ρ'X'
XXXXX
      A←'BIONIC SIX MILLION DOLLAR'
      B←'''PERSON'''
      ρB
8
      A,B
BIONIC SIX MILLION DOLLAR'PERSON'
      A,' ',B
BIONIC SIX MILLION DOLLAR 'PERSON'
      6ρA←'123A456B789C10111D'
123A45
      'TICK'='TACK'
1 0 1 1
```

Figure 10.52   Functions on character vectors.

```
      S←'A'
      ρS                          (blank line)

      V←0ρ'L'
      V                           (blank line)

      W←''
      W                           (blank line)
      ρW
0
```

Figure 10.53   Special cases of character vectors.

Thus, character arrays may be generated, indexed, compared (for equality only), and used with the same utility functions as numeric arrays. Figure 10.52 gives some additional examples of the processing of character vectors.

Character data require some interpretation. A single character enclosed in quote symbols is a scalar value; all other constructs are interpreted as vectors— including the null sequence, as shown in Figure 10.53.

Character Input and Output

The requirement that literals must be enclosed in quote symbols partially negates the generality-of-use principle of APL. The convention is particularly cumbersome for text-editing applications where the eventual user may not be familiar with the APL language.

The quote-quad symbol ⍞ (formed by overstriking a quad symbol with a quote symbol) is used to enter character data. The function is executed in a manner similar to the quad function with the following exceptions:

1. No input symbol is printed to alert the user.
2. The carriage is not indented.

The user types his character data *without* enclosing it in quote symbols, as shown in Figure 10.54.

```
      T←▯
BIONIC SIX MILLION DOLLAR 'PERSON'
      T
BIONIC SIX MILLION DOLLAR 'PERSON'
      ρT
34
      C←▯
A
      ρC
                                        (blank line)
      C
A
```

Figure 10.54   Character input.

```
      ▯←X←'MICRO',▯
PROCESSOR
MICROPROCESSOR
      A←'ABCDEFGHIJKLMNOPQRSTUVWXYZ'
      NDX←▯←A[1 5 7 9]
AEGI
      ,NDX←▯←A[1 5 7 9]
AEGIAEGI
      NDX←▯←A[1 5 7 9]
AEGI
      ,NDX←▯←A[1 5 7 9]
AEGI
AEGI
```

Figure 10.55   Output using the quote-quad or quad symbols.

A quote-quad symbol appearing to the left of a specification arrow indicates that the value of the expression to its right is to be displayed, as depicted in Figure 10.55. For output, the quad symbol moves the cursor to the next line when the output is complete, whereas the quote-quad symbol does not move the cursor to the next line. In a single statement outside of a defined function, where the output quote-quad or output quad symbol is the leftmost symbol, as in:

$$▯←X$$

or

$$□←X$$

the cursor position does not matter, since the cursor is moved to the next line for the next statement anyway. However, when the output quote-quad or the output quad symbol is imbedded in a statement or is in a defined function, then the cursor position is significant and should be considered. This case is also demonstrated in Figure 10.55.

Mixed Output

Although arrays of mixed data cannot be stored, arrays can be intermixed for output (and for output only) by separating the nonhomogeneous data with a

```
      BETA←¯13.471
      'BETA = ';BETA
BETA = ¯13.471
      'PI SQUARED IS ';(○1)*2
PI SQUARED IS 9.8696
```

Figure 10.56   Mixed output.

semicolon. Spaces are not inserted between the mixed data items in the line that is typed by the computer. Figure 10.56 gives some examples of mixed output.

10.4 VECTOR FUNCTIONS

The class of vector functions is divided into two groups:

1. Composite functions, which are extensions to arrays of the scalar dyadic functions, and
2. Mixed functions, which are functions defined only on arrays.

Collectively, the composite and mixed functions permit arrays to be used in APL programs without having to manipulate individual data items.

Vector Reduction

Assume that the market researcher mentioned in the beginning of this chapter wanted to perform some elementary calculations on his data. For example, he might be interested in the total number of observations, the maximum value, and the minimum value for a given day. Ordinarily, he would have to prepare a repetitive program as follows:

Sum	*Maximum*	*Minimum*
1. Set $SUM\leftarrow0$.	1. Set $MAX\leftarrow0$.	1. Set $MIN\leftarrow10E10$, or a very high value.
2. Set $I\leftarrow1$.	2. Set $I\leftarrow1$.	
3. Add the Ith element to SUM.	3. Compare the Ith element with MAX.	2. Set $I\leftarrow1$.
4. Set $I\leftarrow I+1$.	4. If MAX is greater than or equal to it, go to step 5; otherwise, replace MAX with the Ith element.	3. Compare the Ith element with MIN.
5. If I is greater than the size of the vector, stop; otherwise, go to step 3.		4. If MIN is less than or equal to it, go to step 5; otherwise, replace MIN with the Ith element.
	5. Set $I\leftarrow I+1$.	5. Set $I\leftarrow I+1$.
	6. If I is greater than the size of the vector, stop; otherwise, go to step 3.	6. If I is greater than the size of the vector, stop; otherwise, go to step 3.

In APL, a composite function called *reduction* achieves the same result in one operation. The general form of the *reduction function* is: ⊕/V, where ⊕ is a scalar dyadic function, the character / is known as the solidus, and V is a vector

```
      DAY1←7 4 6 5 2
      SUM←+/DAY1
      MAX←⌈/DAY1
      MIN←⌊/DAY1
      SUM,MAX,MIN
24 7 2
      !3
6
      ×/⍳3
6
      V←6 4 10 17 3
      AV←(+/V)÷⍴V
      AV
8
      □←SD←(((+/V*2)÷⍴V)-((+/V)÷⍴V)*2)*.5
5.099
```

Figure 10.57 Vector reduction.

—expressed as a variable or the result of an expression. Reduction is defined as follows:

$$⊕/V≡V[1]⊕V[2]⊕V[3] \ldots V[(⍴V)-1]⊕V[⍴V]$$

The scalar dyadic function is executed from right to left in the usual fashion. Figure 10.57 depicts some simple examples of reduction and two obvious applications—average and standard deviation—in addition to programming the three algorithms given above.

A defined function may not be used as the scalar dyadic function in reduction, and the concept of reduction is extended, appropriately, to arrays of higher dimension. Clearly, the reduction function applied to a vector reduces it to a scalar, hence the name. In general, reduction reduces the number of dimensions in an array by one. The capability of applying the same function to all elements of an array is very useful. Thus far, it has been used for summation, product, maximum, and minimum. It can also be used in a logical sense to determine if *all* elements possess a given property or if *any* element possesses another property. For an example of logical reduction, see Fig. 10.58.

Reduction of an empty vector gives the identity element for the functions used in reduction, as listed in Table 10.5. Reduction of a scalar or a vector of one element gives that value (see Figure 10.59).

```
      X←¯1 2 5 ¯4 19
      N←⍳⍴X
      ∧/(X*N)≥0
0
      ∨/(X*N)≤0
1
      ∧/1 2 3 4=⍳4
1
      ∨/(⍳⍴A)≠A←1 2 3 4 5 6 7
0
```

Figure 10.58 Logical reduction.

TABLE 10.5   IDENTITY ELEMENTS OR PRIMITIVE
SCALAR DYADIC FUNCTIONS

Function	Identity Element	Left or Right	
+	0	L R	
−	0	R	
×	1	L R	
÷	1	R	
*	1	R	
Γ	(See Note a.)	L R	
L	(See Note b.)	L R	
|	0	L	
!	1	L	
∧	1	L R	
∨	0	L R	
=	1	L R	⎫
≠	0	L R	⎬ Logical
>	0	R	Arguments
≥	1	R	Only
<	0	L	⎭
≤	1	L	
⊛	None		
○	None		
⋏	None		
⋎	None		

a Minimum number representable in APL.
b Maximum number representable in APL.

```
                    +/\0
           0
                    */0ρ1
           1
                    ×/⁻5
          ⁻5
                    −/1ρ5
           5
```

Figure 10.59   Reduction of an empty vector, a vector with one element, and a scalar.

Applications.   A single statement without parentheses that computes:

$$e = 1 + \frac{1}{2!} + \frac{1}{3!} + \frac{1}{4!} + \cdots + \frac{1}{n!}$$

is given as follows:

$$E \leftarrow +/÷!\iota N$$

Similarly, a one-statement program to count the number of E's in a message named M is specified as:

$$COUND \leftarrow +/'E'=M$$

and a one-statement program to add the components of ιN that are divisible by 3 is specified as:

$$SUM \leftarrow +/(\iota N) \times 0 = 3 | \iota N$$

In the latter case, only functions given thus far are used. Lastly, given a vector SALARY containing employee's salary, a one-statement program that counts the number of employees with salaries over \$20,000 is given as follows:

$$NUM \leftarrow +/SALARY > 20000$$

Reversal and Rotation

The notion of *reversal* is important for applications requiring that the elements of a vector be reversed. A descending sequence of integers can be generated with an expression of the form:

$$(N+1) - \iota N$$

and if $N \leftarrow 7$, then $(N+1) - \iota N$ is equal to 7 6 5 4 3 2 1. However, the development of a defined function to reverse the elements of any vector, although certainly possible, is indeed cumbersome. The monadic *reversal function*, provided in APL, uses the composite symbol ϕ (formed from the circle symbol $\circ$ and the vertical stroke |) and reverses the elements of its argument. For example, $\phi \iota 3$ is equal to 3 2 1. If R is the result of the vector rotation ϕV, then

$$R \equiv V[1 + (\rho V) - \iota \rho V]$$

Reversal does not change the dimension of the argument, so the result assumes its dimension.

The dyadic form of the symbol ϕ is used to rotate a vector cyclically and is called *rotation*. If V is a vector and K is a scalar, then the expression $K \phi V$ rotates V to the left $(\rho V) | K$ elements. Thus, if K is positive, rotation is to the left whereas if K is negative, rotation is to the right. If $V \leftarrow \iota 6$, then $2 \phi \iota 6$ is equal to the vector 3 4 5 6 1 2. The result R of the rotation function $K \phi V$ is defined as follows:

$$R \equiv V[1 + (\rho V) | ^- 1 + K + \iota \rho V]$$

As with reversal, rotation does not change the structure of the argument and $(\rho R) = \rho V$.

Figure 10.60 gives additional examples of reversal and rotation.

```
        Φι5
5 4 3 2 1
        C←'OWT ROF AET'
        ΦC
TEA FOR TWO
        V←ι7
        2ΦV
3 4 5 6 7 1 2
        ¯3ΦV
5 6 7 1 2 3 4
        (4ΦV)=¯3ΦV
1 1 1 1 1 1 1
        7Φ'ATE'
TEA
```

Figure 10.60   Reversal and rotation.

Compression and Expansion

The *compression* function provides a means of suppressing some elements of a vector while retaining others. The general form of compression is:

$$U/V$$

where U is a logical vector that has the same dimension as V, the vector being compressed. If either argument is a scalar or a one-element array, it is extended to apply to all components of the other argument. Elements of V corresponding to a 1 in U are retained while those corresponding to a 0 in U are suppressed. Thus, 1 0 1/ι3 produces the result 1 3. (Note: The right-to-left convention applies here also.) The result of vector compression is always a vector. The result R of compression U/V has the following property:

$$(\rho R)= +/U$$

Figure 10.61 gives examples of compression.

Expansion is the converse of compression and is written as follows:

$$U\backslash V$$

```
        U←1 0 1 0
        V←'ABCD'
        U/V
AC
        U/Φι4
4 2
        U/5
5 5
        1/ι4
1 2 3 4
```

Figure 10.61   Vector compression.

```
            C←'TEA FOR TWO'
            []←[]←(U←~' '=C)/C
      TEAFORTWO
            U\[]
      TEA FOR TWO
            (11ρ1 1 1 0)\[]
      TEA FOR TWO
            U←9ρ1 0
            Y←U/⍳9
            Z←(~U)/⍳9
            Y
      1 3 5 7 9
            Z
      2 4 6 8
            (U\Y)+(~U)\Z
      1 2 3 4 5 6 7 8 9
            1 1 1 1\5
      5 5 5 5
```

Figure 10.62   Vector expansion.

where U is a logical vector. U\V expands V to the form given by U, so that $(\rho(U\backslash V))=\rho U$, by inserting padding for elements that correspond to zero elements of U. U and V must be conformable in the sense: $(+/U)=\rho V$. If the right argument is a scalar, it is extended to apply to all elements of the left argument. Numeric vectors are padded with zeros and character vectors are padded with space characters. Thus, the expression 1 0 1\7 9 produces the result 7 0 9. Figure 10.62 gives additional examples of vector expansion.

Applications. Given vectors of employee numbers and salaries as follows:

EMPL∆NO← 57 239 637 712 841 910 1059
SALARY← 9380 26140 19239 21630 4389 54553 12500

Statements that display the number of employees with salaries over $20,000 and the employee numbers of employees with salaries over $20,000 are given as follows:

'NO OF EMPLOYEES>$20,000';+/(SALARY>20000)
'EMPLOYEE NUMBERS:' (SALARY>20000)/EMPL∆NO

respectively. Given two numeric vectors X and Y of the same size, a one-statement program that merges the elements of X and Y is given as follows:

RESULT←((1=2|⍳D)\X)+(0=2|⍳D←(ρX)+ρY)\Y

Take and Drop—The Selection of Leading and Trailing Elements

To a limited extent, the capability of selecting the leading or trailing elements of a vector is provided with prefix and suffix vectors and the compression function. A *prefix vector* of order *n* is a logical vector containing *n* leading ones; the remaining elements are zero. Similarly, a *suffix vector* of order *n*

```
            X←¯7 3 9 6 5 1 4 3
            □←U←(3ρ1),((ρX)-3)ρ0
1 1 1 0 0 0 0 0
            U/X
¯7 3 9
            (~U)/X
6 5 1 4 3
            □←V←(((ρX)-3)ρ0),3ρ1
0 0 0 0 0 0 1 1 1
            V/X
1 4 3
            (~V)/X
¯7 3 9 6 5
```

Figure 10.63   Examples of prefix and suffix vectors.

```
            V←¯7 3 9 6 5 1 4 3
            3↑V
¯7 3 9
            ¯5↑V
6 5 1 4 3
            ρρ0↑V
1
            W←'IRREGARDLESS'
            ¯6↑(8↑W)
REGARD
```

Figure 10.64   The take function.

contains n trailing ones. For example, compound expressions to take or drop elements of a vector are given in Figure 10.63.

The *take* and *drop* functions in APL eliminate the need for compound expressions of this sort. The general form of the *take function* is:

$$T↑V$$

where T is a scalar value, which is restricted to being an integer, and V is a vector. T can also be a one-element array. If T is positive, then T↑V selects the first T elements of V. If T is negative, then the trailing T elements are selected. If T=0, then the result is an empty vector. Lastly, if $(|T|) > \rho V$, then the right argument is padded on the left or the right, as required. Thus, ¯2↑4 produces the vector 3 4 and 4↑3 produces 1 2 3 0. Figure 10.64 gives additional examples.

The *drop* function is defined analogously but drops the indicated elements instead of selecting them. The form of drop is:

$$T↓V$$

where T is a scalar or one-element array (again restricted to being an integer) and V is a vector. If $(|T|) \geq \rho V$, the function yields an empty vector. Thus, 2↓4 produces 3 4 and ¯3↓5 yields 1 2. Figure 10.65 depicts other examples.

```
          V←¯7 3 9 6 5 1 4 3
          3↓V
    6 5 1 4 3
          ¯5↓V
    ¯7 3 9
          ρρ(ρV)↓V
    1
          C←'/*COMMENT*/'
          ¯2↓(2↓C)
    COMMENT
```
Figure 10.65   The drop function.

Application. A single statement that adds an element to the Fibonacci sequence without using indexing is given as follows:

$$\text{FIB} \leftarrow \text{FIB},+/(\,\!^{-}2\!\uparrow\!\text{FIB})$$

Set Operations—Index Of and Membership

The *index of* function is written

$$V\iota S$$

and gives the index of the leftmost occurrence of argument S in Vector V. Thus, the function ¯7 3 9 6 5ι6 produces the value 4. The right argument can be a scalar, vector, or array and the result has the same shape. If the right argument is a vector, the result is a vector of the same size—the elements of the result are the indices of the right argument in V. If an element of the right argument in VιW is not found in V, it is given the index $1+\lceil/\iota\rho V$. For example, the expression 'ABCDE' ι 'ATE' yields 1 6 5 with 1-origin indexing and 0 5 4 with 0-origin indexing. Various examples are depicted in Figure 10.66.

The *membership* function yields a logical value (i.e., 0 or 1) if a given element (or scalar quantity) is an element of a specified vector. The function, written AεB, gives a result that is the same shape as A. If an element of A is contained

```
          V←¯7 3 9 6 5 1 4 3
          Vι3
    2
          Vιι5
    6 9 2 7 5
          []IO←0
          Vι3
    1
          (ι2)ι5
    2
          []IO←1
          A←'ABCDEFGHIJKLMNOPQRSTUVWXYZ
          Aι'TEA FOR TWO'
    20 5 1 27 6 15 18 27 20 23 15
```
Figure 10.66   Index of function.

```
        C←'ABCDEFGHIJKLMNOPQRSTUVWXYZ'
        D←'TEA FOR TWO'
        D∊C
1 1 1 0 1 1 1 0 1 1 1
        □←E←(D∊C)/D
TEAFORTWO
        E∊C
1 1 1 1 1 1 1 1 1
        V←¯7 3 9 6 5 1 4 3
        V∊ι5
0 1 0 0 1 1 1 1
```

Figure 10.67 The membership function.

in B, then the respective element of the result is 1; otherwise, it is given the value 0. B can be a scalar, vector, matrix, or higher-dimensional array. The membership function applies to numeric and character arguments. In the case of numeric values, two arguments are considered equal if their absolute values are within a tolerance of □CT and their signs are the same (Figure 10.67).

Grade Up and Down—Sequencing of Elements

The need to sort a trivial list of values occurs frequently in computer applications —yet it is one of the more cumbersome and time-consuming operations. The *grade up* function uses the monadic symbol ⍋ (formed by overstriking a delta △ with a vertical stroke) and yields a vector of indices that would order the vector right argument in ascending sequence. The general form of grade up is:

$$R \equiv \text{⍋} V$$

where the result R is the same dimension as V. Consider, for example, Figure 10.68. In the example, the index of the smallest element in V, that is, ¯7, is 1, the index of the next-highest element, that is, 1, is 6, etc. The ordering of duplicate elements is determined by their position in V.

The *grade down* function:

$$R = \text{⍒} V$$

is analogous to the grade up function except that the ordering is given in descending sequence, and the function symbol is formed from a del (∇) and a vertical stroke. Figure 10.69 contains examples of the use of the grade down function.

```
        V←¯7 3 9 6 5 1 4 3
        ⍋V
1 6 2 8 7 5 4 3
        V[⍋V]
¯7 1 3 3 4 5 6 9
```

Figure 10.68 The grade up function.

```
          V←¯7 3 9 6 5 1 4 3
          ΦV
3 4 5 7 2 8 6 1
          V[ΦV]
9 6 5 4 3 3 1 ¯7
```

Figure 10.69   The grade down function.

The argument for grade up and grade down is limited to vectors, and the dimension of the result is the dimension of the argument. The indices in the vector are affected by the index origin.

Deal—Generation of Numbers at Random Without Replacement

The roll function, discussed previously, generates numbers pseudo-randomly from a given set with replacement. Therefore, the probability of drawing a unique element from the given set by this process exists within probabilistic limits. The *deal function*, A?B, where A and B are integer scalars or one-element arrays, generates a vector of A elements from the vector ιB without replacement. Thus, each element generated is unique. The result is dependent upon the index origin. Some examples of deal are given in Figure 10.70.

Decode and Encode—Base Value and Representation

The ordinary polynomial of the form:

$$a_n x^n + a_{n-1} x^{n-1} \cdots a_2 x^2 + a_1 x + a_0$$

arises in a variety of ways in computing, the most frequent being with regard to the positional number system—or a fixed base value representation. Given a vector whose elements represent coefficients of *descending* powers of a *base* value, then the base ten value of the polynomial is usually computed using nested multiplication or an element-by-element vector multiplication and a sum reduction. In the latter case, it is first necessary to develop a weighting vector of successive powers of the base value. For example, the coefficient vector A←1 2 3 4 to the base 10 is computed using a weighting vector in Figure 10.71.

Similarly, B←1 0 1 to the base 2 and C←1 0 0 to the base 8 are computed by using a similar technique in the same figure. Actually, the operation is more general and applies to: the hours, minutes, and seconds in a day; the gallons, quarts, pints, and ounces in a barrel; the yards, feet, and inches in a mile,

```
          3?5
5 1 2
          7?7
4 5 6 2 1 3 7
```

Figure 10.70   The deal function.

```
      A←ι4
      X←1000  100  10  1
      +/A×X
1234
      B←1  0  1
      Y←4  2  1
      +/B×Y
5
      C←1  0  0
      Z←64  8  1
      +/C×Z
64
```

Figure 10.71   Use of a weighting vector.

```
      A←3  4  17
      B←3600  60  1
      []←S←+/A×B
11057
```

Figure 10.72   Conversion of hours, minutes, and seconds to seconds.

etc. That is, the radix vector need not be successive powers of a given base value. For example, the seconds in 3 hours, 4 minutes, and 17 seconds are computed in Figure 10.72. Yet, in this example, the most natural way of representing the days, hours, and minutes is:

> 24 hours per day,
> 60 minutes per hour, and
> 60 seconds per minute

which is termed a *radix vector*. The *base value* function allows the radix vector to be expressed in natural order and delegates the intermediate calculations to the computer. Base value is often called the *decode* function and is expressed as:

$$B \perp A$$

where B represents the radix and A is the vector of the coefficients. If B is a scalar, then it is extended to all elements of A. If B is a vector, then it must be the same size as A. Figure 10.73 contains the same computation as Figures 10.71 and 10.72 except that the decode function is used. The function utilizes

```
      A←ι4
      10⊥A
1234
      2⊥1  0  1
5
      24  60  60⊥3  4  17
11057
```

Figure 10.73   The decode function.

a weighting vector, internally, which is developed as follows:

$$W[\rho W] = 1$$
$$W[I-1] = B[I] \times W[I]$$

Here, B is the radix vector. The result R of the decode function is defined as:

$$R \equiv +/A \times W$$

The *representation function*, also called *encode*, provides the converse of decode. The function is expressed as:

$$B \top S$$

where B is the radix vector and S is a scalar value. The dimension of the result is the size of B (see Figure 10.74).

R[1] is not used in either function and the components of the radix or coefficient vectors are not restricted to integral or positive values, as shown in Figure 10.75.

Applications. A hexadecimal number uses the base 16 and the characters 0123456789ABCDEF. A one-statement program that converts a positive decimal number N to a hexadecimal number H, stored as a vector of 4 characters, is given as follows:

$$H \leftarrow \text{'0123456789ABCDEF'}[1+(4\rho16)\top N]$$

A one-statement program that converts a hexadecimal number, as defined above, back to decimal is given as:

$$N \leftarrow 16\bot^-1+\text{'0123456789ABCDEF'}\iota H$$

```
            10  10  10  10⊤1234
    1  2  3  4
            2  2  2⊤5
    1  0  1
            2  2⊤5
    0  1
```

Figure 10.74 The encode function.

```
            109  3  .5⊥3  2  0
    5.5
            109  3  .5⊤5.5
    3  2  0
            ‾3  ‾3  ‾3⊥1  3  5
    5
            2  2  2  2⊤‾5
    1  0  1  1
```

Figure 10.75 The arguments for the decode and encode function are not restricted to integral or positive values.

```
        A←ι5
        +\A
1 3 6 10 15
        +\ΦA
5 9 12 14 15
```

Figure 10.76 The scan function.

Scan

The *scan* function takes the form:

$$\oplus\backslash V$$

where V is a numeric vector and $\oplus$ is a scalar dyadic function. The scan function generates a vector of the same size as V; the elements of the result R are defined as follows:

$$R[I] \equiv \oplus/V[\iota I]$$

where $I = 1, 2, \ldots, (\rho V)$ and $R[0] \equiv V[0]$ if $0 = \Box IO$. Figure 10.76 gives an example of the scan function.

Execute

The *execute* function is used to execute a string of characters as though it were an APL expression. The form of the monadic execute function is:

$$\pm C$$

where $\pm$ is a composite character formed from the $\perp$ and small circle (○) symbols. (The small circle ○ is found over the J on the APL keyboard.) The argument C can be a character scalar or a character vector. Figure 10.77 gives several examples of the execute function. If the argument is a null vector, then the execute function is not executed. (An execute function that is not executed cannot be used as an argument, as demonstrated in the last statement of Figure 10.77.

```
        []←C←'2+2'
2+2
        ⊥C
4
        ⁻1+⊥C
3
        ⊥[]
A←54 ⁻47 3
        A
54 ⁻47 3
        ⊥ι0
        1+⊥ι0
VALUE ERROR
        1+⊥ι0
        ^
```

Figure 10.77 The execute function.

```
                        A←¯47 53 39 6
                        B←⌽A
                        B
              ¯47 53 39 6
                        B[1 2]
              ¯4
                        B[6 7 8]
              3 3
                        C←123456
                        D←D←⌽C
              123456
                        2⌽D
              345612
```

Figure 10.78   The monadic format function.

Format

The *format* function is used to format the right argument as a character array; it has both monadic and dyadic forms. The monadic format function takes the form

$$\Phi B$$

where Φ is a composite symbol formed from the $\top$ and $\circ$ symbols, and B is a scalar, vector, or array. The result of the function is a character array that is identical in appearance to the characters displayed when the output of B is specified. Figure 10.78 demonstrates how the monadic format function is used.

The dyadic format function takes the form:

$$A\Phi B$$

where A controls the format and B serves as the argument to the function. The argument B can be a scalar, vector, or an array. The result of the dyadic function is a character array representing a formatted form of the right argument according to the format specified by the left argument. The left argument A is a pair of numbers, used as follows:

$$n_1 n_2 \ \Phi B$$

→Precision
→Field width

The left argument can be specified as a vector variable or a vector constant. Consider the following statements:

$$W \leftarrow 13.412 \quad 16.215 \quad {}^{-}93.8471 \quad .169304$$
$$V \leftarrow 8 \ 2 \Phi W$$

The format function specifies that each value is to be displayed with a field width of 8 with two decimal places to the right of the decimal point. The follow-

```
      P←¯764.3126
      Q←9 3τP
      Q
¯764.313
      W←¯13.412 16.215 ¯93.8471 1.69304
      □←V←8 2τW
¯13.41    16.21   ¯93.85    1.69
      □←U←12 ¯4τW
¯1.341E01    1.621E01    ¯9.385E01    1.693E00
      G←248.61452 97.370126
      □←H←10 3 9 2τG
248.615    97.37
```

Figure 10.79 The dyadic format function.

ing rules apply to the dyadic format function:

1. If the precision number is positive, the result is in decimal form with the number of decimal places specified by the precision number.
2. If the precision number is negative, the result is in scaled representation with the number of digits to the left of the E specified by the precision number.
3. If the field width entry in the left argument (i.e., A in the above format) is zero, then the computer selects a field width such that at least one space separates adjacent numbers.
4. If the left argument contains only one number, then it represents the precision and a field width of zero, as in rule 3, is assumed.
5. When scaled representation is used, the field width must include character positions for the exponent.

Several examples of the dyadic format function are given in Figure 10.79.

The columns of a vector or array can be formatted differently by including a control pair, i.e., ⟨width precision⟩, for each column of the array. This case is also demonstrated in Figure 10.79. If a single control pair is specified, then it applies to all columns. If more than one control pair is desired, then a control pair must be specified for *each* column of the array.

REFERENCES

Katzan, H., *APL User's Guide*, Van Nostrand Reinhold Company, New York, 1971.
IBM 5100 Portable Computer publication: *IBM 5100 APL Reference Manual*, Form #SA21-9213.
IBM Corporation, Rochester, Minnesota 55901.

11 | APL PROGRAMMING II:

Defined Functions, System Variables, and Related Concepts

It is neither practical nor desirable to include, as built-in functions, all sequences of calculations that any user might want to have executed by the computer. Moreover, a large number of language primitives would indeed by confusing to the user. On the other hand, it is necessary that a means be provided so that a user or group of users does not have to enter, or even prepare, a single function more than once. The APL system allows the user to define a function, give it a name, and have it stored in the active workspace. System commands are available for transferring entire workspaces and individual functions between the main storage unit and a tape cartridge. This chapter is primarily concerned with how functions are defined, used, modified, and checked.

11.1 DEFINED FUNCTIONS

The notion of exactly what constitutes a program in the APL language is frequently of concern, particularly to those readers familiar with other programming systems. In the execution mode, statements can be entered by the user and are executed immediately by the computer. Since a program is nothing more than a sequence of statements and programming is the synthesis of meaningful calculations from a sequence of ordinary statements, statements entered and executed in the execution mode satisfy the basic definition of a program even though the sequence in which statements are processed is determined explicitly by the user. Most computer users, however, regard a program as something that, once initiated, is executed automatically with no intervention. This facility is permitted through a *defined function*. When a defined function is executed by the computer, statements are selected from the defined function automatically as executed progresses. Execution of a defined function is always initiated by entering a statement when the computer is in the execution mode.

Overview

The APL system operates in two modes: the execution mode and the definition mode. In the execution mode, as covered previously, statements are executed immediately upon being entered. In the definition mode, statements are saved as part of a defined function. A defined function can then be used in one of two ways:

1. As a stand-alone program that is executed by entering the function name, or
2. As a mathematical function which can be used in an expression, much like the common arithmetic operations + and ×.

The APL system enters the definition mode when the user enters the ∇ character (called *del*) followed by a *function header* statement, which gives the form of the function being developed and the syntax of how it should be used. The APL system leaves the definition mode and re-enters the execution mode when the next ∇ is received. Figure 11.1 shows a "simple" defined function that displays the name of a well-known computer. The name of the defined function is COMPUTER and it is executed by entering the function name COMPUTER. Figure 11.2 shows another "simple" defined function that adds two values. The name of the second function is PLUS, which required two arguments (X and Y) and returns a result so that it may be used in an expression.

```
        ∇COMPUTER
[1]  []←'IBM 5100 PORTABLE COMPUTER'
[2]  ∇
        COMPUTER
IBM 5100 PORTABLE COMPUTER
```
Figure 11.1   A defined function that displays the name of a well-known computer.

```
        ∇R←X PLUS Y
[1]  R←X+Y
[2]  ∇
        2 PLUS 2
4
        A←5
        []←B←A PLUS 3
8
        []←B←20−A PLUS 3
12
```
Figure 11.2   A defined function that can be used in an expression.

Introduction Examples

Consider a right triangle program that computes the diagonal, perimeter, and area when the height and base are given, as follows:

$$d = \sqrt{h^2 + b^2}$$
$$p = h + b + d$$
$$a = \tfrac{1}{2} bh$$

when $h = 3$ and $b = 4$, then

$$d = \sqrt{3^2 + 4^2} = 5$$
$$p = 3 + 4 + 5 = 12$$
$$a = \tfrac{1}{2}(4)(3) = 6$$

The right triangle program is given as a defined function in Figure 11.3. The statements that comprise the function TRIANGLE are described further. Statement (1) puts the APL system into the definition mode and denotes that TRIANGLE is the name of the program. To be completely accurate, here, TRIANGLE is actually a function—but one without parameters and which does not return an explicit result. Statements (2) through (4) comprise the body of the function and are executed sequentially. Statement (5), which is simply the del (∇) symbol, takes the system out of the definition mode and into the execution mode. After statement (5), TRIANGLE exists in the active workspace as a *defined function*. The function TRIANGLE is executed by typing its name (statement 6), and the statements in TRIANGLE are executed sequentially. The system exits from the function after the execution of the last statement has been completed.

```
          ∇TRIANGLE              (1)
     [1]  □←D←((H*2)+B*2)*.5     (2)
     [2]  □←H+B+D                (3)
     [3]  □←.5×B×H               (4)
     [4]  ∇                      (5)
          H←3
          B←4
          TRIANGLE               (6)
     5
     12
     6
          H←5
          B←12
          TRIANGLE
     13
     30
     30
```

Figure 11.3 Program for the right triangle problem entered in the definition mode and executed by a statement entered in the execution mode.

Earlier in this chapter it was stated that a function could be defined so that it could be used as a mathematical function. In fact, the dyadic function PLUS with those characteristics was given. This section goes into more detail on how a function of that type is developed. Consider the mathematical function:

$$f(x) = x^2 + 1$$

It has one argument (or operand) and should be defined so that it can be used as a constituent of an arithmetic expression, that is, in an expression such as

$$f(7) + 1$$

or

$$y = \frac{f(z + 1)}{2}$$

A suitable APL function to compute $f(x)$ is given as Figure 11.4. Statement (1) puts the APL system into the defintion mode and establishes the syntax of the function. Its name is F; it requires one argument (denoted by X, which is a dummy variable); and it returns an explicit result (denoted by the left arrow and R, which is also a dummy variable) so that it can be used in an arithmetic expression. Statement (2) computes $x^2 + 1$ and statement (3) ends the function. In statement (4), the function F is applied to the value 7, as a monadic function, and the partial result of 50 (i.e., $7^2 + 1$) is added to 1, giving the result 51. Statement (5) is processed in a similar manner.

The facility for defining functions is a powerful one, indeed, and Figure 11.5 computes the composite function:

$$f(x) = g(x)^2$$

when

$$g(x) = x + 1$$

The function f denoted by the APL function FX and the function g is denoted by GX.

```
        ∇R←F  X            (1)
   [1]  R←1+X*2            (2)
   [2]  ∇                  (3)
        1+F  7             (4)
   51
        Z←2
        □←Y←(F  Z+1)÷2     (5)
   5
```

Figure 11.4 Function with one argument defined as a mathematical operation.

```
        ∇A←GX X
[1]  A←X+1
[2]  ∇
        ∇B←FX Y
[1]  B←(GX Y)*2
[2]  ∇
            []←ANS←FX 3
16
           ‾1+FX 3
15
```

Figure 11.5 Using one defined function in the body of another defined function.

Mechanics of Function Definition

Ordinarily, the APL system is in the execution mode so that it can respond to requests for computation by the user. The *definition mode* is used for defining functions and is entered by keying in the character ∇, the del, followed by a function header statement, which contains the name of that function. The system leaves the definition mode when the next del is received, that is, if it is not contained in the literal or a comment line. Figure 11.6 gives a state diagram illustrating the execution and definition modes.

After the function header is entered in a function definition, the system responds with a number enclosed in brackets as follows:

∇RTRNGLE

[1]

Statements within functions are sequenced by a decimal number, and the number of the next statement to be entered is given by the computer. The user enters the statements, comprising the function, successively until the function is completed. The statements are not checked as they are received by the computer and are stored in the active workspace under the function name. A final del then completes the function. Figure 11.7 gives a complete function and some examples of how it is used. It should be noted here that *this* function is invoked by entering its name and that it requires no arguments. However, RTRNGL does not return an explicit result, so its appearance in a compound expression results in an appropriate error message. Figure 11.8 depicts an attempt to use RTRNGL in an erroneous manner.

Functions can be modified in a variety of ways. The most elementary form of modification is given here; more extensive procedures are given later in this chapter. Since D, P, and A were displayed after each execution of RTRNGL in the preceding example, it seems reasonable to reopen the function definition and simply add the necessary statement. A function is reopened by entering a del followed by the function name; the system responds with the number of the next statement to be entered. In Figure 11.9, an output statement is added to RTRNGL and the function is again closed. Although the characteristics of that

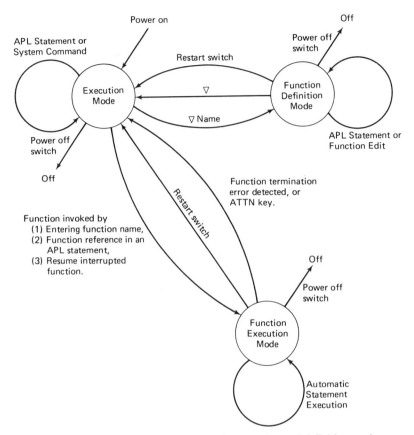

Figure 11.6   State diagram illustrating the execution and definition modes.

```
      ∇RTRNGL
[1]   D←((H*2)+B*2)*.5
[2]   P←H+B+D
[3]   A←.5×B×H
[4]   ∇
      H←3
      B←4
      RTRNGL
      D,P,A
5 12 6
```

Figure 11.7   A defined function with no arguments that does not return an explicit result.

```
      2×RTRNGL
VALUE ERROR
      2×RTRNGL
      ∧
```

Figure 11.8   An attempt to use a function with an implicit result in a compound expression.

```
                    ∇RTRNGL
             [4]   D,P,A
             [5]   ∇
```

Figure 11.9 Adding a statement to a closed function.

```
                    H←3
                    B←4
                    RTRNGL
           5  12  6
                    H←5
                    B←12
                    RTRNGL
           13  30  30
```

Figure 11.10 Output from the defined function RTRNGL with an embedded output statement.

function remain the same (no arguments, implicit result), it now contains embedded output statements and displays the computed results automatically, as shown in Figure 11.10.

After a few changes, it is usually desirable to obtain a listing of the function to insure that future modifications are made from a known base. This is achieved by using the window symbol ▯ as follows:

$$∇RTRNGL[▯] ∇$$

Figure 11.11 gives a complete listing of RTRNGL.

APL also contains facilities for inserting, replacing, or deleting statements and for obtaining a more precise listing of a function. These facilities are introduced in this chapter under the topic, "Function Modification."

The Syntax of Defined Functions

Given a function f and arguments A and B, the syntax of the different forms of functions can be listed as follows:

Number of Formal Arguments	Syntax
Two	$A f B$
One	$f B$
None	f

```
                  ∇RTRNGL[▯]∇
             ∇  RTRNGL
        [1]     D←((H*2)+B*2)*0.5
        [2]     P←H+B+D
        [3]     A←0.5×B×H
        [4]     D,P,A
             ∇
```

Figure 11.11 Listing of a defined function.

Functions of these types are termed dyadic, monadic, and niladic, respectively. When more than two arguments are required, one or both of the formal arguments can be made a vector, a matrix, or a higher-dimensioned array. It is also possible to design a function that accepts either scalar arguments or array arguments; in this case, the function is said to be *defined on arrays*. Similar conventions apply to the result of a function.

The components of a function definition have names which make it easier to discuss them. The statement following the initial *del* is termed the *function header*. The numbers in brackets are called the *statement numbers* and the associated statements are the *body* of the function. The function header essentially controls the form of the function. Six possibilities exist which are grouped into two classes depending on whether or not the function returns an explicit result. The forms are summarized in Table 11.1. An *explicit result* function produces a result and may appear as a constituent of an expression, much like the primitive functions. The different types of defined functions are introduced separately.

Implicit Argument–Explicit Result. This form requires no arguments but produces a result that can be used in an expression, as shown in Figure 11.12. An explicit result function without arguments is analogous to a constant in that it can be used anywhere that an argument can be used, except to the left of a specification operation. The specification symbol in the function header denotes an explicit result; and the dummy variable to its left, called a dummy result, is ordinarily assigned a value during the execution of the function.

TABLE 11.1 SYNTAX OF DEFINED FUNCTIONS

| | Form of Function Header | |
Arguments	Explicit Result	No Explicit Result
0	∇R←FCN	∇FCN
1	∇R←FCN Y	∇FCN Y
2	∇R←X FCN Y	∇X FCN Y

FCN = function name; X, Y = dummy arguments; R = dummy result.

```
        ∇R←RTR1
[1]  D←((H*2)+B*2)*.5
[2]  P←H+B+D
[3]  A←.5×B×H
[4]  R←D,P,A
[5]  ∇
        B←1+H←3
        ▯←T←RTR1
5  12  6
        RTR1+2
7  14  8
```

Figure 11.12 An implicit argument—explicit result function.

```
        ∇X RTR2 Y
[1] D←((X*2)+Y*2)*.5
[2] P←X+Y+D
[3] A←.5×X×Y
[4] D,P,A
[5] ∇
        5 RTR2 12
13 30 30
        (25*.5) RTR2 3×4
13 30 30
```

Figure 11.13   An explicit argument—implicit result function.

Explicit Argument–Implicit Result. This form allows more flexibility in the values to which the function can be applied but restricts the function from being used as a constituent of a compound expression. Figure 11.13 gives an example of this type of function. This example is the first in which formal arguments have been used. Formal arguments, such as X and Y, above, are used during function definition as *dummy variables.* When the function is used, they must be replaced with expressions that have a value. Every occurrence of a dummy variable within a function is effectively replaced by the value that the argument assumes at the point of activation. The use of a dummy variable within a function definition does not affect its value outside the function definition. Figure 11.14 shows how a variable X retains its value even though the same name is used as a dummy variable in a function.

Explicit Argument–Explicit Result. This form requires one or more arguments and returns a result that can be used in a compound expression. Figures, 11.14, 11.15, and 11.16 depict this form of defined function. Careful attention should be given to the function header, since it gives a prototype of how the function *must* be used. If the function header denotes two arguments (i.e., a dyadic function), then the function must be used as a dyadic function. This philosophy applies to monadic and niladic functions, as well.

The user must also be aware of the arguments to which a function is applied and the result that is returned. In general, an argument may be any constituent that is acceptable to the body of the function and is analogous, in that sense, to a primitive function. Consider again the PLUS function given above and listed in Figure 11.16 along with some uses of it. Clearly, the values which replace

```
        ∇R←X PLUS Y
[1] R←X+Y
[2] ∇
        Y←2×X←10
        17 PLUS ¯4
13
        X,Y
10 20
```

Figure 11.14   The use of a dummy variable in a function does not change its value outside of the function.

```
        ∇R←X RTR3 Y
[1]  D←((X*2)+Y*2)*.5
[2]  P←X+Y+D
[3]  A←.5×X×Y
[4]  R←D,P,A
[5]  ∇
        T←3 RTR3 4
        T
5 12 6
        (3 RTR3 4)*2
25 144 36
```

Figure 11.15   An explicit argument-explicit result function.

```
        ∇R←X PLUS Y
[1]  R←X+Y
[2]  ∇
        2 PLUS ⍳5
3 4 5 6 7
        (⍳5) PLUS ⌽⍳5
6 6 6 6 6
```

Figure 11.16   A function defined for use with scalar or array arguments.

dummy variables X and Y can be any values in the range of the dyadic function +. In other functions, the argument(s) must be of a specific type. The SORT function given in Figure 11.17 requires that the single argument be a vector and produces an error message (Figure 11.18) if applied to a scalar value. This error could have been avoided by judicious use of the ravel function as shown in Figure 11.19.

```
        ∇DONE←SORT LIST
[1]  DONE←LIST[⍋LIST]
[2]  ∇
        SORT ¯7 3 9 6 5 1 4 3
¯7 1 3 3 4 5 6 9
        ⌽ SORT ¯7 3 9 6
9 6 3 ¯7
```

Figure 11.17   A sort function defined on a vector argument.

```
        SORT 5
RANK ERROR
SORT[1] DONE←LIST[⍋LIST]
              ∧
```

Figure 11.18   The SORT function of Figure 11.17 applied to a scalar argument.

```
        ∇D←SRT L
[1]  D←(,L)[⍋,L]
[2]  ∇
        SRT ¯7 3 9 6
¯7 3 6 9
        SRT 5
5
```

Figure 11.19   Use of the ravel function to make a function applicable to scalar and vector arguments.

Local and Global Variables

In APL, all variables are *global* unless specified otherwise. Essentially, this means that a variable used inside and outside of a function refers to the same data item, that is, unless it is a dummy variable. In Figure 11.20, for example, H is global to functions SETH and GETH, and all references are made to the same variable. Another example is the RTR3 function considered previously and repeated in Figure 11.21. In the function, the variables D, P, and A are used as temporary variables—but ones that might conflict with important variables outside of the function definition. In Figure 11.22, for example, the values for D, P, and A could have been declared as local variables. A *local variable* is one that retains its value only within the function in which it is declared. A variable which is local to a function is *dominant* over global variables with the same name when that function is active. Local variables for a function are placed as a list after the function prototype in the function header statement. Each local variable listed in the function header must be preceded by a semicolon. Figure

```
        ∇SETH Y
[1]  H←Y
[2]  ∇
        ∇Z←GETH
[1]  Z←H
[2]  ∇
        H←2
        SETH 5
        GETH
5
        H
5
```

Figure 11.20   The use of a global variable H.

```
        ∇R←X RTR3 Y
[1]  D←((X*2)+Y*2)*.5
[2]  P←X+Y+D
[3]  A←.5×X×Y
[4]  R←D,P,A
[5]  ∇
```

Figure 11.21   A function containing global variables D, P, and A.

```
        P←777
        A←888
        D←999
        T←3 RTR3 4
        P
12
        A
6
        D
5
```

Figure 11.22   Conflict between global and temporary variables.

```
        ∇R←X RTR4 Y;P;A;D
[1]  D←((X*2)+Y*2)*.5
[2]  P←X+Y+D
[3]  A←.5×X×Y
[4]  R←D,P,A
[5]  ∇
        P←777
        A←888
        D←999
        T←3 RTR4 4
        P,A,D
777 888 999
```

Figure 11.23   An example of the use of local variables.

```
        ∇LOCAL;□IO;□PP
[1]  '*** □IO AND □PP SPECIFIES LOCALLY AS 0 AND 3 ***'
[2]  □IO←0
[3]  □PP←3
[4]  ι5
[5]  o1
[6]  '*** EXIT FROM LOCAL ***'
[7]  ∇
        □IO←1
        □PP←10
        ι5
1 2 3 4 5
        o1
3.141592654
        LOCAL
*** □IO AND □PP SPECIFIES LOCALLY AS 0 AND 3 ***
0 1 2 3 4
3.14
*** EXIT FROM LOCAL ***
        ι5
1 2 3 4 5
        o1
3.141592654
```

Figure 11.24 Sample function in which the system variable □IO and □PP are declared as local variables.

11.23 depicts the function of Figure 11.21 with variables P, A, and D declared as local variables. Before RTR4 is invoked, the variables P, A, and D are assigned values. During the execution of RTR4, global variables P, A, and D are figuratively "pushed down" and local variables P, A, and D are established and used as temporary variables. When the execution of RTR4 has been completed, the local variables are eliminated and the global variables P, A, and D are "popped up" with their original values.

Local variables are particularly useful when developing a function that is to be used by a number of people to avoid conflict with variables that might otherwise be in use as global variables.

Variables that may be declared as local are not restricted to those defined by the user and may include systems variables. Figure 11.24, for example, depicts a defined function in which the index origion ($\Box$IO) and the printing precision ($\Box$PP) are declared as local variables.

Sequence and Control

Normally, statements in a function are executed sequentially, that is, in the order indicated by the statement numbers, and the execution of that function terminates after the last statement is processed. On the other hand, many algorithmic processes require that parts of a function be repeated. The branch statement in APL provides a facility whereby the normal sequence of operations is interrupted and execution of the function is resumed with another statement. It can also be used to exit from a function by branching to a statement numbered 0 or to a nonexistent statement number.

The general form of the *branch statement* is:

$$\rightarrow S$$

where S is an expression that reduces to an integral value. The branch is a monadic function and causes execution of the defined function to be directed to the statement numbered by the value of the expression to the right of the branch arrow. In a branch statement, no expression can appear to the left of the arrow. If the argument of the branch function is omitted, then the current function is terminated as well as the entire sequence of functions (if any) which invoked the current function.

Branching can be used in a variety of ways. If $N \leftarrow 3$ and $V \leftarrow 3\ 4\ 5\ 7$, for example, then all of the following branch statements transfer function control to the statement number 3:

$$\rightarrow 3$$
$$\rightarrow N$$
$$\rightarrow V$$

In the latter case, the system always uses the first element of a vector to determine the number of the statement to which to branch. This convention is described more formally, later. The argument to the branch function can also be an expression. If $N \leftarrow 3$, then the following statement:

$$\rightarrow (N * 2) + 1$$

denotes a branch to statement numbered 10. In the following example, the computer branches to the statement numbered 10 if $A > B$ and to statement number 20 if $A \leq B$:

$$\rightarrow ((A > B) \times 10) + (A \leq B) \times 20$$

The APL script of Figure 11.25 contains a function to compute gross pay and uses a branch statement similar to the ones just mentioned. Statement number

```
          ∇PAY←HOURS GROSSPAY RATE
[1]  →((HOURS≤40)×2)+(HOURS>40)×4
[2]  PAY←7 2⊤HOURS×RATE
[3]  →0
[4]  PAY←7 2⊤RATE×40+1.5×HOURS-40
[5]  ∇
          35 GROSSPAY 1.00
     35.00
          40 GROSSPAY 2.50
    100.00
          50 GROSSPAY 1.63
     89.65
          32 GROSSPAY 2.19
     70.08
```

Figure 11.25   An example of a multiconditional branch statement.

```
          ∇TABLE N;I
[1]  →(N>0)×2
[2]  I←1
[3]  4 0⊤I,(I*2),I*3
[4]  →((I←I+1)≤N)×3
[5]  ∇
          TABLE 6
     1   1    1
     2   4    8
     3   9   27
     4  16   64
     5  25  125
     6  36  216
```

Figure 11.26   A defined function exhibiting a program loop, a branch statement, and a local variable.

1 reduces to a branch to statement 2 if HOURS ≤ 40 and a branch to statement 4 if HOURS > 40. Statement 3 causes an exit from the function. The GROSS-PAY function uses the format function to round the gross pay to two decimal places.

The program in Figure 11.26*, which builds a table of integers along with their squares and cubes, includes the two statements:

$$\to(N>0)\times 2$$

and

$$\to((I\gets I+1)\leq N)\times 3$$

in which a branch is taken to an existing statement or to zero, which causes an exit from the function. In the first case, a branch is taken to statement 2 or statement 0, depending upon whether N is greater than zero, or not greater than zero, respectively. In the second case, a branch is taken to statement 3 or state-

*A superior version of this function using matrices is given in chapter twelve.

ment 0 depending upon whether I is less than or equal to N, or greater than N, respectively. It should be remembered here, that a branch to 0 terminates the function.

The *branch* function can now be treated more formally. In the statement:

$$\rightarrow S$$

the numeric value of S determines the statement number of the statement to be executed next. S may also indicate that the function is to be terminated, in which case a statement from a calling function is executed next. The following rules apply:

1. If the value of $1\uparrow S$ is a statement number in the function being executed, then the next statement executed is the one numbered as $1\uparrow S$.
2. If the value of $1\uparrow S$ is not a statement number in the function being executed, then the execution of that function terminates.
3. If S is an empty vector, then no branch takes place and the next statement in sequence is executed.

The last case has not been seen before and can take a variety of forms. In general, an empty vector can be computed in the following ways: $0/S$, $0\rho S$, and $S \times \iota 0$. Given a comparison expression $X\,r\,Y$ which can produce the value 0 or 1, then the following statements:

$$\rightarrow (X\,r\,Y)/S$$
$$\rightarrow (X\,r\,Y)\rho S$$
$$\rightarrow S \times \iota X\,r\,Y$$

branch to statement number S or execute the next statement depending upon whether $X\,r\,Y$ produces the value 1 or 0, respectively.[†] Note here that S can be zero, resulting in a branch out of the function if the relationship $X\,r\,Y$ is true. Figure 11.27 gives some variations in the way that a conditional branch can be used.

A branch to one of two statements S1 or S2 can be specified in the following ways:

$$\rightarrow (S1,S2)[1+X\,r\,Y]$$
$$\rightarrow ((X\,r\,Y),\sim X\,r\,Y)/S1,S2$$

Clearly, the last form can be extended to include additional statement numbers, as required. Similarly, a branch to one of several statements can be specified as:

$$\rightarrow N\phi L$$

[†] Ordinarily, r will be one of the operators: $< \leq = \geq > \neq \vee \wedge \forall \wedge \in$.

```
              ∇BFCN
        [1]  'ENTRY'
        [2]  →(X>Y)/S
        [3]  →0,ρ□←'DROPPED THROUGH'
        [4]  'BRANCH TAKEN'
        [5]  ∇
              X←10
              Y←5
              S←4
              BFCN
        ENTRY
        BRANCH TAKEN
              X←0
              BFCN
        ENTRY
        DROPPED THROUGH
              X←3
              Y←2
              S←0
              BFCN
        ENTRY
```

Figure 11.27 Variations in a conditional branch statement.

where N is a counter, L is a vector of statement numbers, ϕ is the rotation function, and the branch function selects $1 \uparrow L$ as the statement number of the next statement to be executed.

As examples of the preceding variations, three simple problems are given in Figure 11.28. The sample problems are defined as follows:

1. Generation of N terms in the Fibonacci sequence.
2. Evaluating the step function:

$$y = 0, \text{if } x \leq 0$$
$$y = 13.2, \text{if } 0 < x < 131.4$$
$$y = 50, \text{if } x \geq 131.4$$

3. Providing a multibranch function TROUBLE-REPORT whose argument is an integer indicating an error message to be selected.

All three functions are provided in that script.

Statement Labels

One of the disadvantages of branching, as it has been presented thus far, is that function modification* can rearrange the statement numbers, requiring a probable modification of some branching statements as well. APL obviates this dif-

---

*APL contains extensive facilities for function modification such that statements can be inserted into or deleted from an existing defined function. This operation requires, eventually, that the statement numbers be resequenced in accordance with the latest version of the function.

```
          ∇L←FIB N;I
[1]  →(N≥2)/3
[2]  →0,ρ□←'VALUE ERROR'
[3]  I←1↑L←1 2
[4]  →((I←I+1)≥N)/0
[5]  →4,L←L,+/¯2↑L
[6]  ∇
       FIB 5
1 2 3 5 8
       FIB 10
1 2 3 5 8 13 21 34 55 89
```

```
          ∇Y←STPFCN X
[1]  →((X≤0),((X>0)∧X≤131.4),X>131.4)/2 3 4
[2]  →Y←0
[3]  →0,Y←13.2
[4]  →0,Y←50
[5]  ∇
       STPFCN ¯1
0
       STPFCN 100
13.2
       STPFCN 1E3
50
```

```
          ∇E←TROUBLEREPORT I
[1]  →((I>5)∨I≤0)/8
[2]  →(I-1)⌽2↓⍳7
[3]  →0,ρE←'VALUE ERROR'
[4]  →0,ρE←'DOMAIN ERROR'
[5]  →0,ρE←'SYNTAX ERROR'
[6]  →0,ρE←'CHARACTER ERROR'
[7]  →0,ρE←'RANK ERROR'
[8]  'IMPROPER TROUBLE REPORT'
[9]  →
[10] ∇
       TROUBLEREPORT 2
DOMAIN ERROR
       TROUBLEREPORT 5
RANK ERROR
       TROUBLEREPORT 10
IMPROPER TROUBLE REPORT
```

Figure 11.28 Sample problems exhibiting the use of the branch statement.

ficulty by permitting a statement to be given a name, called a statement label (or simply a label). A *statement label* is an ordinary scalar variable which has the value of the statement number with which it is associated and is assigned that value automatically by the APL system. Therefore, if a label is used with branching instead of a statement number, then the branch is always valid, regardless of the actual numbering of statements.

```
      ∇PAY←HOURS GROSSPAY RATE
[1]  →(HOURS≥40)/OVTIME
[2]  →0,ρPAY←7 2⊤HOURS×RATE
[3]  OVTIME: PAY←7 2⊤RATE×40+1.5×HOURS-40
[4]  ∇
      40 GROSSPAY 2.50
 100.00
      50 GROSSPAY 1.00
  55.00
```

Figure 11.29 An application of a statement label and conditional branching.

A statement is given a label by preceding the body of the statement by a name and separating the two with a colon as follows:

$$\text{LOOP: } A \leftarrow B+C$$

.

.

.

$$\rightarrow \text{LOOP}$$

A label is local to the function in which it is used. The GROSSPAY example given in Figure 11.25 is modified to use a label and a conditional branch and is included as Figure 11.29. Additional examples are given in subsequent figures.

The IF Function

Branch statements are cumbersome to write and more frustrating to read—even with the use of statement labels. A simple IF function that takes the form:

$$\nabla R \leftarrow A \text{ IF } B$$
[1] $R \leftarrow B/A$
[2] ∇

where A is a statement number or a scalar variable, representing a statement number, and B is a logical scalar value,* can be used to facilitate the writing of conditional statements. The IF statement is used as follows:

→(HOURS>40)/OVTIME   →OVTIME IF HOURS>40
Without IF Function   *With IF Function*

If the value of the scalar expression is false, program control drops through to the next sequential statement. Several examples of the IF function are given in the succeeding section on looping.

*Briefly, B is either 0 or 1.

```
      ∇R←X PLUS Y
[1] ⍝ THIS IS A VERY SIMPLE FUNCTION
[2] R←X+Y
[3] ⍝ THIS DEL DOES NOT END FCN ∇
[4] ⍝ BUT THE NEXT ONE DOES ...
[5] ∇
      1 PLUS 2
3
```

Figure 11.30   Use of a comment line.

Comments

A *comment line* may be inserted in a defined function by making the first character of that line the composite character ⍝, the lamp symbol, formed by overstriking the small circle ○ with the character ∩. In a defined function, a comment line is given a statement number but that line is never executed. Figure 11.30 depicts an appropriate example.

Looping

When the algorithm requires that a sequence of steps be repeated, the corresponding program can be constructed in one of two ways: (1) The program steps can be duplicated the necessary number of times; and (2) the program can be written to execute the same steps iteratively. For long or complex programs, or when the exact number of iterations is not known beforehand, the iterative method is usually preferred.

A series of statements to be executed many times is called a *loop*, and the statements in the loop are called the *range of the loop* or the *body of the loop*. One pass through the loop is termed an *iteration*. A loop must be executed a certain number of times and some mechanism must determine whether the required number has been reached. One of the mechanisms for doing this is a *control variable* which is set to a given value initially (usually zero) and is increased by another value (usually one) for each iteration that is to be made. The process also requires a *limit value*, which determines the upper limit on the number of iterations. Loops may also be programmed in another manner. The control variable may be set initially to the limit value and it is decreased for each iteration until zero is reached. If the control variable is used as an index or data value in the loop, this use frequently determines the direction in which the control variable should be sequenced. In still other cases, a control variable is not required and the program iterates until a specified condition is met—such as a residual value being less than a certain tolerance value. Figure 11.31 depicts the required steps in a loop; they are summarized as follows:

1. *Initialization*. Variables are given initial values; special conditions are checked; and control variables are given appropriate values. Program control is never returned here.

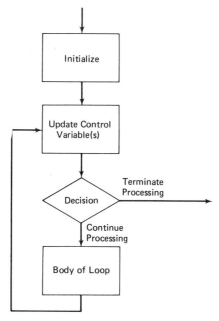

Figure 11.31   Program loop.

2. *Update*. The control variable is updated to correspond to the next iteration.
3. *Decision*. A test is made to determine whether the necessary number of iterations has been made. If so, then an exit is made from the loop; otherwise, control passes to the body of the loop.
4. *Body of the loop*. The required calculations are made for each iteration. Control passes to the update step.

The preceding steps have described the *method of leading decisions*. Clearly, it is feasible to place the decision step after the body of the loop—except in one case. That is when a check should be made to determine if the loop should be executed zero times. Because of the array functions in APL, the need for loops is diminished significantly. The script contained in Figure 11.32 computes the square root R of a value X and uses the following relationship:

$$R \leftarrow R + .5 \times (X \div R) - R$$

The program uses an initial guess $(R = 1)$ and iterates until the residual $|(R * 2) - X$ is less than a given tolerance E.

The example in Figure 11.33 uses a control variable and smooths a given function by a simple averaging method. Consider a vector X with indices running

```
        ∇R←SQRT X;E
[1]  →INIT IF X>0
[2]  →0,ρ□←'VALUE ERROR'
[3]  INIT: E←.001
[4]  R←1
[5]  TEST: →0 IF (|(R*2)-X)≤E
[6]  →TEST,R←R+.5×(X÷R)-R
[7]  ∇
        ∇R←A IF B
[1]  R←B/A
[2]  ∇
        SQRT 1
1
        SQRT 25
5
        SQRT 6.25
2.5
```

Figure 11.32   An iterative function to compute the square root of an argument.

```
        ∇S←SMOOTH X;I;L
[1]  →INIT IF (ρX)>3
[2]  →0,ρ□←'DATA ERROR'
[3]  INIT: I←1
[4]  L←(ρX)-1
[5]  S←ι0
[6]  LOOP: →0 IF (I←I+1)>L
[7]  S←S,(X[I-1]+X[I]+X[I+1])÷3
[8]  →LOOP
[9]  ∇
        SMOOTH 2 10 6 8 16 12 2 4 6 8 7
6 8 10 12 10 6 4 6 7
```

Figure 11.33   A smoothing program containing a program loop.

from 1 to ρX. A given component X[I], for I>1 and I< ρX, is smoothed by expression:

$$S[I] = (X[I-1] + X[I] + X[I+1]) \div 3$$

The function returns a vector which has two less components than the original vector.

Collectively, defined functions and sequence and control facilities enable APL to be used as a programming system and enhance its interactive capabilities.

Sample APL Defined Functions

This section gives a collection of relatively short APL defined functions designed to give an idea of the various techniques that can be used in the construction of APL programs. A "good" defined function is a blend of program size and execution time, which are correlated to some degree.

Adding Machine. Figure 11.34 depicts an adding machine program named ADD that sums a column of numbers entered by the user. When the column is

```
            ∇ADD[□]∇
       ∇ ADD;□IO;S;C;K
  [1]    □IO←1
  [2]    S←⍳0
  [3]    C←'0123456789.+-¯E
  [4]    AGN:→(0=ρK←□)/SUM
  [5]     →((⌈/C⍳K)>ρC)/ERR
  [6]    →AGN,S←S,⍋K
  [7]    SUM:→0,ρ□←+/S
  [8]    ERR:→AGN,ρ□←'CHARACTER ERROR'
       ∇
```

Figure 11.34   Listing of an adding machine simulator.

```
              ADD
       123.50
       ¯100
       4

       27.5
```

Figure 11.35   Sample run of the function ADD defined in Figure 11.34.

complete, the user presses the EXECUTE key without entering any characters and the values are added. A sample run is given in Figure 11.35. The defined function demonstrates the following techniques:

1. □IO as a local variable.
2. Use of a null vector, i.e., $S←⍳0$, to initiate the formation of a vector of values that are later added.
3. Character input and a check for a null character string:

$$AGN: →(0=ρK←□)/SUM$$

4. A test, using the *index of* function, to verify that a character string is in an allowable set:

$$→((⌈/C⍳K)>ρC)/ERR$$

5. Use of the *execute* function to execute an APL expression:

$$→AGN, S←S, ⍋K$$

(This statement also combines a branch and a specification statement.)
6. Combined branch and output statements:

$$SUM:→0, ρ□←+/S$$

and

$$ERR:→AGN, ρ□←\text{'CHARACTER ERROR'}$$

Techniques numbered 4, 5, and 6 use the fact that a branch function of the form →V always branches to the statement number selected at $1↑V$.

```
      ∇FVALUE[□]∇
    ∇ V←FVALUE D
[1]   V← 10 2 ⊤D[1]×(1+(D[2]÷100)÷D[4])*D[3]×D[4]
    ∇
      FVALUE 1000 8 20 12
   4926.80
```

Figure 11.36 Function that computes the future value of $1000 at 8% interest for 20 years compounded 12 times per year.

```
      ∇INVEST[□]∇
    ∇ V←INVEST D
[1]   V← 8 2 ⊤D[1]÷(1+(D[2]÷100)÷D[4])*D[3]×D[4]
    ∇
      INVEST 3000 8 20 12
   608.91
```

Figure 11.37 Function that computes the value that must be invested now to be worth $3000 at 8% interest in 20 years compounded 12 times per year.

Future Value and Investment. Figures 11.36 and 11.37 give two business programs: future value (FVALUE) and investment (INVEST). FVALUE computes the future value of an amount if compounded periodically at a given interest. The syntax of FVALUE is:

$$A←FVALUE\ D$$

where $(\rho D)=4$ and A is a scalar. D[1] is the amount to be invested; D[2] is the interest rate in percent; D[3] is the number of years; and D[4] is the number of times per year that interest is to be compounded. INVEST computes the value that must be invested at a given interest to be worth a specified amount in the future. The syntax of INVEST is:

$$A←INVEST\ D$$

where $(\rho D)=4$ and A is a scalar. D[1] is the future value; D[2] is the interest rate in percent; D[3] is the number of years; and D[4] is the number of times per year that interest is compounded.

Rounding and Significant Digits. Figure 11.38 gives two functions: rounding (RND) and significant digits (SIG). The syntax of RND and SIG are:

$$V←N\ RND\ X$$
$$V←N\ SIG\ \ X$$

where N is the number of places to the right of the decimal point in RND or the number of significant digits in SIG. Both functions return a result that is the same shape as the argument.

Triangular Numbers. The numbers $1, 3, 6, 10, 15, 21, 28, 36, \ldots$ are called triangular numbers because the number of units in each can be displayed as a triangular pyramid of dots. The ith triangular number p_i is computed from:

```
        ∇RND[☐]∇
     ∇ R←N RND X
[1]    →3×ι∧/(N≤0),,(2*31)≥X
[2]    →0,,R←X-N⌊X←X+0.5×N←10*-N
[3]    R←⌊0.5+N×⌊0.5+X÷N←10*-N
     ∇
        ∇SIG[☐]∇
     ∇ R←N SIG X
[1]    R←X-N⌊X←X+0.5×N←10*1-N-⌊10⍟⌈X+X=0
     ∇
        3 RND 78.12356
78.124
        ¯3 RND 123578
124000
        6 SIG 658.23456
658.235
```

Figure 11.38   Utility RND (rounding) and SIG (significant digits).

```
        ∇TRINOA[☐]∇
     ∇ R←TRINOA N;I
[1]    R←,I←1
[2]    NXT:R←R,(¯1↑R)+I←I+1
[3]    →(I<N)/NXT
     ∇
        ∇TRINOB[☐]∇
     ∇ R←TRINOB N
[1]    R←,1
[2]    NXT:R←R,(¯1↑R)+(⍴R)+1
[3]    →(N>⍴R)/NXT
     ∇
        ∇TRINOC[☐]∇
     ∇ R←TRINOC N
[1]    R←+\ιN
     ∇
        TRINOA 5
1 3 6 10 15
        TRINOB 10
1 3 6 10 15 21 28 36 45 55
        TRINOC 20
1 3 6 10 15 21 28 36 45 55 66 78 91 105 120 136 153
     171 190 210
```

Figure 11.39   A function that computes a vector of length N of triangular numbers.

$p_i = p_{i-1} + i$. For example, the 8th triangular number 36 is computed as 28+8. Figure 11.39 contains three versions of a monadic explicit result function that computes a vector containing the first N triangular numbers.

Common Divisor. Figure 11.40 depicts a function that computes the common divisor of two scalar integers using Euclid's algorithm.

Processing of Character Data. Many useful applications involve the manipulation of textual information—such as prose text or a list of character items. For these cases, it is advantageous to store the information as a single character vector and maintain indices to it, as appropriate. Figure 11.41 lists two functions: one to *store* character data items and another to *fetch* them on request. A sim-

```
            ∇EUCLID[□]∇
         ∇ R←A EUCLID B
    [1]    L:R←A
    [2]      A←A|B
    [3]      B←R
    [4]      →(A≠0)/L
         ∇
            12 EUCLID 18
      6
            7 EUCLID 13
      1
```

Figure 11.40 A function that computes the common divisor of two scalar integers A and B using Euclid's algorithm.

```
            ∇INIT[□]∇
         ∇ INIT
    [1]    ID←LENGTH←TEXT←\0
    [2]    START←,0
         ∇

            ∇STORE[□]∇
         ∇ STORE;I;A
    [1]    'ENTER INTEGER ID FOLLOWED BY TEXT ON THE NEXT LINE'
    [2]    →(0=I←□)/0
    [3]    →(0=ρA←□)/0
    [4]    LENGTH←LENGTH,ρA
    [5]    ID←ID,I
    [6]    →2,START←START,ρTEXT←TEXT,A
         ∇

            ∇FETCH[□]∇
         ∇ FETCH LIST;IND;I;L
    [1]    L←ρIND←ID\LIST←,LIST
    [2]    →(1=v/IND>ρID)/ERR
    [3]    I←0
    [4]    LOOP:→(L<I←I+1)/0
    [5]    TEXT[START[IND[I]]+\LENGTH[IND[I]]]
    [6]    →LOOP,ρ□←' '
    [7]    ERR:'INVALID ID'
         ∇
```

Figure 11.41 APL functions STORE and FETCH for the storage and retrieval of character data.

ple application of the functions is given in Figure 11.42. Each character item entered is given a numeric identification by the user. The text is stored in a character vector named TEXT, and its associated identification number is stored in the vector ID. The first position of each item in TEXT is stored in START, and the length of each item is stored in LENGTH. The vectors in Figure 11.42 are related as follows:

```
        ID
3  17  10  57  40
        START
0  24  50  72  95  115
        LENGTH
24  26  22  23  20
        TEXT
INVENTORY CONTROL SYSTEMACCOUNTS RECEIVABLE SYSTEM5100 PORTABLE
    COMPUTERAPL AND BASIC LANGUAGESAMORTIZATION PROGRAM
```

```
            INIT
            STORE
    ENTER INTEGER ID FOLLOWED BY TEXT ON THE NEXT LINE
    □:
            3
    INVENTORY CONTROL SYSTEM
    □:
            17
    ACCOUNTS RECEIVABLE SYSTEM
    □:
            10
    5100 PORTABLE COMPUTER
    □:
            57
    APL AND BASIC LANGUAGES
    □:
            40
    AMORTIZATION PROGRAM
    □:
            0
            FETCH 40 17 57
    AMORTIZATION PROGRAM

    ACCOUNTS RECEIVABLE SYSTEM

    APL AND BASIC LANGUAGES
```

Figure 11.42 Application of functions STORE and FETCH to sample character data.

```
                ∇HIST[□]∇
        ∇ HIST X;I
    [1]    I←⌈/X
    [2]    ' □'[1+I≤X]
    [3]    →2 IF 0<I←I-1
        ∇
            V←1 2 3 4 10 8 6 3 7 9 11 8 5 3 2 1
            HIST V
                    □
        □        □
        □        □□
        □□      □□□
        □□      □□□□
        □□□    □□□□
        □□□    □□□□□
        □□□□    □□□□□
        □□□□□□□□□□□□
        □□□□□□□□□□□□□
        □□□□□□□□□□□□□□
```

Figure 11.43 Function HIST for plotting of frequency histograms for integer values with abscissa running horizontally.

Graph Plotting. A vector of integers is plotted as a histogram with the abscissa running horizontally across the display screen and the ordinate running vertically. Figure 11.43 gives a defined function HIST that plots a frequency histrogram. Often, the information to be plotted must be scaled and reduced to integral values. If X is a vector of values to be plotted and S is a scale factor,

```
              ∇CURVE[□]∇
          ∇ CURVE X;I
      [1]     I←⌈/X
      [2]     '| ',' °'[1+I=X]
      [3]     →2 IF(I←I-1)>0
      [4]     ' ',((ρX)+1)ρ'_'
          ∇

          PTS←1 1 2 3 5 7 8 8 7 5 3 2 1 1
          CURVE PTS
      |        ° °
      |       °   °
      |
      |      °     °
      |
      |     °       °
      |    °         °
      |  ° °         ° °
      _____
```

Figure 11.44 Function CURVE for plotting a continuous curve against its own indices.

then the following statement prepares the statement for use with one of the plotting functions:

$$Y←\lfloor 0.5+X÷S$$

A vector of integers is plotted as a continuous curve in a similar fashion. Figure 11.44 lists a short function, CURVE, which plots a vector against its own indices.

Character Output

Consider the function, given in Figure 11.45, that displays a message, requests input, and displays the data entered. The problem is that the input data is prefixed with the message displayed. Therefore, if quote-quad input follows character output and only the input is to be processed, the character output must be removed from the input line. The function OUTIN in Figure 11.46 solves the problem by dropping the character output from the input line. The OUTIN program will work as long as the character output is less than 64 characters and

```
              ∇EXTRA[□]∇
          ∇ EXTRA
      [1]     □←'ENTER PATIENT''S NAME'
      [2]     NAME←□
      [3]     'THE FOLLOWING DATA IS STORED IN ''NAME'':'
      [4]     NAME
          ∇
          EXTRA
      ENTER PATIENT'S NAME JOHN DOE'
      THE FOLLOWING DATA IS STORED IN 'NAME':
      ENTER PATIENT'S NAME JOHN DOE'
```

Figure 11.45 Demonstration of a problem wherein an input line is prefixed with preceding character output.

```
      ∇ R←OUTIN MSG
[1]     □←MSG
[2]     R←(ρMSG)↓□
      ∇
        ∇NOEXTRA[□]∇
      ∇ NOEXTRA
[1]     NAME←OUTIN 'ENTER PATIENT''S NAME'
[2]     'THE FOLLOWING DATA IS STORED IN ''NAME'':'
[3]     NAME
      ∇
        NOEXTRA
ENTER PATIENT'S NAME JOHN DOE'
THE FOLLOWING DATA IS STORED IN 'NAME':
 JOHN DOE'
```

Figure 11.46 A function OUTIN that removes character output from an input line.

does not include cursor returns. If the message is possibly longer than 64 characters, then OUTIN would have to be modified as follows:

$$R \leftarrow (64 \mid \rho MSG) \downarrow \square$$

Lastly, if the message can include a cursor return, which is element 157 of the atomic vector, i.e., $\square AV[157]$, the function OUTIN would have to be written as follows:

```
      ∇R←OUTIN MSG; □IO;PTR
[1]     □IO←1
[2]     PTR← ̄1+(ϕ□←MSG)ι□AV[157]
[3]     R←(64|PTR)↓□
      ∇
```

The revised function operates by removing the residual of the message after the cursor return.

Locked Functions

A *locked function* is a function that can be executed, copied, or erased, but cannot be revised or displayed. Moreover, a locked function cannot be unlocked, so that if it contains an error, it cannot be edited or corrected. The use of locked functions provides a means of securing proprietary programs.

A function is locked by opening or closing a function definition with a del (∇) overstuck with the tilde symbol (∼).

11.2 FUNCTION MODIFICATION

In the course of developing a function, many problems arise which require that the function be modified in some way. In most cases, the modification involves a display of the function (or part of it) followed by an addition, deletion, insertion, or replacement of one or more statements. The body of a function is

```
        ∇DUMMYFCN
   [1] LINE1
   [2] LINE2
   [3] LINE3
   [4] LINE4
   [5] LINE5
   [6] LINE6
   [7] ∇
```

Figure 11.47 A dummy function defined for use in function modification examples.

not checked by the computer as it is entered—however, the function header is. This fact is used with examples of function editing. The function in Figure 11.47 is defined for use in subsequent examples. The various conventions for modifying a function are presented in the following form:

> Type of modification or operation,
> General form, and
> An example

Throughout this section, FCN is used as a dummy function name and N is a statement number.

Entering and Leaving the Definition Mode

The definition mode is entered for a *new defined function* by entering a del followed by the function header, which gives the syntax of the defined function. When entering the definition mode for an *existing function*, the user must enter a del followed only by the function name. For example, if the function header for a defined function is:

$$∇R←X \text{ PLUS } Y$$

then the following statement is entered to reenter the definition mode for that function:

$$∇PLUS$$

In a defined function, the function header is given a statement number of zero for purposes of editing only, and statements in the function body are numbered consecutively. If the definition mode is reentered for a function, the computer responds with the number of the next statement that would ordinarily be entered. For example, if a function body contained six statements and the definition mode were reentered for that function, then the computer would respond with line number seven, that is, [7]. Figure 11.48 gives an example of how the definition mode is reentered for an existing function.

The APL system leaves the definition mode anytime another del is entered—except when it is in a literal or a comment line. Thus, the PLUS function, which

$$\nabla DUMMYFCN$$
$$[7]$$

Figure 11.48   Reentering the definition mode for an existing function.

has been used as an example several times, could have been entered as follows:

$$\nabla R \leftarrow X \text{ PLUS } Y$$
$$[1] \qquad R \leftarrow X + Y \nabla$$

When the APL system is in the definition mode for a function, that function definition is said to be *open*. Similarly, when the system leaves the definition mode for a function, that function definition is said to be *closed*.

Display of a Function

Several variations exist in the way that a function can be displayed:

1. A single statement can be displayed.
2. An entire function can be displayed.
3. Statements of a function can be displayed beginning with a designed statement number.

Moreover, the statements of a function can be displayed if that function is open or if it is closed.

The quad symbol enclosed in brackets, $[\Box]$, is used to denote that a statement or a series of statements should be displayed. In some cases, such as $[3\Box]$ for example, the convention is altered to denote a specific statement. Each convention for displaying a defined function is identified and presented separately.

1. *Display a closed function.*
   General form:

$$\nabla FCN[\Box] \nabla$$

   Example: Figure 11.49.
2. *Display a closed function and leave it open to perform additional modifications.*
   General form:

$$\nabla FCN[\Box]$$

   Example: Figure 11.50.
3. *Display an open function.*
   General form:

$$[\Box]$$

   Example: Figure 11.51.

```
                ∇DUMMYFCN[□]∇
              ∇ DUMMYFCN
        [1]     LINE1
        [2]     LINE2
        [3]     LINE3
        [4]     LINE4
        [5]     LINE5
        [6]     LINE6
              ∇
```

Figure 11.49 Displaying a closed function.

```
                ∇DUMMYFCN[□]
              ∇ DUMMYFCN
        [1]     LINE1
        [2]     LINE2
        [3]     LINE3
        [4]     LINE4
        [5]     LINE5
        [6]     LINE6
              ∇
        [7]
```

Figure 11.50 Displaying a closed function and leaving the defintion open.

```
              ∇LISTFCN
        [1] LINE1
        [2] LINE2
        [3] [□]
              ∇ LISTFCN
        [1]     LINE1
        [2]     LINE2
              ∇
        [3]
```

Figure 11.51 Displaying an open function.

4. *Display an open function and leave definition mode.*
   General form:

$$[□] \nabla$$

   Example: Figure 11.52.
5. *Display a statement of a closed function.*
   General form:

$$\nabla FCN[N□] \nabla$$

   Example: Figure 11.53.
6. *Display a statement of a closed function and leave it open for further modification.*
   General form:

$$\nabla FCN[N□]$$

   Example: Figure 11.54.

```
        ∇LISTFCN
    [1] LINE1
    [2] LINE2
    [3] [□]∇
        ∇ LISTFCN
    [1]    LINE1
    [2]    LINE2
        ∇
```

Figure 11.52 Displaying an open function and leaving the definition mode.

```
        ∇DUMMYFCN[4□]∇
    [4]    LINE4
```

Figure 11.53 Displaying a statement of a closed function.

```
        ∇DUMMYFCN[3□]
    [3]    LINE3
```

Figure 11.54 Displaying a statement of a closed function and leaving the definition open.

7. *Display a statement of an open function and leave definition mode.*
   General form:

$$[N□] \triangledown$$

   Example: Figure 11.55
8. *Display a statement of an open function and change it.*
   General form:

$$[N□]$$

   Example: Figure 11.56.
9. *Display a closed function beginning with statement number N leaving it open or closed.*
   General forms:

$$\triangledown FCN[□N]$$
$$\triangledown FCN[□N] \triangledown$$

   Examples: Figure 11.57.
10. *Display a function header.*
    General forms:

$$\triangledown FCN[0□] \triangledown$$
$$[0□]$$

    Example: Figure 11.58.

Statement Replacement and Insertion

A statement in a defined function is replaced by entering another statement with the same number. A statement is inserted between existing statements by using

```
                    ∇LISTFCN
              [1] LINE1
              [2] LINE2
              [3] LINE3
              [4] [2□]∇
              [2]    LINE2
```

Figure 11.55 Displaying a statement of an open function and leaving the definition mode.

```
                    ∇LISTFCN
              [1] LINE1
              [2] LINE2
              [3] LINE3
              [4] [2□]
              [2] LINE TWO
              [3] [□]∇
                  ∇ LISTFCN
              [1]    LINE1
              [2]    LINE TWO
              [3]    LINE3
                  ∇
```

Figure 11.56 Displaying a statement of an open function and changing it.

```
                    ∇DUMMYFCN[□4]∇
              [4]    LINE4
              [5]    LINE5
              [6]    LINE6

                    ∇DUMMYFCN[□5]
              [5]    LINE5
              [6]    LINE6
              [6]
```

Figure 11.57 Displaying a closed function beginning with a specified statement number.

```
                    ∇DUMMYFCN[0□]∇
              [0]    DUMMYFCN

                    ∇LISTFCN
              [1] LINE1
              [2] [0□]
              [0]    LISTFCN
```

Figure 11.58 Displaying a function header.

a statement number, with up to four decimal places, that numerically falls between the statement numbers of the existing statements. For example, statement number [4.1] might be used to insert a statement between statement numbered [4] and statement numbered [5]. After an inserted statement, the *next* statement number is determined by adding 1 to the rightmost place of the inserted statement number.* If the statement number [10.001], for example, is used to insert a statement between statement numbered [10] and statement

---

*The last valid statement number is 9999.9999.

```
          ∇DUMMYFCN
    [7]  [3]  LINE  THREE
    [4]  [7]  LINE7
    [8]
```

Figure 11.59 Overriding a statement number.

numbered [11], then the computer would next ask for statement number [10,002]. When the definition of a function is closed, the statements are re-numbered with consecutive integers to satisfy the requirement that statement numbers have integral values.

Convections for replacing and inserting a statement are presented separately in the following paragraphs.

1. *Override a statement number.†*
   General form:

$$[N] \ldots$$

   Example: Figure 11.59.
2. *Insert a statement.*
   General form:

$$[N.M] \ldots$$

   Example: Figure 11.60.
3. *Open a function, replace a statement, and leave the definition mode.*
   General form:

$$\nabla FCN[N] \ldots \nabla$$

   Example: Figure 11.61.
4. *Open a function, replace a statement, and remain in the definition mode.*
   General form:

$$\nabla FCN[N] \ldots$$

   Example: Figure 11.62.

The procedures outlined in cases 3 and 4 also apply to insertion, in a similar manner.

---

†If more than one statement number is entered on the same line, only the last statement number is used. For example, if a line contains [4] [9] [5] A←1, only statement [5] is re-placed when the EXECUTE key is pressed.

```
                    ∇DUMMYFCN
        [8] [4.2] INSERT LINE
        [4.3] [□]
              ∇ DUMMYFCN
        [1]     LINE1
        [2]     LINE2
        [3]     LINE THREE
        [4]     LINE4
        [4.2] INSERT LINE
        [5]     LINE5
        [6]     LINE6
        [7]     LINE7
              ∇
        [8]  ∇
                    ∇DUMMYFCN[□]∇
              ∇ DUMMYFCN
        [1]     LINE1
        [2]     LINE2
        [3]     LINE THREE
        [4]     LINE4
        [5]     INSERT LINE
        [6]     LINE5
        [7]     LINE6
        [8]     LINE7
              ∇
```

Figure 11.60   Inserting a statement in a defined function and resequencing after the definition is closed.

```
                    ∇DUMMYFCN[1] LINE ONE∇
                    ∇DUMMYFCN[□]∇
              ∇ DUMMYFCN
        [1]     LINE ONE
        [2]     LINE2
        [3]     LINE THREE
        [4]     LINE4
        [5]     INSERT LINE
        [6]     LINE5
        [7]     LINE6
        [8]     LINE7
              ∇
```

Figure 11.61   Opening a function definition, replacing a statement, and closing the definition—all in one statement.

Statement Deletion

A statement can be deleted from a closed or an open function by entering one of the following forms:

$$\nabla FCN[\Delta N]$$
$$[\Delta N]$$

If it is desired to close the function immediately after the deletion, then the closing ∇ must be entered on the next line. Example: Figure 11.63.

```
          ∇DUMMYFCN[1] LINE WON
   [2] [□]
      ∇ DUMMYFCN
   [1]    LINE WON
   [2]    LINE2
   [3]    LINE THREE
   [4]    LINE4
   [5]    INSERT LINE
   [6]    LINE5
   [7]    LINE6
   [8]    LINE7
      ∇
   [9]
```

Figure 11.62 Opening a function definition, replacing a statement, and remaining in the definition mode.

```
            ∇DUMMYFCN
   [9] [△5]
   [6] [□]
      ∇ DUMMYFCN
   [1]    LINE WON
   [2]    LINE2
   [3]    LINE THREE
   [4]    LINE4
   [6]    LINE5
   [7]    LINE6
   [8]    LINE7
      ∇
   [9] ∇
            ∇DUMMYFCN[□]∇
      ∇ DUMMYFCN
   [1]    LINE WON
   [2]    LINE2
   [3]    LINE THREE
   [4]    LINE4
   [5]    LINE5
   [6]    LINE6
   [7]    LINE7
      ∇
```

Figure 11.63 Deleting a statement of a function.

Statement Editing

Statement editing is performed by employing facilities presented earlier in this chapter and in chapter nine. The following steps comprise the procedure for line editing:

1. Display the statement to be edited by entering one of the following forms:

$$[N\square]$$
$$\nabla FCN\ [N\square]$$

depending upon whether the function is open or closed, respectively. (N is the number of the statement to be edited.) The statement is displayed in the input line.

2. Edit the statement using the procedures given in chapter nine for line editing.

3. Press the EXECUTE key. The statement in the defined function is replaced and the next statement number is displayed.

When a function is being edited, the scroll up and scroll down keys are inactive. All other keys on the keyboard, however, continue to be active.

11.3 PROGRAM CHECKOUT

Errors exist for a variety of reasons, ranging from simple typing mistakes to major errors in logical or mathematical reasoning. These errors are collectively termed *bugs* and the process of removing them is termed *debugging* or *program checkout*. The APL system contains two facilities, trace control and stop control, which greatly reduce the effort required to check out a program.

The symptoms of an error are usually obvious: An error message is received, the program stops, or incorrect results are computed. With an error message or a halted function the user can diagnose the difficulty, modify his function, and continue. The reasons for incorrect results can be detected by a perusal of the statements, by tracing the function, or by inserting stops at various statements to investigate the function at those points during the course of execution.

Halted Functions

A function is halted for one of two reasons: (1) The execution of a statement cannot be completed; and (2) the function runs for an inordinate length of time and the user presses the ATTN key to halt execution. Case (2) is actually part of case (1).

If the execution of a statement cannot be completed, the following actions are taken by the computer:

1. An error message is printed identifying the error that was encountered.
2. The name of the function and the statement number of the statement being processed is printed.
3. The erroneous statement is printed.
4. A caret is printed to indicate how far exeuction has progressed in that statement.

Thus, the execution of the active function is *suspended* and the sequence of functions which led to the execution of that function (either directly or indirectly) are left *pending*. A function in the latter state is said to be *pendent*. If a function is halted by the ATTN key, then only step 2 takes place. A suspended function remains suspended until one of three actions is taken: (1) A branch, →S, is entered to resume execution at the statement whose number is S; (2) a branch to zero, →0, is given to terminate that function; and (3) a branch without a right argument, →, is entered to clear that suspended function and its pendent functions.

When a function is suspended, the system is in the execution mode and the user can perform calculations, define functions, and even modify the suspended function. Modification of a pendent function, however, engenders a SI DAMAGE error report. Consider the example given in Figure 11.64. While EFCN is suspended, the user is able to define and execute another function. Then EFCN is modified and execution is resumed.

Variables that are local to a function remain active when that function is suspended and may be used as arguments in the usual fashion. Figure 11.65 gives an example in which local variable A is displayed when the function is suspended and another local variable B is specified. They remain active when the function is suspended. When the function is eventually completed, they are undefined.

State Indicator

The APL system contains a *state indicator* which gives a list of pendent and suspended functions. The state indicator is displayed with the system command)SI, which may be used at any time the system is in the execution mode. The

```
          ∇EFCN
     [1]  A←1
     [2]  B←2
     [3]  U←1∧∧1
     [4]  A,B,U
     [5]  ∇
          EFCN
     SYNTAX ERROR
     EFCN[3] U←1∧∧1
              ∧
          5.5*2
     30.25
          ∇R←X PLUS Y
     [1]  R←X+Y
     [2]  ∇
          1 PLUS 2
     3
          ∇EFCN[3]U←1∧1∇
          →3
     1 2 1
```

Figure 11.64 When a function is suspended, the system enters the execution mode and the user has access to all of the facilities of the APL system.

```
          )CLEAR
CLEAR WS
          ∇AFCN;A;B;C
[1] A←1
[2] C←A+B
[3] []←A,B,C
[4] ∇
          AFCN
VALUE ERROR
AFCN[2] C←A+B
                ^
          A
1
          B←2
          →2
1 2 3
          A
VALUE ERROR
          A
          ^
```

Figure 11.65 When a function is suspended, local variables remain active.

)SI display requires some explanation. Consider the following display:

$$\begin{array}{ll} & \text{)SI} \\ A[5] & * \\ B[6] & \\ C[7] & \end{array}$$

Entries marked with an asterisk indicate suspended functions; other entries denote pendent functions. A[5] denotes that function A was suspended just before statement 5 was completed. B[6] means that function A was invoked in statement 6 of function B. C[7] indicates that function B was invoked from statement 7 of function C.

Since a suspended function puts the APL system in the execution mode, other functions can be invoked (and defined, as well) and they can become suspended also. Thus, a situation such as the following might result:

$$\begin{array}{ll} & \text{)SI} \\ H[3] & * \\ I[4] & \\ J[5] & \\ A[10] & * \\ XY[7] & \\ H[3] & * \end{array}$$

where the asterisk again denotes a suspended function and entries without an asterisk indicate a function that is pendent. A function can be invoked more than once and become suspended or pendent that many times.

Since local variables remain active when a function is suspended, the question of what variables are accessible is frequently of concern. The system command)SIV displays the *state indicator vector*, a list of variables local to suspended and pendent functions. In the above case, the)SIV might give the following information:

```
        )SIV
H[3]    *  X  Y        (Last invocation of H)
I[4]       Z
J[5]
A[10]   *  X  W
XY[7]
H[3]    *  X  Y        (First invocation of H)
```

Here, the variables X and Y that are local to the last invocation of function H are accessible while the X local to function A and the X and Y local to the first invocation of H are not.

The state indicator and state indicator vecor can be cleared using the branch arrow without an argument (i.e., →). Each branch arrow clears one suspended function and associated pendent functions. Applied to the above example, it would give:

```
            →
          )SI
A[10]   *
XY[7]
H[3]    *
```

and another branch without an argument would give:

```
          )SI
H[3]   *
```

The state indicator is cleared completely by entering a → without an argument for each asterisk in the list.

Tracing Execution of a Function

If a program gives incorrect results and the reason is not obvious from reviewing the statements, then the user has good reason to trace the execution of that function.

The trace of a function FCN is specified as follows:*

$$T\Delta FCN \leftarrow V$$

---

*It should be obvious now why names cannot begin with T∆.

where V is a vector whose components correspond to the statement numbers in FCN that are to be traced. The trace function works as follows: (1) the value of each statement, whether or not the last operation is a specification, is printed; and (2) the value of the expression to the right of each branch statement that is taken is printed. All output is identified by function and statement number. Figure 11.66 gives an example of how the execution of a function can be traced. The expression TΔFCN←0 or TΔFCN←ι0 discontinues the trace.

Stop Control

When program errors cannot be detected with the trace function, it is necessary to halt execution at specific statements so that the user can "poke" around to ascertain the status of variables and indicators. The stop control feature operates very similarly to the trace function and serves that purpose. A statement of the form:

$$S\Delta FCN \leftarrow V$$

is used to establish stop control. Here, FCN is the function under study and V is a vector of statement numbers. Execution of the function is halted *just before* each statement whose statement number is in V. Figure 11.67 depicts an example of the use of the stop control feature. The function name and statement number are printed each time the function is halted. Stop control is discontinued by SΔFCN←0 or SΔFCN←ι0.

Program checkout in an APL environment is affected significantly by the interactive mode of operation. Ordinarily, checkout would be performed by inserting output statements at appropriate places in the program. When the program is completely verified, then the output statements are removed. The trace and stop control facilities in APL eliminate the need for this type of activity.

Execution of a Halted Function

Execution of a halted function is resumed by branching to the statement number given in the suspension report (e.g., EFCN[3]) displayed when that function was halted. A branch to any other statement resumes execution at that point. A branch to zero or to a statement number outside the range of those in the function terminates execution of that function.

The system variable $\Box$LC contains the statement number currently being executed. When a function is halted, $\Box$LC contains the same statement number as in the suspension report. Therefore, it is possible to resume execution of a halted function by entering the following statement:

$$\rightarrow \Box LC$$

The system variable $\Box$LC is covered in the next section.

```
        ∇R←SQRT X;E
[1]  →(X>0)/INIT
[2]  →0,ρ□←'VALUE ERROR'
[3]  INIT: E←.001
[4]  R←1
[5]  TEST: →((|(R*2)-X)<E/0
[6]  R←R+.5×(X÷R)-R
[7]  →TEST
[8]  ∇
        SQRT 1
DOMAIN ERROR
SQRT[5]TEST:→((|(R*2)-X)<E/0
                                ∧
        )SI
SQRT[5] *
        ∇SQRT[5] TEST: →((|(R*2)-X)<E)/0∇
        →5
1
        SQRT 1
1
        □PP←3
        SQRT 25
5
        T∆SQRT←5 6 7
        SQRT 9
SQRT[5] →6
SQRT[6] 5
SQRT[7] →5
SQRT[5] →6
SQRT[6] 3.4
SQRT[7] →5
SQRT[5] →6
SQRT[6] 3.02
SQRT[7] →5
SQRT[5] →6
SQRT[6] 3
SQRT[7] →5
SQRT[5] →0
3
        SQRT 16
SQRT[5] →6
SQRT[6] 8.5
SQRT[7] →5
SQRT[5] →6
SQRT[6] 5.19
SQRT[7] →5
SQRT[5] →6
SQRT[6] 4.14
SQRT[7] →5
SQRT[5] →6
SQRT[6] 4
SQRT[7] →5
SQRT[5] →6
SQRT[6] 4
SQRT[7] →5
SQRT[5] →0
4
        T∆SQRT←ι0
        SQRT 4
2
```

Figure 11.66 Tracing the execution of a function.

```
        A←B←C←D←0
        ∇SFCN
[1] A←1
[2] B←2
[3] C←3
[4] D←4
[5] 'FINI'
[6] ∇
        SΔSFCN←2 4
        SFCN

SFCN[2]
        B
0
        →□LC

SFCN[4]
        D
0
        →□LC
FINI
        A,B,C,D
1 2 3 4
        SΔSFCN←ι0
        SFCN
FINI
```

Figure 11.67   Analyzing a function using the stop control feature.

11.4 SYSTEM VARIABLES

System variables govern the operation of the APL system and provide information about the system to the user. Each system variable begins with the quad symbol, and a reference to a system variable causes a corresponding entry to be made in the system symbol table. The value assigned to a system variable can be displayed by entering the system variable name. The values of some system variables, such as □PP—printing precision, can be changed; others may not be modified.

Comparison Tolerance

Comparison tolerance is controlled by the system variable □CT, which can be set by the user. With a clear workspace, □CT is set to 1E⁻13 by the APL system. The value of □CT gives the maximum tolerance in testing for equality. If the absolute value of the difference between two numbers is greater than □CT, then the numbers are unequal. □CT is used in the computation for the floor and ceiling functions.

Index Origin

The index origin is controlled by the system variable □IO, which can be set to 0 or 1 by the user. The index origin affects the following functions: indexing

([ ]), index generator (ι), index of (ι), roll (?), deal (?), grade up ($\spadesuit$), and grade down (ψ).

Printing Precision

The printing precision is controlled by the system variable ⎕PP, which can be set by the user. The value of ⎕PP determines the number of digits of precision displayed for numbers in decimal or scaled representation and for integers greater than $2^{31}-1$. With a clear workspace, ⎕PP is set to 5. ⎕PP can be set to any integer value between 1 and 16, inclusive.

Print Width

The width of the output line for display or printing is controlled by the system variable ⎕PW, which can be set by the user to any value from 30 to 390. ⎕PW is set to 64 with a clear workspace. When the length of an output line is greater than ⎕PW, the line overflow to the next line. When the system is in the function definition mode, ⎕PW is temporarily set to 390. When the system leaves the function definition mode, ⎕PW reverts to its previous value.

Random Link

The seed value for generating random numbers is controlled by the system variable ⎕RL, which can be set by the user from 1 to $2^{31}-1$. With a clear workspace, ⎕RL is set to $7*5$ which is 16807.

Line Counter

The line counter is maintained in the system variable ⎕LC, which is a vector that cannot be set by the user. The first element of ⎕LC is the statement number currently being executed.   Succeeding elements in ⎕LC are the statement numbers of statements from pendent functions by reverse order of function references. An attempt to modify ⎕LC is ignored by the system.

Workspace Available

The amount of unused space in bytes in the active workspace is stored in system variable ⎕WA, which cannot be set by the user. An attempt to modify ⎕WA is ignored by the system.

Latent Expression

The character vector assigned to the system variable ⎕LX is executed with the execute function ($\pm$) when the stored workspace containing the latent expression is loaded into the active workspace. Thus, if ⎕LX←'ABC', then function named ABC would be executed automatically when the workspace containing the state-

```
      ⎕AVι'ABC'
87 88 89
      ⎕AV[88]
B
      ⎕←A←'FIRST LINE THEN CURSOR RETURN',⎕AV[157],'SECOND LINE'
FIRST LINE THEN CURSOR RETURN
SECOND LINE
      ⎕←A←'FIRST LINE THEN LINEFEED',⎕AV[160],'SECOND LINE'
FIRST LINE THEN LINEFEED
                       SECOND LINE
```

Figure 11.68 Examples of the use of the atomic vector (⎕AV). ⎕AV[157] is the cursor return character; ⎕AV[160] is the linefeed character.

ment ⎕LX←'ABC' and defined function ABC is loaded. If the latent expression is intended to display a message, then a double set of quotes must be used as follows:

$$⎕LX←' "MOUNT TAPE \#123 ON BUILT-IN UNIT" '$$

The system variable ⎕LX can be used for security by assigning a function that requests a password from the user and terminates execution if it is supplied incorrectly.

Atomic Vector

A 256-character vector containing all possible APL characters is stored in system variable ⎕AV, which cannot be set by the user. A list of characters in ⎕AV is given in the appendices.

⎕AV can be used as any other character vector, as depicted in Figure 11.68. Two of the most frequent uses of the atomic vector are in character sorting and for inserting cursor return and linefeed characters into the output line.

REFERENCES

Hellerman, H., and Smith, I. A., *APL/360: Programming and Applications*, McGraw-Hill Book Company, New York, 1976.

Katzan, H., *APL Programming and Computer Techniques*, Van Nostrand Reinhold Company, New York, 1970.

Katzan, H., *APL User's Guide*, Van Nostrand Reinhold Company, New York, 1971.

IBM 5100 Portable Computer publications:

IBM 5100 APL Reference Manual, Form \#SA21-9213

IBM Corporation, Rochester, Minnesota, 1976.

12 | ADVANCED TOPICS IN APL PROGRAMMING

This chapter covers four important topics in APL programming: matrices and arrays of higher dimension; tape input and output, and printer output; system functions; and the representation of data structures in APL. The subject of *matrices and arrays of higher dimension* extends the concept of vector functions, covered earlier, and provides much of the power of the APL system. A well-written APL program using the full complement of applicable facilities in the language can be notably efficient in terms of storage requirements and processing time. Knowledge of tape operations permits data files to be stored and retrieved from a magnetic tape cartridge and provides the facility for storing large amounts of data. Printer operations permit the user to control the manner in which APL output is printed. System functions provide APL language-related operations that are outside of the scope of the language but which are executable from an executing APL function, in contrast to system commands that can only be entered by a user at the keyboard. The subject of the representation of data structures in APL is presented as a useful programming technique, which additionally gives examples of APL defined functions. The subject matter presented in this chapter assumes a familiarity with the introductory material on APL programming covered in chapters nine, ten, and eleven.

12.1 MATRICES AND ARRAYS OF HIGHER DIMENSION

Functions defined previously on vectors are extended systematically to *n*-dimensional arrays. The distinction between vectors, matrices, and arrays is a pedagogical one, and the basic concepts apply to all arrays—regardless of their shape or size.

Fundamental Concepts

Nearly everyone is familiar with matrices and their indexing properties. In the matrix A, for example, the element A[I;J] is the scalar value found in the Ith row and the Jth column. In arrays of higher dimension, however, indexing properties are not as well known—and frequently lead to some confusion.

Consider the problem of stringing out the elements of a matrix in some order. Two methods can be identified by inspection: row major order and column major order. Applied to the matrix

$$A = \begin{pmatrix} 8 & 7 & 1 & 9 \\ ^-4 & 2 & 3 & 6 \\ 0 & ^-5 & 4 & 1 \end{pmatrix}$$

the two lists would appear as follows:

Row Major Order		Column Major Order	
Element	*Indices*	*Element*	*Indices*
8	A[1;1]	8	A[1;1]
7	A[1;2]	⁻4	A[2;1]
1	A[1;3]	0	A[3;1]
9	A[1;4]	7	A[1;2]
⁻4	A[2;1]	2	A[2;2]
2	A[2;2]	⁻5	A[3;2]
3	A[2;3]	1	A[1;3]
6	A[2;4]	3	A[2;3]
0	A[3;1]	4	A[3;3]
⁻5	A[3;2]	9	A[1;4]
4	A[3;3]	6	[2;4]
1	A[3;4]	1	3;4]

The indices appear most naturally in row major order and that method is referred to in APL as *index order*. Whenever the elements of an array are unraveled, they always appear in index order. Similarly, consider a three-dimensional array as follows:

B =

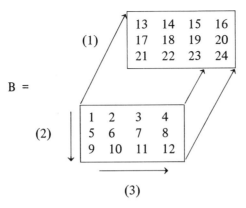

(3)

where the numbers in parentheses indicate the first coordinate, the second coordinate, and the third coordinate, respectively. For example, A[2;1;3]=15.
In index order, the array is listed as follows:

Element	Indices
1	B[1;1;1]
2	B[1;1;2]
3	B[1;1;3]
4	B[1;1;4]
5	B[1;2;1]
6	B[1;2;2]
7	B[1;2;3]
8	B[1;2;4]
9	B[1;3;1]
10	B[1;3;2]
11	B[1;3;3]
12	B[1;3;4]
13	B[2;1;1]
14	B[2;1;2]
15	B[2;1;3]
16	B[2;1;4]
17	B[2;2;1]
18	B[2;2;2]
19	B[2;2;3]
20	B[2;2;4]
21	B[2;3;1]
22	B[2;3;2]
23	B[2;3;3]
24	B[2;3;4]

While there is no general means of visualizing a higher-dimensional array, the following technique will usually suffice:

1. Visualize a *vector* as a horizontal row of elements.
2. Visualize a *matrix* as a rectangular arrangement of elements.
3. Visualize a *three-dimensional* array as a sheet of paper containing one or more matrices—each of which is termed a plane (as shown above).
4. Visualize a *four-dimensional* array as a book of sheets of paper, each containing a three-dimensional array.
5. Visualize a *five-dimensional* array as a library of books (or four-dimensional arrays)—rarely will the user need to go beyond five dimensions, although the idea can be easily extended.

Thus, an element of an array is conceptualized as follows:

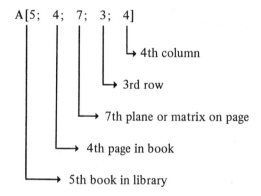

It should be noted that higher-dimensional arrays are synthesized on a right-to-left basis from vectors, matrices, three-dimensional arrays, etc.

Generating a Matrix or an Array of Higher Dimension

In the discussion of vectors, the reshape function of the form $M\rho N$ was used to generate a vector from a scalar or another vector. The left argument, that is, M, was a scalar and determined the dimension of the vector. A logical question might be, "What structure would be generated if the left argument were a vector?" The answer is that an array would be generated, and the dimension of each coordinate is determined by the value of the respective element in the vector. For example, the expression:

$$3 \quad 4\rho 1$$

generates a matrix with 3 rows and 4 columns where each element is the value 1. Use of the reshape function is frequently referred to as *restructuring* because the

```
      ∏←M←3 4ρ1
1 1 1 1
1 1 1 1
1 1 1 1
      M[2;3]←0
      M
1 1 1 1
1 1 0 1
1 1 1 1
      ∏←N←2 2ρ⍳4
1 2
3 4
      3 4ρ⍳12
1  2  3  4
5  6  7  8
9 10 11 12
      I←4
      J←2
      (I,J)ρ¯7 3 9 6 5 1 4 3
¯7  3
 9  6
 5  1
 4  3
      V←2 4 6
      2 3ρV
2 4 6
2 4 6
```

Figure 12.1   Generation of matrices.

function does indeed change the structure of the right argument. Thus, the Ith element of the vector left argument indicates the extent of the Ith coordinate of the generated array. In the examples of Figure 12.1, a matrix is displayed for the first time. A matrix is printed as a rectangular arrangement of elements and is indented from the left margin. It should be noted that the matrices in Figure 12.1 are formed from the right argument in *index order*. As with vectors, the right argument is used cyclically. If it contains more than the necessary number of elements, then only those that are required are used. The concepts apply to character arrays and higher-dimensional arrays as shown in Figure 12.2. Higher-dimensional arrays are printed as successive matrices.

In the reshape function, that is, MρN, the result is an empty array if any element of M is zero. If M is an empty vector, then the result is a scalar. These concepts are further clarified in Figure 12.3. If N is a matrix or an array of higher dimension, then the elements of N are taken in index order and treated as a vector. Figure 12.4 depicts some examples of this convention.

Application. A 4×4 identity matrix of the form:

$$
\begin{matrix}
1 & 0 & 0 & 0 \\
0 & 1 & 0 & 0 \\
0 & 0 & 1 & 0 \\
0 & 0 & 0 & 1
\end{matrix}
$$

```
      2 3 4ρι24
 1  2  3  4
 5  6  7  8
 9 10 11 12

13 14 15 16
17 18 19 20
21 22 23 24
      □←W←3 2 2ρ'ABCDEFGHIJKLMNOPQRSTUVWXYZ'
AB
CD

EF
GH

IJ
KL
```

Figure 12.2   Generation of higher-dimensional arrays.

```
          1 5ρι5
1 2 3 4 5
          5 1ρι5
1
2
3
4
5
          3 1 1ρι3
1

2

3
          A←5 0ρ3
          A


          ρA
5 0
          □←A←(ι0)ρ3
3
          ρA
```

Figure 12.3   Special cases of the reshape function.

is generated with the expression: 4 4 ρ 1 0 0 0 0. Similarly, the character matrices

TOP   and   TEA
CAT   FOR
              TWO

```
      ⎕←A←2 2ρι4
1 2
3 4
      3 2 2ρA
1 2
3 4

1 2
3 4

1 2
3 4
      B←2 3ρι6
      B
1 2 3
4 5 6
      3 2ρB
1 2
3 4
5 6
      B←2 6ρA←4 3ρ¯7 3 9 6 5 1 4 3 8 0 2 7
      A
¯7  3  9
 6  5  1
 4  3  8
 0  2  7
      B
¯7  3  9  6  5  1
 4  3  8  0  2  7
```

Figure 12.4   In the reshape function, MρN, elements from N are taken in index order.

are generated with the expressions 2 3ρ 'TOPCAT' and 3 3ρ 'TEAFORTWO', respectively. Lastly, the matrix

$$\begin{array}{ccc} ^-5 & ^-5 & ^-5 \\ 0 & ^-5 & ^-5 \\ ^-5 & 0 & ^-5 \\ ^-5 & ^-5 & 0 \\ ^-5 & ^-5 & ^-5 \end{array}$$

is generated with the expression 5 3ρ (3ρ ¯5), 0.

Shape of an Array

The monadic rho function, ρ, applied to a vector gives the dimension of that vector. The result is always a vector so that, when dealing with a nonempty vector V, $(\rho\rho V)=1$. When applied to a matrix or higher-dimensional array, the monadic rho function (often called the *dimension* function) gives a vector whose elements are the dimensions of the array. Figure 12.5 gives some examples of the dimension function applied to matrices.

```
M←3 4ρ5
ρM
```
3 4
```
N←1 1ρ7
ρN
```
1 1
```
N
```
7

Figure 12.5   Dimensions of a matrix.

```
M←3 4ρ5
ρρM
```
2
```
N←1 1ρ7
ρρN
```
2
```
ρρ1 2 3 4ρ'CAT'
```
4

Figure 12.6   Rank of an array.

The *rank* of an array A is specified as:

$$\rho\rho A$$

and gives the number of indices (i.e., subscripts) necessary to select an element of **A**. Some examples of rank are given in Figure 12.6.

Table 12.1 gives dimension and rank vectors for frequently used arrays.

Application. The following function displays the number of elements in an argument, and if the argument is a scalar, prints that fact:

```
        ∇DSPLY ARG
[1]     → ( (ρρARG) >0)/3
[2]     →0 ,ρ☐←'ARGUMENT IS SCALAR'
[3]     'NO. OF ELEMENTS IS'; × /ρARG
[4]     ∇
```

The function uses the fact that the rank of an array A (i.e., $\rho\rho A$) gives its dimension.

TABLE 12.1   DIMENSION AND RANK VECTORS FOR FREQUENTLY USED ARRAYS.

Argument (A)	ρA	ρρA	ρρρA
Scalar		0	1
Vector	I	1	1
Matrix	I J	2	1
Three-dimensional	I J K	3	1

Selection and Indexing

Although indexing is essentially a dyadic function, it appears differently from other dyadic functions in that left and right brackets are used as symbols and that indices, which are actually arguments, are separated by semicolons. The use of square brackets to enclose indices is reasonably familar but the use of a semicolon to separate them has probably puzzled the curious reader. The answer lies in the fact that an index which is ordinarily taken to be a scalar has been extended, in APL, to include arrays. Thus an index can be a vector or a matrix or a higher-dimensional array and the quantity selected has the same form. Therefore, a semicolon is used to separate structured indices.

When the array being indexed is a vector, the result R of the indexing function V[N] has the following properties:

1. R is formed by selecting from vector V those elements whose indices are the argument N.
2. $(\rho R) = \rho N$ and $(\rho\rho R) = \rho\rho N$.

Figure 12.7 depicts examples where the index to a vector is a scalar, a vector, and a matrix.

When the array being indexed is a matrix, then the result R of the indexing function W[M;N] has the following properties:

1. R is formed by selecting from W those elements whose row index is M and column index is N.
2. $(\rho R)=(\rho M),\rho N$ and $(\rho\rho R)=(\rho\rho M)+\rho\rho N$.

Careful analysis of the second property reveals that succeedingly complex results are developed by using higher-dimensional arrays as indices (Figure 12.8). If the row index is omitted, all rows are assumed, and if the column index is omitted, all columns are assumed (Figure 12.9).

The concepts are extended systematically to arrays of higher dimension, both as arrays being indexed and as the indices themselves.

An indexed variable, of the variety presently being discussed, may also appear to the left of the specification arrow, and only the selected elements are affected. Thus, as shown in Figure 12.10, entire rows or columns of a matrix, entire planes of a three-dimensional array, or portions of a vector can be replaced.

The indexing origin affects the indexing of matrices and higher-dimensional arrays in the same way that vector indexing is affected. Ordinarily, the lower bound for a coordinate index is 1 and the upper bound is the dimension of that coordinate. If 0-origin indexing is used, then the indices for all coordinates begin at zero. Figure 12.11 gives an example of 0-origin indexing for a vector, matrix, and three-dimensional array.

```
              V←¯7 3 9 6 5 1 4 3
              V[1 3 4 7 8]
         ¯7 9 6 4 3
              I←ι3
              V[I]
         ¯7 3 9
              □←V[6ρ2 6]
         3 1 3 1 3 1
              □←W←V[4]
         6
              ρW

              □←WW←V[,4]
         6
              ρWW
         1
              V[ιρV]
         ¯7 3 9 6 5 1 4 3
              M←3 2ρ6 2 7 5 4 3
              V[M]
           1 3
           4 5
           6 9
              A←'AEFORTW'
              M←3 3ρ6 2 1 3 4 5 6 7 4
              M
           6 2 1
           3 4 5
           6 7 4
              A[M]
         TEA
         FOR
         TWO
```

Figure 12.7 Indexing of a vector.

Application. Some typical applications of the preceding concepts involve the following expressions, using 1-origin indexing:

Expression	Operation Performed
A[2;]	Select the second row of matrix A.
T[3;;]	Select the third plane of array T.
C[;1]←V	Replace the first column of matrix C with vector V.
F[3;4;10]	Select the element in the third plane, fourth row, and tenth column of rank-3 array F.

The rightmost index in a subscript is always the column index, the index that is second from the right in a subscript is always the row index. Other indices in a subscript are interpreted in a similar manner from right to left.

Primitive Scalar Functions Extended to Arrays

As with vectors, element-by-element operations apply to arrays in the usual manner, as depicted in Figure 12.12. Clearly, the extension of monadic scalar

```
      ⎕←M←3 4ρ¯7 3 9 6 5 1 4 3 8 0 2 7
¯7  3  9  6
 5  1  4  3
 8  0  2  7
      M[2;3]
4
      M[1 2;1 2]
¯7  3
 5  1
      M[1 3;2 4]
 3  6
 0  7
      M[2;1 3]
5 4
      N←2 2ρ1 2 3 2
      A←M[N;2]
      ρA
2 2
      ρρA
2
      A
 3  1
 0  1
      M[2;N]
 5  1
 4  1
      B←M[,2;N]
      ρB
1 2 2
      ρρB
3
      B
 5  1
 4  1
      A←M[N;1 3]
      ρA
2 2 2
      ρρA
3
      A
¯7  9
 5  4

 8  2
 5  4
```

Figure 12.8   Indexing of a matrix.

```
        M←3 4ρ⍳12
        M[;2 4]
  2   4
  6   8
 10  12
        M[3;]
 9  10  11  12
```

Figure 12.9   Indexing of a matrix where a row or column index is omitted.

```
      V←'TEAAFORTTWO'
      V[4 8]←' '
      V
TEA FOR TWO
      V[\3]←'GIN'
      V
GIN FOR TWO
      □←M←2 3ρ1
 1 1 1
 1 1 1
      M[;2]←5
      M
 1 5 1
 1 5 1
      □←A←3 2 2ρ0
 0 0
 0 0

 0 0
 0 0

 0 0
 0 0
      A[2;;]←2 2ρ\4
      A
 0 0
 0 0

 1 2
 3 4

 0 0
 0 0
```

Figure 12.10   Indexing to the left of specification.


```
      □IO←0
      □←V←¯7 3 9 6
¯7 3 9 6
      V[1]
3
      □←M←2 3ρ\6
 0 1 2
 3 4 5
      M[1;1]
4
      □←A←2 3 4ρ\24
 0  1  2  3
 4  5  6  7
 8  9 10 11

12 13 14 15
16 17 18 19
20 21 22 23
      A[1;1;1]
17
      □IO←1
```

Figure 12.11   0-origin indexing.

```
        M←3 4ρι12
          2×M+1
  4    6    8   10
 12   14   16   18
 20   22   24   26
          -M
 ¯1   ¯2   ¯3   ¯4
 ¯5   ¯6   ¯7   ¯8
 ¯9  ¯10  ¯11  ¯12
          ⌊M÷3
 0   0   1   1
 1   2   2   2
 3   3   3   4
          3|M
 1   2   0   1
 2   0   1   2
 0   1   2   0
          ⎕←N←3 4ρΦι12
 12  11  10    9
  8   7   6    5
  4   3   2    1
          M>N
 0   0   0   0
 0   0   1   1
 1   1   1   1
          ⎕←U←3 5ρ1 0 1
 1   0   1   1   0
 1   1   0   1   1
 0   1   1   0   1
          ⎕←V←3 5ρ1 1 0 1 1
 1   1   0   1   1
 1   1   0   1   1
 1   1   0   1   1
          U∧V
 1   0   0   1   0
 1   1   0   1   1
 0   1   0   0   1
          ⎕←C←2 2 3ρι12
  1    2    3
  4    5    6

  7    8    9
 10   11   12
          C-3
 ¯2   ¯1    0
  1    2    3

  4    5    6
  7    8    9
```

Figure 12.12   Scalar functions are extended to arrays on an element-by-element basis.

functions to arrays does not require further definition. Dyadic functions are extended to an element-by-element basis but only under the following conditions:

1. One of the arguments is a scalar.
2. The arrays are *conformable*, that is, the same size.
3. One of the arrays is a single-element array of any rank.

```
        M←2 3ρι6
        M+N←1 1 1ρ10
    11  12  13
    14  15  16
        N
    10
        ρN
  1 1 1
        P←1 1ρ5
        []←Q←N+P
    15
        ρQ
  1 1 1
        ρρQ
  3
```

Figure 12.13   Single-element arrays.

```
        []←M←3 4ρι12
  1   2   3   4
  5   6   7   8
  9  10  11  12
        ,M
  1 2 3 4 5 6 7 8 9 10 11 12
```

Figure 12.14   Ravel of an array.

Further, if two single-element arrays are used as arguments, then the rank of the argument with the greatest rank is chosen for the result. Figure 12.13 depicts some results when single-element arrays are used as arguments.

The *ravel* function when applied to a matrix or an array of higher dimension generates a vector whose elements are the elements of the array taken in *index order* (Figure 12.14). The result R of the ravel function on M is always a vector, so the following relationships hold:

$$(\rho R)=\times /\rho M$$
$$(\rho\rho R)=1$$

Applications. A one-statement function to add the elements of an array ARY is given as follows:

```
        ∇R←ADDUP ARY
  [1]   R←+/ ,ARY
  [2]   ∇
```

The function is applicable, regardless of the rank of the argument. A statement that multiplies two conformable matrices A and B on an element-by-element basis, then subtracts 1 from the result, and finds the largest element is given as ⌈/ , ¯1+A×B. A function that displays a table of N integers, squares, and cubes with the columns aligned without using the format function is given as follows:

```
    ∇TABLE N;I
[1]   →(N≤0)/ERR,LST←ιI←0
[2]   NXT:→(N<I←I+1)/PRT
[3]   →NXT,LST←LST,I,(I*2),(I*3)
[4]   PRT:→0,ρ□←(N,3)ρLST
[5]   ERR: 'INVALID ARGUMENT'
[6]   ∇
```

The function accumulates the values as a vector and uses the reshape function to form the required matrix. The function can even be simplified further using other matrix operations.

Coordinates

Several functions on arrays, such as reduction, perform an operation along one of the coordinates of an array. Therefore, it is important to identify which number goes with which coordinate. In the matrix generated by the expression,

$$M←3\ 4ρι12$$

there are 3 rows and 4 columns. The coordinates are numbered by their index in the vector generated by the monadic rho function. Thus, $ρM$ is equal to 3 4; the dimension of the first coordinate is 3 and the dimension of the second coordinate is 4. Similary, for the three-dimensional array $2\ 3\ 4ρι24$, the following dimensions apply:

Coordinate	Dimension
1	2
2	3
3	4

If 0-origin indexing is used, then there is a 0 coordinate. The versatility inherent in origin indexing requires, minimally, that the first and last coordinate be identified. Therefore, if no coordinate is specified for a function on an array, then the *last* coordinate is assumed. Special provisions apply to the first coordinate. For example, reduction along the first coordinate (covered in the next section) is indicated by the composite symbol $\neq$, which is a solidus overstruck by a minus symbol.

Reduction

Reduction is applied along the Ith coordinate of an array with an expression of the form

$$⊕/[I]\ A$$

where $\oplus$ is a primitive dyadic function and A is an array. Reduction along the last coordinate is denoted by $\oplus/A$; the notation is also simplified along the first coordinate with $\oplus \neq A$, where the composite symbol $\neq$ has been mentioned previously. Figure 12.15 gives some illustrative examples of reduction applied to a matrix and a rank 3 array. Reduction effectively reduces the rank of an array by one.

Application. Assume that dollar sales by month and by salesperson are given by a table of the form:

		Month			
		JAN	FEB	MAR	APR
	BAKER	4320.50	3505.60	4987.25	1625.00
Salesperson	JONES	1274.20	1580.10	1917.50	2560.25
	SMITH	6321.50	5720.50	4731.20	4280.50

and that the matrix is generated with a statement such as:

```
    SALES←3 4ρ4320.50 3505.60 4897.25 1625.00 1274.20 1580.10
1917.50 2560.25 6321.50 5720.50 4731.20 4280.50
```

The row index is the salesperson number and the column index is the number of the month. A total of sales by month would then be given as $+\neq$SALES or as $+/[1]$SALES and the total sales by salesperson is given as $+/$SALES. A simple function to display sales by month is:

```
          ∇MONTH
     [1]  '    JAN      FEB       MAR       APR'
     [2]  9 2⊤+≠SALES
     [3]  ∇
          MONTH
     JAN        FEB       MAR       APR
    11916.20  10806.20  11545.95   8465.75
```

and similarly, a simple function to display sales by salesperson is:

```
          ∇PERSON
     [1]  '    BAKER    JONES     SMITH'
     [2]  9 2⊤+/SALES
     [3]  ∇
          PERSON
     BAKER     JONES     SMITH
    14348.35   7332.05  21053.70
```

The APL system does not distinguish between a column vector and a row vector, as shown in the PERSON function. Through reduction, the array was reduced to a column vector that is displayed horizontally.

```
      []←M←2 3ρι6
 1 2 3
 4 5 6
      +/[1]M
 5 7 9
      +/[2]M
 6 15
      (+/[2]M)=+/M
 1 1
      []←N←2 2 3ρι12
 1  2  3
 4  5  6

 7  8  9
10 11 12
      ×/N
 7 16 27
40 55 72
```

Figure 12.15 Array reduction.

Scan

The scan function is applied along the Ith coordinate of an array with an expression of the form

$$\oplus \backslash [I] A$$

where $\oplus$ is a primitive dyadic function and A is an array. The scan operator applied along the last coordinate is denoted by $\oplus \backslash A$; the notation is simplified along the first coordinate as $\oplus \bar{\backslash} A$, where $\bar{\backslash}$ is a composite symbol formed from $\backslash$ and $-$. Figure 12.16 contains examples of the scan function.

Inner Product

The familiar matrix product of the form:

$$\begin{bmatrix} a_{11} a_{12} a_{13} \\ a_{21} a_{22} a_{23} \end{bmatrix} \begin{bmatrix} b_{11} b_{12} \\ b_{21} b_{22} \\ b_{31} b_{32} \end{bmatrix} = \begin{bmatrix} a_{11} b_{11} + a_{12} b_{21} + a_{13} b_{31} & a_{11} b_{12} + a_{12} b_{22} + a_{13} b_{32} \\ a_{21} b_{11} + a_{22} b_{21} + a_{23} b_{31} & a_{21} b_{12} + a_{22} b_{22} + a_{23} b_{32} \end{bmatrix}$$

where the (I,J)th element of the product C is expressed in APL as:

$$C[I;J] \leftarrow +/A[I;] \times B[;J]$$

The preceding operation is termed the *inner product*. It is written more succinctly in APL as:

$$A + . \times B$$

and is characteristic of the class of functions:

$$Af.gB$$

```
        ☐←M←2 3ρι6
 1  2  3
 4  5  6
        +\[1]M
 1  2  3
 5  7  9
        +\M
 1  2  3
 5  7  9
        +\[2]M
 1   3   6
 4   9  15
        ☐←N←2 3 4ρι24
 1   2   3   4
 5   6   7   8
 9  10  11  12

13  14  15  16
17  18  19  20
21  22  23  24
        +\N
 1   2   3   4
 5   6   7   8
 9  10  11  12

14  16  18  20
22  24  26  28
30  32  34  36
        +\[2]N
 1   2   3   4
 6   8  10  12
15  18  21  24

13  14  15  16
30  32  34  36
51  54  57  60
        +\[3]N
 1   3   6  10
 5  11  18  26
 9  19  30  42

13  27  42  58
17  35  54  74
21  43  66  90
        ☐←P←2 2 3ρι12
 1   2   3
 4   5   6

 7   8   9
10  11  12
        ×\[1]P
 1   2   3
 4   5   6

 7  16  27
40  55  72
```

Figure 12.16 Scan function.

```
      A←2 3ρι6
      B←3 2ρΦι6
      □←C←A+.×B
20 14
56 41
      B←3 3ρι9
      A+.×B
30 36 42
66 81 96
      □←U←2 2ρ1 0 0 1
1 0
0 1
      □←V←2 2ρ1 1 1 0
1 1
1 0
      U∧.∨V
1 0
1 1
```

Figure 12.17   Inner product.

```
      A←3 3ρι9
      X←2 4 6
      □←B←A+.×X
28 64 100
      X+.×A
60 72 84
      X+.×3 5 7
68
      □←U←2 2ρ1 0 0 1
 1 0
 0 1
      V←1 0
      U∧.∨V
 0 1
```

Figure 12.18   Inner product can be used with vector and matrix arguments.

where f and g are primitive scalar dyadic functions. Introductory examples of the inner product are given in Figure 12.17.

The dimension of the last coordinate of the first argument must agree with the dimension of the first coordinate of the second argument to satisfy a conformality requirement. As shown in Figure 12.18, the inner product can be used with a combination of vector and matrix arguments.

Given the result R of the inner product Af.gB, the following definitions apply:

Type of Arguments	Definition
Vector	$R \equiv f/AgB$
Vector and matrix	$R[I] \equiv f/AgB[;I]$
Matrix and vector	$R[I] \equiv f/A[I;]gB$
Matrix and matrix	$R[I;J] \equiv f/A[I;]gB[;J]$

In all cases, the following identities are true:

$$(\rho R) = (\bar{\,}1 \downarrow \rho A), 1 \downarrow \rho B$$
$$(\rho \rho R) = ((\rho \rho A) + \rho \rho B) - 2$$

Matrix Division

Matrix division is a primitive function that uses the domino symbol (⌹), formed by overstriking the quad symbol (⎕) and the division sign (÷). As a dyadic function, matrix division is written

$$X \leftarrow B ⌹ A$$

where the following conditions must hold:

$$2 \leftrightarrow \rho \rho A$$
$$(1 \uparrow \rho A) \geq 1 \downarrow \rho A$$
$$\vee/1 \quad 2 = \rho \rho B$$

and

$$(1 \uparrow \rho A) \leftrightarrow 1 \uparrow \rho B$$

The result X of the function is the least squares solution to the system of simultaneous linear equations

$$(A +. \times X) = B$$

X is computed such that the expression

$$R \leftarrow +/(, B - A +. \times X) * 2$$

is minimized and $\rho X \leftrightarrow N, 1 \downarrow \rho B$, where $\rho A \leftrightarrow M, N$.

If A is a nonsingular square matrix, then R is zero and X is the solution to the set of equations. If $M > N$, then the system of equations is overdetermined and R is minimized.

As a monadic function of the form

$$X \leftarrow ⌹ A$$

the matrix divide function is equivalent to

$$X \leftarrow I ⌹ A$$

where I is an identity matrix of order $1 \uparrow \rho A$. If A is nonsingular, then X is the left inverse of A. If A is a nonsquare matrix, then the solution X minimizes the expression

$$+/(, I - A +. \times X) * 2$$

As an example of dyadic matrix division, consider the set of equations

$$x_1 + x_2 + x_3 = 2$$
$$2x_1 + x_2 + 2x_3 = 3$$
$$x_1 + 3x_2 + 2x_3 = 4$$

If

$$A = \begin{pmatrix} 1 & 1 & 1 \\ 2 & 1 & 2 \\ 1 & 3 & 2 \end{pmatrix}, \quad X = \begin{pmatrix} x_1 \\ x_2 \\ x_3 \end{pmatrix}, \quad \text{and} \quad B = \begin{pmatrix} 2 \\ 3 \\ 3 \end{pmatrix}$$

then the system of equations can be expressed as

$$AX = B$$

or in APL notation as

$$(A+ .\times X) = B$$

A solution X is computed as follows.

```
A← 3 3ρ1 1 1 2 1 2 1 3 2
B← 2 3 3
▯← X ← B ⌹ A
```

2   1   ‾1

A computer printout of this example is given as Figure 12.19.

Outer Product

The familiar multiplication table is an example of multiplying each element of one vector by *all* elements of another. That is:

×	1	2	3	4
1	1	2	3	4
2	2	4	6	8
3	3	6	9	12
4	4	8	12	16

In APL, the outer product of vectors A and B with respect to multiplication is written A∘.× B where the element in the Ith row and the Jth column is defined as:

$$R[I;J] \equiv A[I] \times B[J]$$

As with inner product, the definition applies to all of the scalar dyadic functions. Figure 12.20 contains illustrative examples of outer product. In general,

```
        □←A←3 3ρ1 1 1 2 1 2 1 3 2
  1 1 1
  2 1 2
  1 3 2
        □←Y←⊟A
  4.0000E0     ¯1.0000E0    ¯1.0000E0
  2.0000E0     ¯1.0000E0    ¯2.6780E¯16
 ¯5.0000E0      2.0000E0     1.0000E0
        Y+.×A
  1.0000E0      1.7764E¯15   1.5543E¯15
  6.6613E¯16    1.0000E0     4.4409E¯16
 ¯1.7764E¯15   ¯2.2204E¯15   1.0000E0
        B←2 3 3
        □←X←B⊟A
  2 1 ¯1
        A+.×X
  2 3 3
```

Figure 12.19 Matrix division.

```
        (ι4)∘.×ι4
  1   2   3   4
  2   4   6   8
  3   6   9  12
  4   8  12  16
        (2 2ρι4)∘.+10 20
 11  21
 12  22

 13  23
 14  24
```

Figure 12.20 Outer product.

outer product is regarded as each element of the first argument applied to every element of the second argument. The result R of the outer product A∘.fB is defined as:

Type of Arguments	Definition
Vector	$R[I;J] \equiv A[I] fB[J]$
Vector and matrix	$R[I;J;K] \equiv A[I] fB[J;K]$
Matrix and vector	$R[I;J;K] \equiv A[I;J] fB[K]$
Matrix and matrix	$R[I;J;K;L] \equiv A[I;J] fB[K;L]$

where

$$(\rho R) = (\rho A), \rho B$$
$$(\rho\rho R) = (\rho\rho A) + \rho\rho B$$

Application. The following defined function with one argument N:

$$\nabla R \leftarrow DIAG\ N$$
[1] $R \leftarrow (\iota N) \circ .= \iota N$
[2] ∇

generates a square matrix of order N with 1's in the main diagonal and zero elements elsewhere. (This is known as the identity matrix.)

Transposition

The notion of interchanging the rows and columns in a matrix is a fundamental concept in mathematics and is useful in many data analysis programs. For example, a program designed to group data by row for analysis, that is,

		Subject		
		A	B	C
Variable	1	X	X	X
	2	X	X	X
	3	X	X	X
	4	X	X	X

would be useful for grouping the data by subject. All that is needed is a means of transposing the data matrix.

The *row column* transposition of a matrix in APL is written ⍉M and produces a matrix whose rows are the columns of M and whose columns are the rows of M. For an example, see Figure 12.21. The monadic function symbol is the circle symbol overstruck with the reverse solidus. More generally, the monadic transpose function reverses the order of all the coordinates of its argument. Figure 12.22 depicts an example of monadic transposition applied to a rank-3 array.

Application. The familiar problem of augmenting a matrix A with columns from a matrix B, depicted as:

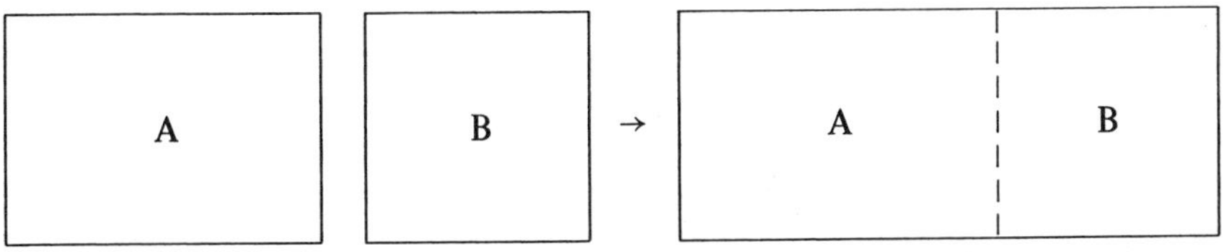


```
      ⎕←M←3 4⍴⍳12
 1  2  3  4
 5  6  7  8
 9 10 11 12
      ⍉M
 1  5  9
 2  6 10
 3  7 11
 4  8 12
```

Figure 12.21 Monadic transposition applied to a matrix argument.

```
               []←N←2 3 4ρ\24
    1    2    3    4
    5    6    7    8
    9   10   11   12

   13   14   15   16
   17   18   19   20
   21   22   23   24
               []←NTR←⍉N
    1   13
    5   17
    9   21

    2   14
    6   18
   10   22

    3   15
    7   19
   11   23

    4   16
    8   20
   12   24
                   ρN
     2   3   4
                   ρNTR
       4   3   2
```

Figure 12.22 Monadic transposition applied to a rank-3 array.

```
       A←3 4ρ\12
       B←3 2ρ0
       C←⍉(((ρA)+ρB)[2],(ρA)[1])ρ(,⍉A),,⍉B
       A
   1    2    3    4
   5    6    7    8
   9   10   11   12
         B
   0   0
   0   0
   0   0
         C
   1    2    3    4    0    0
   5    6    7    8    0    0
   9   10   11   12    0    0
```

Figure 12.23 Augmenting one matrix by another using the ravel, catenation, and transpose
functions.

is easily solved with the ravel, catenation, and transpose functions, as given in
Figure 12.23.

The dyadic form of transposition uses a left argument which specifies the
coordinates that should be interchanged, as shown in Figure 12.24. Given the
dyadic transposition function $N \lozenge M$, then ρN must equal $\rho \rho M$ and the $N[I]$ th
coordinate of the result is the Ith coordinate of M. Therefore, the elements of

```
      M←3 4ρι12
       2 1⍉M
 1   5   9
 2   6  10
 3   7  11
 4   8  12
      (⍉M)=2 1⍉M
 1 1 1
 1 1 1
 1 1 1
 1 1 1
```

Figure 12.24 Dyadic transposition applied to a matrix argument.

N must specify all the coordinates of the array result. If $(\rho\rho M)=3$, then 1 2 3 or 1 1 2 or 1 2 1 or 3 1 2 would be a suitable value for N, whereas 1 1 3 would be illegal. Figure 12.25 gives additional examples of the dyadic transposition func-tion. The result R of dyadic transposition of M is defined as follows:

Operation	ρρM	ρρR	Result	Notes
1 1⍉M	2	1	R[I]=M[I;I]	Main diagonal of M
1 2⍉M	2	2	R[I;J]=M[I;J]	No transposition specified
2 1⍉M	2	2	R[I;J]=M[J;I]	Same as ⍉M
1 1 1⍉M	3	1	R[I]=M[I;I;I]	Main diagonal of M
1 1 2⍉M	3	2	R[I;J]=M[I;I;J]	
1 2 1⍉M	3	2	R[I;J]=M[I;J;I]	
1 2 2⍉M	3	2	R[I;J]=M[I;J;J]	
1 2 3⍉M	3	3	R[I;J;K]=M[I;J;K]	No transposition specified
1 3 2⍉M	3	3	R[I;J;K]=M[I;K;J]	Same as ⍉M
2 1 1⍉M	3	2	R[I;J]=M[J;I;I]	
2 1 2⍉M	3	2	R[I;J]=M[J;I;J]	
2 1 3⍉M	3	3	R[I;J;K]=M[J;I;K]	
2 2 1⍉M	3	2	R[I;J]=M[J;J;I]	
2 3 1⍉M	3	3	R[I;J;K]=M[J;K;I]	
3 1 2⍉M	3	3	R[I;J;K]=M[K;I;J]	
3 2 1⍉M	3	3	R[I;J;K]=M[K;J;I]	

The following values for N where $(\rho\rho M)=3$ are illegal: 1 1 3, 1 3 1, 1 3 3, 2 2 2, 2 2 3, 2 3 2, 2 3 3, 3 1 1, 3 1 3, 3 2 2, 3 2 3, 3 3 1, 3 3 2, and 3 3 3.

Application. The following expression:

$$+/1\ 1\ ⍉\ M$$

sums the elements of the main diagonal of a matrix M.

Reversal and Rotation

Reversal of the elements of a rank-n array is accomplished in a similar manner to the way elements of a vector are reversed. Given an array A, then ϕA denotes a

```
            ⎕←A←2 3 4ρι24·
  1   2   3   4
  5   6   7   8
  9  10  11  12

 13  14  15  16
 17  18  19  20
 21  22  23  24
            ⎕←Q←3 1 2⍉A
  1  13
  2  14
  3  15
  4  16

  5  17
  6  18
  7  19
  8  20

  9  21
 10  22
 11  23
 12  24
            ρA
 2  3  4
            ρQ
 3  4  2
```

Figure 12.25   Dyadic transposition applied to a rank-3 array.

reversal along the last coordinate and ⊖A denotes a reversal along the first coordinate (⊖ is formed by overstriking a o with a ⁻). If reversal along an axis other than the first or last coordinate is desired, then a coordinate index must be specified. Thus, reversal along the Ith axis is written as $\phi[I]$ A so that $\phi[3] = \phi$A and $\phi[1] = \ominus$A, for a rank-3 array using 1-origin indexing. Figure 12.26 depicts examples of array reversal.

Rotation is applied along the Ith coordinate of an array with an expression of the form

$$K\phi[I]A$$

where A is an array and K denotes the rotation that is applied to the other dimensions of A. The dimension of K must agree with the dimension of the specified coordinate of the right argument, that is, $(\rho K) = (\rho A)[I]$. The sign and magnitude of each element of K determine the amount and direction of rotation that is applied. Again, a positive element denotes rotation toward the elements with lowest-numbered indices. If K is a scalar, then it is extended to all indices of A. If the coordinate index is elided, then the last coordinate is assumed; K⊖A denotes rotation along the first coordinate. Several examples of array rotation are given in Figure 12.27.

The dimension and rank of the result of reversal or rotation are taken from the right argument since its structure is not changed by either function.

```
        ⎕←B←2 3ρ⍳6
1  2  3
4  5  6
        Φ[1]B
4  5  6
1  2  3
        Φ[2]B
3  2  1
6  5  4
        (Φ[2]B)=ΦB
1  1  1
1  1  1
        ⎕←C←2 3 4ρ⍳24
 1   2   3   4
 5   6   7   8
 9  10  11  12

13  14  15  16
17  18  19  20
21  22  23  24
        Φ[2]C
 9  10  11  12
 5   6   7   8
 1   2   3   4

21  22  23  24
17  18  19  20
13  14  15  16
        ⎕←A←3 3ρ'TEAFORTWO'
TEA
FOR
TWO
        Φ[1]A
TWO
FOR
TEA
```

Figure 12.26 Reversal of an array.

Compression and Expansion

Arrays are compressed with an expression of the form

$$U/[I]A$$

where U is a logical vector, A is an array, I is the coordinate along which compression is applied, and the dimension of U is the same as the dimension of the Ith coordinate of A. If either argument is a scalar or a one-element array, then it is extended to apply to all elements of the other argument. U⌿A and U/A denote the first and last coordinates, respectively. As shown in the examples of Figure 12.28, compression along the first coordinate of a matrix suppresses rows, and compression along the last coordinate of a matrix suppresses columns. In the compression of a rank-3 array, compression operates along a coordinate and entire matrices are suppressed, as shown in Figure 12.29. The concepts are extended to higher-dimensional arrays so that compression of a rank-4 array

```
      ⎕←A←3 4ρ⍳12
 1   2   3   4
 5   6   7   8
 9  10  11  12
      2Φ[2]A
 3   4   1   2
 7   8   5   6
11  12   9  10
      (¯1ΦA)=¯1Φ[2]A
1 1 1 1
1 1 1 1
1 1 1 1
      1Φ[1]A
 5   6   7   8
 9  10  11  12
 1   2   3   4
      1 0 2ΦA
 2   3   4   1
 5   6   7   8
11  12   9  10
      3 1 2 0Φ[1]A
 1   6  11   4
 5  10   3   8
 9   2   7  12
      ⎕←B←2 3 4ρ⍳24
 1   2   3   4
 5   6   7   8
 9  10  11  12

13  14  15  16
17  18  19  20
21  22  23  24
      1Φ[2]B
 5   6   7   8
 9  10  11  12
 1   2   3   4

17  18  19  20
21  22  23  24
13  14  15  16
      3Φ[1]B
13  14  15  16
17  18  19  20
21  22  23  24

 1   2   3   4
 5   6   7   8
 9  10  11  12
      2ΦB
 3   4   1   2
 7   8   5   6
11  12   9  10

15  16  13  14
19  20  17  18
23  24  21  22
```

Figure 12.27   Rotation of an array.

```
      □←M←3 4ρι12
 1  2  3  4
 5  6  7  8
 9 10 11 12
      1 0 1/[1]M
 1  2  3  4
 9 10 11 12
      1 1 0 1/M
 1  2  4
 5  6  8
 9 10 12
      □←N←3 4ρ'TAEAFBORTCWO'
TAEA
FBOR
TCWO
      □←P←1 0 1 1/N
TEA
FOR
TWO

      0 1 1/[1]P
FOR
TWO
```

Figure 12.28   Compression of a matrix.

```
       □←Q←2 3 3ρι18
 1  2  3
 4  5  6
 7  8  9

10 11 12
13 14 15
16 17 18
      1 0/[1]Q
1 2 3
4 5 6
7 8 9
       0 1 1/[2]Q
 4  5  6
 7  8  9

13 14 15
16 17 18
      1 0 1/Q
 1  3
 4  6
 7  9

10 12
13 15
16 18
```

Figure 12.29   Compression of a rank-3 array.

```
          □←M←2 4ρ⍳8
 1 2 3 4
 5 6 7 8
          1 0 1\[1]M
 1 2 3 4
 0 0 0 0
 5 6 7 8
          1 0 1 1 1\M
 1 0 2 3 4
 5 0 6 7 8
          □←Q←2 2 2ρ⍳8
 1 2
 3 4

 5 6
 7 8
          1 1 0\[2]Q
 1 2
 3 4
 0 0

 5 6
 7 8
 0 0
          1 0 1\[1]Q
 1 2
 3 4

 0 0
 0 0

 5 6
 7 8
```

Figure 12.30 Expansion of an array.

suppresses entire rank-3 arrays.   In general, the rank of the result of compression is always equal to the rank of the right argument.

Similarly, expansion of an array is denoted by

$$U\backslash[I]A$$

and provides the converse of compression. The conformability requirement for $U\backslash[I]A$ is that $(+/U) = (\rho A)[I]$. The established convention for the first and last coordinates apply here, as well, so that $U\bar{+}A$ denotes the first coordinate and $U\backslash A$ the last. Figure 12.30 gives examples of array expansion. The padding for elements of the result that correspond to zero elements in U are the same as those used for vector expansion, that is, numeric arrays are padded with zeros and character arrays are padded with space characters.

Take and Drop

The extension of the take function

$$T\uparrow A$$

to arrays requires that ρT equals $\rho\rho A$. The value of element $T[I]$ determines the

```
      []←M←3 4ρι12
1   2   3   4
5   6   7   8
9  10  11  12
      N←1 3
      N↑M
1 2 3
      ¯2 2↑M
5   6
9  10
      ρ3 0↑M
3  0
      []←A←2 3 4ρι24
1   2   3   4
5   6   7   8
9  10  11  12

13  14  15  16
17  18  19  20
21  22  23  24
       ¯1 3 4↑A
13  14  15  16
17  18  19  20
21  22  23  24
       2 2 ¯2↑A
3   4
7   8

15  16
19  20
```

Figure 12.31   The take function applied to matrix and rank-3 arguments.

elements selected along the Ith coordinate of A. The elements of T may be positive or negative and indicate first or last elements, respectively. Figure 12.31 depicts examples in which the take function is applied to matrix and rank-3 arguments.

The drop function, T↓A, is defined analogously, except the element T[I] determines the elements dropped along the Ith coordinate of A. As with the drop function on vectors, a positive value for T[I] indicates that leading elements are dropped and a negative value for T[I] indicates that trailing elements should be dropped. Again, ρT must equal $\rho\rho$A. Figure 12.32 gives examples of the drop function applied to array arguments.

Some special cases of take and drop can be identified. If +/T equals 0, the take function returns an empty array and the drop function yields the right argument A, without modification. If ∧/(T = ρA) equals 1, the take function yields the right argument A and the drop function returns an empty array.

Set Operations

The index and membership functions are also defined to accept rank-n arrays as arguments. The result R of the *index* of function

$$V\iota A$$

```
        []←M←3 4ρι12
 1   2   3   4
 5   6   7   8
 9  10  11  12
        N←1 3
        N↓M
 8
12
        ‾2 2↓M
 3  4
        ρ3 0↓M
 0  4
        []←A←2 3 4ρι24
 1   2   3   4
 5   6   7   8
 9  10  11  12

13  14  15  16
17  18  19  20
21  22  23  24
        ‾1 0 0↓A
 1   2   3   4
 5   6   7   8
 9  10  11  12
        0 ‾1 2↓A
 3   4
 7   8

15  16
19  20
```

Figure 12.32   The drop function applied to matrix and rank-3 arguments.

(where V is a vector and A is a rank-n array) has the following properties:

$$(\rho R) = \rho A$$
$$(\rho\rho R) = \rho\rho A$$

The elements of R are the indices of the right argument in V, which must always be a vector. If an element of A is not found in V, then it is given the index $1 + \lceil \iota\rho V$. Thus, the result is affected by the indexing origin.

The membership function, written

$$A \epsilon B$$

yields a result that is the same size as A. B can be a scalar, vector, or rank-n array. If an element of A is contained in B, then the respective element of the result is 1; otherwise, it is given the result 0.

Figure 12.33 gives examples of the index of and membership functions applied to arrays as arguments.

```
      V←¯7 3 9 6 5 1 4 3
      V⍳2 3⍴⍳6
 6 9 2
 7 5 4
      ⎕IO←0
      V⍳2 3⍴⍳6
 8 5 8
 1 6 4
      ⎕IO←1
      (3 4⍴⍳12)∊⍳6
 1 1 1 1
 1 1 0 0
 0 0 0 0
      ((5⍳⍳25)∊0)/⍳25
 5 10 15 20 25
      (2 4 6 8 10 12 14 16)∊3 4⍴⍳12
 1 1 1 1 1 1 0 0
```

Figure 12.33   Index of and membership functions applied to array arguments.

Applications. The defined function PRIME, listed and executed as follows:

```
      ∇PRIME[⎕]∇
    ∇ R←PRIME N
[1]   R←(~N∊N∘.×N)/N←1+⍳N-1
    ∇
      PRIME 13
2 3 5 7 11 13
```

generates prime numbers less than or equal to an argument N. The function
operates by creating a matrix of composite numbers using the outer product
function and by testing whether an index vector of natural numbers is contained
in the matrix using the membership function. The defined function WHEREIN,
listed and executed as follows:*

```
      ∇WHEREIN[⎕]∇
    ∇ I←A WHEREIN B
[1]   I←(∧/[1](¯1+⍳⍴A)⌽A∘.=B)⍳1
    ∇

      'ISS' WHEREIN 'MISSISSIPPI'
2
      3 4 5 WHEREIN ⍳10
3
```

gives the first occurrence in succession of the elements of vector A in vector B.
The function applies to both numeric and character vectors. This application
presents the opportunity of displaying a straightforward method of determining

*Pakin, S., *APL\360 Reference Manual*, Chicago, Science Research Associates, 1972,
p. 103. (Ms. Pakin credits Jules Kaplan for the function WHEREIN.)

how a defined function operates, which may become necessary because of the conciseness of APL notation. As applied to the function WHEREIN, each step is executed manually as follows:

```
                    ∇WHEREIN[□]∇
            ∇ I←A WHEREIN B
       [1]    I←(∧/[1]( ¯1+⍳⍴A)⊖A∘.=B)⍳1
         ∇
            A←'ISS'
            B←'MISSISSIPPI'
            □←C←A∘.=B
      0 1 0 0 1 0 0 1 0 0 1
      0 0 1 1 0 1 1 0 0 0 0
      0 0 1 1 0 1 1 0 0 0 0
            □←D← ¯1+⍳⍴A
      0 1 2
            □←E←D⊖C
      0 1 0 0 1 0 0 1 0 0 1
      0 1 1 0 1 1 0 0 0 0 0
      1 1 0 1 1 0 0 0 0 0 0
            □←F←∧/[1]E
      0 1 0 0 1 0 0 0 0 0 0
            F⍳1
      2
```

which is more accurate and efficient than going through the computations by hand.

Catenation and Lamination

Two arrays can be joined along an existing coordinate with the *catenation function* extended to rank-n arrays. The catenation of two arrays is specified as

$$A,[K]B$$

where A and B are arrays, and is permitted for arrays of the same rank and dimension, except along the Kth coordinate. If the arrays have different ranks, then the coordinates in common must be of the same size. Figure 12.34 gives examples of array catenation. If [K] is elided, then the last coordinate is assumed.

Lamination joins two arguments along a new coordinate and is specified as follows:

$$A,[K]B$$

The function inserts after the $(\lceil/\iota\lfloor K)$th coordinate, a new coordinate with the range $\iota 2$, used to distinguish elements of A from elements of B. The process is depicted as follows.

```
      C←2 3ρ⍳6
      D←2 3ρ1
      C,[1]D
1 2 3
4 5 6
1 1 1
1 1 1
      C,D
1 2 3 1 1 1
4 5 6 1 1 1
      L←2 2 3ρ⍳12
      R←2 3 3ρ0
      L,[2]R
1    2    3
4    5    6
0    0    0
0    0    0
0    0    0

7    8    9
10   11   12
0    0    0
0    0    0
0    0    0
```

Figure 12.34   Array catenation.

A,[.5]B   as

A,[1.5]B   as

A,[2.5]B   as

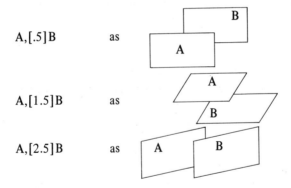

Figure 12.35 gives examples of lamination. Both catenation and lamination can be used with character arrays.

Application. The simplified defined function, mentioned earlier, that displays a table of N integers, squares, and cubes with columns aligned without using the format function is given as follows:

```
      ∇STABLE N
[1]   ⍕(N≤0)/'→0,ρ⎕←"INVALID ARGUMENT"'
[2]   N,(N*2),(N←⍳N)*3
      ∇
```

```
        A←3 4ρι12
        B←3 4ρ1
        □←C←A,[.5]B
    1   2   3   4
    5   6   7   8
    9  10  11  12

    1   1   1   1
    1   1   1   1
    1   1   1   1
        ρC
  2 3 4
        □←D←A,[1.5]B
    1   2   3   4
    1   1   1   1

    5   6   7   8
    1   1   1   1

    9  10  11  12
    1   1   1   1
        ρD
  3 2 4
```

Figure 12.35 Lamination.

This application uses the execute function to display a message if the argument is invalid and the array catenation function to construct the desired table.

Decode and Encode

The decode and encode functions are extended to apply to cases when the left and right arguments are arrays, other than the limited case presented previously for vectors. The decode function is specified as

$$A⊥B$$

When the left argument is a vector (or an extended scalar) and the right argument is an array, then the result is the base value computation along the first coordinate of B using the radix vector A. If the left argument is a matrix, the computation is made using the rows of A as radix vectors.

Encode is written

$$A⊤B$$

When the left argument is a vector and the right argument is a vector, then each column of the result is the representation of the corresponding column of B using radix vector A. When the left argument is a matrix and the right argument is a vector, then the result R[;I;J] is the representation in base A[;I] of the component B[J]. Figure 12.36 gives examples of the decode and encode functions applied to arrays.

```
          []←B←3 4ρ3 2 0 9 5 4 1 8 7 6 2 7
 3 2 0 9
 5 4 1 8
 7 6 2 7
          10⊥B
357 246 12 987
          5⊥B
107 76 7 272
          []←C←2 3ρ10 10 10 5 5 5
 10 10 10
  5  5  5
          C⊥B
357 246   12 987
107  76    7 272
          A←357 246 12 987
          10 10 10⊤A
 3 2 0 9
 5 4 1 8
 7 6 2 7
          []←D←2 2ρA
357 246
 12 987
          10 10 10⊤D
 3 2
 0 9

 5 4
 1 8

 7 6
 2 7
```

Figure 12.36   Decode and encode functions extended to arrays.

Application. An amazingly simple APL program can be constructed to sort strings that are stored as a two-dimensional array. Each row of the matrix represents a distinct string as depicted in Figure 12.37. The function uses the base-value function to compute the permutation of indices that would order the rows in ascending sequence.

Format Function

The operating conventions that givern the execution of the format function are given in Chapter 10. The syntax of the monadic format function is

$$⍕B$$

where B is a scalar or array, and the function generates a character array that is identical in appearance to the characters displayed when the output of B is specified. Figure 12.38 demonstrates the monadic form of the format function.

The syntax of the dyadic format function is

$$A⍕B$$

```
        ∇FILLΔANDΔSORT[□]∇
    ∇ FILLΔANDΔSORT;M
[1]    FORMΔLIST
[2]    SORT M
    ∇

        ∇FORMΔLIST[□]∇
    ∇ FORMΔLIST
[1]    M← 0 18 ρ□←'ENTER CHAR STRINGS -- HIT EXECUTE WHEN FINISHED'
[2]    NXT:→(0=ρC←□)/0
[3]    →NXT,ρM←M,[1] 18↑C,17ρ' '
    ∇

        ∇SORT[□]∇
    ∇ R←SORT A;S
[1]    S←' ABCDEFGHIJKLMNOPQRSTUVWXYZ0123456789'
[2]    R←A[⍋(2+ρS)⊥⍋S⍳A;]
    ∇

    FILLΔANDΔSORT
ENTER CHAR STRINGS -- HIT EXECUTE WHEN FINISHED
MAGIC SQUARE
5100 COMPUTER
BASIC LANGUAGE
APL LANGUAGE
LAMINATE
CATENATE

APL LANGUAGE
BASIC LANGUAGE
CATENATE
LAMINATE
MAGIC SQUARE
5100 COMPUTER
```

Figure 12.37   Alphabetic sort.

```
            □←B←2 3ρ⍳6
    1 2 3
    4 5 6
            □←C←⍕B
    1 2 3
    4 5 6
        C[2;]
    4 5 6
```

Figure 12.38   Monadic form of the format function.

```
        □←B←2 3ρ1.23 6.1 5 3.71362 ¯4.9162 11.38146
    1.23          6.1          5
    3.71362      ¯4.9162      11.3815
        □←C←6 2 7 3 8 4⍕B
    1.23   6.100   5.0000
    3.71  ¯4.916  11.3815
        C[;7+⍳6]
    6.100
   ¯4.916
```

Figure 12.39   Dyadic form of the format function.

where B is a scalar or array and A is a set of control pairs that control the field width and precision of values displayed. (See chapter ten.) When A is a single control pair, it applies to all elements of B. If A represents more than one control pair, then a control pair must exist for each column of B. If B is a matrix or a rank-*n* array, then the control vector A applies to *each* row of B. This is demonstrated in Figure 12.39. The argument A, in the above syntax, may not be a matrix or a rank-*n* array.

12.2 TAPE INPUT AND OUTPUT AND PRINTER OUTPUT

There are two ways of saving information on tape. The first method is straight-forward and involves saving the entire workspace—both functions and data—with the)SAVE or) CONTINUE command. The second method is to create a tape file that only contains data. The first method is satisfactory only if used within reasonable limits because multiple copies of functions exist, which becomes cumbersome when programming changes are required. Another consideration is that the size of a workspace is limited by the size of main storage. When large amounts of data are involved, then the use of tape files is necessary. Printer out-put is generated with the)OUTSEL ALL and the)OUTSEL OUT options, which means that output displayed on the display screen is also printed. Thus, the display unit and the printer cannot be used for different purposes. Printer output facilities in APL permit printer output to be explicitly controlled by an executing function, so that the user may interact with the computer via the display screen and reports can be printed on the printer.

Shared Variables

Tape and printer operations are implemented through the "shared variable" con-cept in APL. The term *shared variable* refers to an operating environment in which several users access the same APL system concurrently. Through the use of a shared variable, two or more users may reference the same data. The 5100 APL system services a single user and the shared variable facility is employed to transfer information between tape and main storage and from main storage to the printer. Thus, a shared variable in 5100 APL is one that is shared between an active workspace and the tape or printer units. During an output operation, data assigned to a shared variable is either written to tape or printed—depending upon whether the shared variable is established for the printer unit or one of the tape units. For an input operation, data is read from tape each time a shared variable, established for input, is referenced.

Because the name of a shared variable takes the same form as any other vari-able name, the APL system must first be notified that a specific variable is going to be used as a shared variable. This process is termed "establishing a shared variable." For example, the following statement:

$$A \leftarrow 1 \; \square SVO \; \text{'OUTPUT'}$$

establishes the variable OUTPUT as a shared variable. Next, the APL system must be informed whether the mode of operation is input or output and the physical address of the peripheral device involved. This process is termed "opening the file" or "activating the file." The use of the two terms is synonomous. For example, the following statement:

$$\text{OUTPUT} \leftarrow \text{'OUT 1006 ID} = (\text{PMASTER}) \; \text{TYPE} = \text{A'}$$

opens shared variable OUTPUT as an output file on tape unit 1, which is the built-in tape unit, and file 6. The file identification is PMASTER and the file type is A, which denotes that data is to be stored in internal format. After a shared variable is established and opened, the corresponding file is read or written, depending upon the mode of operation, each time the variable is referenced in an executed APL statement. For example, each of the following statements:

$$\text{OUTPUT} \leftarrow \text{EMPLNO,NAME,ADDRESS}$$

.

.

.

$$\text{OUTPUT} \leftarrow \text{PAYREC}$$

causes the values of the respective variables, regardless of their shape, to be transferred to the device and file that was opened. After a series of input or output operations has been completed, a file or printer operation is deactivated by assigning an empty vector to the shared variable, such as

$$\text{OUTPUT} \leftarrow \iota 0$$

This completes the file or printer operation. However, the shared variable remains established as a shared variable for subsequent input or output operations. A shared variable is withdrawn as a shared variable with a statement, such as

$$A \leftarrow \square SVR \; \text{'OUTPUT'}$$

This process is termed "retracting a shared variable," which means that the specified variable can again be used as a normal APL variable.

Case Study—Data Storage and Retrieval

A hypothetical case study is given to demonstrate how shared variables are used and some of the required programming techniques. The case study involves the entry, storage, retrieval, and printing of textual information. The system consists of five functions, listed and described as follows:

MAIN—This function serves only to invoke the other four functions.

ENTER—This function permits the user to enter textual information from the keyboard. The information is stored as a matrix in which each row corresponds to a line of text.

WRITE—This function writes the matrix constructed by the ENTER function to a tape file.

READ—This function reads the data matrix from the tape file and assigns it to an array variable.

PRINT—This function prints the information, which was read from tape on a row-by-row basis, on the printer unit.

The five functions, mentioned here, are listed in Figure 12.40, and a script of a sample execution is given as Figure 12.41. Each function is described separately. The emphasis is on input and output processing.

Main Function. The function MAIN is comprised of references to the following four niladic implicit result functions: ENTER, WRITE, READ, and PRINT. Use of this function simply eliminates the need of invoking the functions separately.

Enter Function. The function ENTER makes an input request with the quote-quad sumbol ▯, appends trailing blanks, and catenates the first 64 characters of the result to the first coordinate of the data matrix. An exit is made from the function when an empty string of characters is entered by pressing the EXECUTE key without entering any information.

Write Function. The function WRITE is the first that uses a shared variable. The name of the shared variable is OUTP. One of the characteristics of the shared variable facility is that a variable name must be undefined before it is established as a shared variable, otherwise, a diagnostic message is generated by the APL system. Statement numbered [1], listed as follows:

$$A \leftarrow \Box EX \text{ 'OUTP'}$$

insures that OUTP is undefined by using the ▯EX system function to expunge, i.e., remove, the named referent from the active workspace. Statement numbered [2], listed as follows:

$$\rightarrow (2 \neq 1 \Box SVO \text{ 'OUTP'})/ERR1$$

establishes OUTP as a shared variable with the system function ▯SVO, which returns an explicit result. A successful operation causes a value of two to be returned, so that the statement branches to the statement labeled ERR1 if the explicit result of the ▯SVO function is not equal to 2. At this point, OUTP is committed as a shared variable and may not be used in computational state-

```
        ∇MAIN[∏]∇
     ∇ MAIN
[1]    ENTER
[2]    WRITE
[3]    READ
[4]    PRINT
     ∇



        ∇ENTER[∏]∇
     ∇ ENTER;C
[1]    M← 0 64 ρ∏←'ENTER CHAR DATA - PRESS EXECUTE WHEN FINISHED'
[2]    NXT:→(0=ρC←∏)/0
[3]    →NXT,ρM←M,[1] 64↑C,63ρ' '
     ∇




        ∇WRITE[∏]∇
     ∇ WRITE;A
[1]    A←∏EX 'OUTP'
[2]    →(2≠1 ∏SVO 'OUTP')/ERR1
[3]    OUTP←'OUT 1003 ID=(DFILE) MSG=OFF TYPE=A'
[4]    →(1≠∧/ 0 0 =A←OUTP)/ERR2
[5]    OUTP←M
[6]    →(1≠∧/ 0 0 =A←OUTP)/ERR3
[7]    OUTP←ι0
[8]    →(1≠∧/ 0 0 =A←OUTP)/ERR4
[9]    →(2=∏SVR 'OUTP')/0
[10] ERR5:→OUT,ρ∏←'WRITE: ERROR RETRACTING SHARED VARIABLE'
[11] ERR1:→OUT,ρ∏←'WRITE: ERROR ESTABLISHING SHARED VARIABLE'
[12] ERR2:→OUT,ρ∏←'WRITE: ERROR OPENING FILE 1003'
[13] ERR3:→OUT,ρ∏←'WRITE: ERROR WRITING FILE 1003'
[14] ERR4:→OUT,ρ∏←'WRITE: ERROR CLOSING FILE 1003'
[15] OUT:A←∏SVR 'OUTP'
[16]   →
     ∇
        ∇READ[∏]∇
     ∇ READ;A
[1]    A←∏EX 'INPT'
[2]    →(2≠1 ∏SVO 'INPT')/ERR1
[3]    INPT←'IN 1003 ID=(DFILE) MSG=OFF'
[4]    →(1≠∧/ 0 0 =A←INPT)/ERR2
[5]    →(0=ρN←INPT)/ERR3
[6]    INPT←ι0
[7]    →(1≠∧/ 0 0 =A←INPT)/ERR4
[8]    →(2=∏SVR 'INPT')/0
[9]  ERR5:→OUT,ρ∏←'READ: ERROR RETRACTING SHARED VARIABLE'
[10] ERR1:→OUT,ρ∏←'READ: ERROR ESTABLISHING SHARED VARIABLE'
[11] ERR2:→OUT,ρ∏←'READ: ERROR OPENING FILE 1003'
[12] ERR3:→OUT,ρ∏←'READ: END OF FILE 1003'
[13] ERR4:→OUT,ρ∏←'READ: ERROR CLOSING FILE 1003'
[14] OUT:A←∏SVR 'INPT'
[15]   →
     ∇
```

Figure 12.40 APL defined functions for the storage and retrieval case study.

```
        ∇PRINT[□]∇
      ∇ PRINT;A;I;□IO
 [1]    A←□EX 'PRNT'
 [2]    □IO←1
 [3]    →(2≠1 □SVO 'PRNT')/ERR1
 [4]    PRNT←'PRT MSG=OFF'
 [5]    →(1≠∧/ 0 0 =A←PRNT)/ERR2
 [6]    PRNT←(10ρ' '),'DATA LISTING',□AV[157],'
 [7]    →(1≠∧/ 0 0 =A←PRNT)/ERR3
 [8]    I←1
 [9]  AGN:PRNT←N[I;]
 [10]   →(1≠∧/ 0 0 =A←PRNT)/ERR3
 [11]   →((I←I+1)≤1↑ρN)/AGN
 [12]   PRNT←ι0
 [13]   →(1≠∧/ 0 0 =A←PRNT)/ERR4
 [14]   →(2=□SVR 'PRNT')/0
 [15] ERR5:→OUT,ρ□←'PRINT: ERROR RETRACTING SHARED VARIABLE'
 [16] ERR1:→OUT,ρ□←'PRINT: ERROR ESTABLISHING SHARED VARIABLE'
 [17] ERR2:→OUT,ρ□←'PRINT: ERROR OPENING PRINTER'
 [18] ERR3:→OUT,ρ□←'PRINT: PRINT ERROR'
 [19] ERR4:→OUT,ρ□←'PRINT: ERROR CLOSING PRINTER'
 [20] OUT:→0,A←□SVR 'PRNT'
      ∇
```

Figure 12.40 (Continued)

```
        MAIN
ENTER CHAR DATA - PRESS EXECUTE WHEN FINISHED
...THERE IS NOTHING MORE DIFFICULT TO TAKE IN HAND, MORE PERIL-
OUS TO CONDUCT, OR MORE UNCERTAIN IN ITS SUCCESS, THAN TO TAKE
THE LEAD IN THE INTRODUCTION OF A NEW ORDER OF THINGS.  BECAUSE
THE INNOVATOR HAS FOR ENEMIES ALL THOSE WHO HAVE DONE WELL UNDER
THE OLD CONDITIONS, AND THE LUKEWARM DEFENDERS IN THOSE WHO MAY
DO WELL UNDER THE NEW.  THIS COOLNESS ARISES PARTLY FROM FEAR OF
THE OPPONENTS, WHO HAVE THE LAWS ON THEIR SIDE, AND PARTLY FROM
THE INCREDULITY OF MEN, WHO DO NOT READILY BELIEVE IN NEW THINGS
UNTIL THEY HAVE A LONG EXPERIENCE OF THEM.
                                        MACHIAVELLI IN THE PRINCE
```

```
        DATA LISTING

...THERE IS NOTHING MORE DIFFICULT TO TAKE IN HAND, MORE PERIL-
OUS TO CONDUCT, OR MORE UNCERTAIN IN ITS SUCCESS, THAN TO TAKE
THE LEAD IN THE INTRODUCTION OF A NEW ORDER OF THINGS.  BECAUSE
THE INNOVATOR HAS FOR ENEMIES ALL THOSE WHO HAVE DONE WELL UNDER
THE OLD CONDITIONS, AND THE LUKEWARM DEFENDERS IN THOSE WHO MAY
DO WELL UNDER THE NEW.  THIS COOLNESS ARISES PARTLY FROM FEAR OF
THE OPPONENTS, WHO HAVE THE LAWS ON THEIR SIDE, AND PARTLY FROM
THE INCREDULITY OF MEN, WHO DO NOT READILY BELIEVE IN NEW THINGS
UNTIL THEY HAVE A LONG EXPERIENCE OF THEM.
                                        MACHIAVELLI IN THE PRINCE
```

Figure 12.41 Sample execution of the storage and retrieval case study.

ments. Statement numbered [3], listed as follows:

OUTP ← 'OUT 1003 ID=(DFILE) MSG=OFF TYPE=A'

opens file numbered 3 on tape unit number 1, the built-in unit, for output and assigns a file identification of DFILE. Error messages are not to be printed and the file type is A, which denotes that data will be recorded in internal APL form. A return code is assigned to OUTP after the open operation has been completed, wherein a vector of 0 0 denotes successful completion. Statement numbered [4], listed as follows:

→ (1≠∧/0 0=A←OUTP)/ERR2

checks the return code generated during the open operation and causes a branch to statement labeled ERR2 if the return is not 0 0. Statement numbered [5], listed as follows:

OUTP←M

assigns the data to be written—which is M in this case—to the shared variable OUTP. OUTP is opened for output so that the assignment causes M to be written to the tape file specified in the open statement. After an output operation, a completion vector is assigned to the shared variable. If the completion vector contains 0 0, then the output operation is successful. Otherwise, an output error has occurred. Statement numbered [6] inspects the completion vector and branches to statement labeled ERR3 if it is not 0 0. Statement numbered [7] listed as follows:

OUTP←ι0

closes the output file by assigning a null vector to the shared variable. Again, a completion vector of 0 0 is returned for a successful operation and statement numbered [8], listed as

→ (1≠∧/0 0=A←OUTP)/ERR4

branches to ERR4 if the close operation was not successful. Statement numbered [9] listed as

→ (2=□SVR 'OUTP')/0

uses the system function □SVR to retract the shared variable OUTP and branches out of the function if a successful completion code of 2 is returned. Statements numbered [10] through [14] display an error message and branch to statement labeled OUT, listed as follows:

OUT: A←□SVR 'OUTP'

which retracts the shared variable. Statement numbered [16] is comprised of a branch arrow without an argument. This statement causes the APL system to revert to the execution mode directly without returning through the chain of function references. When a variable is written to a type A file, as in statement numbered [5], the shape of the variable is also recorded. Thus, when the data is subsequently read back in and assigned to a variable, the receiving variable has the same shape.

Read Function. The READ function uses the shared variable INPT and is intended to read the file written by the WRITE function. Return codes are not repeated in this section. However, a successful return code for ⎕SVO or ⎕SVR is 2 and a successful completion vector for the open, read, and close operations is a 0 0 vector. In the READ function, statement numbered [1] listed as

$$A \leftarrow \Box EX \ 'INPT'$$

insures that INPT is undefined and statement numbered [2] listed as:

$$\rightarrow (2 \neq 1 \ \Box SVO \ 'INPT')/ERR1$$

establishes INPT as a shared variable and branches to ERR1 if the operation is not successful. Statement numbered [3] listed as

$$INPT \leftarrow 'IN \ 1003 \ ID = (DFILE) \ MSG = OFF'$$

opens file 3 on tape unit 1 for input. If the specified file identification does not match the actual file header, then the open fails and an unsuccessful completion vector is generated. Statement number [5] listed as

$$\rightarrow (0 = \rho N \leftarrow INPT)/ERR3$$

reads the specified file and assigns the next set of input values to N. (Each time the shared variable is referenced, as in N←INPT, the file is read.) An end-of-file condition is denoted by a null vector so that the subexpression $0 = \rho N$ checks for a null vector with a shape of 0 and the statement branches to ERR3 if the condition is true. Statement numbered [6] listed as

$$INPT \leftarrow \iota 0$$

closes the file and statement numbered [8] retracts the shared variable INPT. The remainder of the function is similar to the WRITE function. At this point in the execution of the sequence of functions, the data has been read back in and assigned to N.

Print Function. The PRINT function prints the matrix N on a line-by-line basis. *When a shared variable is opened for printer output, it can only be assigned a character scalar or character vector.* Thus, the PRINT function loops through the matrix printing each row at a time. The function uses 1-origin indexing and ⎕IO is declared as a local variable so that the function will operate successfully regardless of the setting of ⎕IO in the calling program. Again, completion codes are not covered but the conventions given previously apply. Statements [1], [2], and [3] listed as

> A←⎕EX 'PRNT'
> ⎕IO←1
> → (2≠1 ⎕SVO 'PRNT')/ERR1

expunge the shared variable name, set the indexing origin to 1, and establish the shared variable PRNT, respectively. Statement numbered [4] listed as

> PRNT←'PRT MSG=OFF'

opens the shared variable PRNT for printer output. Now, whenever a character string is assigned to PRNT, it is printed. Statement numbered [6] listed as

> PRNT←(10ρ' '), 'DATA LISTING', ⎕AV[157],' '

assigns a character vector to PRNT to be printed. However, the character vector includes ⎕AV[157], which is the cursor return. Therefore, the statement causes the message to be printed followed by a blank line. Statements numbered [8] through [11] listed as:

> I←1
> AGN: PRNT←N[I;]
> → (1≠∧/ 0 0 =A←PRNT)/ERR3
> → ((I←I+1)≤1 ↑ρN)/AGN

successively print each row of matrix N. Lastly, statements [12] and [14] close the printer operation and retract the shared variable PRNT, respectively.

In all of the above functions, the diagnostic messages are important because they serve to inform the user of special circumstances—such as when the printer is not turned on.

Establishing a Shared Variable

The dyadic system function ⎕SVO is used to establish a shared variable and is entered as an expression, as follows:

> 1 ⎕SVO *char-arg*

where *char-arg* is a character variable, a character expression, or a character constant scalar or vector. The left argument must be a 1 and the function returns a value of 2 for each variable that is established successfully as a shared variable. For example, the expression:

> 1 ⎕SVO 'OUTP'

2

establishes OUTP as a shared variable and an explicit result of 2 is generated. In a defined function, the above expression would cause the value 2 to be displayed. To eliminate the display, the result could be assigned to a local variable as in A←1 ☐SVO 'OUTP'. The right argument may also be a character variable, as in

DUM←'FLOUT'
1 ☐SVO DUM
2

which establishes FLOUT as a shared variable. If the right argument is a matrix, as in:

TV←3 5ρ 'FLOUTFLIN1FLIN2'
TV

```
    FLOUT
    FLIN1
    FLIN2
        1  ☐SVO TV
    2 2 2
```

each row of the matrix represents a shared variable. In the preceding example, FLOUT, FLIN1, and FLIN2 are established and a success code of 2 is generated for *each* shared variable successfully established and a zero or a one value for each variable that was not successfully established. The right argument may also be a character expression, as in

1 ☐SVO 4 2ρ'ABCDEFGH'
2 2 2 2

which establishes AB, CD, EF, and GH as shared variables. The right argument to ☐SVO may specify up to eight variables to be shared.

Opening a Shared Variable

A shared variable is opened for input or output by assigning a special character string to it that specifies the following information:

1. Mode of operation
2. Device/file number
3. File identification
4. Message option
5. Type of data format to be used in the input or output operation.

This information is specified in a character vector of a specification function that has the following format:

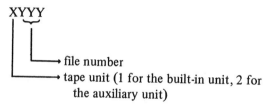

where:

name is the shared variable
IN denotes an input operation from tape
OUT denotes an output operation to tape
ADD denotes an output operation to the end of a currently existing file
PRT denotes printer output
device/file number specifies the tape unit and file number of a tape cartridge on the unit as follows:

XYYY

→ file number
→ tape unit (1 for the built-in unit, 2 for the auxiliary unit)

For example, device/file number 1013 denotes tape unit 1, the built-in unit, and file numbered 13. Similarly, 2117 denotes file 117 on tape unit 2, the auxiliary unit. If fewer than 4 digits are used for the device/file number, the built-in tape unit is assumed.

ID=(file ID) specifies from 1 to 17 characters enclosed in parenthesis. The *file ID* represents the file identification which must match the existing file identification for an IN or ADD operation. For an OUT operation to an existing file, the file identification specified must match the existing file identification, or the existing file identification must have been previously nullified with the)DROP command. (This field is not specified with PRT files.)

MSG=OFF denotes that no error messages are to be displayed for nonzero return codes.

TYPE=A denotes a file written in APL internal data format.

TYPE=I denotes a file written in data exchange format, meaning it can be read by a BASIC program if the data is formatted appropriately.

TYPE=I1 denotes a data exchange file and is exactly the same as a type I file.

TYPE=I2 denotes a file written in general exchange format, meaning it can be used to store a BASIC language source program.

Data formats can be specified only with OUT operations; with other file operations, the data format is picked up from the existing file. If no data format is specified with an OUT operation, a type A file is assumed. With printer output, the only options that can be specified are PRT and MSG=OFF. Only character scalars or vectors may be assigned to type I, I1, or I2 files. Therefore, numeric data must have been previously formatted with the ⌽ function and rank-2 or higher arrays must be written on a row-by-row basis.

In general, there is no need to use type I, I1, or I2 files in APL except when communicating with the BASIC language system. In the latter case, data must always be formatted so that it is compatible between the two systems.

The requirement, given previously, that a shared variable must be previously defined can now be amplified. A shared variable must be undefined *or* it must have been assigned the correct information to be opened, prior to the execution of the ☐SVO function; otherwise an INVALID DATA TYPE message will be generated. The message, however, does not affect an input or an output operation. Thus, a shared variable effectively can be opened before or after it is established as a shared variable. Both cases are demonstrated in Figure 12.42.

Data Transfer Operations

Data is transferred between main storage and a tape cartridge in blocks of 512 bytes.   For an input operation, a block of data is read into a buffer. Sets of data from a block are assigned to variables in response to subsequent IN operations. When a block is exhausted, another block is read. For an output operation, data is held in a buffer until a block is full. The block is then written to tape and another block is started. When the file is closed, the last block is written. For printer output operations, character vectors are transferred to the printer in blocks governed by the print width (system variable ☐PW). When the output mode is ADD, then data to be added to a file always begins on a new 512-byte boundary.

Output.   Data is transferred from a variable in main storage to a tape of printer unit by assigning it to a shared variable that is opened for the OUT, ADD, or PRT options. When a type A file is involved, data is written in an internal form and no formatting is required. For type I, I1, and I2 files and for printer output, only character scalars or character vectors may be written and use of the format function (⌽) may be necessary to convert numeric data to its displayed equivalent.

Input.   Data is transferred from tape to a variable in main storage by referencing the corresponding shared variable in an APL expression, such as

$$V \leftarrow D$$

or

$$+/D[I;]$$

```
      CLEAR WS
            PRNT←'PRT'
            1 □SVO 'PRNT'
2
            PRNT←'THE SQUARE ROOT OF 1296 IS ',⍕1296*.5
```
                        Contents of Display Screen

```
                  CLEAR WS
                        PRNT←'PRT'
                        1 □SVO 'PRNT'
                  THE SQUARE ROOT OF 1296 IS 36
```
                            Printed Output

        (a) Opened before being established as a shared variable.

```
      CLEAR WS
            1 □SVO 'PRNT'
2
            PRNT←'PRT'
            PRNT
0  0
            PRNT←'THE SQUARE ROOT OF 1296 IS ',⍕1296*.5
```
                        Contents of Display Screen

```
                  CLEAR WS
                        1 □SVO 'PRNT'
                  2
                        PRNT←'PRT'
                  THE SQUARE ROOT OF 1296 IS 36
```
                            Printed Output

        (b) Opened after being established as a shared variable.

Figure 12.42 An input or output operation may be opened before or after a shared variable is established.

where V is an APL variable and D is a shared variable. However, the data "in" a shared variable is not retained since the next time the shared variable is referenced, another set of data* is read. Therefore, if input data is to be referenced more than once, it should be assigned to an APL variable, as in V←D given above. The cursor return character (□AV[157]) and the end-of-block character (□AV[158]) embedded in a character vector have special meaning for tape input on data exchange files. The cursor return character denotes an end-of-record and the end-of-block character denotes the end-of-data in a 512-byte block. Data written after the end-of-block character cannot be read since the APL system skips automatically to the next block.

---

*A set of data refers to a scalar data item or an array.

Closing a Shared Variable

A file is closed by assigning a null vector to the shared variable, as in FL10←ι0, where FL10 is a shared variable. A successful close operation is indicated by completion vector of 0 0 assigned to the shared variable. For an IN operation, a file is closed after an end-of-file condition or after an error return code is generated.

For a tape output operation, the closing of a file serves to write the final block to the tape cartridge. After OUT and ADD operations, data files that are not closed properly cannot be read and are unusable.

A tape cartridge should never be removed from the built-in tape unit or from the auxiliary tape unit during the time that there is an open output operation on that tape unit. However, a file that has been closed for output may be opened for input, or vice versa, using the same or a different shared variable. After tape and printed operations have been completed, shared variables used therein should be retracted.

Retracting a Shared Variable

A shared variable is retracted from being shared with the monadic □SVR function, which takes the following form:

$$\text{□SVR } \textit{char-arg}$$

where *char-arg* is a character variable, a character expression, or a character constant scalar or vector. The right argument takes the same form as in the □SVO function. The □SVR returns a value of 2 if the shared variable has been retracted successfully and a zero or a one if the shared variable was not retracted successfully. Most cases in which a shared variable is not retracted successfully result from the fact that the shared variable is not currently established due to an error condition of some kind. If a □SVR is issued to a file before it is closed, the file is closed automatically.

As an example, the expression:

$$\text{□SVR 'OUTP'}$$
$$2$$

would return a value of 2, as indicated, denoting a successful retracted shared variable, if OUTP had been previously established. In a defined function, the above expression would cause the value 2 to be displayed. To eliminate the display, the result could be assigned to a local variable as in A←□SVR 'OUTP'. The argument may also be a character variable, as in

$$\text{DUM←'FLOUT'}$$
$$\text{□SVR DUM}$$
$$2$$

which retracts FLOUT as a shared variable. If the right argument is a matrix, as in:

$$TV \leftarrow 2\ 2\rho\text{'F1F2'}$$
$$TV$$

F1
F2

$$\square SVR\ TV$$

2 2

each row of the matrix represents a shared variable to be retracted. In the preceding example, shared variables F1 and F2 are retracted and a success code of 2 is generated for *each* shared variable that is successfully retracted and a zero or a one value for each shared variable that was not successfully retracted—as covered previously. The right argument may also be a character expression, as in:

$$\square SVR\ 3\ 1\rho\ \text{'FQT'}$$

2 2 2

which retracts F, Q, and T as shared variables. The argument to $\square SVR$ may specify up to eight shared variables to be retracted.

Types of Files

The following types of files are permitted on the 5100 Portable Computer:

Type	File Description
0	Marked but unused file
1	Data exchange file
2	General exchange file
3	BASIC source file
4	BASIC work area file
5	BASIC keys file
6	APL continued file
7	APL save file
8	APL internal data file
16	Patch/tape recovery/tape copy file
17	Diagnostic file
18	IMF file (Internal Machine Fix)
72	Tape storage dump

Each type of file is described in appropriate portions of the book. Thus far, however, file types 0, 1, 2, 7, and 8 have been covered—either explicitly or implicitly. A file that has been initialized with the)MARK command but not used is a type 0 file. An APL output file of type I or I1 is a type 1 data exchange file; an APL output file of type I2 is a type 2 general exchange file. An APL workspace stored on tape with the)SAVE command is a type 7 APL save file and an APL output file of type A is a type 8 APL internal data file. It is more efficient to save data as a type 8 file than as either a type 1 or a type 2 file for two reasons. First, it requires less tape space, and second, the APL program to write or read it takes less space in main storage and executes more quickly.

Tape Capacity

A tape cartridge has the capacity for holding many tape files. Each file has an overhead of approximately .5K bytes so that the 200K byte capacity of the tape cartridge can hold 132 1K byte files, 80 2K byte files, 44 4K byte files, etc., or any combination thereof. Estimation of the file size required for an argument is cumbersome but a close approximation can be determined from the following algorithm. The amount of tape storage (S) in bytes required for an argument (A) is computed as:

if A is a scalar *then*

$$S \leftarrow \lceil T+12$$

elseif A is an array and $(\lceil 12+(4\times\rho\rho A)+(T\times/\rho A)) \leqslant 500$ *then*

$$S \leftarrow \lceil 12+(4+\rho\rho A)+(T\times/\rho A)$$

otherwise

$$B \leftarrow \lceil T\times/\rho A \qquad \text{(total bytes required for data)}$$
$$F \leftarrow 12+4\times\rho\rho A \qquad \text{(overhead for each logical record)}$$
$$S \leftarrow B+F\times\lceil B\div500-F$$

where

$$T = \begin{cases} \frac{1}{8} & \text{if A is logical data} \\ 4 & \text{if A is integer data} \\ 1 & \text{if A is character data} \\ 8 & \text{if A is data in scaled representation} \end{cases}$$

The latter quantity T represents the amount of storage in bytes required for the various types of data in main storage as well as on a tape cartridge.

12.3 SYSTEM FUNCTIONS

System functions provide facilities that are outside the scope of the APL language—as are system commands—but can be invoked from within an APL statement. A system function always begins with the quad symbol and consists of a two character function name. A typical example is the expunge function,

TABLE 12.2 SYSTEM FUNCTIONS IN THE 5100 APL SYSTEM.

Syntax of Function	Function Performed
□CR *name*	Canonical representation
□FX *name*	Fix
□EX *name*	Expunge
□NL *class*	Name list
char □NL *class*	Name list beginning with the specified character
□NC *name*	Name classification

covered in the previous section, that is denoted by □EX. Table 12.2 lists the system functions in the 5100 APL system.

Canonical Representation Function

The □CR, *canonical representation*, function generates a character matrix representation of a user-defined function. The monadic system function □CR takes one argument, which is the name of the user-defined function that is to be formatted as the character matrix, and returns the character matrix as an explicit result. Figure 12.43 gives a user-defined function DET which computes the determinant of a matrix. Using the system function □CR, the function DET is formatted into a character matrix, assigned to the variable BLT, and is displayed. The resulting character matrix is characterized by the fact that the line numbers in the function along with the opening and closing del (∇) symbols are removed. All statements, as well as statement labels, are aligned at the left margin. After a

```
        ∇DET[□]∇
     ∇ C←DET Z;J;Q
[1]     →(1=ρ,Z)ρ0,C←,Z
[2]     →L2×ι(2=ρρZ)∧=/ρZ
[3]     →0,ρ□←'ILLEGAL STRUCTURE'
[4]   L2:→0×ι(1↑ρZ)<J←(Z[1;]=0)ιC←,0
[5]     Z←(J-1)ΦZ
[6]     Z←Z-Z[;1]∘.×Z[1;]÷C←Z[1;1]
[7]     C←(¯1*J-1)×C×DET 1 1 ↓Z
     ∇
        □←BLT←□CR 'DET'
C←DET Z;J;Q
→(1=ρ,Z)ρ0,C←,Z
→L2×ι(2=ρρZ)∧=/ρZ
→0,ρ□←'ILLEGAL STRUCTURE'
L2:→0×ι(1↑ρZ)<J←(Z[1;]=0)ιC←,0
Z←(J-1)ΦZ
Z←Z-Z[;1]∘.×Z[1;]÷C←Z[1;1]
C←(¯1*J-1)×C×DET 1 1 ↓Z
     ρBLT
8 30
```

Figure 12.43 An example of the canonical representation (□CR) system function.

function is formatted as a character matrix, it can be utilized in APL statements as any other character matrix. The ⎕FX function, described in the next section, provides the inverse operation to the ⎕CR function.

Fix Function

The ⎕FX, *fix*, function converts a character matrix representing a user-defined function to an actual user-defined function. The monadic system function ⎕FX takes one argument, which is the name of the character matrix, and returns either of the following as an explicit result:

1. The name of the user-defined function as a character vector—if the execution of the fix function was successful—and a new or replacement function definition is created.
2. The number of the row being processed minus one of the character matrix is displayed—if an error occurs during the execution of the fix function. A function definition is not created in this case. A typical error is a missing quote or an invalid APL character symbol.

Figure 12.44 gives the ⎕FX function applied to the BLT matrix created for the DET function in Figure 12.43. The ⎕CR function, described in the preceding section, provides the inverse operation to the ⎕FX function.

Expunge Function

The ⎕EX, *expunge*, function erases the named objects from the active workspace. The monadic system function ⎕EX takes one argument, which must be character scalar, character vector, or character matrix representing the names of

```
        )ERASE DET
        ⎕FX BLT
DET
        ∇DET[⎕]∇
    ∇ C←DET Z;J;Q
[1]    →(1=ρ,Z)ρ0,C←,Z
[2]    →L2×ι(2=ρρZ)∧=/ρZ
[3]    →0,ρ⎕←'ILLEGAL STRUCTURE'
[4]    L2:→0×ι(1↑ρZ)<J←(Z[1;]=0)ιC←,0
[5]    Z←(J-1)⌽Z
[6]    Z←Z-Z[;1]∘.×Z[1;]÷C←Z[1;1]
[7]    C←(¯1*J-1)×C×DET 1 1 ↓Z
    ∇
        ⎕←M←3 3ρ3 2 4 2 4 1 0 2 3
    3 2 4
    2 4 1
    0 2 3
        DET M
    34
```

Figure 12.44   An example of the fix (⎕FX) system function.

```
      A←13.465
      A
13.465
      ▯EX 'A'
1
      A
VALUE ERROR
      A
      ^
      ∇R←A PLUS B
[1] R←A+B
[2] ∇
      2 PLUS 3
5
      T1←'PLUS'
      ▯EX T1
1
      2 PLUS 3
SYNTAX ERROR
      2 PLUS 3
      ^
      C←2+B←1+A←3
      C,B,A
6 4 3
      ▯EX 3 1ρ'ABC'
1 1 1
      C,B,A
VALUE ERROR
      C,B,A
      ^
```

Figure 12.45 Examples of the use of the expunge (▯EX) system function.

objects to be erased. The argument may be expressed as a character constant or a character variable. For each object that is successfully erased, the ▯EX function returns an explicit result of one; if the object is not successfully erased, the ▯EX function returns an explicit result of zero. Figure 12.45 gives several examples of the use of the expunge function.

If the argument to the ▯EX function is a character matrix, then each row of the matrix represents the name of an object to be erased from the active workspace, as demonstrated in Figure 12.45. The object to be erased with ▯EX cannot be a pendent or a suspended function.

Name List

The ▯NL, *name list*, function generates a character matrix wherein each row represents the name of an object in the active workspace. The monadic form of ▯NL takes the following form:

▯NL *class*

where *class* is a numeric scalar or vector limited to the values 1, 2, or 3. The values 1, 2, and 3 have the following meaning:

Argument	Name Class
1	Labels
2	Variables
3	User-defined functions

For example, consider the following statements:

```
      CLEAR WS
          C←2+B←1+A←3
          ⎕NL 2
      A
      B
      C
```

The monadic form of ⎕NL with an argument of 2 yields the variable names in the active workspace as an explicit result. If the argument had been a one or a three, the function ⎕NL would have yielded the names of labels or user-defined functions, respectively. If the argument is a vector, such as ⎕NL 1 3, then the values in the vector determine the classes of names that are included in the result. Thus ⎕NL 1 3 generates the names of all labels and user-defined functions.

The dyadic form of ⎕NL takes the following form:

$$char \; ⎕NL \; class$$

where *char* is a character scalar or a character vector that specifies that only names with the initial characters contained in the argument are to be produced, and *class* is the same as given above. Thus, for example,

$$\text{'BLT'} \; ⎕NL \; 2$$

will yield a matrix of variable names starting with the letters B, L, or T as the explicit result. The following statement

$$⎕EX \; \text{'QR'} \; ⎕NL \; 2$$

erases all variables from the active workspace that begin with the letters Q and R.

Name Classification

The ⎕NC, *name classification*, function gives the class number of the names contained in the argument. The class numbers are listed as follows:

Class Number	Class
0	Available for use, i.e., undefined
1	Name of statement label

```
          )CLEAR
   CLEAR  WS
          ∇R←X PLUS Y
   [1] R←X+Y
   [2] ∇
          C←2+B←1+A←3
          □NC 4 4ρ'PLUSA    B    C
    3 2 2 2
```

Figure 12.46   Example of the name classification (□NC) system function.

Class Number	Class
2	Name of a variable
3	Name of a user-defined function
4	Nonstandard name, i.e., cannot be used.

The argument to the monadic □NC function can be character scalar, vector, or matrix. If the argument is a matrix, then each row represents a name. Thus, for example, the □NC function in the following statements:

$$A←2$$
$$□NC \text{ 'A'}$$
$$2$$

yields an explicit result of 2 because A is a variable name. Figure 12.46 gives other examples of the name classification function.

12.4 REPRESENTATION OF DATA STRUCTURES IN APL

The key to effective computer utilization is the representation of data structures. Thus far, scalers, arrays, and files have been covered. This section covers several user-oriented data structures that facilitate computer programming and depend upon the APL system for implementation.

Strings and Sets

The most primitive type of data structure, other than the scalar numeric data item, is the string comprised of a sequence of characters. In APL, a character string is stored as a vector so that a list of strings is stored as a two-dimensional array or as a long vector with the strings catenated. A set is stored in a similar manner but its elements are restricted to be of the same type—either character or numeric data items.

Substring Function. The STR function in the BASIC language (and the STR defined function in the APL language) selects a portion of a character string in

```
        ∇STR[□]∇
     ∇ R←S STR A;□IO
[1]     □IO←1
[2]     R←S[¯1+A[1]+⍳A[2]]
     ∇
        D←'ALL COWS EAT GRASS'
        D STR 5 4
COWS
        D STR 1 3
ALL
```

Figure 12.47   The substring function.

the following manner:

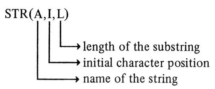

Thus, if A='TEA FOR TWO', then STR(A,5,3) yields the substring 'TEA'. The substring function is simulated in APL as shown in Figure 12.47. The function returns the substring as an explicit result.

Pattern Matching and Replacement. Pattern matching and replacement functions provide the ability to search a given string for a sequence of characters and perform a replacement operation, as implied by the following syntaz:

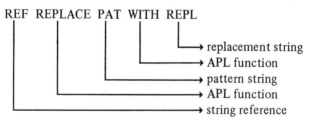

Implementation of pattern matching involves three functions: FIND, REPLACE, and WITH, as demonstrated in Figure 12.48. FIND gives the index of the first occurrence of one string in another. REPLACE replaces one sequence of characters with another. WITH is used as a utility function that permits the REPLACE function to have three arguments.

Set Union and Intersection. Set union (UNION) and intersection (INTERS) functions are not restricted to character values and are demonstrated in Figure 12.49.

Character Translation. A conceptually simple operation is the translation of character values from one set to another. Figure 12.50 gives an APL function that performs a character translation on a string argument.

```
        ∇REPLACE[□]∇
     ∇ R←STR REPLACE A;I;J;□IO
[1]    □IO←1
[2]    →((ρSTR)≥I←1↑,(A←,A) FIND(STR←,STR))/L1
[3]    →0,ρR←STR
[4]   L1:R←STR[ιI-1],U135V,STR[J+ι(ρSTR)-J←⁻1+I+ρA]
     ∇

        ∇FIND[□]∇
     ∇ P←C FIND D;□IO
[1]    □IO←1
[2]    P←(∧/[1](⁻1+ιρC)⌽(C←,C)∘.=D)ι1
     ∇

        ∇WITH[□]∇
     ∇ R←A WITH B
[1]    U135V←B
[2]    R←A
     ∇

        TEXT←'TAKE AND DROP'
        TEXT REPLACE 'AND' WITH 'OR'
TAKE OR DROP
        TEXT REPLACE 'TAKE' WITH ')ERASE'
)ERASE AND DROP
        TEXT REPLACE 'AND' WITH ''
TAKE  DROP
```

Figure 12.48 Pattern matching and replacement.

```
        ∇UNION[□]∇
     ∇ R←U UNION V
[1]    R←U,(~V∈U←,U)/V←,V
     ∇
        ∇INTERS[□]∇
     ∇ R←U INTERS V
[1]    R←(U∈V)/U
     ∇
        6 8 10 UNION 8 9 10 11
6 8 10 9 11
        'STVEW' INTERS 'TEX'
TE
        (ι7) INTERS 3 5
3 5
```

Figure 12.49 Set union and intersection.

Queues and Stacks

Storage is maintained dynamically in APL and this feature is useful for implementing stacks and queues. In each case, the data structure is represented as a vector without requiring a list pointer.

Queues. A *queue* is a data structure in which additions are made at one end and deletions are made at the other. A queue is commonly known as a *First-In-First-Out* (FIFO) list. Functions QUEUE and DEQUEUE used for adding elements to a queue and removing elements from a queue, respectively, are given in Figure 12.51.

```
       ∇TRANSC⎕⎕∇
    ∇ B←TRANS A;A1;A2;⎕IO
[1]    ⎕IO←1
[2]    A1←'¯α⍳∩⌊∊‗∇Δ⍳∘''⎕⍳⊤○*?ρ⌈~↓∪⍵⊃↑∊∧¨¯<≤=≥>≠∨'
[3]    A2←' ABCDEFGHIJKLMNOPQRSTUVWXYZ0123456789 '
[4]    B←A2[A1⍳A]
    ∇

       TRANS 'I∝∇⍳∩'
MAGIC
       TRANS '∝⎕⎕¯L○∇⌈¯∊∝~'
ALL DOGS EAT
```

Figure 12.50   Character translation.

```
                 ∇QUEUEC⎕⎕∇
            ∇ QUEUE A
       [1]    Q←Q,A
            ∇
                 ∇DEQUEUEC⎕⎕∇
            ∇ R←DEQUEUE
       [1]    R←1↑Q
       [2]    Q←1↓Q
            ∇

            Q←⍳0
            QUEUE 83
            QUEUE 7
            QUEUE ¯50
            DEQUEUE
       83
            DEQUEUE
       7
            QUEUE 341
            DEQUEUE
       ¯50
```

Figure 12.51   Queue functions.

Stacks. A *stack* is a data structure in which entries and deletions are made at the same end. A stack is commonly known as a *Last-In-First-Out* list. Functions PUSH and PULL, used for adding elements to a stack and deleting elements from a stack, respectively, are given in Figure 12.52.

Tables

A table is a set of ordered pairs (k_i, v_i) with unique first components k_i. Here, the key k_i and the value v_i can be numeric values or character strings. An entry v_i is said to be associated with the key k_i. Table lookup involves determining, for a key k^1, the table entry (k_i, v_i) where $k^1 = k_i$. This process makes available the desired value v_i.

Numeric Values. A numeric table is stored as an $n \times 2$ matrix where the first column represents the keys and the second column represents the values. Given

```
            ∇PUSH[□]∇
        ∇  PUSH A
   [1]     STACK←A,STACK
        ∇
            ∇PULL[□]∇
        ∇  R←PULL
   [1]     R←1↑STACK
   [2]     STACK←1↓STACK
        ∇

            STACK←⍳0
            PUSH 83
            PUSH 7
            PUSH ¯50
            PULL
  ¯50

            PULL
  7

            PUSH 341
            PULL
  341
```

Figure 12.52 Stack functions.

a key K and a table T, it is determined if the key is found in the table through an expression of the form:

$$K \epsilon T[;1]$$

Replacement, deletion, addition, and fetch functions for numeric tables stored as matrices are given in Figure 12.53.

Fixed-Length Character Values with Numeric Keys. A fixed-length character string table with numeric keys is stored as a character matrix (A) and a numeric vector (L), where $(1 \uparrow \rho A) = \rho L$, so that if the key $K \epsilon L$ then the desired character string in A is $A[L \iota K;]$. Replacement, deletion, addition, and fetch functions are given in Figure 12.54 for fixed-length character strings of 18 characters.

Numeric Values and Fixed-Length Character Keys. Fixed-length character keys and numeric values are stored in a character matrix (M) and a numeric vector (N), where $(1 \uparrow \rho M) = \rho N$, so that if the key $K = M[I;]$ for some I, then the desired numeric value is $N[I]$. Replacement, deletion, addition, and fetch functions are given in Figure 12.55 for 6-character keys.

Variable-Length Character Values. The case of numeric keys and variable-length character values is given in chapter 11. The functions are repeated in Figure 12.56 for completeness with the addition of a function REMOVE that deletes a key and corresponding variable-length character value.

Extensions. The preceding material covers all of the necessary programming techniques to extend the concepts to any combination of keys and values. For example, several values of either type can correspond to a single key and several keys may correspond to two or more values, depending upon the needs of a particular application.

```
      ∇CHECK[□]∇
    ∇ L←T CHECK K;□IO
[1]    □IO←1
[2]    L←K∊T[;1]
    ∇
      ∇INDEX[□]∇
    ∇ I←T INDEX K;□IO
[1]    □IO←1
[2]    I←T[;1]⍳K
    ∇
      ∇REPL[□]∇
    ∇ REPL V;□IO
[1]    □IO←1
[2]    →(TABLE CHECK V[1])/L1
[3]    →0,ρ□←'KEY NOT IN TABLE'
[4]  L1:TABLE[TABLE INDEX V[1];2]←V[2]
    ∇
      ∇ADD[□]∇
    ∇ ADD V;□IO
[1]    □IO←1
[2]    →(~TABLE CHECK V[1])/L1
[3]    →0,ρ□←'DUPLICATE KEY'
[4]  L1:TABLE←TABLE,[1] V
    ∇
      ∇FETCH[□]∇
    ∇ R←FETCH K;□IO
[1]    □IO←1
[2]    →(TABLE CHECK K)/L1
[3]    →0,ρ□←'KEY NOT IN TABLE'
[4]  L1:R←TABLE[TABLE INDEX K;2]
    ∇
      ∇DELETE[□]∇
    ∇ DELETE K;I;□IO
[1]    □IO←1
[2]    →(TABLE CHECK K)/L1
[3]    →0,ρ□←'KEY NOT IN TABLE'
[4]  L1:TABLE←(((I-1),2)↑TABLE),[1]((-((1↑ρTABLE)-I←TABLE INDEX K)),2)↑TABLE
    ∇
      TABLE←0 2ρ⍳0
      ADD 3 16
      ADD 7 45
      ADD 9 34
      TABLE
   3 16
   7 45
   9 34
      REPL 7 83
      ADD 15 0
      TABLE
   3 16
   7 83
   9 34
  15  0
      FETCH 9
34
      DELETE 9
      TABLE
   3 16
   7 83
  15  0
```

Figure 12.53 Functions for use with numeric tables.

```
        ∇REPLC[□]∇
    ∇ K REPLC S
[1]    →(K∈LIST)/L1
[2]    →0ρ□←'KEY NOT IN TABLE'
[3]    L1:DATA[LIST⍳K;]←18↑S,18ρ' '
    ∇

        ∇ADDC[□]∇
    ∇ K ADDC S;□IO
[1]    □IO←1
[2]    →(~K∈LIST)/L1
[3]    →0,ρ□←'DUPLICATE KEY'
[4]    L1:LIST←LIST,K
[5]    DATA←DATA,[1] 18↑S,18ρ' '
    ∇

        ∇FETCHC[□]∇
    ∇ R←FETCHC K
[1]    →(K∈LIST)/L1
[2]    →0,ρ□←'KEY NOT IN TABLE'
[3]    L1:R←DATA[LIST⍳K;]
    ∇

        ∇DELETEC[□]∇
    ∇ DELETEC K;I;□IO
[1]    □IO←1
[2]    →(K∈LIST)/L1
[3]    →0,ρ□←'KEY NOT IN TABLE'
[4]    L1:DATA←(((I-1),18)↑DATA),[1]((-((1↑ρDATA)-I←LIST⍳K)),18)↑DATA
[5]    LIST←((I-1)↑LIST),(-(ρLIST)-I)↑LIST
    ∇

        LIST←⍳0
        DATA←0 18ρ' '
        5 ADDC 'COMPUTER'
        17 ADDC 'TAPE CARTRIDGE'
        23 ADDC 'PRINTER'
        LIST
5 17 23
        DATA
COMPUTER
TAPE CARTRIDGE
PRINTER
        17 REPLC 'KEYBOARD'
        10 ADDC 'PAPER'
        DELETEC 23
        LIST
5 17 10
        DATA
COMPUTER
KEYBOARD
PAPER
```

Figure 12.54 Functions for tables of fixed-length character values with numeric keys.

Lists

A *list* is a data structure in which a pointer associated with each value gives the index of the next element on the list. This type of structure is useful for large sorting jobs because the pointers can be adjusted without having to move data. The data part of a list is stored as numeric or character data, as required. Pointer data is stored as a numeric array with indices to succeeding elements. For

```
      ∇VERIFY[□]∇
    ∇ R←M VERIFY K;S;□IO;J
[1]   □IO←1
[2]   J←2+ρS←' ABCDEFGHIJKLMNOPQRSTUVWXYZ0123456789'
[3]   R←(J⍳S⍳6↑K,5ρ' ')∊J⍳⍵S⍳M
    ∇
      ∇CFIND[□]∇
    ∇ R←M CFIND K;S;□IO,J
[1]   □IO←1
[2]   J←2+ρS←' ABCDEFGHIJKLMNOPQRSTUVWXYZ0123456789'
[3]   R←(J⍳⍵S⍳M)⍳J⍳S⍳6↑K,5ρ' '
    ∇
      ∇CREPL[□]∇
    ∇ K CREPL V;□IO
[1]   □IO←1
[2]   →(M VERIFY K)/L1
[3]   →0,ρ□←'KEY NOT IN TABLE'
[4]  L1:N[M CFIND K]←V
    ∇
      ∇CADD[□]∇
    ∇ K CADD V;□IO
[1]   □IO←1
[2]   →(~M VERIFY K)/L1
[3]   →0,ρ□←'DUPLICATE KEY'
[4]  L1:N←N,V
[5]   M←M,[1] 6↑K,5ρ' '
    ∇
      ∇CFETCH[□]∇
    ∇ R←CFETCH K;□IO
[1]   □IO←1
[2]   →(M VERIFY K)/L1
[3]   →0,ρ□←'KEY NOT IN TABLE'
[4]  L1:R←N[M CFIND K]
    ∇
      ∇CDELETE[□]∇
    ∇ CDELETE K;J;□IO
[1]   □IO←1
[2]   →(M VERIFY K)/L1
[3]   →0,ρ□←'KEY NOT IN TABLE'
[4]  L1:J←M CFIND K
[5]   N←((J-1)↑N),(-(ρN)-J)↑N
[6]   M←(((J-1),6)↑M),[1]((-((1↑ρM)-J)),6)↑M
    ∇
      M←0 6ρ' '
      N←⍳0
      'BOLT' CADD 256
      'NUT' CADD 375
      'NAIL' CADD 5281
      CFETCH 'NUT'
375
      'BOLT' CREPL 526
      N
526 375 5281
      M
BOLT
NUT
NAIL
      CDELETE 'NUT'
      N
526 5281
      M
BOLT
NAIL
```

Figure 12.55 Functions for tables with numeric values and fixed-length character keys.

```
      ∇INIT[□]∇
    ∇ INIT
[1]   ID←LENGTH←TEXT←⍳0
[2]   START←,0
    ∇
      ∇STORE[□]∇
    ∇ STORE;I;A;□IO
[1]   □IO←1
[2]   'ENTER INTEGER ID FOLLOWED BY TEXT ON THE NEXT LINE'
[3]   →(0=I←□)/0
[4]   →(0=ρA←□)/0
[5]   LENGTH←LENGTH,ρA
[6]   ID←ID,I
[7]   →2,START←START,ρTEXT←TEXT,A
    ∇
      ∇FETCH[□]∇
    ∇ FETCH LIST;IND;I;L;□IO
[1]   □IO←1
[2]   L←ρIND←ID⍳LIST←,LIST
[3]   →(1=∨/IND>ρID)/ERR
[4]   I←0
[5]   LOOP:→(L<I←I+1)/0
[6]   TEXT[START[IND[I]]+⍳LENGTH[IND[I]]]
[7]   →LOOP,ρ□←' '
[8]   ERR:'INVALID ID'
    ∇
      ∇REMOVE[□]∇
    ∇ REMOVE KEY;I;J;□IO
[1]   □IO←1
[2]   →((ρID)≥I←ID⍳KEY)/GO
[3]   →0,ρ□←'INVALID ID'
[4]   GO:TEXT←TEXT[⍳START[I]],TEXT[J+⍳(ρTEXT)-J←START[I]+LENGTH[I]]
[5]   ID←ID[⍳I-1],ID[I+⍳(ρID)-I]
[6]   START←START[⍳I-1],((START[I+⍳(ρSTART)-I])-LENGTH[I])
[7]   LENGTH←LENGTH[⍳I-1],LENGTH[I+⍳(ρLENGTH)-I]
    ∇
```

Figure 12.56 Functions for use with tables with variable-length character values.

example, consider the following numeric list: ⟨25,40,13⟩. It can be represented conceptually as:

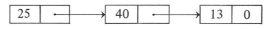

and stored in APL as:

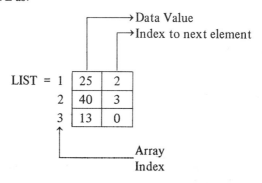

Adding an element after the second one is depicted as:

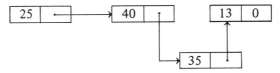

and in APL as:

$$
\text{LIST} = \begin{array}{c|c|c}
1 & 25 & 2 \\
\hline
2 & 40 & 4 \\
\hline
3 & 13 & 0 \\
\hline
4 & 35 & 3 \\
\end{array}
$$

Thus, deletions and additions can be made without requiring that other data items be moved. Figure 12.57 gives functions for listing, adding, and deleting elements from a list of this type. The list techniques can be combined with table processing methods for storing fixed and variable-length character data.

12.5 MISCELLANEA

This section covers miscellaneous APL programming techniques that are best covered after prerequisite material has been absorbed. Each topic relates to a practical problem encountered during routine APL programming.

Input Loops

Figure 12.58 depicts a case known as an *input loop*. It is possible to escape from the input loop by entering → as was done in the figure. This entry does the job because the input quad (⎕) specifies evaluated input and the branch arrow causes an exit from the function.

An input loop can also occur with character input, and an attempt to escape from the loop with the symbol → is interpreted as a character and not as a way out of the loop. An escape is provided with the "out" character formed from the characters O, U, and T as follows ⍒. This character is entered by holding down the CMD key and pressing the ⍫ key. Figure 12.59 depicts a character input loop.

Storage Space

The storage space required by APL data items is listed in Table 12.3. Calculations are performed using general arithmetic functions so that the specification function may not necessarily store the result of an arithmetic computation in the most optimum form. For example, the statement:

$$A \leftarrow 2*30$$

```
      ∇LIST[□]∇
    ∇ R←LIST L;I;J;□IO
[1]    □IO←1
[2]    I←J←1
[3]  LOOP:→(L[J;2]=0)/PRINT
[4]    I←I,J←L[J;2]
[5]    →LOOP
[6]  PRINT:R←L[I;1]
    ∇
      ∇INSERT[□]∇
    ∇ INSERT N;□IO
[1]    □IO←1
[2]  ⍝ N[1] NODE AFTER WHICH NEW NODE SHOULD BE INSERTED
[3]  ⍝ N[2] NEW NODE
[4]    L[N[1];2]←1↑⍴L←L,[1] N[2],L[N[1];2]
    ∇
      ∇INDEXOF[□]∇
    ∇ R←INDEXOF A;□IO
[1]    □IO←1
[2]    R←L[;1]⍳A
    ∇
      ∇PRED[□]∇
    ∇ R←PRED I;□IO
[1]    □IO←1
[2]    R←L[;2]⍳I
    ∇
      ∇DELNODE[□]∇
    ∇ DELNODE N;□IO
[1]    □IO←1
[2]  ⍝ N[1] NODE TO BE DELETED
[3]  ⍝ N[2] PRECEDING NODE
[4]    L[N[2];2]←L[N[1];2]
    ∇
      ∇APPEND[□]∇
    ∇ APPEND A;I;J;□IO
[1]    □IO←1
[2]    I←1
[3]  L1:→((I←L[J←I;2])≠0)/L1
[4]    L←L,[1](A,0)
[5]    L[J;2]←1↑⍴L
    ∇
```

(a) Listing of functions.

Figure 12.57 Functions for listing, adding, or deleting elements from a list.

stores the result as eight bytes, even though it is an integer $\leqslant 2^{31}-1$. To insure that four bytes are sued for storage, the floor function can be used as follows:

$$A←⌊2*30$$

With logical data, the APL system may not know that logical values are desirable, as in the following case:

```
      VCT←24⍴3-2
      VCT
1 1 1 1 1 1 1 1 1 1 1 1 1 1 1 1 1 1 1 1 1 1 1 1
```

```
      L←1 2ρ45 0
      APPEND 36
      APPEND 13
      INSERT (INDEXOF 36),67
      LIST L
45 36 67 13
      L
 45   2
 36   4
 13   0
 67   3
      PRED 2
1
      PRED 3
4
      APPEND 5
      APPEND 34
      LIST L
45 36 67 13 5 34
      L
 45   2
 36   4
 13   5
 67   3
  5   6
 34   0
      DELNODE (INDEXOF 13),PRED INDEXOF 13
      LIST L
45 36 67 5 34
```

(b) Execution

Figure 12.57 (Continued)

```
      ∇ROOT[□]∇
      ∇ ROOT;X
 [1]   LOOP:X←□*0.5
 [2]   X
 [3]   →LOOP
      ∇
      ROOT
 □:
      1296
 36
 □:
       5
 2.23607
 □:
       →
```

Figure 12.58 Numeric input loop.

which stores the result as 24 ones, each occupying four bytes for a total of 96 bytes. The result can be changed to a logical vector as follows:

```
      VCT←VCT∧1
      VCT
1 1 1 1 1 1 1 1 1 1 1 1 1 1 1 1 1 1 1 1 1 1 1 1
```

so that the result occupies only three bytes of storage.

```
          ∇ABC[⎕]∇
       ∇ ABC;B
[1]     B←,⎕
[2]     ρB
[3]     →1
       ∇
       ABC
COMPUTER
8
QUOTE-QUAD (⎕) INPUT
20
Φ
1
1 2 3
5
→
1
⍙
INTERRUPT
ABC[1] B←,⎕
        ^
```

Figure 12.59 Character input loop.

TABLE 12.3 STORAGE USED BY APL DATA ITEMS

Data Type	Number of Bytes Required
Character	1
Integer $\leqslant 2^{31} - 1$	4
Integer $> 2^{31} - 1$	8
Decimal number	8
Logical	$\frac{1}{8}$ byte (1 byte contains 8 ones or zeros)

Chaining

The facility for permitting one function to dynamically reference another function stored on tape is available through the canonical representation (⎕CR) and fix (⎕FX) functions covered earlier. Consider the following program structure:

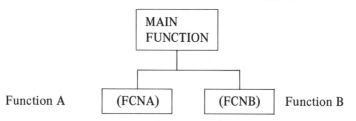

in which it is impossible to have all three functions loaded into the active workspace at one time. The situation can be resolved by defining Function A, converting it to a character matrix with the ⎕CR function, and writing it to a tape file. Similarly, Function B is also defined, converted to a character matrix with the ⎕CR function, and is written to another tape file. During program execution, the main function can "call" one of the subordinate functions by reading in the character matrix representing that function and by converting it to a defined function with the fix system function (⎕FX). It may be necessary in some cases to expunge the previously called function with the expunge system function (⎕EX).

Update in Place

In computer systems with limited file capability, one method of doing file processing is to update in place. Normally, a file update program operates in the following general fashion:

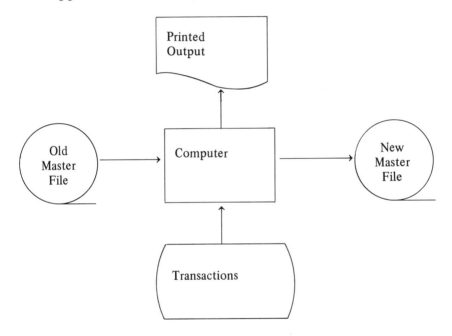

When a tape file is not available for the new master, an update-in-place procedure can be used as described in the following procedure:

1. OPEN file #*n*
2. READ entire file into main storage
3. CLOSE file #*n*
4. UPDATE data records
5. OPEN file #*n* (Same file as in step 1.)
6. WRITE updated records back to file #*n*

7. CLOSE file #*n*
8. GO on to file #*n*+1

Normally, data can be read and written as entire arrays so that a complete file can often be read in or written out with a few statements. The 5100 system always locates files by number so that the file sequence is implicitly taken care of. As far as file structure is concerned, either a one-record-per-file or a many-record-per-file structure can be used depending upon the size of the records involved.

REFERENCES

Katzan, H., *APL User's Guide*, Van Nostrand Reinhold Company, New York, 1971.
Katzan, H., "An APL Approach to the Representation and Manipulation of Data Structures," *International Journal of Computer and Information Sciences*, 1 (2), June, 1972, pp. 93–113.
Pakin, S., APL\360 Reference Manual, Science Research Associates, Chicago, 1972.
IBM 5100 Portable Computer publications:
IBM 5100 APL Reference Manual, Form #SA21-9213
IBM Corporation, Rochester, Minnesota, 1976.

13 | APL SYSTEM COMMANDS

The IBM 5100 Portable Computer system includes a comprehensive set of system commands that provide functions that are outside the scope of the APL language. These commands are grouped into the following categories:

1. Workspace control,
2. Workspace management,
3. Inquiry, and
4. System control.

Workspace control commands govern the information that is stored in the active workspace. Workspace management commands concern tape files and the storage of workspaces and data files on tape. Inquiry commands provide information on the 5100 APL system, and system control commands permit the user to control various aspects of the operation of the 5100 Portable Computer.

13.1 GENERAL CONSIDERATIONS

Each system command begins with a right parenthesis followed by a keyword denoting the function performed by that command and by additional parameters, as required. The following list gives the major functions performed by each command:

Command	Major Function(s)
)CLEAR	Clears the active workspace.
)CONTINUE	Stores the active workspace on tape without changing that workspace.

Command	*Major Function(s)*
)COPY	Copies objects (i.e., functions or variables) from a stored workspace to the active workspace.
)DROP	Deletes a stored workspace or data file from tape by marking it as an unused file.
)ERASE	Erases named objects from the active workspace.
)FNS	Displays the names of user-defined functions in the active workspace.
)LIB	Displays the file headers of files on a tape cartridge.
)LOAD	Loads a stored workspace from a tape cartridge to the main storage unit.
)MARK	Formats a tape cartridge so that an active workspace or a data file can be saved on it.
)MODE	Loads the 5100 communications program or the serial I/O adapter program from a tape cartridge to the main storage unit.
)OUTSEL	Specifies the kinds of data that are displayed on the printer.
)PATCH	Invokes execution of special 5100 system programs that permit system modifications, tape recovery, or tape copying.
)PCOPY	Copies objects from a stored workspace to the active workspace while protecting objects in the active workspace.
)REWIND	Rewinds the tape cartridge on the specified tape unit.
)SAVE	Saves the contents of the active workspace as a file on a tape cartridge.
)SI	Displays the names of suspended and pendent user-defined functions.
)SIV	Displays the names of suspended and pendent user-defined functions and names local to those functions.
)SYMBOLS	Displays or changes the number of function names and statement labels in the active workspace.
)VARS	Displays the names of all global variables in the active workspace.
)WSID	Changes or displays the tape/file number and workspace identification of the active workspace.

Each command is described separately.

Entering of Commands

A command keyword and the preceding right parenthesis may be entered on a character-by-character basis from the keyboard or by holding down the CMD key and pressing the number key below the name of the function above the keyboard. *The result in either case is exactly the same.* Ten keywords cannot be entered with the CMD key:)CLEAR,)DROP,)ERASE,)MARK,)MODE,)PATCH,)PCOPY,)SI,)SIV, and)SYMBOLS. These command keywords, which are less frequently used than the others, must always be entered on a character-by-character basis. Depending upon a particular command, the keyword is followed by appropriate parameters for that command.

After a system command is entered into line position 1 of the display screen, it is executed by pressing the EXECUTE key. A system command is always processed immediately by the computer.

Rules for Entering Commands

Five rules govern the manner in which system commands are entered:

1. A system command always begins with a right parenthesis followed by the appropriate keyword.
2. Each command must begin on a new line.
3. No statement number is needed or required with a system command and will cause an error if used. A system command may not be used in a user-defined function.
4. Blank characters are not permitted within parameters.
5. All parameters must be separated by at least one blank character, and more than one blank character in succession is logically equivalent to one blank character.

The following example demonstrates these rules:

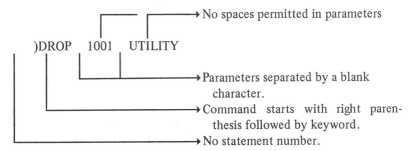

Errors

When a command is entered, it is immediately checked for syntax errors. If an error is detected, an error report is displayed as in the following invalid example of a system command:

```
)MARK 2,3,4
INVALID PARAMETER
```

At this point, the correct form of the command can be reentered or the original command can be corrected through scroll and editing operations.

It is also possible to generate an error during the execution of a system command. These errors are diagnosed and corrected in a manner specific to a particular command.

Parameters

In the description of system commands, the following parameters and their definitions are used:

1. The *device/file number* specifies the tape unit and file number. The form of this parameter is:

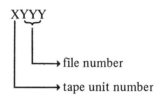

The file number can be 1 through 999 and the tape unit number can be 1 or 2. Tape unit number 1 refers to the built-in tape unit; tape unit number 2 refers to the auxiliary tape unit. If the parameter contains less than four digits, tape unit number 1 is assumed. The following examples demonstrate valid device/file numbers:

Device/file number	*Interpretation*
2	Built-in tape unit, file 2
54	Built-in tape unit, file 54
1013	Built-in tape unit, file 13
2105	Auxiliary tape unit, file 105
2001	Auxiliary tape unit, file 1

The following example shows the way that a device/file number would be used:

)SAVE 9 PAYROLL

which specifies that the active workspace is to be saved as file 9 on the built-in tape unit and given the identification PAYROLL.

2. The *workspace ID* is any sequence up to 11 APL alphabetic of numeric characters, without embedded blank characters. The first character must be alphabetic. If more than 11 characters are entered, only the first 11 are

retained. The following are valid examples:

$$T$$
$$T34$$
$$INVPROG$$

The following example demonstrates how a workspace ID would be used:

$$)LOAD \quad 2015 \quad ARRAYFCNS$$

which specifies that the workspace stored as file 15 and identified as AR-RAYFCNS on the tape cartridge in the auxiliary tape unit is to be loaded as the active workspace.

3. The *password* is any sequence of up to 8 APL alphabetic or numeric characters, without embedded blank characters. If more than 8 characters are entered, only the first 8 are retained. The following are valid examples:

$$5B$$
$$C$$
$$SECRET$$
$$999999$$

The following example demonstrates how a password would be used:

$$)SAVE \quad 6 \quad PERSONNEL \quad :BOSTON$$

which specifies that the active workspace is to be saved as file 6 on the built-in tape unit, given the identification PERSONNEL and the password BOSTON. The password BOSTON must be supplied whenever the stored workspace is referenced, as in a)LOAD or)COPY command.

4. The *object* (or *objects*) is a variable name or a user-defined function name, used in a system command as in the following example:

$$)COPY \quad 2010 \quad MATH \quad :NEWYORK \; DET \; SALES$$

In this case, the)COPY command references workspace named MATH stored as file 10 of the tape cartridge in the auxiliary tape unit. The password for the workspace is NEWYORK and objects DET and SALES are copied into the active workspace. If several objects are specified, they must be separated by a blank character.

In the syntax of system commands, parameters enclosed in brackets are optional and may be omitted.

13.2 WORKSPACE CONTROL COMMANDS

The set of workspace control commands governs the information that is stored in the active workspace. Depending upon the command involved, information may be read from tape or entered from the keyboard.

The)CLEAR Command

The)CLEAR command clears the active workspace and initializes the system attributes. The command has the following syntax:

)CLEAR

and requires no parameters. Then the)CLEAR command is entered explicitly by the user or implicitly through the power up sequence, the following attributes are assigned:

Attribute	Value
Index origin (□IO)	1
Workspace ID	CLEAR WS
Comparison tolerance (□CT)	1E⁻13
Printing width (□PW)	64
Printing precision (□PP)	5
Random number seed (□RL)	16807
Data printed ( )OUTSEL)	ALL
Number of symbols allowed	125

The system always responds with CLEAR WS when)CLEAR is entered.

The)COPY Command

The)COPY command copies the specified objects from the specified stored workspace to the active workspace. Only objects saved on tape with the)SAVE command may be copied. The syntax of the)COPY command is:

)COPY *device/file number workspace ID* [*:password*] [*objects*]

The *password* must be given if the workspace was saved with a password. If *objects* are specified, then only the specified objects are copied. If no objects are specified, then all objects from the stored workspace are copied. The following are valid examples:

```
)COPY  39  ALLFCNS
)COPY  5  TABLES SALES IDS PROJ
)COPY  2001  LISTFCNS :PW SORT
```

When the execution of the)COPY command is successfully completed, the message COPIED *device/file number workspace ID* is displayed.

The)ERASE Command

The)ERASE command erases the specified objects from the active workspace. The syntax of the)ERASE command is:

)ERASE *objects*

where *objects* is one or more variable of function names separated by at least one blank character. Specified objects are removed from the workspace but corresponding symbol table entries are not deleted. (Symbol table entries are also erased when the workspace is saved and then loaded again.) The following are valid examples:

)ERASE DET SORT LIST
)ERASE T34

The)LOAD Command

The)LOAD command loads a stored workspace from tape into the active workspace. The previous contents of the active workspace are lost. The syntax of the)LOAD command is:

)LOAD *device/file number workspace ID* [*:password*]

where the *password* may be used only if the stored workspace was stored with a password. The following are valid examples:

)LOAD 23 INVENSYS
)LOAD 2002 DATASYS :ALPINE

When the execution of the)LOAD command is successfully completed, the message LOADED *device/file number workspace ID* is displayed.

The)PCOPY Command

The)PCOPY command copies the specified objects from the specified stored workspace to the active workspace. Only objects saved on tape with the)SAVE command may be copied. The syntax of the)PCOPY command is:

)PCOPY *device/file number workspace ID* [*:password*] [*objects*]

The *password* must be given if the workspace was saved with a password. If *objects* are specified, then only the specified objects are copied. If no objects are specified, then all objects from the stored workspace are copied. This command is the same as)COPY except that an object is not copied if it currently exists in the active workspace, supplying protection from having an object inadvertently overlaid and destroyed. The following are valid examples:

)PCOPY 2 MISCFCNS
)PCOPY 2015 MATHLIB SIMP TRAP TSERIES
)PCOPY 101 STATPACK :231K ANOVA REGRESS

When the execution of the)PCOPY is successfully completed, the message COPIED *device/file number workspace ID* is displayed.

The)SYMBOLS Command

The)SYMBOLS command is used to change the number of symbols permitted in a workspace. [A symbol is a variable name, function name, or statement label.] With a clear workspace, the allowed number of symbols is set to 125. The syntax of the)SYMBOLS command is:

$$)\text{SYMBOLS } n$$

where *n* is an integer $\geqslant 26$ that gives the number of symbols to be allowed in an active workspace. The following are valid examples:

)SYMBOLS 256
)SYMBOLS 50

The allowed number of symbols can only be changed in a clear workspace and symbols are assigned in multiples of 21. Each symbol requires eight bytes of storage. After the execution of a)SYMBOLS command has been successfully completed, the message WAS *former number of symbols* is displayed.

A variation of the)SYMBOLS command is also used as an inquiry command.

The)WSID Command

As with a stored workspace, an *active* workspace has an identification, which is assigned in one of three ways:

1. By loading a workspace from tape. The active workspace assumes the *device/file number*, *workspace ID*, and *password* (if used) of the workspace loaded.
2. By saving an unnamed active workspace on tape. The active workspace, although it is not modified in any way, assumes the name under which it was saved.
3. By using the)WSID command followed by appropriate parameters.

The)WSID command affects only the active workspace and takes the following form:

$$)\text{WSID } [device/file\ number]\ [workspace\ ID]\ [:password]$$

If all parameters are omitted, then the command becomes an inquiry command—covered later. If the device/file number is omitted, then it is cleared as far as the active workspace is concerned and must be specified with a subsequent)SAVE or)CONTINUE command. The workspace ID parameter specifies a *new* name for the active workspace; this parameter must be present if any other parameter is used. The password is optional. The following are valid examples:

)WSID NEWFCNS
)WSID 2035 MISC
)WSID MATPAK :SIGMA

After the execution of the)WSID command with parameters has been successfully completed, the message WAS *device/file number workspace ID* is displayed.
A variation of the)WSID command is also used as an inquiry command.

13.3 WORKSPACE MANAGEMENT COMMANDS

The set of workspace management commands governs the storing of workspaces
on tape and the initializing of a tape cartridge prior to the saving of a workspace.

The)CONTINUE Command

The)CONTINUE command permits a user to discontinue a work session and
save the *current* state of the active workspace on tape. Everything is saved on
tape—including open shared variables and suspended functions. Therefore, when
the continued workspace is loaded, the work session can be resumed from the
point of discontinuation. The syntax of the)CONTINUE command is:

)CONTINUE [*device/file number*] [*workspace ID*] [:*password*]

The various parameters must be specified if the desired specifications differ from
those of the active workspace. The following are valid examples:

)CONTINUE 5 TEMP
)CONTINUE
)CONTINUE 2015
)CONTINUE 23 LINALG :MYFCNS

After the execution of the)CONTINUE command has been successfully completed, the message CONTINUED *device/file number workspace ID* is displayed.

The)DROP Command

The)DROP command deletes a file from tape by marking it as "unused." After
a file is dropped, it cannot be read and the prior contents are lost. The file may
be a stored workspace or an output file containing data. The syntax of the
)DROP command is:

)DROP *device/file number* [*file ID*]

where *file ID* is a workspace ID or a file name. In the case of a file name, the
file ID parameter is ignored. The following are valid examples:

)DROP 29
)DROP 2001 NEWFCNS
)DROP 3 MATPAK :SIGMA

After the execution of the)DROP command has been successfully completed,
the message DROPPED *device/file number file ID* is displayed.

The)MARK Command

The)MARK command is used to initialize a tape cartridge for storing work-spaces and data files. If a tape cartridge has not been previously marked to store information, an attempt to save a workspace or write a data file will result in an error condition. A tape cartridge is always marked in increments of 1,024 characters of storage. The syntax of the)MARK command is:

)MARK *size number of files starting file number* [*device*]

where:

size is an integer specifying the number of 1,024 character blocks to be re-served for each file.

number of files is the number of files of the specified size to be marked.

starting file number is the lowest-numbered file to be marked.

device is the number of the tape unit on which the tape cartridge to be marked has been placed. This parameter can be 1 for the built-in tape unit or 2 for the auxiliary tape unit. (The default device number is 1.)

A sample)MARK command is:

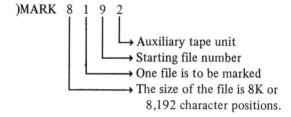

Similarly, another valid)MARK command is:

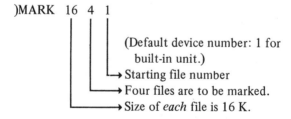

If a file specified in the)MARK command has already been marked, the message ALREADY MARKED is displayed. To continue with the operation and remark the file, the word GO should be entered followed by pressing the EXECUTE key. If the file should not be re-marked, the EXECUTE key should be pressed without entering the word GO.

If an existing file is re-marked, then that file on the tape and all succeeding files are inaccessible. *This means that the storage positions occupied by those files have been reformatted and the previously stored information cannot be read.* However, old files preceding the newly marked files continue to be accessible. In this respect, the tape cartridge is similar to recorder tape since information is always stored sequentially.

When the execution of the)MARK command has been successfully completed, the message MARKED *last file number size* is displayed.

Before a tape file can be marked to hold a workspace or data file, the required amount of storage must be estimated. In general, this is not a problem since an educated guess is usually satisfactory. The size of a workspace can be calculated as follows:

$$m = 3 + \lceil (c-a) \div 1024$$

where:

m is the size of the workspace in 1024 character blocks.
c is the value of □WA with a clear workspace.
a is the current value of □WA.

The size of a data file can be estimated as:

$$n = \lceil (w-u) \div 1024$$

where:

n is the size of the file in 1024 byte blocks.
w is the value of □WA when the data is in the active workspace.
u is the value of □WA without the data in the active workspace.

All tape files require an overhead of .5K bytes for the file header.

The)SAVE Command

The)SAVE command is used to save an active workspace on tape. If the active workspace contains a suspended function, then it cannot be saved with the)SAVE command. (However, it can be stored with the)CONTINUE command.) Also, open shared variables are not stored with the)SAVE command. The syntax of the)SAVE command is:

)SAVE [*device/file number*] [*workspace ID*] [:*password*]

The various parameters must be specified if the desired specifications differ from those of the active workspace. The following are valid examples:

```
)SAVE
)SAVE  1  LISTSPACE
)SAVE 2057
)SAVE  15  LINALG  :MYFCNS
```

After the execution of the)SAVE command has been successfully completed, the message SAVED *device/file number workspace ID* is displayed.

13.4 INQUIRY COMMANDS

Inquiry commands provide information about the APL system and the state of executing functions. The use of inquiry commands does not affect the active workspace or the contents of a tape cartridge.

The)FNS Command

The)FNS command displays the names of user-defined functions in the active workspace. The syntax of the)FNS command is:

)FNS [characters]

where *characters* is a sequence of alphabetic and numeric characters that serves as a starting point for the alphabetic listing of names. If no parameter is used, the names of all functions are displayed alphabetically. If the parameter is specified, then the alphabetic listing begins at that point. The following are valid examples:

)FNS

)FNS A

)FNS TL

The execution of the)FNS command can be discontinued at any time by pressing the ATTN key.

The)LIB Command

The)LIB command is used to display a directory of the contents of a tape cartridge. The syntax of the)LIB command is:

)LIB [device/file number]

where *device/file number* gives the number of the tape unit and the starting file. All file headers from the starting file to the end of the tape are displayed. The default tape number is 1 and the default file number is the current tape position. The following are valid examples:

)LIB

)LIB 41

)LIB 2003

The directory displayed with the)LIB command consists of the following information:

File number
File identification
File type

Number of contiguous 1,024 byte segments assigned to the file

Number of contiguous 1,024 byte segments unused in the file

Number of defective 512 byte areas in the file (If the number of defective areas is greater than 9, an asterisk is printed.)

First and last statement numbers for BASIC user work area and SOURCE files

Key numbers saved for KEYS or KEY(0-9) files

The file types are listed in Table 13.1 and Figure 13.1 gives a sample annotated directory.

The)SI and)SIV Commands

The)SI command gives the names of suspended and pendent user-defined functions. The syntax of the)SI command is:

$$)SI$$

which requires no parameters. Suspended functions are indicated with an asterisk (*).

The)SIV command gives the names of suspended and pendent user-defined functions and lists names of variables local to those functions. The syntax of the)SIV command is:

$$)SIV$$

which requires no parameters. The suspended functions are denoted with an asterisk (*) and the function list is generated in the reverse order of execution.

TABLE 13.1   FILE TYPES.

Type	File
0	Marked or unused file
1	Data exchange file
2	General exchange file
3	BASIC source file
4	BASIC user work area file
5	BASIC KEYS file
6	APL continued file
7	APL SAVE file
8	APL internal data
16	Customer Support File (Patch/recovery/copy)
17	Diagnostic file
18	IMF file
72	Tape storage dump

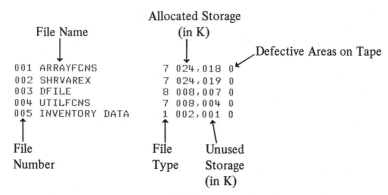

Figure 13.1   Annotated directory. (See also Figure 8.5.)

The)SYMBOLS Command

The)SYMBOLS command gives the number of symbols permitted in the active workspace and has the following syntax:

$$\text{)SYMBOLS}$$

This form of the command requires no parameters. After the execution of the)SYMBOLS command is successfully completed, the message IS *number of symbols* is displayed.

The)VARS Command

The)VARS command displays the names of all global variables in the active workspace. The syntax of the)VARS command is:

$$\text{)VARS } [\textit{characters}]$$

where *characters* is a sequence of alphabetic and numeric characters that serves as a starting point for the alphabetic listing of names. If no parameter is used, the names of all global variables are displayed alphabetically. If the parameter is specified, then the alphabetic listing begins at that point. The following are valid examples:

$$\begin{array}{l}\text{)VARS} \\ \text{)VARS F} \\ \text{)VARS PR34}\end{array}$$

The execution of the)VARS command can be discontinued at any time by pressing the ATTN key.

The)WSID Command

The)WSID command gives the name of the active workspace and has the following syntax:

)WSID

This form of the)WSID command requires no parameters. After the execution of the)WSID command is successfully completed, the message *file number workspace ID* is displayed.

13.5 SYSTEM CONTROL COMMANDS

The set of system control commands is used to control various aspects of 5100 APL system operation and to execute IBM supplied utility programs.

The)MODE Command

The)MODE command is used to load an auxiliary program from a tape cartridge mounted in the built-in tape unit. Two types of programs can be loaded: the communications program and the serial I/O adapter program. The syntax of this command for the communications mode is:

)MODE COM

After the command is executed, the 5100 Portable Computer leaves the APL mode and enters the communications mode. This topic is covered further in chapter 14.

The)OUTSEL Command

The)OUTSEL command is used to specify the data that is printed in addition to being displayed. The syntax of the)OUTSEL command is:

)OUTSEL [*option*]

where *option* is:

ALL if all displayed information is to be printed.
OUT if only displayed *output* is to be printed.
OFF if no information is to be printed.

If the *option* is omitted, the ALL entry is selected. The following are valid examples:

)OUTSEL OFF
)OUTSEL
)OUTSEL ALL

With a clear workspace, the ALL option is selected.

The)PATCH Command

The)PATCH command is used to invoke an IBM supplied serviceability program or to copy a tape. More specifically, the)PATCH command permits the following options:

1. Copy IMF tape
2. Load IMFs
3. Display EC version
4. Key enter an IMF
5. End of job
6. Tape recovery
7. Tape copy program

The)PATCH command does not require parameters and has the following syntax:

)PATCH

The command is used by placing an IBM supplied "Customer Support Cartridge" into the built-in tape unit and then entering the PATCH command on a character-by-character basis. After the EXECUTE key is pressed, the computer responds with the options given in Figure 13.2. Three of the options deal with Internal Machine Fixes (IMFs) that rectify system-based errors. In general, it is only necessary to apply an IMF if the user encounters a corresponding system problem. The directory of a customer support cartridge is given in Figure 13.3.

Copy IMF Tape. The copy IMF option is used to copy the first two files of the "Customer Support Cartridge." The remaining files cannot be copied—except by service personnel. When this option is selected, the copy IMF program directs the user on the action that should be taken. Before files 1 and 2 can be copied, the tape cartridge onto which they will be copied must be marked with the)MARK command for two files of the correct size. The required sizes can be determined by issuing the)LIB command for the "Customer Support Cartridge." (An example of this directory was given in Figure 13.3.)

Load IMFs. The load IMFs option loads the applicable internal machine fixes (IMFs) from the Customer Support Cartridge into the computer. The IMFs occupy space in the user work area and utilize processing time—as required. Therefore, IMFs should only be used when they affect the user's task. The load IMFs program directs the user on the action that should be taken.

Display EC Version. This option is used by service personnel to display the latest engineering change (EC) level of the computer.

Key Enter IMF. This option is used by service personnel to enter an IMF from the keyboard into the computer. After the IMF is loaded, it is written onto the Customer Support Cartridge so that it can be loaded with the "Load IMFs" option, covered above.

```
ENTER OPTION NO.
1. COPY IMF TAPE
2. LOAD IMF'S
3. DISP EC VER.
4. KEY ENTER IMF
5. END OF JOB
6. TAPE RECOVERY
7. TAPE COPY PGM
```

Figure 13.2   Options available with the)PATCH command.

```
      )LIB
001 IMF COPY/LOAD     16 008,000 0
002 IMF FILE          19 008,000 0
003 TAPE RECOVERY     16 014,000 0
004 TAPE COPY         16 005,000 0
005 APLAIDS           07 008,000 0
```

Figure 13.3   Directory of the customer support cartridge.

End of Job.   This option terminates processing of the)PATCH command and returns the computer to normal operation. This is the option that permits the user to escape from the)PATCH command; after the processing of the other options, the computer always displays the)PATCH options in preparation for another operation.

Tape Recovery.   This option permits data to be recovered from a tape cartridge on which errors are occurring and as a result of which the data cannot be read. The following file types can be recovered:

> Type 01—Data exchange file
> Type 02—General exchange file
> Type 03—BASIC source file
> Type 08—APL internal data file

The tape recovery program is used by inserting the tape cartridge containing the errors into the built-in tape unit. The program then directs the user on the action that should be taken.

Tape Copy.   This option permits a tape to be copied and can operate with or without the auxiliary tape unit. The program also marks the tape onto which the copy is made. The program directs the user on the action that should be taken.

APL Aids.   The fifth file of the customer support cartridge is a set of APL aids that permits the following functions:

$\triangle\triangle$TRACE—traces all statements in a specified user-defined function.

$\triangle\triangle$TRACEALL—traces the first executable statement in each user-defined function in the active workspace.

$\triangle\triangle$TRACEOFF—turns off tracing.

$\triangle\triangle$SHARED—displays active shared variables.

These functions can be copied into the active workspace with the)COPY command, as in the following example:

$$\text{)COPY 5 APLAIDS } \Delta\Delta\text{SHARED}$$

If the)COPY command is used without objects, i.e.,

$$\text{)COPY 5 APLAIDS}$$

then the following variables describe the various options:

DESCRIBE
DESCRIBE$\Delta\Delta$TRACE
DESCRIBE$\Delta\Delta$TRACEALL
DESCRIBE$\Delta\Delta$TRACEOFF
DESCRIBE$\Delta\Delta$SHARED

Figure 13.4 displays the variable DESCRIBE$\Delta\Delta$TRACE.

The)REWIND Command

The)REWIND command rewinds the tape cartridge on the specified tape unit and has the following syntax:

$$\text{)REWIND } [device\ number]$$

where *device number* is 1 for the built-in tape unit and 2 for the auxiliary tape unit. The default value for this parameter is 1. The following are valid examples:

)REWIND
)REWIND 1
)REWIND 2

The)LIB command without the *device/file number* displays a directory of the contents of the tape cartridge on the built-in tape unit—starting at its current position. The)REWIND command can be used prior to the)LIB command so that the directory begins with the first file on the cartridge, as follows:

)REWIND
)LIB

This sequence of commands is an alternate to using:

)LIB 1001

or

)LIB 1

which give equivalent results.

```
    )COPY 5 APLAIDS
COPIED 1005 APLAIDS


    DESCRIBEΔΔTRACE


THE ΔΔTRACE FUNCTION HAS THE FOLLOWING INPUTS AND OUTPUTS

    INPUTS:
       THE NAME OF THE FUNCTION ENCLOSED IN QUOTES.

    OUTPUTS:
       A TRACE VECTOR WILL BE SET UP FOR ALL LINES OF THE
       FUNCTION.  THIS ALLOWS THE USER TO FOLLOW THE PATH OF ALL
       INSTRUCTIONS WITHIN THE DESIGNATED FUNCTION.
```

Figure 13.4   Description of one of the APLAIDS.

It is not necessary to rewind a tape cartridge before removing it from the tape unit. Moreover, all file operations require that files be referenced by number and the computer is designed to search for a needed file—regardless of the current position of a tape cartridge. During normal operations, the)REWIND command is infrequently used.

The)REWIND command *can* be used, however, as a convenience. If, for example, a work session normally begins with a)LOAD 1 . . . command, then the tape cartridge can be rewound prior to the end of the previous session so as to minimize subsequent startup time.

REFERENCES

Katzan, H., *APL User's Guide*, Van Nostrand Reinhold Company, New York, 1971.
IBM 5100 Portable Computer publication: *IBM 5100 APL Reference Manual*, Form #SA21-9213.
IBM Corporation, Rochester, Minnesota, 1975.

PART IV:
Miscellanea

PART IV
Miscellaneous

14 | DATA COMMUNICATIONS

The IBM 5100 Portable Computer equipped with the Communications Adapter can be used to communicate with another computer system via telecommunications facilities. Data can be transmitted or received by the 5100, which can serve as a remote terminal or a distributed processor. This chapter covers basic data communications concepts and gives some practical examples of the use of the 5100 in the communications mode. A familiarity with the section "Communications Adapter," included in chapter 3 is assumed. However, all of the technical details of data communications that could possibly pertain to a particular application may not be covered. The *main* objective here is to present overall concepts without the distraction of operational details that are normally subordinated to the implementation phase of systems development.

14.1 DATA COMMUNICATIONS CONCEPTS

The term data communications refers to the use of teleprocessing facilities for the transmission of data. Facilities of this type are used for three major reasons:

1. To provide computational facilities to a user at a remote location.
2. To allow information to be entered or retrieved from a data base system on a dynamic basis.
3. To transfer data between locations at a high rate of speed.

Obviously, other reasons for using data communications facilities exist. However, the three reasons listed above have given rise to the more "popular" applications, such as time sharing, computer networks, message transmission and switching, and information-based systems.

Communications System

Arthur D. Hall[1] defines a communications system as having five functions (or components):

1. A message source.
2. An encoder.
3. A signal channel.
4. A decoder.
5. A message destination.

The model of a communications system defined by Hall is depicted in Figure 14.1. The purpose of the *channel* is to transport data from one location to another. The services used to transmit data are telegraph, telephone, microwave, and broadband telephone.[2]   Telegraph and telephone facilities usually exist as open wires, coaxial cable circuits, and microwave systems.

Communications lines are classed as simplex, half-duplex, and full-duplex. An example of each is given in Figure 14.2. *Simplex lines* transmit in one direction only. *Half-duplex lines* can transmit in either direction but not simultaneously. *Full-duplex lines* can transmit in both directions at the same time. Public telephone lines are half-duplex, and full-duplex transmission is available only through leased facilities. Simplex lines are not used in data communications because control signals must be sent back to the transmitter. Most data communications systems use half-duplex lines so that a two-way dialogue is possible.

Codes and Transmission Modes

For data transmission, data can be represented as a train of bits, as depicted in Figure 14.3.   Successive bits denote a specific character according to a predetermined method of coding.   The number of bits necessary to represent a character generally ranges from 5 to 8 plus a vertical parity bit. Longitudinal redundancy check (i.e., a longitudinal parity bit) and cyclic check codes are also frequently used to aid in error detection.

Data are transmitted in one of three modes: asynchronous start-stop, synchronous, and parallel.   With *asynchronous transmission*, one character is tranamitted at a time and start and stop codes are used to achieve calibration between transmitter and receiver. The *start code* is a zero bit with a one bit-unit

---

[1] Hall, A. D., *A Methodology for Systems Engineering*, New York, Van Nostrand Reinhold Co., 1962, p. 381.
[2] Martin, J., *Design of Real-Time Computer Systems*, Englewood Cliffs, N.J., Prentice-Hall, Inc., 1967, p. 278.

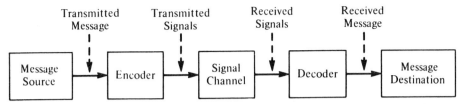

Figure 14.1 Model of an elementary communication system. (Hall, *op. cit.*, p. 381.)

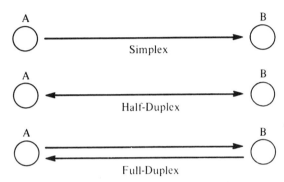

Figure 14.2 Classes of communications lines.

time duration. The *stop code* is a one bit with a time duration of 1.42 bit units.*

With *synchronous transmission*, a block is accumulated in a buffer prior to transmission and the synchronization of transmitter is controlled by oscillators. Synchronous transmission is more efficient since there are no start and stop bits and no pauses. Block lengths varies and is usually dependent upon the physical characteristics of the hardware.

Parallel transmission uses several communications channels to transmit a character. Usually, a channel exists for each bit in the code structure.

Types of Data Lines

Communications lines are classified according to the data rate that they can sustain. Data rates are measured in bits per second. Three classifications are usually used: subvoice grade, voice grade, and wide band. *Subvoice-grade lines* transmit at rates that range from 45 to 180 bits per second; lines in this category are customarily used for teletype service. *Voice-grade lines* can sustain data rates from 110 to 9600 bits per second; public telephone lines fall into this category. *Wide band lines* (also called *broadband lines*) are used to transmit data at line

---

*The stop code time duration varies from 1.00 to 2.00 bit units depending on line speed and character length in bits.

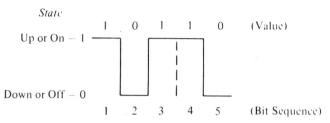

Figure 14.3   Representation of data as a bit train.

speeds of from 12,500 to 250,000 bits per second; broadband facilities operate in the duplex mode and are supplied by common carriers such as Western Union and The Bell System.

A significant characteristic of communication lines is whether they are switched or private. Telegraph and public telephone lines are switched through public exchanges—even though they may be used to transmit data. Private or leased lines avoid the public switching network. The advantage of switched lines is the fact that they are located practically everywhere. Leased lines can be less expensive than switched lines depending upon volume and distance. Leased lines can also be "conditioned" to reduce transmission errors.

Signal Representation and Modulation

Data can be transmitted in a digital form or an analog form. With a digital form of transmission, a sequence of on/off pulses is transmitted in much the same manner that data are moved in the computer, since it is a digital device. Figure 14.4(a) depicts a digital signal that contains two voltage levels—representing 0 and 1. The original telegraph system used digital transmission. One of the disadvantages of digital transmission is that the pulses become distorted, as depicted in Figure 14.4(b) when they have to travel long distances and at a high rate of speed over communications lines. Regenerative repeaters are used to reconstruct the bits and pass them on.

With an analog signal, a continuous range of frequencies is transmitted, as depicted in the oversimplified example in Figure 14.4(c). Analog signals can be distorted through attenuation, delay characteristics of the signal, and noise on the communications line. Amplifiers are used to increase the signal strength of analog signals.

Most communications lines that can be used for data transmission are designed to carry analog signals and the computer is a digital device. The process of converting digital data to analog form is called *modulation*. The reverse process of converting analog signals to digital data is called *demodulation*. A small hardware device that performs modulation/demodulation is called a *modem*. Two types of modems are used: a dataset and an acoustical coupler.

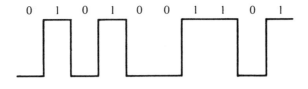

(a) Digital Pulse

(b) Digital Pulses Distorted at the Receiver

(c) Analog Signal

Figure 14.4   Analog and digital transmission signals.

A *dataset* is supplied by the telephone company and is connected to the telephone and the data source—either a terminal device, a high-speed transmission unit, or a transmission control unit of a computer. A dataset establishes a fixed connection between one terminal and one telephone line. When a user desires to make a data communications connection to the computer using a dataset, he pushes the TALK button and dials the number of the computer. After the telephone rings, it is answered by the computer and a high-pitched sound is heard. Next, the DATA button is pushed and the receiver is cradled. A line connection is made.

An *acoustical coupler* is a device that converts digital signals to audible tones. The acoustical coupler must be attached to the transmitting device but not to a telephone line. Thus, the terminal can be portable. When a user desires to make a data communications connection to the computer using an acoustical coupler he simply dials the computer over an ordinary telephone. After the computer answers the telephone and produces a high-pitched sound, the receiver of the telephone is clamped in to the coupler mechanism and a line connection is made.

The different types of lines used for data transmission vary widely in the amount of information that can be transmitted over them in a fixed unit of time. This capacity is frequently referred to as *bandwidth*. Bandwidth is measured in cycles per second (or Hertz as it is usually called). In general, cycles of the analog signal are used to represent data; the amount of data that can be transmitted over a given line is directly proportional to the bandwidth.

Modulation can take several forms: amplitude modulation, frequency modulation, phase modulation, and pulse modulation. IBM's data communications primer[3] presents a good overview of modulation techniques. One of the best sources of information on data communications is a book by James Martin entitled, *Introduction to Teleprocessing*.[4]

Structure of a Sample System

A sample data communications system is depicted in Figure 14.5. Several concepts are depicted: leased lines, datasets, acoustical coupler, transmission control unit, the main computer system, and a remote computer system.

Computer programs that utilize data communications facilities are similar to conventional programs. Generally speaking, a data communications line is treated as an input/output device, and telecommunications access methods, similar to data management access methods, are used to handle input and output operations.

14.2 5100 COMMUNICATIONS MODE

In order to enter the 5100 communications mode, two things are necessary:

1. The 5100 Communications Adapter, and
2. The 5100 Communications Programs.

The Communications Adapter is a hardware feature that is built into a 5100 Portable Computer equipped with the communications option. The only external evidence of the communications feature on the 5100 Portable Computer is a communications connector on the rear panel of the computer that is used to attach the computer to either an acoustical coupler or a data set modem. The communications programs are provided on a communications tape cartridge that is supplied with a machine equipped with the communications feature.

Loading the Communications Program

The communications program operates in either the APL or BASIC modes and is loaded by inserting the communications tape cartridge into the built-in tape unit and by entering the following command:

)MODE COM

[3]*Data Communications Primer*, White Plains, N.Y., IBM Corporation, Form C20-1668,). 9ff.
[4]Martin, J., *Introduction to Teleprocessing*, Englewood Cliffs, N.J., Prentice-Hall, Inc., 1972.

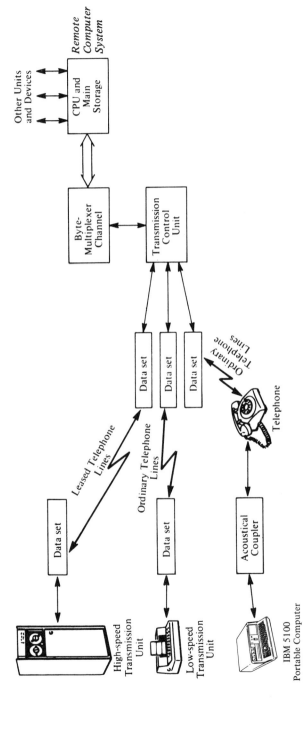

Figure 14.5   Sample data communications system.

when in the APL mode, or

UTIL MODE COM

when in the BASIC mode. After the command is entered into the input line, the EXECUTE key must be pressed. The communications program is then read in from tape and the computer enters the communications mode.

Communications Options

After the loading of the communications program has been completed, the set of options depicted in Figure 14.6 is displayed. In the set of options, the terms EBCD and CORRESPONDENCE refer to methods for coding character information, and the method that applies in a given case depends upon the remote system. Otherwise, there are two processing options: the print option and the tape option. With the *print option*, messages received from or sent to the remote system are printed during transmission. All data transmitted is also placed in the extended display, which can also be printed. The tape unit cannot be used with the print option. With the *tape option*, the tape unit can be used during data communications, so that outgoing messages are sent from the specified tape unit and incoming messages are written to the specified tape unit. The printer can also be used with the tape option. The *communications adapter test* is used to check the operational readiness of the communications feature.

States of the 5100 Communications System

The 5100 communications system operates in five states:

State	Designation
Home	HOME
Edit	EDIT
Scroll	SCRL
Transmit	XMIT
Process	PROC

The various states are associated with the communications commands, located above the keyboard, that are entered through the use of the CMD key and the corresponding numeric key.

The meanings of the various states are generally self-explanatory. The *home state* is used to terminate a prior operation and must be entered before performing a scroll operation or entering a communications command. The *edit state* is entered before line editing, line deletion, and must be used prior to printing and tape operations. The *scroll*, *transmit*, and *process* states are entered automatically by the 5100 communications system during the execution of a corresponding operation.

ENTER:
```
        1  FOR EBCD TAPE OPTION
        2  FOR EBCD PRINT OPTION
        3  FOR CORRESPONDENCE TAPE OPTION
        4  FOR CORRESPONDENCE PRINT OPTION
        5  FOR COMMUNICATIONS ADAPTER TEST
```
Figure 14.6 Communications options.

Communications Status Line

Line position 0 of the display screen is known as the *Communications Status Line* when the system is in the communications mode. During system operations, the communications status line contains several indicators so that the user can quickly determine the status of the communications system. Character positions 58 and 60 are particularly useful for determining what the system is doing, as indicated by the following list:

Character Positions *58 and 60*	*Status*
☐↓	No line connection; the 5100 system is offline.
☐↑	A line connection has been made; the 5100 system is online.
☐←	The 5100 system is receiving.
☐→	The 5100 system is transmitting.

Character positions 53–56 of the communications status line give the state of the communications system. For example, the following information in character positions 53–60:

HOME ☐ ↓

indicates that the system is offline in the home state. Similarly, the following information in character positions 53–60:

XMIT ☐ →

indicates that the 5100 system is online and transmitting data.

Command Processing

All 5100 communications system commands, given in chapter 3, begin with the command character (&), which is a composite symbol constructed from the and (&) and underscore ( ) characters. The 5100 system recognizes the command character and processes the associated command. When the 5100 system is online, messages starting with the command character are not transmitted to the remote system, but are processed as system commands. All information entered from the keyboard, including commands, is placed in the extended display.

14.3 OFFLINE OPERATIONS

Offline 5100 communications operations include the capability for printing messages and writing messages on tape, in addition to line editing operations, which are covered briefly here, and the entering of information into the extended display.

Entering Information into the Extended Display

Once the 5100 system is in the communications mode but not online, data is entered on a line-by-line basis into the extended display through the use of the following procedure:

1. Place the system in the home state by holding the CMD key down and pressing the home key.
2. While holding the CMD key down, press the edit key. (The system is then in the edit state.)
3. Enter a line of data into the input line.
4. Move the line of data to the extended display by holding the CMD key down and pressing the home key.
5. Continue with step 2 to enter additional lines.

Input lines are placed in the extended display in the order in which they are entered.

Simple Editing

A line from the extended display is edited by placing the system in the home state and scrolling up or down until the line to be edited is in the input line. The following procedure can then be used for line editing:

1. Hold the CMD key down and press the edit key.
2. Edit the line in the usual fashion or while holding the CMD key down, press the line delete key.
3. Hold the CMD key down and press the home key.

Special precautions should be taken with editing for the following reason: *When a line is edited, all lines from the point of editing to the end of the contents of the extended display are deleted.* Thus, only the last line entered can effectively be edited.

Printing Messages

Lines from the extended display can be printed through the use of the following procedure:

1. Place the 5100 system in the home state.
2. Scroll up or down until the first line to be printed is in the input line.
3. Hold the CMD key down and press the edit key.
4. Hold the CMD key down and press the print key.

The contents of the extended display from the line shown to the end of the extended display are then printed.

Placing Messages on Tape

When the tape mode has been selected, the contents of the extended display can be written to tape using the following procedure:

1. Insert an appropriately marked tape cartridge into the built-in or auxiliary tape units.
2. Use the &OPEN command to open the file for output, as in the following example:

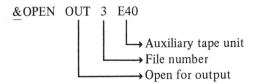

&OPEN OUT 3 E40

→ Auxiliary tape unit
→ File number
→ Open for output

   (A communications command may be entered only when the system is in the home state.)
3. Using the procedure given above, delete the &OPEN command from the extended display. Remember, *all* information entered is placed in the extended display. (This operation should leave the 5100 system in the home state.)
4. Scroll up or down until the first line to be written to tape is in the input line.
5. Hold the CMD key down and press the edit key.
6. Hold the CMD key down and press the write key. (This step causes the contents of the extended display to be written to tape.)
7. Hold the CMD key down and press the home key.
8. Enter a &CLOSE command to complete the tape write operation.

The tape write capability permits messages to be constructed offline for later transmission to a remote system.

14.4 ONLINE OPERATIONS

The 5100 Portable Computer can be used as a terminal device or as a message input and output device. In the latter case, successive lines are transmitted without intervening operator action.

Keyboard/Display Operations

When the 5100 system is used as a terminal device, the keyboard is used for input to the remote system and the display screen is used to display output from the remote system. If the print option has been selected, then remote system output is also printed if the printer unit is turned on. The steps required for using the 5100 as a terminal device are outlined as follows:

1. Place the 5100 Portable Computer in the communications mode. Select the print option.
2. Initialize the 5100 system by entering &SYSTEM and &RATE commands, as required.
3. Establish a line connection to the remote system.
4. Enter into a dialogue with the remote system as would be done with a conventional terminal.

5100 data is transmitted to or received from the remote system on a character-by-character basis. After an input line to the remote system has been placed in the input line of the 5100 system, the end-of-message code is transmitted by pressing the EXECUTE key—as in normal terminal operations. Each line transmitted to or received from the remote system is stored in the extended display. Figure 14.7 depicts a simple dialogue with a remote system; the script in Figure 14.7 was listed through the use of the technique for printing messages given above. Figure 14.7 represents a complete dialogue in the sense that *all* data passing through the 5100 is placed in the extended display. If it were desired to only place messages from the remote systems in the extended display, then the following command should be entered:

&OUTSEL SYS

when the 5100 communications system is in the home state.

Tape Input

Data stored on tape locally, i.e., on a 5100 tape cartridge, can be transmitted to a remote system through the use of the following procedure:

1. Place the 5100 Portable Computer in the communications mode. Select the tape option.

```
&SYSTEM BASIC
&RATE 300


CALLDATA SYSTEMS
GOOD AFTERNOON!  GRUMMAN-DTSS LINE 1/0317;
FRIDAY, 08 OCT 76, 13:41; 040 USERS
USER NUMBER---G52004

NEW OR OLD---NEW SERIES
READY

10 FOR I=2 TO 100 STEP 0
20 PRINT I;
30 LET I=2*I-1
40 NEXT I
50 PRINT "AD INFINITUM"
60 END
RUN

SERIES     08 OCT 76   13:42

2  3  5  9  17  33  65 AD INFINITUM

0.062 SEC.   28 I/O
READY
```

Figure 14.7 A listing from the extended display of a dialogue with a remote system using the 5100 as a terminal device.

2. Initialize the 5100 system by entering &SYSTEM and &RATE commands, as required.
3. Open the 5100 input tape with an &OPEN command such as:

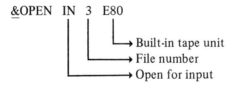

```
&OPEN  IN  3  E80
```
→ Built-in tape unit
→ File number
→ Open for input

4. Establish a line connection to the remote system.
5. Gain access to the remote system through the use of identification codes and passwords, as appropriate.
6. Enter information appropriate to the remote system to prepare it for accepting data from the 5100 system.
7. Enter a &TAPEIN command.

At this point, successive lines from the 5100 tape cartridge will be transmitted to the remote system automatically without intervening operator action. When transmission has been completed, the input file is automatically closed.

```
G52004
NEW SORT
10   DIM W(100)
20   READ N
30   FOR I=1 TO N
40   READ W(I)
50   NEXT I
60   LET F=0
70   FOR I=1 TO N-1 STEP 2
80       IF W(I)<=W(I+1) THEN 130
90       LET T=W(I)
100      LET W(I)=W(I+1)
110      LET W(I+1)=T
120      LET F=1
130  NEXT I
140  FOR I=2 TO N-1 STEP 2
150      IF W(I)<=W(I+1) THEN 200
160      LET T=W(I)
170      LET W(I)=W(I+1)
180      LET W(I+1)=T
190      LET F=1
200  NEXT I
210  IF F<>0 THEN 60
220  PRINT "SORTED VALUES"
230  FOR I=1 TO N
240  PRINT W(I)
250  NEXT I
260  DATA 8
270  DATA -7,3,9,6,5,1,4,3
280  END
RUN
```

Figure 14.8   A complete dialogue transmitted with the tape input feature.

Tape input can be used to transmit a complete dialogue to the remote system, as is the case in Figure 14.8, or to transmit a portion of a dialogue, such as a program or a data set. The 5100 communication system tape option must be selected in order to perform tape input.

Tape Output

Data stored at the remote system can be transmitted to the 5100 system and be placed on tape through the use of the following procedure:

1. Place the 5100 Portable Computer in the communications mode. Select the tape option.
2. Initialize the system by entering &SYSTEM and &RATE commands, as required.
3. Open the 5100 output tape with an &OPEN command such as:

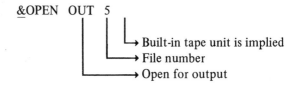

&OPEN OUT 5

→ Built-in tape unit is implied
→ File number
→ Open for output

or as:

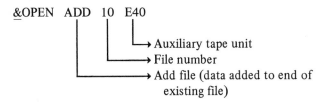

&OPEN ADD 10 E40

→ Auxiliary tape unit
→ File number
→ Add file (data added to end of existing file)

4. Enter an &OUTSEL SYS command so that only data from the remote system is written to tape.
5. Establish a line connection to the remote system.
6. Gain access to the remote system through the use of identification codes and passwords, as appropriate.
7. Enter information appropriate to the remote system to cause it to transmit the required data to the 5100 system. (In a BASIC operating environment, for example, a user might enter a LIST command to have the remote system send a BASIC program to the 5100 system.)

At this point, successive lines from the remote system are transmitted to the extended display of the 5100 system without intervening operator action. The "total" amount of data that can be transmitted is limited by the size of the extended display. After transmission has been completed, the transmitted data is printed, if the printer is attached and turned on, and then it is written to the tape file opened in step 3. One final step is required, as follows:

8. The output file must be closed with a command of the form:

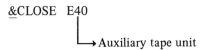

&CLOSE E40

→ Auxiliary tape unit

The data received from the remote system is written as a type 2 file, which can subsequently be read by a BASIC or APL program. If the data is a BASIC program, it can be loaded with a LOAD n, SOURCE command, where n is the file number. Similarly, the data can be inspected by a LOAD n, DATA command when the system is in the BASIC mode. Figure 14.9 gives an example of a BASIC program received from a remote system with the tape output feature and listed after it was loaded with a LOAD n, DATA command.

14.5 COMMUNICATIONS MISCELLANEA

This section includes miscellaneous topics relevant to data communications in a 5100 Portable Computer system environment. Most applications require a knowledge of the remote system, which for obvious reasons, cannot be covered here. Therefore, the topics covered present only an idea of the scope of possible applications.

```
0 01 D..A 10    DIM W(100)
0002 DATA 20    READ N
0003 DATA 30    FOR I=1 TO N
0004 DATA 40        READ W(I)
0005 DATA 50    NEXT I
0006 DATA 60    LET F=0
0007 DATA 70    FOR I=1 TO N-1 STEP 2
0008 DATA 80        IF W(I)<=W(I+1) THEN 130
0009 DATA 90        LET T=W(I)
0010 DATA 100       LET W(I)=W(I+1)
0011 DATA 110       LET W(I+1)=T
0012 DATA 120       LET F=1
0013 DATA 130   NEXT I
0014 DATA 140   FOR I=2 TO N-1 STEP 2
0015 DATA 150       IF W(I)<=W(I+1) THEN 200
0016 DATA 160       LET T=W(I)
0017 DATA 170       LET W(I)=W(I+1)
0018 DATA 180       LET W(I+1)=T
0019 DATA 190       LET F=1
0020 DATA 200   NEXT I
0021 DATA 210   IF F<>0 THEN 60
0022 DATA 220   PRINT "SORTED VALUES"
0023 DATA         FOR I=1 TO N
0024 DATA 240       PRINT W(I);
0025 DATA 250   NEXT I
0026 DATA 260   STOP
0027 DATA 270   DATA 8
0028 DATA 280   DATA -7,3,9,6,5,1,4,3
0029 DATA 290   END
```

Figure 14.9   Example of a BASIC program received from a remote system with the tape output feature and listed after it was loaded with a LOAD *n*, DATA command.

Syntax of Communications System Commands

Table 14.1 lists the syntax of 5100 communications system commands. The functions performed by the various commands are covered in chapter 3.

Program Development

Computer programs can be placed on tape locally with the 5100 system and then be transmitted to the remote system for processing. The scope of this activity is not restricted to the APL and BASIC languages and may include programs written in any language, such as COBOL, FORTRAN, and PL/I. When messages are constructed offline with the 5100 system, the computer does not recognize the content of the messages.

Data Collection

Data can be collected locally with the 5100 system in the offline mode through the use of tape files and the &OPEN ADD . . . option. In this case, data is added

TABLE 14.1   SYNTAX OF COMMUNICATION SYSTEM COMMANDS.

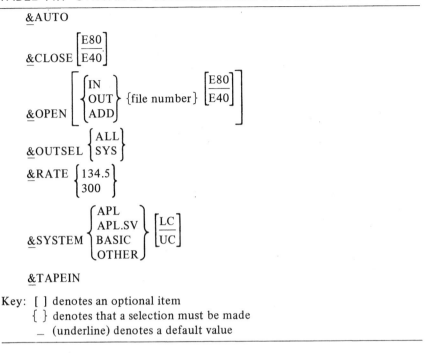

Key: [ ] denotes an optional item
     { } denotes that a selection must be made
     _ (underline) denotes a default value

to the end of a local file as it is collected. After collection has been completed, it can be transmitted to a remote system for entry into a central data base.

Local Data Bases

A local data base can be constructed from a large central data base at a remote location by using the tape output option in an online mode. Data transmitted to the 5100 can subsequently be queried through a specially prepared APL or BASIC program.

Transmission of BASIC Programs

BASIC programs constructed locally can be transmitted to a remote system by simply saving the BASIC program as a SOURCE file, as follows:

$$\text{SAVE } n, \text{SOURCE}$$

where n is a file number. The BASIC program is stored in character form and can be transmitted to the remote system with the tape input option in the online mode. With tape input, the following character translations:

| Character from | Character Displayed and Transmitted | |
5100 Tape	EBCD Mode	CORRESPONDENCE Mode
≤	<=	[=
≥	>=	]=
≠	<>	[]
↑	**	**
<	<	[
>	>	]

are made automatically prior to transmission to the remote system, if the &SYSTEM BASIC or the &SYSTEM OTHER command has been entered.

Transmission of APL Functions

APL functions are best transmitted in character form through the use of the ⎕CR and ⎕FX system functions. The procedures are straightforward but require a detailed knowledge of APL file input and output operations.

Remote System to 5100 APL. The steps required to transmit an APL function from a remote APL system to the 5100 are outlined as follows:

1. Place the 5100 Portable Computer in the communications mode. Select the tape option.
2. Initialize the 5100 system by entering the &SYSTEM APL and &RATE commands, as required.
3. Open the 5100 output tape with an &OPEN command.
4. Enter the &OUTSEL SYS command so that only remote APL system output will be written to tape.
5. Enter a statement to the remote APL system to convert the function to be transmitted to a character matrix. The command would take the following general form:

$$VAR \leftarrow \square CR \text{ 'FUNCTION'}$$

6. Enter the following expression:

$$\rho VAR$$

to the remote APL system so that the size of the character matrix is sent to the local 5100 system.

7. Transmit the character matrix representation to the local 5100 system by entering the variable name. The function is then transmitted as successive lines in character format without intervening operator action. (When the transmission is complete, the function is listed, if the printer is attached and turned on, and written to tape.)
8. Close the local 5100 file with the &CLOSE command.
9. Sign off the remote system.

The function from the remote system is now stored on tape and can be converted to a 5100 APL function through the use of the following procedure:

1. Establish an APL shared variable to read the designated file and open it for input.
2. Read the first record of the file to obtain the size of the matrix representing the function.
3. Read in the remainder of the file as character records and create the corresponding character matrix.
4. Convert the character matrix to a 5100 APL function using the system function ⎕FX.

Figure 14.10 lists an APL function, READLCL, that reads a character representation of an APL function from a communications file and converts it to an APL function.

5100 System to Remote APL System. The process of transmitting an APL function from the 5100 to a remote APL system involves three distinct but related tasks:

1. A procedure to write the APL function in character form to a local file. This procedure requires an APL function that actually writes a type 2 file that can be transmitted via the 5100 communications feature. (This

```
       ∇READLCL[⎕]∇
    ∇ READLCL;FCN;A;SIZE;⎕IO;I
[1]    ⎕IO←1
[2]    A←⎕EX 'FILE'
[3]    →(2≠1 ⎕SVO 'FILE')/ERR1
[4]    FILE←'IN 1001 MSG=OFF'
[5]    →(1≠∧/ 0 0 =A←FILE)/ERR2
[6]    →(0=ρSIZE←FILE)/ERR3
[7]    FCN←(SIZE←↓SIZE)ρ' '
[8]    I←1
[9]    AGN:→(0=ρA←FILE)/ERR3
[10]   FCN[I;]←A
[11]   →((I←I+1)≤1↑ρSIZE)/AGN
[12]   FILE←10
[13]   →(1≠∧/ 0 0 =A←FILE)/ERR4
[14]   ⎕←'SUCCESSFUL TRANSMISSION OF FUNCTION: ',⎕FX FCN
[15]   →(2=⎕SVR 'FILE')/0
[16]   ERR5:→OUT,ρ⎕←'READLCL: ERROR RETRACTING SHARED VARIABLE'
[17]   ERR1:→OUT,ρ⎕←'READLCL: ERROR ESTABLISHING SHARED VARIABLE'
[18]   ERR2:→OUT,ρ⎕←'READLCL: ERROR OPENING FILE 1001'
[19]   ERR3:→OUT,ρ⎕←'READLCL: END OF FILE 1001'
[20]   ERR4:→OUT,ρ⎕←'READLCL: ERROR CLOSING FILE 1001'
[21]   OUT:A←⎕SVR 'FILE'
[22]   →
    ∇
```

Figure 14.10 An APL function that reads a character representation of a function from a communications file and converts it to an APL function.

```
          ∇WRITELCL[□]∇
      ∇ WRITELCL;FCN;A;SIZE;□IO;I
[1]     □IO←1
[2]     A←□EX 'FILE'
[3]     →(2≠1 □SVO 'FILE')/ERR1
[4]     FILE←'OUT 1001 MSG=OFF TYPE=I2'
[5]     →(1≠∧/ 0 0 =A←FILE)/ERR2
[6]     FILE←↑SIZE←ρFCN←□CR 'TRANSFCN'
[7]     →(1≠∧/ 0 0 =A←FILE)/ERR3
[8]     I←1
[9]  NXT:FILE←FCN[I;]
[10]    →(1≠∧/ 0 0 =A←FILE)/ERR3
[11]    →((I←I+1)≤1↑ρSIZE)/NXT
[12]    FILE←ι0
[13]    →(1≠∧/ 0 0 =A←FILE)/ERR4
[14]    □←'SUCCESSFUL □CR AND WRITE OF TRANSFCN'
[15]    →(2=□SVR 'FILE')/0
[16] ERR5:→OUT,ρ□←'WRITELCL: ERROR RETRACTING SHARED VARIABLE'
[17] ERR1:→OUT,ρ□←'WRITELCL: ERROR ESTABLISHING SHARED VARIABLE'
[18] ERR2:→OUT,ρ□←'WRITELCL: ERROR OPENING FILE 1001'
[19] ERR3:→OUT,ρ□←'WRITELCL: ERROR WRITING FILE 1001'
[20] ERR4:→OUT,ρ□←'WRITELCL: ERROR CLOSING FILE 1001'
[21] OUT:A←□SVR 'FILE'
[22]    →
      ∇
```

Figure 14.11 An APL function that converts an APL function to canonical representation and writes it to a local file.

```
          ∇READRMT[□]∇
      ∇ READRMT;FCN;SIZE;□IO;I
[1]     □IO←1
[2]     FCN←(SIZE←ιℕ)ρ' '
[3]     I←1
[4]  RPT:FCN[I;]←ℕ
[5]     →((I←I+1)≤1↑ρSIZE)/RPT
[6]     □←'SUCCESSFUL TRANSMISSION OF FUNCTION: ',□FX FCN
      ∇
```

Figure 14.12 An APL function that runs on a remote APL system and reads a transmitted function in character form and converts it to an APL function.

function is referred to as WRITELCL. The function to be transmitted is referred to as TRANSFCN.)

2. An APL function that runs on the remote APL system to read the transmitted function in character form and convert it to an APL function. (This function is referred to as READRMT.)

3. A communications procedure for performing the transmission operations.

The APL functions for performing tasks 1 and 2 are given in Figures 14.11 and 14.12, respectively. The steps that comprise the operational procedure for actually transmitting the function via communications facilities is outlined as follows:

1. In the APL mode, copy functions WRITELCL and TRANSFCN into the active workspace.
2. Execute WRITELCL, which converts TRANSFCN to character form and writes it to a local 5100 tape file.
3. Place the 5100 Portable Computer in the communications mode. Select the tape option.
4. Initialize the 5100 system by entering &SYSTEM, &RATE, and &OPEN commands as covered previously.
5. Establish a line connection and gain access to the remote APL system.
6. Load and execute the READRMT function on the remote APL system. [This function reads the size of the character matrix and the character matrix using the quote-quad (⎕) form of input.]
7. Enter a &TAPEIN command to initiate local 5100 data transmission.
8. After transmission has been completed, send a)SAVE command to the remote APL system to save the transmitted function.

The procedure is fairly involved but is considerably less tedious than re-entering a lengthy APL function.

REFERENCES

Hall, A. D., *A Methodology for Systems Engineering*, Van Nostrand Reinhold Company, New York, 1962.

Katzan, H., *Computer Data Security*, Van Nostrand Reinhold Company, New York, 1973.

Martin, J., *Design of Real-Time Computer Systems*, Prentice-Hall, Inc., Englewood Cliffs, N.J., 1967.

Martin, J., *Introduction to Teleprocessing*, Prentice-Hall, Inc., Englewood Cliffs, N.J., 1972.

Data Communications Primer, White Plains, N.Y., IBM Corporation, Form #C20-1668.

IBM 5100 Portable Computer publications:
  a. *IBM 5100 APL Reference Manual*, Form #SA21-9213.
  b. *IBM 5100 Communications Adapter Feature*, Form #SA21-9215.
  c. *IBM 5100 BASIC Reference Manual*, Form #SA21-9217.

IBM Corporation, Rochester, Minnesota.

15 | SYSTEM DEVELOPMENT LIFE CYCLE

15.1 INTRODUCTION

Most applications evolve through a set of successive stages from initial conception of the system idea to final cessation of system utilization. The set of stages is known as the *system life cycle*, and a high degree of commonalty exists between the stages of development of different systems, especially in the areas of computers, data processing, and information systems. Rubin* lists the eight stages in the system life cycle as:

1. Conception
2. Preliminary analysis
3. System design
4. Programming
5. System documentation
6. System installation
7. System operation
8. System cessation

To a large degree, the above stages only approximate real life and serve as a model for organization and planning. For example, the class of activities generally known as "controlling and implementing the solution"† is not included in

---

*Rubin, p. 4.
†For example, see Churchman, et al., pp. 595–622.

the system life cycle. The practicalities of system development are such that the solution (i.e., system) must be monitored and controlled because it may lose some of its effectiveness due to changes in the operating environment. The process of monitoring and controlling the effectiveness of a system necessarily involves a feedback cycle, which is not included in Rubin's system life cycle. The need for monitoring and control may become necessary as a result of three possible conditions:

1. A previously irrelevant system variable may become relevant.
2. The value of one or more system variables may change and affect the operational logic of the system.
3. The functional components of the system may change or need to be adjusted.

Thus, the feedback cycle is a practical reality that can be viewed both from within the life cycle and from outside the life cycle in its operating environment. As a result, the design and development methodology does not include methods for describing this aspect of the system development life cycle.

15.2 CONCEPTION

The conception stage is used to determine whether or not a need exists for the new system. The need can be recognized by the system design and development group (e.g., the data processing department) or by the organization that the new system is expected to service. In the latter case, the manager involved is usually aware of a need, but is not certain that a new or improved system is feasible.

The conception stage is formalized when the systems department and the operational group meet to identify the specific need and to determine whether the systems approach supports the goals of the organization.

When a new system is to exist as a product or service, the conception stage represents a preliminary market analysis and a summarization of the relevant business conditions. In organizations that normally deal in products and services, ideas for "new business" occur frequently and the conception stage serves to sort out ideas that warrant further study. The conception stage is summarized in a convenient form in Figure 15.1.

The result of the conception stage of the system life cycle is normally a report to the sponsoring department that summarizes the needs, resources, and other pertinent information about the proposed system. The report serves as a medium for deciding whether to pursue the proposed system development effort or to drop the idea altogether.

15.3 PRELIMINARY ANALYSIS

Preliminary analysis is popularly known as the "feasibility study" and is primarily concerned with three areas:

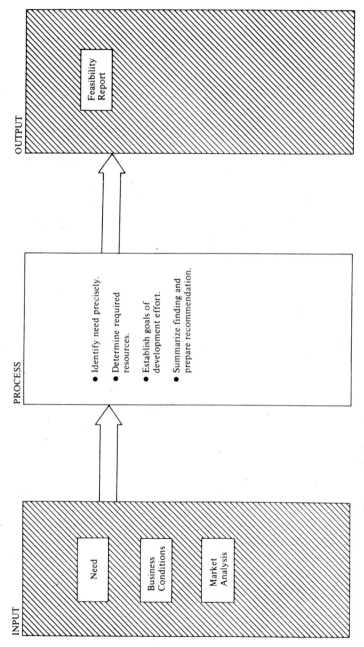

Figure 15.1 Overview diagram of the conception stage of the system life cycle.

1. The characteristics of the present system or operating environment.
2. Consideration of whether a new system should be developed or the present system should be revised.
3. Whether the proposed system is viable for the sponsoring organization.

Even though the preliminary analysis function is commonly performed by a systems analyst, it is usually assisted through management participation by the sponsoring organization, either through direct participation or by permitting the analyst to work through members of the sponsoring organization. Figure 15.2 gives an overview diagram of the preliminary design stage of the system life cycle.

Inputs to the preliminary design stage are listed as follows:

1. Characteristics of the current system (i.e., the existing system if one exists).
2. Ideas for the proposed system.
3. Organization factors.
4. Financial considerations.

Characteristics of the current system are determined through existing documentation, and in the event that it does not exist, through extensive analysis by the systems analyst. This is an instance in the system life cycle in which effective documentation of the existing system is important for ongoing analysis. Clearly, detailed documentation is not necessary, but a general description of the system at the "overview" level is required. *Ideas for the proposed system* are obtained by the analyst as a separate step or as a by-product of the need to describe the existing system. This step is particularly significant when proposed changes to an existing system are planned. In many cases, actual users of a system are the only ones that are aware of its deficiencies. It is also important to recognize that many, if not most, users of a system are unaware of the potentialities of a new system, especially in the case of computer-based systems, and tend to express needs, limitations, and deficiencies in their own language. *Organization factors*, which unfortunately are ignored in many cases, include: organizational politics, resistance to change, previous experience with systems work, and the type of employees involved. Organizational factors can "make or break" a system effort if left unrecognized, but generally do not result in organizational problems if considered during the preliminary analysis state. *Financial considerations* normally include the cost of the current system and standard implementation costs. In the latter case, expected implementation costs are used to determine how much the proposed system development effort will cost in terms of the organization's resources.

The objective of the preliminary analysis stage is to investigate the feasibility of developing a system to satisfy the needs identified during the system conception stage, and if a new or modified system is both desirable and practical, to propose an effective system that satisfies the stated needs. The functions performed in the preliminary analysis stage usually include:

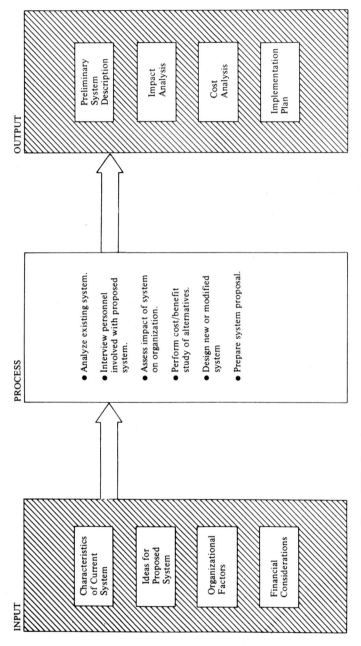

Figure 15.2   Overview diagram of the preliminary design stage of the system life cycle.

1. *Analyze* existing system.
2. *Interview* personnel involved with the proposed system.
3. *Assess* impact of new or modified system on the organization.
4. *Perform* cost/benefit study of alternatives.
5. *Design* new or modified system.
6. *Prepare* system proposal.

The specific functions performed by the analyst during the preliminary analysis stage are self-explanatory and are not discussed further. (The reader is referred to a reference on the system life cycle, such as Rubin* or Benjamin†.) It should be mentioned, however, that an *implementation plan* is necessary for the system design and development stages, because of its importance in the success or failure of a systems effort, and this plan is an output of the feasibility study. When data processing is involved in the systems evaluation, then a special effort should be made to determine the optimum resolution of the problem rather than the course of action that would invariably lead to automation. Clearly, the feasibility study may simply reinforce the use of manual procedures.

The outputs of the preliminary analysis stage are:

1. A preliminary system description.
2. An impact analysis.
3. A cost analysis.
4. An implementation plan.

Each of the four outputs is important, but can realistically be presented to management at different times, depending upon organizational factors. The *preliminary system description* along with the cost analysis are the primary inputs to the management decision-making process and effectively determine whether a proposal is accepted or rejected. The two main reasons that systems proposals are accepted by organizational management are increased functional capability and reduced cost. At this point, management is concerned with function and not specific design details, and many proposals are rejected solely on the basis of cost because the functional capability of the system is not clearly understood. In short, the analyst is presenting structure and implementation rather than function. Required equipment and personnel can be included either in the preliminary system specification or in the cost analysis. *Inpact analysis* concerns the effect of the proposed system upon organizational operations, or in the case of a product or service, justification for the proposed system in the form of a competitive analysis. *Cost analysis* includes both development costs and operational costs, in addition to a summarization of current costs in the case of an in-house system. In the case of a product or service, the cost analysis

*Rubin, *op cit*., pp. 19–59.
† Benjamin.

would necessarily include expected return on investment, a cost/value analysis, and a study of any risk factors that are involved. The *implementation plan* is intended to summarize needed resources and establish dates and schedules. In short, the implementation plan outlines the remainder of the system life cycle for management comments, suggestions, and approval.

15.4 SYSTEM DESIGN

The system design stage of the system cycle is concerned with the hierarchical structure of the system and the functions that are performed at each level and by each component of the system. The system design effort utilizes the preliminary system description, developed during the feasibility study, and molds that description into a set of design specifications that can be used during the development stage.

System design involves five major functions:

1. The analysis of system objectives and the respecification of these objectives as design constraints.
2. The investigation of possible modes of system operation and requirements for physical facilities.
3. The establishment of the operational capability of the system and physical equipment needed.
4. The specification of the functional structure of the system and the development of a precise description of each system component.
5. Documentation of the design of the system.

Figure 15.3 gives an overview diagram of the design stage of the system life cycle.

Input to the design stage includes four major items:

1. The preliminary system description, mentioned above.
2. A set of system objectives.
3. Physical requirements.
4. Operational requirements.

The set of *system objectives* governs the design of a system and serves to aid in insuring that the system that management decided upon is the same system that will be produced. The objectives may be contained in the preliminary system description or they may be developed by the system designer. The system objectives may also specify the inputs and outputs of the system, although perhaps at a relatively high level. In a data processing system, for example, a common objective might be to generate a particular type of management report, which may implicitly dictate that a particular kind of information system be developed from which that report can be obtained.

The task of determining the necessary modes of system operation and the required physical facilities may require an investigation by the system designer

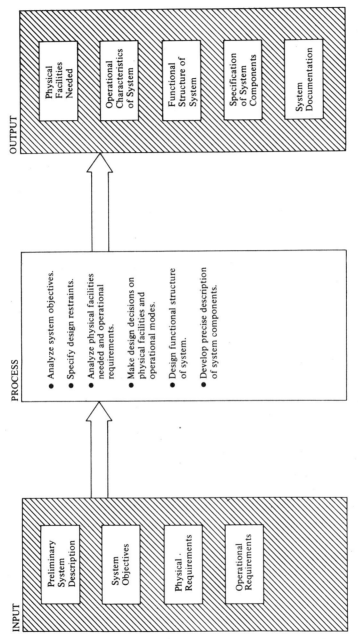

Figure 15.3   Overview diagram of the design stage of the system life cycle.

of the possible modes in which the system can operate and the equipment needed to sustain that type of operation. The investigation may additionally include a study of how inputs to the system will be obtained and how outputs will be used. The investigation phase can be conducted through interviews, questionnaires, and reports. To sum up, if the necessary inputs to the design stage are not available beforehand, then the designer must obtain them himself.

Design decisions regarding physical facilities and operational requirements are based on the preliminary system description, design objectives, and the information obtained in the investigation of physical and operational capabilities. Physical facilities depend upon the system involved but characteristically take the form of computer and storage requirements, physical space needed, vehicles that will be available, etc. Operational capabilities involve the manner in which the physical facilities are used and typically involve how information will be organized and accessed. The physical and operational specifications for a system are established in this step; these specifications serve as the external description of the system.

The process of specifying the functional structure of a system that provides the required operational capability through the physical facilities is referred to as "systems design." Normally, the hierarchical structure of the components that comprise the system is given and each component is described in detail. The inputs, outputs, and internal logic of each component are defined. Internal logic is usually described with equations, flow diagrams, or decision tables, and the system, as a whole, is described with a general "system" flow diagram or a HIPO diagram. Clearly, the internal logic of a component utilizes the design decisions established previously that concern physical facilities, operational capabilities, and information structures.

Effective documentation of a system starts at the design stage—and perhaps earlier as the preliminary system description. The objective of documentation at the design level is to give the implementation group something to work with and to provide management with the needed information for decision making. Clearly, documentation is an important by-product of the design phase and not an effort that takes place after the project has been completed. Another factor that is frequently included in all phases of system design, especially documentation, is a description of the physical environment in which the system is intended to operate.

The design cycle normally includes feedback between the prospective user of the system and the system designer. This type of feedback is healthy and helps to insure that systems are not designed in a vacuum. After the system design phase has been completed, the prospective user of the system should have a set of specifications that are understandable and acceptable to him, and at the same time, are technically practical and satisfy the stated objectives of the system. The same set of specifications serve as input to the implementation stage.

15.5 SYSTEM IMPLEMENTATION

The system implementation stage is the one in which the logic and specifications of a system are put to the test of a realistic development effort. Briefly stated, the integrity of the system design is verified. An accepted practice is for the development team to hold "structured walkthroughs," in which the logic of the system is subjected to the scrutiny of the development team in a face-to-face environment.

The precise nature of the implementation stage is necessarily dependent upon the type of system being developed. In hardware systems development, detailed logic diagrams for the components of the system are constructed before the components are built. After each component is built, it is subjected to a functional test to insure that it operates according to specifications. The various components of a system are assembled according to a preestablished plan and the complete system is "system tested" to insure that the interfaces between the components are properly designed and that the system meets its operational objectives.

In the implementation of computer software systems, detail diagrams of each component are constructed and the design specifications are implemented as software modules. Each module is unit tested, to insure that it functions properly, prior to integration of the modules of the system. The complete system is then system tested, as mentioned above. During software systems implementation, software modules are associated with detail diagrams.

Software systems development has evolved as a bottom-to-top process wherein the "lower-level" modules in the hierarchical structure of a system are implemented before "higher-level" modules, as suggested in Figure 15.4. The difficulties with bottom-to-top development are that many module interfaces must be developed simultaneously, often by more than one person, and that a driver program must be developed to perform the unit testing of a module. Bottom-to-top development is error-prone, because of the module interfaces, and integration of modules to form a complete system is cumbersome because of the fact that all modules must "come together" at the same time.

An alternate approach to systems implementation is to use top-down development, as suggested in Figure 15.5. Top-down development is considered by many professionals to be superior to bottom-to-top development because modules are developed in a natural order from the control structures downward. No driver programs are required and the concept of a stud is employed to test module interfaces. A stub is simply a short module that displays a message stating that program control reached that module and then returns to the calling program. One of the primary advantages of top-down development is that the system is always operable, so an integration effort is not required as the last stage of implementation.

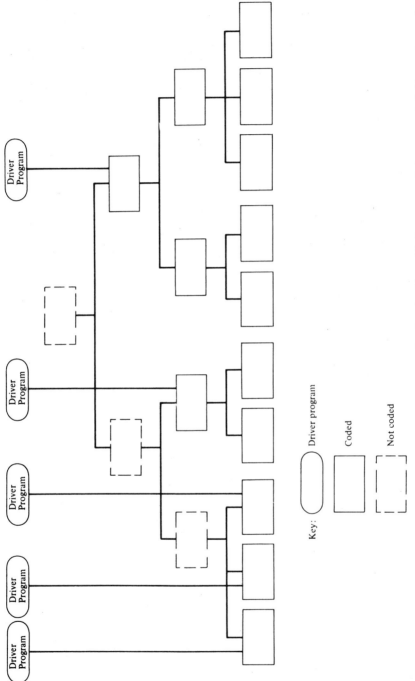

Figure 15.4 · A conceptual view of a bottom-to-top development, showing the hierarchical structure of the system and driver programs for testing purposes.

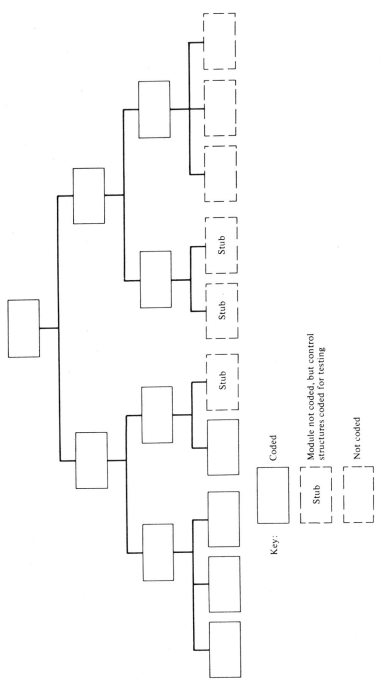

Key:

Coded

Stub — Module not coded, but control structures coded for testing

Not coded

Figure 15.5   A conceptual view of top-down development, showing the hierarchical structure of the system and the use of "stubs" for testing.

Systems implementation also applies to "people systems" in which detailed logic diagrams or detailed module descriptions are replaced by detailed job descriptions. In many human systems, implementation takes the form of reorganization of the management system. Interestingly enough, component and module interfaces in hardware and software systems are analogous to people interfaces in human systems, and the system testing phase of hardware and software systems corresponds to the period in human systems in which the informal structure of a management system is developed.

In the implementation of most systems, there is a considerable amount of feedback between the development effort and the system designers. This is usually a result of the fact that unforeseen circumstances arise and the design of the system must be adjusted accordingly. The need for feedback and adjustment also arises out of limitations in the design of a system, so the implementation stage can also serve as a check on the integrity of the system.

15.6 SYSTEM DOCUMENTATION

System documentation is the set of documents that provide general and detailed information on the system. In general, effective documentation is necessary for installing, maintaining, and using a system and for ongoing analysis of the system's performance. Documentation should satisy four needs:

1. As a reference for management.
2. As a reference for design, implementation, and maintenance personnel.
3. As a reference for operators of the system—in the case of hardware of software systems.
4. As a reference for users of the system.

Unfortunately, system documentation is frequently regarded as a discrete stage in the system life cycle, whereas in reality, effective documentation is achieved by applying a technically sound methodology at the conception, preliminary analysis, design, and implementation stages of the system life cycle, and by "putting it all together" during the documentation stage.

15.7 SYSTEM INSTALLATION, OPERATION, AND CESSATION

System installation, operation, and cessation are the final three stages in the system life cycle. *System installation* refers to the process of putting a system into operation and the activity related to passing shake-down and acceptance tests. In a computer and data processing environment, system installation may also refer to the conversion of data formats to meet the needs of the new system and the adjustment of operating procedures. System installation frequently involves training and demonstrations. Clearly, training usually refers to operations personnel and emphasizes the operational characteristics of the new or modified system. Demonstrations are usually management-oriented and serve to orient the organization with the added capability that is provided with the new system and the impact the new system will have on the day-to-day operations in the organization.

System operation refers to the operation of the new or modified system after installation has been completed. Optimally, the system should be monitored during the initial operational period to insure that the system designers have "zeroed in" on the system needed by the organization. Operator's manuals should be reviewed for accuracy and completeness, and operational standards should be established.

System cessation refers to the practical eventuality that all systems have a finite life, and are either replaced or modified as the operational environment evolves. Because of the reality that system cessation does exist, a system should be controlled and monitored so that the need for replacement or modification is recognized with enough lead time to insure that continued operation of the system does not degrade the performance of the organization. Monitoring for system cessation differs from monitoring of the system during the initial period of operation. The analysis exists at a higher level; in fact, system cessation may actually be a part of the implementation plan developed earlier in the system life cycle.

To sum up, system installation includes training of operators *and* prospective users, acceptance testing, orientation of the organization to the new system, and demonstration of the capability of the new or modified system. System operation is concerned with operational procedures, monitoring, performance evaluation, and standards. Lastly, system cessation is concerned with the ongoing analysis of a system's contribution to the objectives of an organization.

15.8 CONCLUSIONS

There is a definite orientation of the system life cycle to the computer field and the systems analysis function with an organizational environment. However, because of the commonality of systems, the concepts apply in general.

Regardless of the type of system involved, system design and documentation plays a major role in most stages of the system life cycle, and serves as the primary vehicle for passing information between the various stages. Descriptive techniques include verbal descriptions, syntactical specifications, logic diagrams, drawings and schematics, flow diagrams, decision tables, and HIPO diagrams.

REFERENCES

Benjamin, R. I., *Control of the Information System Development Cycle*, John Wiley & Sons, Inc., New York, 1970.

Churchman, C. W., Ackoff, R. L., and Arnoff, E. L. *Introduction to Operations Research*, John Wiley & Sons, Inc., New York, 1957.

Couger, J. D. and Knapp, R. W. (editors), *System Analysis Techniques*, John Wiley & Sons, Inc., New York, 1974.

Katzan, H., *Systems Design and Documentation: An Introduction to the HIPO Method*, Van Nostrand Reinhold Company, New York, 1976.

Rubin, M. L., *Handbook of Data Processing Management, Volume 1, Introduction to the System Life Cycle*, Brandon/Systems Press, Princeton, 1970.

Appendices

APPENDIX A

ILLUSTRATIVE EXAMPLES OF BASIC AND APL PROGRAMS

This appendix gives two illustrative examples, each programmed in the BASIC language and in the APL language. The objective is to introduce typical applications and to demonstrate the elements that constitute corresponding 5100 computer programs. The examples deal with amortization calculations and payroll processing.

AMORTIZATION CALCULATIONS

Programs 1 and 2 give BASIC and APL programs, respectively, that perform amortization calculations and list a payment schedule. The programs are operationally equivalent and serve to demonstrate some of the procedural equivalents in the two languages.

The amortization program initially prompts the user for interest rate, cost of the asset, downpayment percent, sales tax percent, and the number of months to repay the loan. The program computes and displays the monthly payment, the downpayment, and the amount to be financed. Optionally, a payment schedule can be listed.

PAYROLL PROCESSING

Programs 3 and 4 give BASIC and APL programs, respectively, that perform pay roll processing. Both programs, which are operationally equivalent, utilize a pay roll matrix that is optionally read in or created when program execution is initiated. The programs are structured the same and provide the options of listing the payroll file, deleting or adding an employee record, changing employee data, entering hours worked for either one employee or all employees, printing checks, and listing employee names and addresses.

COMMENT

The APL code is more dense and less readable than the BASIC programs. However, the programs are decipherable using the introductory material contained in earlier chapters and the interested reader can learn several advanced APL programming techniques by studying the amortization and payroll programs. The set of APL programs also contains functions for using shared variables for tape input and output and for printer output.

```
0010 REM *****AMORTIZATION PROGRAM*****
0020 GOSUB 0600
0030 PRINT TAB(10),'AMORTIZATION CALCULATION'
0040 PRINT
0050 PRINT 'ENTER YEARLY INTEREST RATE (E.G.-.08)';
0060 INPUT R
0070 PRINT 'ENTER COST OF THE ASSET';
0080 INPUT C
0090 PRINT 'ENTER DOWNPAYMENT PERCENT (E.G.-.25)';
0100 INPUT D
0110 PRINT 'ENTER SALES TAX PERCENT (E.G.-.05)';
0120 INPUT S
0130 PRINT 'ENTER NUMBER OF MONTHS TO REPAY LOAN';
0140 INPUT N
0150 P=C*(1-D)+S*C
0160 M=(P*R/12)/(1-(1+R/12)↑(-N))
0170 GOSUB 0600
0180 PRINT USING 0210,'          MONTHLY PAYMENT IS',M
0190 PRINT USING 0210,'             DOWNPAYMENT IS',C*D
0200 PRINT USING 0210,'AMOUNT TO BE FINANCED IS',P
0210 : ######################## #######.##
0220 PRINT
0230 PRINT 'DO YOU WANT TO PRINT OUT SCHEDULE? 1-YES, 0-NO'
0240 INPUT A
0250 IF A=1 GOTO 0410
0260 IF A=0 GOTO 0320
0270 PRINT 'RESPONSE RESTRICTED TO 1-YES OR 0-NO'
0280 PRINT 'PRESS EXECUTE TO CONTINUE'
0290 PAUSE
0300 GOSUB 0600
0310 GOTO 0230
0320 GOSUB 0600
0330 PRINT 'DO YOU WANT TO PERFORM ANOTHER AMORTIZATION '
0340 PRINT 'CALCULATION?  1-YES, 0-NO'
0350 INPUT A
0360 IF A=1 GOTO 0020
0370 GOSUB 0600
0380 PRINT 'EXECUTION TERMINATED'
0390 STOP
0400 REM *****PRINT AMORTIZATION SCHEDULE*****
0410 GOSUB 0600
0420 PRINT 'READY PRINTER FOR OPERATION.  MOVE PAPER TO THE TOP'
0430 PRINT 'OF THE NEXT PAGE.  PRESS EXECUTE WHEN READY.'
0440 PAUSE
0450 PRINT FLP,TAB(22),'PAYMENT SCHEDULE'
0460 PRINT FLP,
0470 PRINT FLP,
0480 PRINT USING FLP,0570
0490 PRINT FLP,
0500 FOR I=1 TO N
0510 A=(R/12)*P
0520 P=P-(M-A)
0530 PRINT USING FLP,0580,I,M-A,A,M,P
0540 NEXT I
0550 GOTO 0320
```

Program 1. BASIC Amortization Program.

```
0560 REM *****PRINT IMAGES*****
0570 :MONTH   PRINCIPAL     INTEREST     TOT PAYMNT      BALANCE
0580 : ##    ######.##    ######.##    #######.##    #######.##
0590 REM *****CLEAR SCREEN ROUTINE*****
0600 FOR Z9=1 TO 14
0610 PRINT
0620 NEXT Z9
0630 RETURN
0640 END
```

Program 1. BASIC Amortization Program (*continued*).

```
      ∇AMCALC[□]∇
    ∇ AMCALC
[1]   ⍝ CLEAR SCREEN
[2]   START:14ρ□AV[157]
[3]   □←(10ρ' '),'AMORTIZATION CALCULATION',2ρ□AV[157]
[4]   R←1↑□,ρ□←'ENTER YEARLY INTEREST RATE (E.G., .08)'
[5]   C←1↑□,ρ□←'ENTER COST OF THE ASSET'
[6]   D←1↑□,ρ□←'ENTER DOWNPAYMENT PERCENT (E.G., .25)'
[7]   S←1↑□,ρ□←'ENTER SALES TAX PERCENT (E.G., .05)'
[8]   N←1↑□,ρ□←'ENTER NUMBER OF MONTHS TO REPAY LOAN'
[9]   M←((P←(C×(1-D))+S×C)×R÷12)÷1-(1+R÷12)*(-N)
[10]  □←(14ρ□AV[157]),(6ρ' '),'MONTHLY PAYMENT IS ', 9 2 ⊤M
[11]  □←(10ρ' '),'DOWNPAYMENT IS ', 9 2 ⊤C×D
[12]  □←'AMOUNT TO BE FINANCED IS ',(9 2 ⊤P),□AV[157]
[13] RPT:□←'DO YOU WANT TO PRINT OUT SCHEDULE? YES OR NO'
[14]  →((ANS←1↑□)='Y')/LIST
[15]  →(ANS='N')/AGN
[16]  →RPT,ρ□,□←'ANSWER YES OR NO.  PRESS EXECUTE TO CONTINUE.'
[17] AGN:14ρ□AV[157]
[18]  □←'WOULD YOU LIKE TO PERFORM ANOTHER AMORTIZATION'
[19]  □←'CALCULATION? YES OR NO'
[20]  →((ANS←1↑□)='Y')/START
[21]  →0,ρ□←(14ρ□AV[157]),'EXECUTION TERMINATED'
[22] LIST:14ρ□AV[157]
[23]  □←'READY PRINTER FOR OPERATION.  MOVE PAPER TO THE'
[24]  MSG←□,□←'TOP OF THE NEXT PAGE.  PRESS EXECUTE WHEN READY.'
[25]  □←(22ρ' '),'PAYMENT SCHEDULE',2ρ□AV[157]
[26]  □←(3ρ' '),'MONTH',(2ρ' '),'PRINCIPAL',(6ρ' '),'INTEREST'
[27]  □←(4ρ' '),'TOT PAYMNT',(5ρ' '),'BALANCE',□AV[157]
[28]  I←1
[29] LOOP:P←P-M-A←R×P÷12
[30]  □←(6 0 ⊤I),(13 2 ⊤(M-A)),(14 2 ⊤A),(14 2 ⊤M),(14 2 ⊤P)
[31]  →((I←I+1)≤N)/LOOP
[32]  →AGN
    ∇
```

Program 2. APL Amortization Program.

```
0010 REM *****PAYROLL PROGRAM*****
0020 DIM E$(30,4),E(30,20)
0030 $$='PAYROLL DATA'
0040 GOSUB 3330
0050 PRINT TAB(15),'PAYROLL PROGRAM'
0060 PRINT
0070 PRINT 'WOULD YOU LIKE TO USE AS OLD PAYROLL FILE OR CREATE'
0080 PRINT 'A NEW ONE?  1-OLD FILE,  2-NEW FILE'
0090 INPUT A
0100 GOTO 0140,0200 ON A
0110 PRINT 'IMPROPER RESPONSE.  PRESS EXECUTE TO CONTINUE.'
0120 PAUSE
0130 GOTO 0070
0140 PRINT 'GIVE THE FILE NUMBER OF THE EXISTING PAYROLL FILE'
0150 INPUT F9
0160 OPEN FL1,'E80',F9,IN
0170 MAT GET FL1,E$,E,EOF 3280
0180 CLOSE FL1
0190 GOTO 0270
0200 GOSUB 3330
0210 PRINT 'A NEW PAYROLL FILE WILL BE CREATED.  REMEMBER,'
0220 PRINT 'EMPLOYEE DATA MUST BE ENTERED BEFORE PAYROLL'
0230 PRINT 'CALCULATIONS CAN BE PERFORMED.'
0240 PRINT
0250 PRINT 'ENTER THE NEW FILE NUMBER';
0260 INPUT F9
0270 PRINT 'ENTER THE DATE IN QUOTES SEPARATED WITH SLASHES'
0280 INPUT P$
0290 REM THIS ROUTINE IS TO DISPLAY THE OPTIONS
0300 GOSUB 3330
0310 PRINT TAB(15),'MENU'
0320 PRINT 'SELECT ONE OF THE FOLLOWING OPTIONS:'
0330 PRINT 'OPTION 4 COMPUTES THE PAYROLL AS HRS ARE ENTERED'
0340 PRINT 'OPTION 7 WILL SAVE THE NEW PAYROLL DATA'
0350 PRINT '   1 LIST THE PAYROLL FILE'
0360 PRINT '   2 DELETE OR ADD AN EMPLOYEE RECORD'
0370 PRINT '   3 CHANGE EMPLOYEE DATA'
0380 PRINT '   4 INPUT WEEKLY HRS WORKED'
0390 PRINT '   5 PRINT CHECKS'
0400 PRINT '   6 LIST EMPLOYEE NAMES AND ADDRESSES'
0410 PRINT '   7 TERMINATE PAYROLL PROGRAM EXECUTION'
0420 INPUT A
0430 GOSUB 0460,0730,1740,1270,2330,3110,3040 ON A
0440 GOTO 0300
0450 REM ****LIST THE PAYROLL FILE*****
0460 PRINT 'READY THE PRINTER. PRESS EXECUTE WHEN READY.'
0470 PAUSE
0480 PRINT FLP,TAB(50),'PAYROLL FILE'
0490 PRINT FLP,TAB(52),P$
0500 PRINT FLP,
0510 PRINT FLP,'EMP';'  WEEKLY  ';'  WEEKLY  ';TAB(69);'YTD';
0520 PRINT FLP,TAB(78);'YTD';TAB(88);'YTD';TAB(98);'YTD';
0530 PRINT FLP,TAB(108);'YTD'
0540 PRINT FLP,' NO.';'   NET   ';'  GROSS   ';' STATE TAX';
0550 PRINT FLP,'   CITY TAX ';' F.W.H. ';' F.I.C.A.';
```

Program 3. BASIC Payroll Program.

```
0560 PRINT FLP,TAB(68);'GROSS';'   STATE TAX';' CITY TAX ';
0570 PRINT FLP,TAB(96);'F.W.H.';'     F.I.C.A. ';'RATE';'   HRS'
0580 PRINT FLP,
0590 FOR T=1 TO 30
0600 IF E(T,2)=2 GOTO 0680
0610 IF E(T,2)=0 GOTO 0690
0620 PRINT USING FLP,0650,E(T,1),E(T,9),E(T,10),E(T,15),E(T,16);
0630 PRINT USING FLP,0660,E(T,13),E(T,14),E(T,4),E(T,11),E(T,12);
0640 PRINT USING FLP,0670,E(T,5),E(T,6),E(T,3),E(T,8)
0650 : ### ###.##     ###.##         ###.##    ###.##
0660 :'       ###.##    ###.## #####.## #####.## #####.##  .
0670 : #####.##    #####.##   ##.##   ##.#
0680 NEXT T
0690 PRINT FLP,
0700 PRINT FLP,'END OF PAYROLL FILE'
0710 RETURN
0720 REM *****ADD OR DELETE AN EMPLOYEE RECORD*****
0730 GOSUB 3330
0740 PRINT 'SELECT ONE OF THE FOLLOWING OPTIONS:'
0750 PRINT 'ENTER  1 TO RETURN TO THE MENU'
0760 PRINT 'ENTER  2 TO ADD AN EMPLOYEE RECORD'
0770 PRINT 'ENTER  3 TO DELETE AN EMPLOYEE RECORD'
0780 INPUT A
0790 GOTO 1250,0990,0840 ON A
0800 PRINT 'IMPROPER RESPONSE.  PRESS EXECUTE TO CONTINUE.'
0810 PAUSE
0820 GOTO 0730
0830 REM *****DELETE EMPLOYEE RECORD*****
0840 PRINT 'ENTER EMPLOYEE NUMBER'
0850 INPUT N
0860 FOR T=1 TO 30
0870 IF E(T,2)=2 GOTO 0900
0880 IF E(T,2)=0 GOTO 0910
0890 IF E(T,1)=N GOTO 0950
0900 NEXT T
0910 PRINT 'EMPLOYEE NUMBER';N;'NOT FOUND. PRESS EXECUTE TO'
0920 PRINT 'CONTINUE.'
0930 PAUSE
0940 GOTO 0730
0950 LET E(T,2)=2
0960 PRINT 'EMPLOYEE NUMBER';N;'HAS BEEN MADE INACTIVE'
0970 GOTO 0730
0980 REM ****ADD EMPLOYEE RECORD*****
0990 FOR T=1 TO 30
1000 IF E(T,2)=0IE(T,2)=2 GOTO 1070
1010 NEXT T
1020 PRINT 'PAYROLL TABLE FULL.  DELETE AN EMPLOYEE BEFORE EN-'
1030 PRINT 'TERING A NEW EMPLOYEE RECORD.  PRESS EXECUTE TO'
1040 PRINT 'CONTINUE.'
1050 PAUSE
1060 GOTO 0730
1070 PRINT 'ENTER NEW EMPLOYEE DATA'
1080 PRINT 'EMPLOYEE NUMBER';
1090 INPUT E(T,1)
1100 PRINT 'NAME IN QUOTES';
```

Program 3. BASIC Payroll Program (*continued*).

```
1110 INPUT E$(T,1)
1120 PRINT 'STREET ADDRESS IN QUOTES';
1130 INPUT E$(T,2)
1140 PRINT 'CITY STATE & ZIP CODE IN QUOTES';
1150 INPUT E$(T,3)
1160 PRINT 'HOURLY RATE';
1170 INPUT E(T,3)
1180 PRINT 'NUMBER OF DEPENDENTS';
1190 INPUT E(T,7)
1200 PRINT 'SOCIAL SECURITY NUMBER IN QUOTES';
1210 INPUT E$(T,4)
1220 PRINT 'EMPLOYEE NUMBER';E(T,1);'HAS BEEN ACTIVATED'
1230 E(T,2)=1
1240 GOTO 0730
1250 RETURN
1260 REM *****INPUT THE HOURS WORKED*****
1270 GOSUB 3330
1280 PRINT 'HOURS WORKED. SELECT OPTION:'
1290 PRINT '    1 - ALL EMPLOYEES'
1300 PRINT '    2 - ONE EMPLOYEE'
1310 PRINT '    3 - RETURN TO MENU';
1320 INPUT A
1330 GOTO 1620,1380,1600 ON A
1340 PRINT 'INCORRECT RESPONSE. PRESS EXECUTE TO CONTINUE.'
1350 PAUSE
1360 GOTO 1270
1370 REM ONE EMPLOYEE
1380 GOSUB 3330
1390 PRINT 'ENTER EMPLOYEE NUMBER';
1400 INPUT N
1410 FOR T=1 TO 30
1420 IF E(T,2)=2 GOTO 1450
1430 IF E(T,2)=0 GOTO 1460
1440 IF E(T,1)=N GOTO 1490
1450 NEXT T
1460 PRINT 'EMPLOYEE NOT FOUND. PRESS EXECUTE TO CONTINUE.
1470 PAUSE
1480 GOTO 1560
1490 PRINT 'THIS IS:  ';E$(T,1);'      OK?'
1500 PRINT 'IF SO, ENTER 1  OTHERWISE ENTER ANY NUMBER';
1510 INPUT A
1520 IF A≠1 GOTO 1560
1530 PRINT 'ENTER HRS WORKED';
1540 INPUT E(T,8)
1550 GOSUB 2030
1560 PRINT 'ANOTHER EMPLOYEE?'
1570 PRINT 'IF SO, ENTER 1  OTHERWISE ENTER ANY NUMBER';
1580 INPUT A
1590 IF A=1 GOTO 1380
1600 RETURN
1610 REM ALL EMPLOYEES
1620 FOR T=1 TO 30
1630 IF E(T,2)=0 GOTO 1700
1640 IF E(T,2)=2 GOTO 1690
1650 PRINT 'INPUT THE HRS WORKED FOR THIS WEEK'
```

Program 3. BASIC Payroll Program (*continued*).

```
1660 PRINT 'FOR EMPLOYEE NO   ';E(T,1);E$(T,1);
1670 INPUT E(T,8)
1680 GOSUB 2030
1690 NEXT T
1700 PRINT 'END OF PAYROLL FILE. PRESS EXECUTE TO CONTINUE.'
1710 PAUSE
1720 RETURN
1730 REM *****CHANGE EMPLOYEE RECORD*****
1740 GOSUB 3330
1750 PRINT 'CHANGE EMPLOYEE RECORD.  ENTER THE EMPLOYEE NUMBER'
1760 INPUT N
1770 FOR T=1 TO 30
1780 IF E(T,2)=2 GOTO 1810
1790 IF E(T,2)=0 GOTO 1820
1800 IF E(T,1)=N GOTO 1850
1810 NEXT T
1820 PRINT 'EMPLOYEE NOT FOUND. PRESS EXECUTE TO CONTINUE.'
1830 PAUSE
1840 GOTO 1960
1850 PRINT 'ENTER EMPLOYEE DATA'
1860 PRINT 'NAME IN QUOTES';
1870 INPUT E$(T,1)
1880 PRINT 'STREET ADDRESS ENTERED IN QUOTES';
1890 INPUT E$(T,2)
1900 PRINT 'CITY, STATE, AND ZIP CODE ENTERED IN QUOTES';
1910 INPUT E$(T,3)
1920 PRINT 'HOURLY RATE'
1930 INPUT E(T,3)
1940 PRINT 'NUMBER OF DEPENDENTS';
1950 INPUT E(T,7)
1960 PRINT 'ANY MORE CHANGES ?'
1970 PRINT 'ENTER A 1 FOR MORE CHANGES'
1980 PRINT 'IF NO MORE CHANGES ENTER ANY NUMBER'
1990 INPUT A
2000 IF A=1 GOTO 1740
2010 RETURN
2020 REM *****PERFORM PAYROLL CALCULATION*****
2030 E(T,13),E(T,14),E(T,17),E(T,18)=0
2040 IF E(T,8)≤40 GOTO 2090
2050 E(T,17)=E(T,8)-40
2060 E(T,18)=E(T,17)*E(T,3)*1.5
2070 E(T,10)=40*E(T,3)+E(T,18)
2080 GOTO 2100
2090 E(T,10)=E(T,3)*E(T,8)
2100 IF E(T,7)>3 GOTO 2190
2110 GOTO 2140,2160,2180 ON E(T,7)
2120 E(T,13)=E(T,10)*.2
2130 GOTO 2190
2140 E(T,13)=E(T,10)*.16
2150 GOTO 2190
2160 E(T,13)=E(T,10)*.12
2170 GOTO 2190
2180 E(T,13)=E(T,10)*.08
2190 IF E(T,4)≥14100 GOTO 2230
2200 E(T,14)=E(T,10)*.0585
```

Program 3. BASIC Payroll Program (*continued*).

```
2210 IF E(T,4)+E(T,10)≦14100 GOTO 2230
2220 E(T,14)=(14100-E(T,4))*.0585
2230 E(T,15)=E(T,10)*.05
2240 E(T,16)=E(T,10)*.02
2250 E(T,4)=E(T,4)+E(T,10)
2260 E(T,5)=E(T,5)+E(T,13)
2270 E(T,6)=E(T,6)+E(T,14)
2280 E(T,11)=E(T,11)+E(T,15)
2290 E(T,12)=E(T,12)+E(T,16)
2300 E(T,9)=E(T,10)-E(T,13)-E(T,14)-E(T,15)-E(T,16)
2310 RETURN
2320 REM *****PRINT THE CHECKS*****
2330 GOSUB 3330
2340 PRINT 'CHECK PRINTING.  SELECT DESIRED OPTION:'
2350 PRINT '   1 - RETURN TO THE MENU'
2360 PRINT '   2 - PRINT ONE CHECK'
2370 PRINT '   3 - PRINT ALL CHECKS'
2380 INPUT A
2390 GOTO 2310,2440,2590 ON A
2400 PRINT 'IMPROPER RESPONSE.  PRESS EXECUTE TO CONTINUE.'
2410 PAUSE
2420 GOTO 2330
2430 REM *****PRINT ONE CHECK*****
2440 PRINT 'ENTER EMPLOYEE NUMBER'
2450 INPUT A6
2460 FOR T=1 TO 30
2470 IF E(T,2)=0 GOTO 2510
2480 IF E(T,2)=2 GOTO 2500
2490 IF A6=E(T,1) GOTO 2540
2500 NEXT T
2510 PRINT 'EMPLOYEE NOT FOUND.  PRESS EXECUTE TO CONTINUE.'
2520 PAUSE
2530 GOTO 2330
2540 PRINT 'ENTER THE CHECK NUMBER';
2550 INPUT A1
2560 GOSUB 2690
2570 GOTO 2330
2580 REM *****PRINT ALL CHECKS*****
2590 PRINT 'ENTER INITIAL CHECK NUMBER'
2600 INPUT A1
2610 FOR T=1 TO 50
2620 IF E(T,2)=0 GOTO 2670
2630 IF E(T,2)=2 GOTO 2660
2640 GOSUB 2690
2650 A1=A1+1
2660 NEXT T
2670 RETURN
2680 REM CHECK PRINTING SUBROUTINE
2690 T$='EMPL NO'
2700 M$='SOC SEC NO'
2710 PRINT FLP,TAB(40)'CHECK NUMBER';A1
2720 PRINT FLP,TAB(8),T$,TAB(38)'DATE';TAB(52);M$;TAB(73);T$;
2730 PRINT FLP,TAB(103)'DATE';TAB(119);M$
2740 PRINT FLP,TAB(10);E(T,1);TAB(37);P$;TAB(52);E$(T,4);
2750 PRINT FLP,TAB(75);E(T,1);TAB(102);P$;TAB(119);E$(T,4)
```

Program 3. BASIC Payroll Program (*continued*).

```
2760 PRINT FLP,
2770 PRINT USING FLP,2780,E(T,9),E(T,9)
2780 :     PAY************#####.##DOLLARS              $#####.##
2790 PRINT FLP,TAB(71)'NET PAY';TAB(80)'FED W.H.';TAB(93)'FICA';
2800 PRINT FLP,TAB(101)'ST TAX';TAB(112)'CTY TAX';TAB(122)'DEP';
2810 PRINT FLP,' GROSS'
2820 PRINT FLP,TAB(70),
2830 PRINT USING FLP,2850,E(T,9),E(T,13),E(T,14),E(T,15);
2840 PRINT USING FLP,2860,E(T,16),E(T,7),E(T,10)
2850 :#####.## ####.##    ####.##    ###.##
2860 :     ###.##     ## #####.##
2870 PRINT FLP,'  TO THE',TAB(93)' YEAR TO DATE '
2880 PRINT FLP,'ORDER OF',E$(T,1),TAB(80)'FED W.H.';TAB(92)'FICA';
2890 PRINT FLP,TAB(102)'ST. TAX';TAB(112)'CITY TAX';TAB(125);
2900 PRINT FLP,' GROSS'
2910 PRINT FLP,,E$(T,2),TAB(80),
2920 PRINT USING FLP,2940,E(T,5),E(T,6),E(T,11);
2930 PRINT USING FLP,2950,E(T,12),E(T,4)
2940 :####.## ####.##      ###.##
2950 :    ###.##    #####.##
2960 PRINT FLP,,E$(T,3)
2970 PRINT FLP,TAB(40)'------------------------------'
2980 PRINT FLP,TAB(50)'SIGNATURE'
2990 FOR Z9=1 TO 5
3000 PRINT FLP,
3010 NEXT Z9
3020 RETURN
3030 REM *****WRITE PAYROLL FILE*****
3040 OPEN FL1,'E80',F9,$$,OUT
3050 MAT PUT FL1,E$,E
3060 CLOSE FL1
3070 GOSUB 3330
3080 PRINT 'EXECUTION TERMINATED'
3090 STOP
3100 REM *****LIST EMPLOYEE NAMES AND ADDRESSES*****
3110 GOSUB 3330
3120 PRINT 'READY THE PRINTER. PRESS EXECUTE WHEN READY.'
3130 PAUSE
3140 PRINT FLP,TAB(29),'EMPLOYEE LIST'
3150 PRINT FLP,TAB(31),P$
3160 PRINT FLP,
3170 PRINT FLP,'NUMBER','NAME','STREET','LOCATION'
3180 PRINT FLP,
3190 FOR T=1 TO 30
3200 IF E(T,2)=2 GOTO 3230
3210 IF E(T,2)=0 GOTO 3240
3220 PRINT FLP,E(T,1),E$(T,1),E$(T,2),E$(T,3)
3230 NEXT T
3240 PRINT FLP,
3250 PRINT FLP,'END OF EMPLOYEE LIST'
3260 RETURN
3270 REM *****UNEXPECTED END OF FILE*****
3280 GOSUB 3330
3290 PRINT 'UNEXPECTED END OF FILE ON PAYROLL MASTER FILE'
3300 PRINT 'EXECUTION TERMINATED'
```

Program 3. BASIC Payroll Program (*continued*).

```
3310 STOP
3320 REM *****CLEAR SCREEN ROUTINE*****
3330 FOR Z9=1 TO 14
3340 PRINT
3350 NEXT Z9
3360 RETURN
3370 END
```

Program 3. BASIC Payroll Program (*continued*).

```
          ∇PAYROLL[□]∇
       ∇ PAYROLL
  [1]    CR←□AV[157]
  [2]    CLEAR
  [3]    □←(TAB 15),'PAYROLL PROGRAM',CR
  [4]  RPT:□←'WOULD YOU LIKE TO USE AN OLD PAYROLL FILE OR CREATE'
  [5]    □←'A NEW ONE?  ENTER OLD OR NEW.'
  [6]    →((ANS←1↑(ANS≠' ')/ANS←,□)='O')/OLD
  [7]    →(ANS='N')/NEW
  [8]    →RPT MSG 'ANSWER OLD OR NEW'
  [9]  OLD:□←'GIVE FILE NUMBER OF EXISTING FILE'
  [10]   FILE←⍳□
  [11]   READ FILE
  [12]   →CONTINUE
  [13] NEW:CLEAR
  [14]   □←'A NEW PAYROLL FILE WILL BE CREATED.  REMEMBER,'
  [15]   □←'EMPLOYEE DATA MUST BE ENTERED BEFORE PAYROLL '
  [16]   □←'CALCULATIONS CAN BE PERFORMED.',CR
  [17]   □←'ENTER THE NEW FILE NUMBER'
  [18]   FILE←⍳□
  [19]   PAY← 30 20 ρ0
  [20]   AD1←AD2←NAM← 30 18 ρ' '
  [21]   SS← 30 11 ρ' '
  [22] CONTINUE:CLEAR
  [23]   □←'ENTER DATE'
  [24]   DATE←□
  [25] MENU:CLEAR
  [26]   □←(TAB 15),'MENU',CR
  [27]   □←'SELECT ONE OF THE FOLLOWING OPTIONS:'
  [28]   □←'OPTION 4 COMPUTES THE PAYROLL AS HRS ARE ENTERED'
  [29]   □←'OPTION 7 SAVES THE NEW PAYROLL DATA'
  [30]   □←'    1 - LIST THE PAYROLL FILE'
  [31]   □←'    2 - DELETE OR ADD AN EMPLOYEE RECORD'
  [32]   □←'    3 - CHANGE EMPLOYEE DATA'
  [33]   □←'    4 - INPUT WEEKLY HRS WORKED'
  [34]   □←'    5 - PRINT CHECKS'
  [35]   □←'    6 - LIST EMPLOYEE NAMES AND ADDRESSES'
  [36]   □←'    7 - TERMINATE PAYROLL PROGRAM EXECUTION'
  [37]   →((N>7)∨(N←□)<1)/ERR
  [38]   →(N-1)⌽LSP,DEL,CH,IN,PR,LSE,TR
  [39] ERR:→DIAG MENU
  [40] LSP:LISTP
  [41]   →MENU
  [42] DEL:DELADD
  [43]   →MENU
  [44] CH:CHANGE
  [45]   →MENU
  [46] IN:INPUT
  [47]   →MENU
  [48] PR:PRINTC
  [49]   →MENU
  [50] LSE:LISTE
  [51]   →MENU
  [52] TR:EXPUNGE
  [53]   WRITE FILE
  [54]   CLEAR
  [55]   □←CR,'EXECUTION TERMINATED'
       ∇
```

Program 4. APL Payroll Program.

```
      ∇LISTP[□]∇
    ∇ LISTP;□PW
[1]   ⍝ LIST THE PAYROLL FILE
[2]   □PW←132
[3]   →LS1 MSG 'READY THE PRINTER'
[4]   LS1:□←(TAB 50),'PAYROLL FILE'
[5]   □←(TAB 52),DATE,CR
[6]   □←'EMP',(48ρ(TAB 2),'WEEKLY'),(TAB 5),(40ρ'YTD',TAB 7),'YTD'
[7]   A←' NO',(TAB 4),'NET',(TAB 4),'GROSS',(TAB 3),'STATE'
[8]   A←A,(TAB 3),'CITY',(TAB 5),'FED',(TAB 4),'FICA',(TAB 5)
[9]   A←A,'GROSS',(TAB 5),'STATE',(TAB 5),'CITY',(TAB 7),'FED'
[10]  □←A,(TAB 7),'FICA',(TAB 4),'RATE',(TAB 3),'HRS',CR
[11]  U←((,PAY[;2])=1)/ι30
[12]  V← 1 9 10 15 16 13 14 4 11 12 5 6 3 8
[13]  F← 3 0 ,(12ρ 8 2),(10ρ 10 2), 7 2 6 1
[14]  □←F⍕PAY[U;V]
[15]  □←CR,'FND OF PAYROLL FILE'
    ∇


      ∇DELADD[□]∇
    ∇ DELADD
[1]   AGN:CLEAR
[2]   □←'SELECT ONE OF THE FOLLOWING OPTIONS:'
[3]   □←'    1 - RETURN TO THE MENU'
[4]   □←'    2 - ADD AN EMPLOYEE RECORD'
[5]   □←'    3 - DELETE AN EMPLOYEE RECORD'
[6]   →((N>3)∨(N←□)<1)/ERR
[7]   →(N-1)Φ0,ADD,DEL
[8]   ERR:→DIAG AGN
[9]   ⍝ADD EMPLOYEE RECORD
[10]  ADD:→((1↑ρPAY)≥I←(,PAY[;2])ι2)/FILL
[11]  →((1↑ρPAY)≥I←(,PAY[;2])ι0)/FILL
[12]  □←'PAYROLL TABLE FULL.  DELETE AN EMPLOYEE RECORD'
[13]  →AGN MSG 'BEFORE ENTERING A NEW EMPLOYEE RECORD.'
[14]  FILL:□←'ENTER NEW EMPLOYEE DATA'
[15]  □←'EMPLOYEE NUMBER'
[16]  PAY[I;1]←⍎□
[17]  □←'EMPLOYEE NAME'
[18]  NAM[I;]←18ρ□,17ρ' '
[19]  □←'STREET ADDRESS'
[20]  AD1[I;]←18ρ□,17ρ' '
[21]  □←'CITY, STATE, AND ZIP CODE'
[22]  AD2[I;]←18ρ□,17ρ' '
[23]  □←'HOURLY RATE'
[24]  PAY[I;3]←⍎□
[25]  □←'NUMBER OF DEPENDENTS'
[26]  PAY[I;7]←⍎□
[27]  □←'SOCIAL SECURITY NUMBER'
[28]  SS[I;]←11ρ□,10ρ' '
[29]  □←'EMPLOYEE NUMBER',(4 0 ⍕PAY[I;1]),' HAS BEEN ACTIVATED'
[30]  →AGN,PAY[I;2]←1
[31]  ⍝ DELETE EMPLOYEE RECORD
[32]  DEL:□←'ENTER EMPLOYEE NUMBER'
[33]  →((I←(,PAY[;1])ιN←⍎□)≤1↑ρPAY)/EX
[34]  →AGN MSG 'EMPLOYEE NUMBER ',(⍕N),' NOT FOUND'
[35]  EX:PAY[I;2]←2
[36]  PAY[I;1]←0
[37]  →AGN,ρ□←'EMPLOYEE NUMBER ',(⍕N),' HAS BEEN MADE INACTIVE'
    ∇
```

Program 4. APL Payroll Program (*continued*).

```
        ∇CHANGE[□]∇
     ∇ CHANGE
[1]   AGN:CLEAR
[2]     □←'CHANGE EMPLOYEE RECORD. ENTER THE EMPLOYEE NUMBER.'
[3]     →((I←PAY[;1]ι↓□)≤1↑ρPAY)/CH
[4]     →RPT MSG 'EMPLOYEE NOT FOUND'
[5]   CH:□←'ENTER EMPLOYEE DATA'
[6]      □←'EMPLOYEE NAME'
[7]      NAM[I;]←18ρ□,17ρ' '
[8]      □←'STREET ADDRESS'
[9]      AD1[I;]←18ρ□,17ρ' '
[10]     □←'CITY, STATE, AND ZIP CODE'
[11]     AD2[I;]←18ρ□,17ρ' '
[12]     □←'HOURLY RATE'
[13]     PAY[I;3]←ι□
[14]     □←'NUMBER OF DEPENDENTS'
[15]     PAY[I;7]←ι□
[16]  RPT:□←'ANY MORE CHANGES. ENTER YES FOR MORE CHANGES.'
[17]     □←'ENTER NO TO RETURN TO MENU.'
[18]     →((ANS←1↑(ANS≠' ')/ANS←,□)='Y')/AGN
[19]     →(ANS='N')/0
[20]     →RPT MSG 'ANSWER YES OR NO'
     ∇



        ∇INPUT[□]∇
     ∇ INPUT
[1]   ⍝ INPUT HRS WORKED AND PERFORM PAYROLL CALCULATIONS
[2]   AGN:CLEAR
[3]     □←'HOURS WORKED. SELECT OPTION:'
[4]      □←'   1 - ALL EMPLOYEES'
[5]      □←'   2 - ONE EMPLOYEE'
[6]      □←'   3 - RETURN TO MENU'
[7]     →((N>3)∨(N←□)<1)/ERR
[8]     →(N-1)⌽ALL,ONE,0
[9]   ERR:→DIAG AGN
[10]  ⍝ COMPUTE PAYROLL FOR ALL EMPLOYEES
[11]  ALL:I←0
[12]  TST:→((I←I+1)>1↑ρPAY)/DNE
[13]     →(PAY[I;2]=0)/DNE
[14]     →(PAY[I;2]=2)/TST
[15]     □←'INPUT THE HRS WORKED FOR THIS WEEK'
[16]     □←'FOR EMPLOYEE NO ',(⍕PAY[I;1]),' ',NAM[I;]
[17]     →TST,I COMPUTEP PAY[I;8]←ι□
[18]  DNE:→0 MSG 'END OF PAYROLL FILE'
[19]  ⍝ COMPUTE PAYROLL FOR ONE EMPLOYEE
[20]  ONE:□←'ENTER EMPLOYEE NUMBER'
[21]     →((I←PAY[;1]ιι□)≤1↑ρPAY)/OK
[22]     →RPT MSG 'EMPLOYEE NOT FOUND.'
[23]  OK:□←'THIS IS: ',NAM[I;],'   OK?'
[24]     □←'IF SO, ENTER 1  OTHERWISE ENTER ANY NUMBER'
[25]     →(1≠ι□)/RPT
[26]     □←'INPUT THE HRS WORKED FOR THIS WEEK'
[27]     A←I COMPUTEP PAY[I;8]←ι□
[28]  RPT:□←'ANOTHER EMPLOYEE?'
[29]     □←'IF SO, ENTER 1 OTHERWISE ANY NUMBER'
[30]     →((A≠1),1=A←ι□)/0,ONE
     ∇
```

Program 4. APL Payroll Program *(continued)*.

```
     ∇PRINTC[⎕]∇
   ∇ PRINTC;C
[1]    CLEAR
[2]    →OPN MSG 'READY PRINTER.'
[3]  OPN:OPENP
[4]  AGN:CLEAR
[5]    ⎕←'CHECK PRINTING.  SELECT DESIRED OPTION:'
[6]    ⎕←'    1 - RETURN TO MENU'
[7]    ⎕←'    2 - PRINT ONE CHECK'
[8]    ⎕←'    3 - PRINT ALL CHECKS'
[9]    →((N<1)∨(N←⎕)>3)/ERR
[10]   →(N-1)⌽LVE,ONE,ALL
[11] ERR:→DIAG AGN
[12] ⍝ PRINT CHECK FOR ONE EMPLOYEE
[13] ONE:⎕←'ENTER EMPLOYEE NUMBER'
[14]   →((I←PAY[;1]⍳⍳⎕)≤1↑ρPAY)/OK
[15]   →AGN MSG 'EMPLOYEE NOT FOUND'
[16] OK:⎕←'ENTER CHECK NUMBER'
[17]   →AGN,I CHECK⍳⎕
[18] ⍝ PRINT CHECKS FOR ALL EMPLOYEES
[19] ALL:I←1↑0,C←1↑(⎕-1),ρ⎕←'ENTER INITIAL CHECK NUMBER'
[20] TST:→((I←I+1)>1↑ρPAY)/DNE
[21]   →(PAY[I;2]=0)/DNE
[22]   →(PAY[I;2]=2)/TST
[23]   →TST,I CHECK C←C+1
[24] DNE:⎕←'LAST CHECK PRINTED'
[25] LVE:CLOSEP
   ∇
```

```
     ∇LISTE[⎕]∇
   ∇ LISTE;S
[1]  ⍝ LIST EMPLOYEE NAMES AND ADDRESSES
[2]    CLEAR
[3]    →LS1 MSG 'READY THE PRINTER'
[4]  LS1:⎕←(TAB 23),'EMPLOYEE LIST'
[5]    ⎕←(TAB 25),DATE,CR
[6]    A←'NUM',(TAB 8),'NAME',(TAB 14),'STREET',(TAB 12)
[7]    ⎕←A,'LOCATION',CR
[8]    U←((,PAY[;2])=1)/⍳30
[9]    S←((ρU),1)ρ' '
[10]   ⎕←(3 0 ⍕((ρU),1)ρ,PAY[U;1]),S,NAM[U;],S,AD1[U;],S,AD2[U;]
[11]   ⎕←CR,'END OF EMPLOYEE LIST'
   ∇
```

Program 4. APL Payroll Program (*continued*).

```
        ∇CHECK[□]∇
      ∇ R←I CHECK C;A
[1]     PL(TAB 39),'CHECK NUMBER ',⍕C
[2]     A←(TAB 9),'EMPL NO',(TAB 23),'DATE',(TAB 6),'SOC SEC NO'
[3]     A←A,(TAB 10),'EMPL NO',(TAB 23),'DATE',(TAB 11)
[4]     PL A,'SOC SEC NO'
[5]     A←(TAB 10),(3 0 ⍕PAY[I;1]),(TAB 25),DATE,(TAB 4),,SS[I;]
[6]     A←A,(TAB 11),(3 0 ⍕PAY[I;1]),(TAB 25),DATE,(TAB 10)
[7]     PL A,(,SS[I;]),CR,CR
[8]     A←(TAB 4),'PAY**********',(8 2 ⍕PAY[I;9]),'DOLLARS'
[9]     PL A,(TAB 10),'$',(8 2 ⍕PAY[I;9])
[10]    A←(TAB 69),'NET PAY',(TAB 3),'FED W.H.',(TAB 4),'FICA'
[11]    A←A,(TAB 6),'ST TAX',(TAB 4),'CTY TAX',(TAB 3),'DEP'
[12]    PL A,(TAB 2),'GROSS'
[13]    A←(TAB 68),(8 2 ⍕PAY[I;9]),(9 2 ⍕PAY[I;13])
[14]    A←A,(10 2 ⍕PAY[I;14]),(11 2 ⍕PAY[I;15]),(11 2 ⍕PAY[I;16])
[15]    PL A,(6 0 ⍕PAY[I;7]),(9 2 ⍕PAY[I;10])
[16]    PL(TAB 2),'TO THE',(TAB 85),'YEAR TO DATE'
[17]    A←'ORDER OF',(TAB 10),(,NAM[I;]),(TAB 43),'FED W.H.'
[18]    A←A,(TAB 4),'FICA',(TAB 6),'ST TAX',(TAB 3),'CITY TAX'
[19]    PL A,(TAB 8),'GROSS'
[20]    A←(TAB 18),(,AD1[I;]),(TAB 43),(7 2 ⍕PAY[I;5])
[21]    A←A,(9 2 ⍕PAY[I;6]),(12 2 ⍕PAY[I;11]),(10 2 ⍕PAY[I;12])
[22]    PL A,(15 2 ⍕PAY[I;4])
[23]    PL(TAB 18),(,AD2[I;])
[24]    PL(TAB 39),30ρ'_'
[25]    PL(TAB 49),'SIGNATURE'
[26]    PL 5ρ□AV[157]
[27]    →R←0
      ∇
```

```
        ∇COMPUTEP[□]∇
      ∇ R←I COMPUTEP H;B;C;D
[1]     PAY[I;4]←PAY[I;4]+PAY[I;10]←(B×H⌊40)+PAY[I;18]←(B←PAY[I;3]
)×1.5×PAY[I;17]←(C+H>40)×H-40
[2]     PAY[I;5]←PAY[I;5]+PAY[I;13]←PAY[I;10]×(0.2×D<1)+(0.16×D=1)
+(0.12×D=2)+(0.08×D=3)+0×3<D←PAY[I;7]
[3]     ⍝ FICA  14100×.0585=824.85
[4]     PAY[I;14]←(PAY[I;6]←824.85⌊PAY[I;6]+PAY[I;10]×0.0585)-PAY[
I;6]
[5]     PAY[I;11]←PAY[I;11]+PAY[I;15]←PAY[I;10]×0.05
[6]     PAY[I;12]←PAY[I;12]+PAY[I;16]←PAY[I;10]×0.02
[7]     R←PAY[I;9]←PAY[I;10]-+/PAY[I; 13 14 15 16]
      ∇
```

Program 4. APL Payroll Program (*continued*).

```
      ∇READ[□]∇
    ∇ READ F;A
[1]   A←□EX 'INPT'
[2]   →(2≠1 □SVO 'INPT')/ERR1
[3]   INPT←'IN ',(⍕F+1000),' ID=(APL PAYROLL DATA) MSG=OFF'
[4]   →(1≠∧/ 0 0 =A←INPT)/ERR2
[5]   →(0=ρPAY←INPT)/ERR3
[6]   →(0=ρNAM←INPT)/ERR3
[7]   →(0=ρAD1←INPT)/ERR3
[8]   →(0=ρAD2←INPT)/ERR3
[9]   →(0=ρSS←INPT)/ERR3
[10]  INPT←ι0
[11]  →(1≠∧/ 0 0 =A←INPT)/ERR4
[12]  →(2=□SVR 'INPT')/0
[13]  ERR5:→OUT,ρ□←'READ: ERROR RETRACTING SHARED VARIABLE'
[14]  ERR1:→OUT,ρ□←'READ: ERROR ESTABLISHING SHARED VARIABLE'
[15]  ERR2:→OUT,ρ□←'READ: ERROR OPENING FILE ',⍕F
[16]  ERR3:→OUT,ρ□←'READ: END OF FILE ',⍕F
[17]  ERR4:→OUT,ρ□←'READ: ERROR CLOSING FILE ',⍕F
[18]  OUT:A←□SVR 'INPT'
[19]  →
    ∇


      ∇WRITE[□]∇
    ∇ WRITE F;A
[1]   A←□EX 'OUTP'
[2]   →(2≠1 □SVO 'OUTP')/ERR1
[3]   OUTP←'OUT ',(⍕F+1000),' ID=(APL PAYROLL DATA) MSG=OFF'
[4]   →(1≠∧/ 0 0 =A←OUTP)/ERR2
[5]   OUTP←PAY
[6]   →(1≠∧/ 0 0 =A←OUTP)/ERR3
[7]   OUTP←NAM
[8]   →(1≠∧/ 0 0 =A←OUTP)/ERR3
[9]   OUTP←AD1
[10]  →(1≠∧/ 0 0 =A←OUTP)/ERR3
[11]  OUTP←AD2
[12]  →(1≠∧/ 0 0 =A←OUTP)/ERR3
[13]  OUTP←SS
[14]  →(1≠∧/ 0 0 =A←OUTP)/ERR3
[15]  OUTP←ι0
[16]  →(1≠∧/ 0 0 =A←OUTP)/ERR4
[17]  →(2=□SVR 'OUTP')/0
[18]  ERR5:→OUT,ρ□←'WRITE: ERROR RETRACTING SHARED VARIABLE'
[19]  ERR1:→OUT,ρ□←'WRITE: ERROR ESTABLISHING SHARED VARIABLE'
[20]  ERR2:→OUT,ρ□←'WRITE: ERROR OPENING FILE ',⍕F
[21]  ERR3:→OUT,ρ□←'WRITE: ERROR WRITING FILE ',⍕F
[22]  ERR4:→OUT,ρ□←'WRITE: ERROR CLOSING FILE ',⍕F
[23]  OUT:A←□SVR 'OUTP'
[24]  →
    ∇
```

Program 4. APL Payroll Program (*continued*).

```
      ∇OPENP[▯]∇
    ∇ OPENP;A
[1]   A←▯EX 'PRNT'
[2]   →(2≠1 ▯SVO 'PRNT')/ERR
[3]   PRNT←'PRT MSG=OFF'
[4]   →(1=∧/ 0 0 =A←PRNT)/0
[5]   →OUT,ρ▯←'OPENP: ERROR OPENING PRINTER'
[6] ERR:▯←'OPENP: ERROR ESTABLISHING SHARED VARIABLE'
[7] OUT:A←▯SVR 'PRNT'
[8]   →
    ∇


      ∇PL[▯]∇
    ∇ PL L;A
[1]   PRNT←L
[2]   →(1=∧/ 0 0 =A←PRNT)/0
[3]   ▯←'PL: PRINT ERROR'
[4]   A←▯SVR 'PRNT'
[5]   →
    ∇


      ∇CLOSEP[▯]∇
    ∇ CLOSEP;A
[1]   PRNT←⍳0
[2]   →(1≠∧/ 0 0 =A←PRNT)/ERR
[3]   →(2=▯SVR 'PRNT')/0
[4]   →OUT,ρ▯←'CLOSEP: ERROR RETRACTING SHARED VARIABLE'
[5] ERR:▯←'CLOSEP: ERROR CLOSING PRINTER'
[6] OUT:A←▯SVR 'PRNT'
[7]   →
    ∇


      ∇CLEAR[▯]∇
    ∇ CLEAR
[1]   SKIP 14
    ∇


      ∇SKIP[▯]∇
    ∇ SKIP N
[1]   ▯←Nρ▯AV[157]
    ∇


      ∇TAB[▯]∇
    ∇ R←TAB N
[1]   R←Nρ' '
    ∇
```

Program 4. APL Payroll Program (*continued*).

```
      ∇MSG[]∇
    ∇ R←S MSG C
[1]    []←C
[2]    R←1↑S,ρ[],[]←'PRESS EXECUTE TO CONTINUE'
    ∇


      ∇DIAG[]∇
    ∇ R←DIAG S
[1]    R←1↑S,ρ[],[]←'IMPROPER RESPONSE. PRESS EXECUTE TO CONTINUE.'
    ∇


      ∇EXPUNGE[]∇
    ∇ EXPUNGE;A
[1]  A CLEAR WORKSPACE FOR WRITE OPERATION
[2]    A←[]EX 5 8 ρ'CHANGE  COMPUTEPDELADD  DIAG     INPUT    '
[3]    A←[]EX 5 8 ρ'LISTE   LISTP    MSG      OPENP    PL       '
[4]    A←[]EX 5 8 ρ'PRINTC  READ     TAB      CHECK    CLOSEP   '
    ∇
```

Program 4. APL Payroll Program (*continued*).

APPENDIX B

APL ATOMIC VECTOR

The following chart shows the character, the character name, and the index of that character in the atomic vector:

Character	Character Name	Index (□IO←1)
	RESERVED.	1
	RESERVED.	2
	RESERVED.	3
	RESERVED.	4
	RESERVED.	5
	RESERVED.	6
	RESERVED.	7
	RESERVED.	8
	RESERVED.	9
	RESERVED.	10
	RESERVED.	11
	RESERVED.	12
	RESERVED.	13
	RESERVED.	14
[	LEFT BRACKET.	15
]	RIGHT BRACKET	16
(	LEFT PARENTHESIS.	17
)	RIGHT PARENTHESIS	18
;	SEMICOLON	19
/	SLASH	20
\	BACK SLASH.	21
←	LEFT ARROW.	22
→	RIGHT ARROW	23
	RESERVED.	24
	RESERVED.	25
¨	DIERESIS (UPPERSHIFT 1)	26

Character	Character Name	Index ($\square$IO←1)
+	PLUS.	27
-	MINUS	28
x	TIMES	29
÷	DIVIDE.	30
*	STAR.	31
Γ	MAXIMUM	32
L	MINIMUM	33
|	RESIDUE	34
∧	AND	35
∨	OR.	36
<	LESS THAN	37
≤	LESS THAN OR EQUAL.	38
=	EQUAL	39
≥	GREATER THAN OR EQUAL	40
>	GREATER THAN.	41
≠	NOT EQUAL	42
α	ALPHA	43
∈	EPSILON	44
⍳	IOTA.	45
ρ	RHO	46
ω	OMEGA	47
,	COMMA	48
!	SHRIEK (EXCLAMATION).	49
⌽	REVERSAL.	50
⊥	ENCODE (BASE)	51
⊤	DECODE (REPRESENTATION)	52
○	CIRCLE.	53
?	QUERY	54
~	NOT	55
↑	UP ARROW.	56
↓	DOWN ARROW.	57
⊂	SUBSET.	58
⊃	RIGHT SUBSET.	59
∩	CAP	60
∪	CUP	61
_	UNDERSCORE.	62
⍉	TRANSPOSE	63
⌶	I-BEAM.	64
∘	NULL (SMALL CIRCLE)	65
⎕	QUAD.	66
⍞	QUAD QUOTE.	67
⍟	LOG	68
⍲	NAND.	69
⍱	NOR	70
⍝	LAMP-COMMENT.	71
⍋	GRADE UP.	72
⍒	GRADE DOWN.	73
⊖	OVERSTRUCK CIRCLE-HYPHEN. . . .	74
⌿	OVERSTRUCK SLASH-HYPHEN	75
⍀	OVERSTRUCK BACKSLASH-HYPHEN . .	76
⌹	MATRIX DIVIDE	77
⍕	FORMAT.	78
⍎	EXECUTE	79
&	AMPERSAND	80
@	AT.	81
#	POUND	82

Character	Character Name	Index ($\Box IO \leftarrow 1$)
$	DOLLAR.	83
⅏	UNUSED.	84
T∆	TRACE (T DELTA)	85
S∆	STOP (S DELTA).	86
A	A . . . . . : . . . \	87
B	B	88
C	C	89
D	D	90
E	E	91
F	F	92
G	G	93
H	H	94
I	I	95
J	J	96
K	K	97
L	L	98
M	M	99
N	N	100
O	O	101
P	P	102
Q	Q	103
R	R	104
S	S	105
T	T	106
U	U	107
V	V	108
W	W	109
X	X	110
Y	Y	111
Z	Z	112
∆	DELTA	113
A̲	A-UNDERSCORE.	114
B̲	B-UNDERSCORE.	115
C̲	C-UNDERSCORE.	116
D̲	D-UNDERSCORE.	117
E̲	E-UNDERSCORE.	118
F̲	F-UNDERSCORE.	119
G̲	G-UNDERSCORE.	120
H̲	H-UNDERSCORE.	121
I̲	I-UNDERSCORE.	122
J̲	J-UNDERSCORE.	123
K̲	K-UNDERSCORE.	124
L̲	L-UNDERSCORE.	125
M̲	M-UNDERSCORE.	126
N̲	N-UNDERSCORE.	127
O̲	O-UNDERSCORE.	128
P̲	P-UNDERSCORE.	129
Q̲	Q-UNDERSCORE.	130
R̲	R-UNDERSCORE.	131
S̲	S-UNDERSCORE.	132
T̲	T-UNDERSCORE.	133
U̲	U-UNDERSCORE.	134
V̲	V-UNDERSCORE.	135
W̲	W-UNDERSCORE.	136
X̲	X-UNDERSCORE.	137
Y̲	Y-UNDERSCORE.	138
Z̲	Z-UNDERSCORE.	139

Character	Character Name	Index (⎕IO←1)
Ā	DELTA-UNDERSCORE	140
0̈	0	141
1	1	142
2	2	143
3	3	144
4	4	145
5	5	146
6	6	147
7	7	148
8	8	149
9	9	150
.	PERIOD	151
¯	OVERBAR	152
	BLANK	153
'	QUOTE	154
:	COLON	155
∇	DEL (FN DEF CHAR)	156
	CURSOR RETURN	157
	END OF BLOCK(CANNOT BE DISPLAYED)	158
	BACKSPACE	159
	LINEFEED	160
∇̰	PROTECTED DEL	161
	UNUSED	162
	UNUSED	163
	UNUSED	164
	UNUSED	165
	UNUSED	166
	UNUSED	167
	UNUSED	168
	LENGTH OF Z-SYMBOL TABLE	169
⑪	O-U-T FOR COMMUNICATION TAPE . . .	170
¬	LOGICAL NOT	171
"	DOUBLE QUOTE	172
%	PERCENT	173
Ã̰	PROTECTED DELTA	174
⊙	BULLS EYE	175
Ä	A UMLET	176
Ö	O UMLET	177
Ü	U UMLET	178
Å	ANGSTROM	179
Æ	AE DIAGRAPH	180
Pₜ	P SUB T	181
Ñ	N TILDE	182
£	POUND STERLING	183
¢	CENT	184
Õ	O TILDE	185
Ã	A TILDE	186

Note: The remaining elements (187-256) are unused.

APPENDIX C
BASIC HEXADECIMAL CODES

These are the characters that the 5100 can display along with their hexadecimal representations. The second 128 characters are the same as the first 128 with the addition of underscores.

X'00' =	X'2B' = ,	X'56' =)	X'81' = A	X'AC' = .	X'D7' = ;
X'01' = A	X'2C' = .	X'57' = ;	X'82' = B̄	X'AD' = α	X'D8' = :
X'02' = B	X'2D' = α	X'58' = :	X'83' = C̄	X'AE' = ⊥	X'D9' = Φ
X'03' = C	X'2E' = ⊥	X'59' = Φ	X'84' = D̄	X'AF' = n	X'DA' = θ
X'04' = D	X'2F' = n	X'5A' = θ	X'85' = Ē	X'B0' = L	X'DB' = ◊
X'05' = E	X'30' = L	X'5B' = ◊	X'86' = F̄	X'B1' = ∈	X'DC' = ⊕
X'06' = F	X'31' = ∈	X'5C' = ⊕	X'87' = Ḡ	X'B2' =	X'DD' = ↗
X'07' = G	X'32' = _	X'5D' = ↗	X'88' = H̄	X'B3' = ∇̄	X'DE' = ↖
X'08' = H	X'33' = ∇	X'5E' = ↖	X'89' = Ī	X'B4' = Δ̄	X'DF' = □̄
X'09' = I	X'34' = Δ	X'5F' = □	X'8A' = J̄	X'B5' = \	X'E0' = !
X'0A' = J	X'35' = \	X'60' = !	X'8B' = K̄	X'B6' = ◡	X'E1' =
X'0B' = K	X'36' = ◡	X'61' =	X'8C' = L̄	X'B7' = ◠	X'E2' =
X'0C' = L	X'37' = '	X'62' =	X'8D' = M̄	X'B8' = □̄	X'E3' =
X'0D' = M	X'38' = □	X'63' = ⊖	X'8E' = N̄	X'B9' = Ī	X'E4' =
X'0E' = N	X'39' = I	X'64' = ⊟	X'8F' = Ō	X'BA' = τ	X'E5' =
X'0F' = O	X'3A' = τ	X'65' = I	X'90' = P̄	X'BB' = ō	X'E6' =
X'10' = P	X'3B' = o	X'66' = A	X'91' = Q̄	X'BC' = *	X'E7' =
X'11' = Q	X'3C' = *	X'67' =	X'92' = R̄	X'BD' = ?	X'E8' =
X'12' = R	X'3D' = ?	X'68' =	X'93' = S̄	X'BE' = ρ	X'E9' = Ψ̄
X'13' = S	X'3E' = ρ	X'69' = Ψ	X'94' = T̄	X'BF' = Γ̄	X'EA' =
X'14' = T	X'3F' = Γ	X'6A' = ♠	X'95' = Ū	X'C0' = ~	X'EB' =
X'15' = U	X'40' = ~	X'6B' = ↑	X'96' = V̄	X'C1' = ↓	X'EC' =
X'16' = V	X'41' = ↓	X'6C' = ↓	X'97' = W̄	X'C2' = υ	X'ED' =
X'17' = W	X'42' = υ	X'6D' = ¬	X'98' = X̄	X'C3' = ω	X'EE' =

X'18'	=	X	X'43'	=	ω	X'6E'	=	"	X'99'	=	Ȳ

```
X'18'  =  X        X'43'  =  ω        X'6E'  =  "        X'99'  =  Ȳ        X'C4'  =  ⊃̄        X'EF'  =  &̄
X'19'  =  Y        X'44'  =  ⊃        X'6F'  =  &        X'9A'  =  Z̄        X'C5'  =  ↑̄        X'F0'  =  @̄
X'1A'  =  Z        X'45'  =  ↑        X'70'  =  @        X'9B'  =  0̄        X'C6'  =  ⊂̄        X'F1'  =  #̄
X'1B'  =  0        X'46'  =  ⊂        X'71'  =  #        X'9C'  =  1̄        X'C7'  =  ∧̄        X'F2'  =  $̄
X'1C'  =  1        X'47'  =  ∧        X'72'  =  $        X'9D'  =  2̄        X'C8'  =  ¨̄        X'F3'  =  %̄
X'1D'  =  2        X'48'  =  ¨        X'73'  =  %        X'9E'  =  3̄        X'C9'  =  ‾̄        X'F4'  =  Ǟ
X'1E'  =  3        X'49'  =  ‾        X'74'  =  Ä        X'9F'  =  4̄        X'CA'  =  <̄        X'F5'  =  Ů̄
X'1F'  =  4        X'4A'  =  <        X'75'  =  Ů        X'A0'  =  5̄        X'CB'  =  ≤̄        X'F6'  =  ȫ
X'20'  =  5        X'4B'  =  ≤        X'76'  =  ö        X'A1'  =  6̄        X'CC'  =  =̄        X'F7'  =  ǖ
X'21'  =  6        X'4C'  =  =        X'77'  =  ü        X'A2'  =  7̄        X'CD'  =  ≥̄        X'F8'  =  Å̄
X'22'  =  7        X'4D'  =  ≥        X'78'  =  Å        X'A3'  =  8̄        X'CE'  =  >̄        X'F9'  =  Ǣ
X'23'  =  8        X'4E'  =  >        X'79'  =  Æ        X'A4'  =  9̄        X'CF'  =  ≠̄        X'FA'  =  Ñ̄
X'24'  =  9        X'4F'  =  ≠        X'7A'  =  R        X'A5'  =  /̄        X'D0'  =  ∨̄        X'FB'  =  £̄
X'25'  =  /        X'50'  =  ∨        X'7B'  =  ñ        X'A6'  =  +̄        X'D1'  =  \̄        X'FC'  =  ç̄
X'26'  =  +        X'51'  =  \        X'7C'  =  £        X'A7'  =  x̄        X'D2'  =  -̄        X'FD'  =  ȫ
X'27'  =  ×        X'52'  =  -        X'7D'  =  ç        X'A8'  =  ←̄        X'D3'  =  ÷̄        X'FE'  =  ȫ
X'28'  =  ←        X'53'  =  ÷        X'7E'  =  ö        X'A9'  =  [̄        X'D4'  =  →̄        X'FF'  =  Ã̄
X'29'  =  [        X'54'  =  →        X'7F'  =  Ã        X'AA'  =  ]̄        X'D5'  =  (̄
X'2A'  =  ]        X'55'  =  (        X'80'  =  _        X'AB'  =  ,̄        X'D6'  =  )̄
```

APPENDIX D

BASIC COLLATING SEQUENCE

The following chart lists all the characters available on the 5100, BASIC-only keyboard, and their relative value, lowest to highest:

Character	Sequence Number	Character	Sequence Number
(blank)	65	?	112
.	76	:	123
<	77	#	124
(	78	@	125
+	79	'	126
|	80	=	127
&	81	↑	139
!	91	≤	141
$	92	[	174
*	93	≥	175
)	94	]	190
;	95	≠	191
–	97	A	194
/	98	B	195
,	108	C	196
>	111	D	197

Character	Sequence Number	Character	Sequence Number
E	198	U	229
F	199	V	230
G	200	W	231
H	201	X	232
I	202	Y	233
J	210	Z	234
K	211	0	241
L	212	1	242
M	213	2	243
N	214	3	244
O	215	4	245
P	216	5	246
Q	217	6	247
R	218	7	248
\	225	8	249
S	227	9	250
T	228		

APPENDIX E
APL REFERENCE CARD

IBM 5100

APL Reference Card

GX21-9214-0

OVERSTRUCK CHARACTERS

The overstruck characters are formed by pressing one key, backspacing, and pressing the other key. The order in which the keys are pressed does not matter.

Symbol For	Character	Keys Used	
Comment	⍝	∩/C	°/J
Execute	⍎	⊥/B	°/J
Factorial, combination	!	'/K	:/.
Format	⍕	T/N	°/J
Grade down	⍒	∇/G	I/M
Grade up	⍋	Δ/H	I/M
Logarithm	⍟	*/P	O/O
Matrix division	⌹	▫/L	÷/X
Nand	⍲	∧/0	~/T
Nor	⍱	∨/9	~/T
Protected function	⍢	∇/G	~/T
Quad quote	⍞	▫/L	'/K
Rotate, reverse	⌽	I/M	O/O
Transpose	⍉	\//	O/O
Compress	⌿ (See note)	\//	-/+
Expand	⍀ (See note)	\//	-/+
Rotate, reverse	⊖ (See note)	O/O	-/+

Note: These are variations of the symbols for these functions; they are used when the function is acting on the first coordinate of an array.

PRIMITIVE SCALAR FUNCTIONS

Function	Result		Data Types (L=logical, N=numeric, C=character)		
			A	B	Result
+B	B.			N	N
−B	Sign of B is changed.			N	N
×B	Sign of B ($\bar{1}$, 0, 1).			N	N
÷B	Reciprocal of B.			N	N
⌈B	B is rounded up to the next larger integer.			N	N
⌊B	B is rounded down to the next smaller integer.			N	N
|B	Absolute value of B.			N	N
⋆B	2.71828 (e) raised to the power B.			N	N
⊛B	Log of B to the base 2.71828 (e).			N	N
○B	3.14159 (π) times B.			N	N
!B	Product of all the integers from 1 to B.			N	N
?B[1]	Random number between the origin and B.			N	N
∼B	1 when B is 0, 0 when B is 1.			L	L
A+B	B added to A.		N	N	N
A−B	B subtracted from A.		N	N	N
A×B	A multiplied by B.		N	N	N
A÷B	A divided by B.		N	N	N
A⌈B	Larger of A or B.		N	N	N
A⌊B	Smaller of A or B.		N	N	N
A|B	Residue (remainder) when B is divided by A.		N	N	N
A⋆B	A raised to the power B.		N	N	N
A⊛B	Log of B to base A.		N	N	N
A○B	0○B (1−B⋆2)⋆.5 1○B sin B 2○B cos B 3○B tan B 4○B (1+B⋆2)⋆.5 5○B sinh B 6○B cosh B 7○B tanh B $\bar{1}$○B arcsin B $\bar{2}$○B arccos B $\bar{3}$○B arctan B $\bar{4}$○B ($\bar{1}$+B⋆2)⋆.5 $\bar{5}$○B arcsinh B $\bar{6}$○B arccosh B $\bar{7}$○B arctanh B		N	N	N
A!B	Number of combinations of B taken A at a time.		N	N	N

	Arguments		Results						
	A	B	A∧B	A∨B	A∼̃B	A∨̃B			
A∧B	0	0	0	0	1	1	L	L	L
A∨B	0	1	0	1	1	0	L	L	L
A∼̃B	1	0	0	1	1	0	L	L	L
A∨̃B	1	1	1	1	0	0	L	L	L

Function	Result		A	B	Result
A>B	A greater than B.		N	N	L
A=B	A equal to B.		N, C	N, C	L
A<B	A less than B.	Result is 1 if the relation is true; otherwise, the result is 0.	N	N	L
A≥B	A greater than or equal to B.		N	N	L
A≤B	A less than or equal to B.		N	N	L
A≠B	A not equal to B.		N, C	N, C	L

[1] Depends on the index origin (⎕IO).

PRIMITIVE MIXED FUNCTIONS

Function	Result	Data Types (L=logical, N=numeric, C=character)		
		A	B	Result
ρB	Shape of B.		N, C	N
,B	A vector containing the elements of B.		N, C	N, C
⍋B[1]	Index values that select B in ascending order.		N	N
⍒B[1]	Index values that select B in descending order.		N	N
ιB[1]	B consecutive integers from the origin.		N	N
φ[I] B	Elements of B reversed along the Ith coordinate.		N, C	N, C
φB	Elements of B reversed along the last coordinate.		N, C	N, C
⊖B	Elements of B reversed along the first coordinate.		N, C	N, C
⍉B	Reversed coordinates of B.		N, C	N, C
⌹B	Inverted square matrix or pseudo inverse of a rectangular matrix.		N	N
⍎B	B (character string) executed as an APL expression.		C	N, C, L
⍕B	B (an APL expression or variable) converted to character data.		N, C	C
AρB	Reshape B to A.	N	N, C	N, C
A , [I] B	If I is an integer, A and B are joined along an existing (Ith) coordinate. If I is a decimal number, A and B are joined along a new coordinate.	N, C	N, C	N, C
A , B	A and B are joined along the last coordinate.	N, C	N, C	N, C
A / [I] B	Elements of B selected, as specified by A, along the Ith coordinate.	L	N, C	N, C
A / B	Elements of B selected, as specified by A, along the last coordinate.	L	N, C	N, C
A ≠ B	Elements of B selected, as specified by A, along the first coordinate.	L	N, C	N, C
A \ [I] B	B expanded, as specified by A, along the Ith coordinate.	L	N, C	N, C
A \ B	B expanded, as specified by A, along the last coordinate.	L	N, C	N, C
A ⍀ B	B expanded, as specified by A, along the first coordinate.	L	N, C	N, C
A ↑ B	Elements taken from B as specified by A.	N	N, C	N, C
A ↓ B	Elements dropped from B as specified by A (the remaining elements are the result).	N	N, C	N, C
A ι B[1]	Index of the first occurrence in A of the element(s) in B.	N, C	N, C	N
Aφ[I] B	B rotated, as specified by A, along the Ith coordinate.	N	N, C	N, C

[1] Depends on the index origin (□IO).

PRIMITIVE MIXED FUNCTIONS (continued)

Function	Result	A	B	Result
		Data Types (L=logical, N=numeric, C=character)		
$A \phi B$	B rotated, as specified by A, along the last coordinate.	N	N, C	N, C
$A \ominus B$	B rotated, as specified by A, along the first coordinate.	N	N, C	N, C
$A \lozenge B$	Interchanged coordinates of B as specified by A.	N	N, C	N, C
$A \, ? B^1$	A integers selected from ιB without duplication.	N	N	N
$A \perp B$	Values of B in the number system specified by A.	N	N	N
$A \top B$	Representation of B in the number system specified by A.	N	N	N
$A \in B$	A 1 for each element of A that is found in B and a 0 for each element not found.	N, C	N, C	L
$A \boxdiv B$	Solution to one or more sets of linear equations with coefficient matrices or the least squares solution to one or more sets of linear equations.	N	N	N
$A \top B$	B (an expression or variable) converted to character data in the format specified by A.	N	N, C	C

APL OPERATORS

Function	Result	A	B	Result
		Data Types (L=logical, N=numeric, C=character)		
$\text{(f)}/[I]B$	B reduced along the Ith coordinate.		N	N
$\text{(f)}/B$	B reduced along the last coordinate.		N	N
$\text{(f)}\neq B$	B reduced along the first coordinate.		N	N
$\text{(f)}\backslash[I]B$	B scanned along the Ith coordinate.		N	N
$\text{(f)}\backslash B$	B scanned along the last coordinate.		N	N
$\text{(f)}\backslash B$	B scanned along the first coordinate.		N	N
$A\text{(f)}.\text{(g)}B$	Inner product of matrices A and B.	N	N	N
$A \circ .\text{(f)}B$	Outer product of matrices A and B.	N	N	N

Note: (f) and (g) can be any primitive scalar dyadic (two-argument) functions.

FUNCTION DEFINITION

A ▽(del) places the 5100 in function definition mode and another ▽ indicates the end of the function definition and changes the mode back to execution mode.

The function header determines how many arguments the function has and whether or not the function has an explicit result.

Number of Arguments	Without Explicit Result	With Explicit Result
0	▽NAME	▽R←NAME
1	▽NAME B	▽R←NAME B
2	▽A NAME B	▽R←A NAME B

Names are made local to a function by placing them in the function header preceded by a semicolon (;): ▽R←A NAME B;LOCAL

Displaying Functions

The 5100 must be in function definition mode.

[▢]   Display the entire function
[n▢]   Display statement n
[▢n]   Display from statement n to the end of the function

If the 5100 is not in function definition mode, it can be placed in function definition mode, the function displayed, and mode changed back to execution mode with one statement. For example: ▽NAME[▢] ▽ (displays function NAME)

Editing Functions

The 5100 must be in function definition mode.

[n] statement   Replace the original statement n.
[1.5]   Insert a statement between statements 1 and 2.
[n▢]   Display statement n, which can then be edited using the 5100 statement editing capabilities.
[△n]   Delete statement n. (A closing ▽ cannot be on the same line.)

Trace and Stop Controls

T△PROG←n   During execution of PROG, statement n and its results are displayed each time the statement is executed.
S△PROG←n   Halts execution of PROG immediately before statement n is executed.

n can be a scalar, vector, or expression that results in a scalar or vector. Stop and trace controls can be established within a function. For example, [3] T△PROG← 4×I≥N means statement 4 will be traced when I≥N is true.

Trace or stop control is removed by assigning an empty vector: T△PROG← ι 0 or S△ PROG← ι 0

Suspended Function Execution

The following options are available when a function is suspended:

- Execute system commands (except)SAVE,)COPY, and)PCOPY).
- Reopen and edit the suspended function.
- Resume function execution by entering →▢LC or →n (n can be any statement number).
- Execute another function.

INPUT/OUTPUT OPERATIONS

The following procedure is to be used when doing input/output operations using an APL shared variable:

1. Establish variable name(s) to be shared:

   1 □SVO 'NAME(S)'

   A 2 is displayed for each name successfully established to be shared.

2. Open a data file or select printer output:

   Note: The items in brackets are optional; if PRT is specified, the only other item that can be specified is MSG=OFF; TYPE= can only be specified for an OUT operation; a return code vector of 0 0 is assigned to the shared variable if the operation is successful.

3. Transfer data using the APL shared variable (assign data to the variable).

   Note: For OUT, ADD, and PRT operations, a return code vector of 0 0 is assigned to the shared variable if the operation is successful.

4. Close the data file or terminate printer output:

   NAME← ι 0

5. Retract the variable name being shared:

   □SVR 'NAME(S)'

   A 2 is displayed for each name successfully retracted.

NOTES:

SYSTEM COMMANDS

Function	Command	Displayed Response
Clear the active workspace.	)CLEAR	CLEAR WS
Write the contents of the active workspace on tape. The workspace can have suspended functions in it.	)CONTINUE [FILE] [WSID] [:password]	CONTINUED FILE WSID
Copy a saved workspace or objects into the active workspace.	)COPY FILE WSID [:password] [objects]	COPIED FILE WSID
Drop a file from the tape.	)DROP FILE [WSID]	DROPPED FILE WSID
Erase global objects from the active workspace.	)ERASE name(s)	None
Display the names of the user-defined functions.	)FNS [character(s)]	Names of the defined functions
Display the file headers.	)LIB [FILE]	The file headers
Load the active workspace with a stored workspace.	)LOAD FILE WSID [:password]	LOADED FILE WSID
Format the tape.	)MARK size number [device] of file files number	MARKED last size file number marked
Place the 5100 in communications mode.	)MODE COM	Options or 00001 HOME □↓
Select printer output.	)OUTSEL OUT ALL OFF	None
Apply IMFs.	)PATCH	List of options

SYSTEM COMMANDS (continued)

Description	Command	Result
Copy a saved workspace or objects into the active workspace and protect objects in the active workspace from being destroyed.	)PCOPY FILE WSID [:password] [objects]	COPIED FILE WSID
Rewind the tape.	)REWIND [device number]	None
Write the contents of the active workspace on tape. The active workspace cannot contain suspended functions.	)SAVE [FILE] [WSID] [:password]	SAVED FILE WSID
Display the state indicator.	)SI	Names of the suspended functions
Display the state indicator and local names.	)SIV	Names of the suspended functions and local names for each function
Display or change the number of symbols allowed. The number of symbols allowed can only be changed in clear workspace.	)SYMBOLS [number of symbols]	IS number of symbols allowed or WAS former number of symbols allowed
Display the global variable names.	)VARS [character(s)]	Names of the global variables
Display or change the active workspace ID.	)WSID [FILE] [WSID] [:password]	FILE WSID or WAS FILE WSID

Notes:

1. The items in brackets are optional; FILE=device/file number; WSID=workspace ID or file ID.
2. The keywords)LOAD,)SAVE,)CONT,)LIB,)FNS,)VARS,)COPY,)WSID,)OUTSEL, and)REWIND can be entered by holding the CMD key while pressing the top-row key just below the keyword you want.

SYSTEM VARIABLES

Function	Variable	Description	Initial Value[2]	Range
Specifies the tolerance used by the relational and floor and ceiling functions.	□CT	Comparison tolerance	$1E^{-}13$	$0 \leq □CT < 1$
Specifies the index origin.	□IO	Index origin	1	1 or 0
Specifies the significant digits to be displayed.	□PP	Printing precision	5	1 to 16
Specifies the length of the output line.	□PW	Print width	64	30 to 390
Specifies the number seed used in generating random numbers.	□RL	Random link	16807	1 to $2^{31} - 2$
A vector of statement numbers; the first element is the statement number being executed.	□LC[1]	Line counter	10	
Indicates the number of unused bytes (space) in the active workspace.	□WA[1]	Work area available		
Executed as an APL statement when a stored workspace is loaded into the active workspace.	□LX	Latent expression	10	
A 256-element vector of all the possible characters.	□AV[1]	Atomic vector		

[1] These system variables cannot be set by the user.
[2] The value that the variable is set to in a clear workspace.

SYSTEM FUNCTIONS

Result	Function and Format	Description
A user-defined function formatted into a character matrix.	□CR 'function name'	Canonical representation
A character matrix formatted into a user-defined function.	□FX matrix name	Fix
The specified object (can be a local object) is erased from the active workspace. (A 1 is displayed if the object was erased; otherwise, a 0 is displayed.)	□EX name	Expunge
A character matrix of the specified names in the active workspace.	□NL class of names: 1=labels 2=variables 3=functions	Name list
A character matrix of the specified names in the active workspace, beginning with the specified characters.	character □NL class of names: vector 1=labels 2=variables 3=functions	Name list (beginning with the specified characters)
A numerical indication of the type of name represented by each row of a specified matrix: 0=name available 1=label 2=variable 3=function 4=name not available	□NC matrix name	Name classification

SPECIAL SYMBOLS

Symbol	Name	Description
←	Assignment arrow	Causes everything to the right of the arrow to be evaluated and associated with the name to the left of the arrow.
→	Branch arrow	The branch arrow is used to:
		• Change the order in which statements are executed in a user-defined function.
		• Escape from a ▢ input request.
		• Resume execution of a suspended user-defined function (→▢LC).
		• Clear the state indicator.
▢	Quad	Requests input or displays output:
		X←▢ Requests input and assigns it to X.
		▢←X Displays output (X).
▢′	Quad quote	Requests input or displays output. Input is treated as character data and enclosing single quotes are not required. Output is displayed without a cursor return, therefore, more than one character vector or variable can be displayed on the same line.
⍝	Comment	Indicates to APL that the statement is only a comment and is not to be executed. The comment symbol must not be preceded by any other characters on the input line.
( )	Parentheses	Specifies the order of execution within an APL expression.
⍉	OUT	Escapes from a ▢′ request for input. This character is entered by holding the CMD key and pressing the ⌐↓ key.

International Business Machines Corporation
General Systems Division
5775D Glenridge Drive N.E.
Atlanta, Georgia 30301
(USA Only)

IBM World Trade Corporation
821 United Nations Plaza, New York, New York 10017
(International)

APPENDIX F

BASIC REFERENCE CARD

IBM 5100

BASIC Reference Card

GX21-9218-0

BASIC STATEMENTS

All the BASIC statements in the 5100 are listed alphabetically below. Required parameters are in lowercase letters. Optional parameters are enclosed in brackets. Parameters enclosed in braces indicate that you must enter one of the enclosed parameters. Ellipses (. . .) indicate that the preceding parameter(s) can be repeated. Commas must be entered where shown. Remember that each statement must be preceded by a statement number. Single quotation marks and parentheses must also be entered as shown.

Statement	Statement Function
CHAIN 'dev-address',arith-exp	Ends the current program, loads and begins executing a new program from the file indicated by the arithmetic expression.
CLOSE file ref [,file ref]. . .	Closes an open data file(s).
DATA $\left\{\begin{array}{l} \text{arith-con} \\ \text{char-con} \end{array}\right\} \left[,\left\{\begin{array}{l} \text{arith-con} \\ \text{char-con} \end{array}\right\}\right]$. . .	Defines data to be read by READ or MAT READ statements.
DEF FNfunction-name $\left[\text{arith-var [,arith-var] . . .}\right]$ [=arith-exp]	Defines a user function.
DIM array-name (rows [,columns]) $\left[,\text{array-name (rows [,columns])}\right]$. . .	Specifies dimensions of arrays.
END [comment]	Stops program execution.
FNEND [comment]	Ends a user function defined in a DEF statement.
FOR control-var=arith-exp TO arith-exp [STEP arith-exp]	Begins a FOR-NEXT loop and defines number of times loop is executed.

Note: This statement must be paired with a NEXT statement.

```
GET file ref  , { arith-var      } ... [ ,EOF line-num ]
                { arith-arr-var   }
                { char-var        }
                { char-arr-var    }
                { str-func        }
```
Reads data from an input data file.

```
GOTO  line-num [ ,line-num ] ... ON arith-exp
```
Transfers program execution control to a specified line.

```
GOSUB line-num [ ,line-num ] ... ON arith-exp
```
Transfers program execution control to a subroutine.

```
IF { arith-exp rel-opr arith-exp } [ {&} { arith-exp rel-opr arith-exp } ] ... { THEN } line-num
   { char-exp rel-opr char-exp   }  {|} { char-exp rel-opr char-exp   }       { GOTO }
```
Transfers program execution control to a specified line if the specified conditions exist.

```
INPUT { arith-var      } , ...
      { arith-arr-var  }
      { char-var       }
      { char-arr-var   }
      { str-func       }
```
Specifies variables for which you enter data when the statement is executed.

```
[LET] { arith-var      } [ , { arith-var      } ] ... =arith-exp
      { arith-arr-var  }     { arith-arr-var  }
      { char-var       }     { char-var       } ... = { char-exp }
      { char-arr-var   }     { char-arr-var   }        { char-con }
      { str-func       }     { str-func       }
```
Assigns a simple value, or a solution to a formula, to specified variables. Also extracts, concatenates, or replaces selected characters of specified character data items.

```
MAT array-name [ rows [,columns] ] = { array-name     }
                                      { scalar-expr } )
```
Assigns a value to matrix or array elements, or assigns values of one matrix to another matrix.

MAT matrix-name $\left[\text{rows}\left[,\text{columns}\right]\right]$ = matrix-name $\left\{{+\atop-}\right\}$ matrix-name

Adds or subtracts a matrix expression and assigns the results to a specified matrix.

MAT matrix-name $\left[\text{rows}\left[,\text{columns}\right]\right]$ = $\left\{{\text{matrix-name}\atop(\text{arith-exp})}\right\}$ • matrix-name

Multiplies a matrix expression and assigns the results to a specified matrix.

Note: For multiplication, the matrix specified on the left of the equal sign should not be specified on the right.

MAT matrix-name $\left[\text{rows, columns}\right]$ = $\left\{{\text{IDN}\atop\text{INV (matrix-name)}}\right\}$

Produces an identity matrix or inverts a matrix. All specified matrices must be square.

MAT array-name $\left[\text{rows, columns}\right]$ = TRN (array-name)

Transposes an array.

MAT GET file ref, array-name $\left[\text{rows}\left[,\text{columns}\right]\right]$ $\left[\text{array-name}\left[\text{rows}\left[,\text{columns}\right]\right]\right]$ ... $\left[,\text{EOF line-num}\right]$

Reads data from an input data file into the specified matrices.

MAT INPUT array-name $\left[\text{rows}\left[,\text{columns}\right]\right]$ $\left[\text{array-name}\left[\text{rows}\left[,\text{columns}\right]\right]\right]$ ...

Specifies matrices for which you enter data when the statement is executed.

MAT PRINT [file ref,] array-name $\left[\left\{{,\atop;}\right\}\text{array-name}\right]$ ... $\left[\left\{{,\atop;}\right\}\right]$

Displays or prints the contents of specified matrices during program execution.

Note: A semicolon indicates short print zone spacing. See PRINT statement syntax for information about short print zones.

MAT PRINT USING [file ref,] line-num, array-name [{;}{,}[array-name]]... [{;}{,}]

Displays or prints the contents of specified matrices during program execution according to the format specified in the associated image statement.

:[{char-string}{print-image}]...print-image[{char-string}{print-image}]...

Image statement specifying the format for the data to be printed or displayed.

MAT PUT file ref, array-name [array-name]...

Places the contents of the specified matrices in an output data file.

MAT READ array-name [rows [,columns]]] [array-name [rows [,columns]]]]...

Reads data into the specified matrices from a data file created by a DATA statement(s).

NEXT control-var

Last statement of a FOR-NEXT loop.

Note: This statement must be paired with a FOR statement.

OPEN file ref,'dev-address' [,file-num][,{'user ID'}{char-var}]{IN}{OUT}

Opens input/output data files.

PAUSE [comment]

Stops program execution temporarily.

PRINT [file ref.] $\left[\left\{\begin{matrix}\text{arith-exp} \\ \text{char-exp} \\ \text{TAB (exp)}\end{matrix}\right\}\right]$ $\left\{\begin{matrix}\text{char-con} \\ \text{char-con}\end{matrix}\right\}$ $\left[\begin{matrix}: \\ :\end{matrix}\right]$ $\left\{\begin{matrix}\text{arith-exp} \\ \text{char-exp} \\ \text{TAB (exp)}\end{matrix}\right\}$ $\left[\begin{matrix}\text{arith-exp} \\ \text{char-exp} \\ \text{TAB (exp)}\end{matrix}\right]$ $\cdots$ $\left[\begin{matrix}\text{char-con} \\ :\;: \end{matrix}\right]$

Prints or displays specified data during program execution.

Note: A character constant cannot be followed by a character constant.

Print Zone Characteristics

		Maximum number of print zones per:	
		64 character line	132 character line
Short zone size	Number of characters per print zone (includes sign, value, decimal point, and exponent)		
6 spaces	2, 3, or 4 characters	10	22
9 spaces	5, 6, or 7 characters	7	14
12 spaces	8, 9, or 10 characters	5	11
15 spaces	11, 12, or 13 characters	4	8
18 spaces	14, 15, 16, or 17 characters	3	7

Short print zones for character data are exactly as long as the number of characters in a character data item.

PRINT USING [file ref.] line-num $\left[\ , \left\{ {\text{arith-exp} \atop \text{char-exp}} \right\} \left[\left\{ {, \atop ;} \right\} \left\{ {\text{arith-exp} \atop \text{char-exp}} \right\} \right] \cdots \right] \left[\left\{ {, \atop ;} \right\} \right]$

Displays or prints the specified data during program execution according to the format specified in the associated image statement.

$: \left[\left\{ {\text{char-string} \atop \text{print-image}} \right\} \right] \cdots \text{print-image} \left[\left\{ {\text{char-string} \atop \text{print-image}} \right\} \right] \cdots$

Image statement specifying the format for the data to be displayed or printed.

PUT file ref , $\left\{ {\text{arith-exp} \atop \text{char-exp}} \right\} \left[, \left\{ {\text{arith-exp} \atop \text{char-exp}} \right\} \right] \cdots$

Places specified data in an output data file.

READ $\left\{ {\text{arith-var} \atop {\text{arith-arr-var} \atop {\text{char-var} \atop {\text{char-arr-var} \atop \text{str-func}}}}} \right\} \left\{ {\text{arith-var} \atop {\text{arith-arr-var} \atop {\text{char-var} \atop {\text{char-arr-var} \atop \text{str-func}}}}} \right\} \cdots$

Reads data from a data file created by a DATA statement(s).

REM [comment]

Inserts explanatory comments in a program.

RESET file ref [END] [,file ref [END]] $\cdots$

Moves data pointer(s) to beginning or end of an open data file(s).

RESTORE [comment]

Moves data pointer to beginning of a data file created by a DATA statement(s).

RETURN [arith-exp]

Last statement of a subroutine that returns execution control to statement following last GOSUB statement executed (arith-exp not allowed) or to calling function if in a multiline function (arith-exp required).

STOP [comment]

Stops program execution.

USE {arith-var / char-var / arith-arr (rows [,columns]) / char-arr (rows [,columns])} [, {arith-var / char-var / arith-arr (rows [,columns]) / char-arr (rows [,columns])}] . . . .

Stores variables to be used in successive programs or defines array dimensions.

BASIC SYSTEM COMMANDS

COMMAND   FUNCTION

AUTO [line-num [,increment]]

Automatically numbers BASIC statements.

GO [line-num] [, {RUN / STEP / TRACE [,PRINT]} [,RD=n]]

Resumes halted operations (n=1-13).

GO END

Terminates operations.

LIST [PRINT] [, {KEYx / line-num}]

Displays or prints work area contents (x=0-9).

LOAD file-num [, {KEYx / KEYS / DATA / BASIC / SOURCE}] [,dev-address]

Loads saved program into work area, or prepares work area for data or program to be entered from keyboard (x=0-9). *See Example of LOAD Command.*

MARK K-characters,files,starting file [,dev-address]

Prepares tape for storage.

MERGE file-num [,from line-num] [,through line-num] [,new line-num] [,dev-address]

Merges all or part of a saved file with work area contents.

PATCH

Applies internal machine fixes (IMFs).

RD=n

Specifies number of digits for rounding (n=1-13).

RENUM [KEYx] [,first line-num,increment]

Renumbers BASIC statements (including key groups) (x=0-9).

REWIND [dev-address]

Rewinds tape cartridge.

RUN [{STEP / TRACE [,PRINT]}] [,P=D] [,RD=n]

Runs program in normal, step, or trace mode (n=1-13).

SAVE file-num [, {KEYx / KEYS / SOURCE}] [,dev-address] [,'file ID']

Saves work area contents on tape (x=0-9). *See Example of SAVE Command.*

UTIL {MODE COM / [PRINT,]} [DIR [integer]] [,dev-address]

Displays or prints a directory of files on a tape, or transfers control to communications feature. *See Example of UTIL PRINT Command.*

BASIC EDITING FUNCTIONS

From line-num DEL [to line-num]

Deletes all BASIC statement(s) between (and including) the line numbers entered.

KEYx, line-num $\left\{ \begin{array}{l} \text{DEL [line-num]} \\ \text{statement} \end{array} \right\}$

Edits keys files where x=0-9.

International Business Machines Corporation
General Systems Division
5775D Glenridge Drive N.E.
Atlanta, Georgia 30301
(USA Only)

IBM World Trade Corporation
821 United Nations Plaza, New York, New York 10017
(International)

COMMONLY USED TERMS IN STATEMENT SYNTAX

arith-arr-var: An arithmetic-array variable is named with an alphabetic character, A through Z, @, #, or $, immediately followed by subscripts enclosed in parentheses. An arithmetic-array variable represents a numeric value contained in an array at the location indicated by the subscripts.

arith-con: An arithmetic constant is a numeric value.

arith-exp: An arithmetic expression can be an arithmetic constant, variable, array variable, or formula.

arith-var: An arithmetic variable is named with an alphabetic character, A through Z, @, #, or $, or an alphabetic character immediately followed by a numeric character, 0 through 9. An arithmetic variable represents a numeric value.

array-name: An array name is an alphabetic character, A through Z, @, #, or $, that may be followed by a dollar sign, which may or may not be followed by array dimensions enclosed in parentheses.

char-arr-var: A character-array variable is named with an alphabetic character and a dollar sign immediately followed by a subscript enclosed in parentheses. A character-array variable represents a character string contained in an array at the location indicated by the subscript.

char-con: A character constant is a string of characters enclosed in single quotation marks.

char-exp: A character expression can be a substring function, character variable, or character-array variable.

char-var: A character variable is named with an alphabetic character, A through Z, @, #, or $, immediately followed by a dollar sign. A character variable represents a character string.

matrix-name: A matrix name is an alphabetic character, A through Z, @, #, or $, which may or may not be followed by matrix dimensions enclosed in parentheses.

str-function: A string function specifies characters in character data items that are being extracted, concatenated, replaced, or compared with other specified characters. The string function syntax is:

$$\text{STR} \left(\left\{ \begin{matrix} \text{char-var} \\ \text{char-arr-var} \end{matrix} \right\}, \text{arith-exp}, \text{arith-exp} \right)$$

CALCULATOR STATEMENTS

- Assignment statements (without LET specified)

- MAT assignment statements

- PRINT (to display screen or printer)

- MAT PRINT (to display screen or printer)

- DIM statements

- Arithmetic expressions

- Character expressions

FUNCTION KEYS

Numeric keys 0-9 can be assigned functions in the following manner:

- A LOAD command specifies the key: LOAD0, KEY (0-9)

- The following statement is preceded by a statement number of 999 (0-9). The statement specifies:

    NULL-No function for the key.
    CMD-The key function is a system command or calculator expression.
    REM-The key function is a series of BASIC statements.
    TXT-The key function is a character string (enclosed in single quotation marks).

- Each time the specified key (on the right of the keyboard) is pressed with the CMD key, the defined function is activated.

- REM key groups can be executed by a branch from a GOSUB statement, or by pressing the CMD key and the appropriate numeric key.

COMMAND OPERATIONS

Calc Result		Displays result of the last calculation.
Copy Display (This key is blank on a BASIC-only machine.)		Prints the contents of the display screen.
Delete		Deletes character indicated by cursor.
Insert		Creates space for a character insertion.

RELATIONAL ARITHMETIC OPERATORS

Relation	Symbol
Equal	$=$
Not equal	$\neq$ or $<>$
Greater than	$>$
Less than	$<$
Greater/equal	$\geqslant$ or $> =$
Less/equal	$\leqslant$ or $< =$

BASIC CONSTANTS	
Use this symbol	**When you want the value of this constant**
&PI	π (3.141592653590)
&SQR2	$\sqrt{2}$ (1.414213562373)
&E	e (2.718281828459)
&LBKG	pounds-to-kilograms conversion constant (0.45359237)
&INCM	inches-to-centimeters conversion constant (2.54)
&GALI	gallons-to-liters conversion constant (3.7854117840)

BASIC CHARACTER SET	
Alphabetic characters	A, B . . . Z, #, @, $
Digits	0, 1 . . . 9
Alphameric characters	alphabetic character or digit
Special characters	blank , . : ' $<$ $=$ $>$ & $+$ /) (; ? - * | $\geqslant$ $\leqslant$ ↑ $\neq$ and all APL symbols

SYSTEM FUNCTIONS

Function	Meaning
ABS(x)	Absolute value of x
ACS(x)	Arc cosine (in radians) of x
ASN(x)	Arc sine (in radians) of x
ATN(x)	Arc tangent (in radians) of x
COS(x)	Cosine of x radians
COT(x)	Cotangent of x radians
CSC(x)	Cosecant of x radians
DEG(x)	Number of degrees in x radians
DET(x)	Determinant of a square arithmetic array
EXP(x)	Natural exponent of x
HCS(x)	Hyperbolic cosine of the real number x
HSN(x)	Hyperbolic sine of the real number x
HTN(x)	Hyperbolic tangent of the real number x
INT(x)	Integer part of x
LGT(x)	Logarithm of x to the base 10
LOG(x)	Logarithm of x to the base e
LTW(x)	Logarithm of x to the base 2
RAD(x)	Number of radians in x degrees
RND [(x)]	Random number between 0 and 1 (x is optional)
SEC(x)	Secant of x radians
SGN(x)	Sign of x (–1, 0, or 1)
SIN(x)	Sine of x radians
SQR(x)	Square root of x
STR (X$, y, z)	Substring of character variable X$, starting with the yth character, and extending for z characters
TAN(x)	Tangent of x radians

EXAMPLE OF LOAD COMMAND

LOAD1

READY   PAYROLL,002,001,0010,0110   28191

User Identification

First Statement Number

Last Statement Number

Unused Storage (in K)

Allocated Storage (in K)

Number of Characters in Unassigned Work Area

EXAMPLE OF SAVE COMMAND

SAVE1

READY   002,001

Allocated Storage (in K)

Unused Storage (in K)

Note: K=1024 characters

EXAMPLE OF UTIL PRINT COMMAND

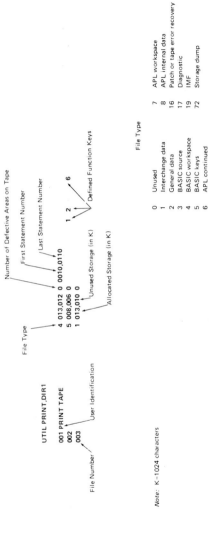

UTIL PRINT,DIR1

001 PRINT TAPE
002
003

File Number

User Identification

File Type

Number of Defective Areas on Tape

First Statement Number

Last Statement Number

4 013,012 0 0010,0110
5 008,006 0
1 013,010 0

Unused Storage (in K)

Allocated Storage (in K)

1 2   6

Defined Function Keys

File Type

0	Unused
1	Interchange data
2	General data
3	BASIC source
4	BASIC workspace
5	BASIC keys
6	APL continued

7	APL workspace
8	APL internal data
16	Patch or tape error recovery
17	Diagnostic
19	IMF
72	Storage dump

Note: K=1024 characters

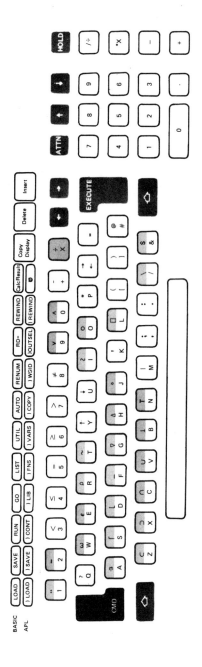

Note: The shaded characters on the alphameric keys are APL symbols, and are not shown on the BASIC-only machine. These symbols can be used in character constants and program input lines and can be displayed and printed (on both a BASIC-only or a BASIC/APL machine), but their APL functions are not active in BASIC operations.

The gray keys perform the following functions:

CMD–The command key is used to select a system command or BASIC statement keyword or activate one of the user-defined key functions.

EXECUTE–This key is used to indicate the end of a program line or to cause execution of a calculator expression.

ATTN–The attention key is used to stop 5100 operations (except I/O).

HOLD–The hold key stops 5100 operations when pressed once and resumes operations when pressed again.

⟡ –These keys are used to select the uppershift symbols.

↑ ↓ –These keys are used to move the lines of data on the display screen up or down.

← → –These keys are used to move the cursor for error correction or changes in a line.

INDEX